127-133 - conventions
355-6 - Name - death of dead - scourge
268 Wood revulsion for name.
uu

SHAKESPEARE

AND THE RENAISSANCE CONCEPT

OF HONOR

SHAKESPEARE AND THE RENAISSANCE CONCEPT OF HONOR

BY CURTIS BROWN WATSON

PRINCETON, NEW JERSEY
PRINCETON UNIVERSITY PRESS
1960

Publication of this book
has been aided by the Ford Foundation program
to support publication, through university presses,
of works in the humanities and social sciences

❖

Printed in the United States of America by
Princeton University Press
Princeton, New Jersey
Second Printing, 1967

TO MY FAMILY

PREFACE

THIS book stems from a thesis presented to the Department of English of Harvard University in 1950. In quoting Shakespeare, I have used *The Complete Works of Shakespeare*, edited by George Lyman Kittredge. I have modernized the spelling of a few words in order to help the reader grasp quickly the meaning of the many passages which are rendered in Elizabethan or Jacobean English. "Receyued," for example, becomes more readily recognizable as "Received." (The archaic u is replaced with the modern v, the i with a y and vice versa, the i with a j, and the modern form of s is used. Otherwise I have left the archaic spelling untouched in order to preserve the integrity of the original passages.)

I have used the Loeb Library edition of the basic classical works by Plato, Aristotle, and Cicero so that the passages cited can be easily compared with the original Greek or Latin version. In the case of Elyot's *The Gouernour*, Castiglione's *The Courtier*, and Florio's translation of Montaigne's *Essays*, I have used the excellent Everyman's Library reprints of the early editions, since many readers may possess these books. They are among the few of the innumerable works on Renaissance moral philosophy still read today. I have also used, where possible, the *Great Books of the Western World*, edited by Robert Maynard Hutchins and published by the *Encyclopedia Britannica*. The first volume (The Syntopicon) includes a discussion of the concept of honor as one of the germinal ideas which have had a decisive influence on the shaping of Western culture.

It is impossible for me to acknowledge adequately my debt to all those who have contributed, directly or indirectly, to the shaping of the ideas which have gone into this book. But since my subject is honor, it is particularly important that I give credit to the deserving—to use the idiom of the Renaissance moralists. A partial list of acknowledgments must include: Professors I. J. Kapstein of Brown, S. F. Johnson of Columbia,

Edward Hubler of Princeton, and Arthur Colby Sprague of Bryn Mawr, who first aroused my interest in Shakespeare; Professors Walter Houghton, Harry Levin, and I. A. Richards, and Mr. Howard Baker, whose inspiring teaching of Harvard graduate students indirectly contributed to this book; Professors Ira Wade and Alfred Foulet of Princeton's Department of Romance Languages and Literatures, Dean Robert Davril, Executive Officer of the Fulbright Commission for France, and Mr. Roger Hibon, formerly assistant director of the Maison Française at Oxford, for many valuable tips in regard to the contributions of French scholars to an understanding of my period; and finally Professor George Fenwick Jones of the Department of German at Goucher College for making available to me his unpublished manuscript, "The Concept of Honor in Medieval German Literature," recently published at Chapel Hill as *Honor in German Literature*. I am particularly indebted to Professor S. F. Johnson for detailed suggestions for revisions and to Professor Richard LeMay, formerly at Columbia and now teaching at the American University of Beirut, for detailed suggestions in regard to revisions of the first chapter. Finally I must thank the long list of harassed professors who have had a look at the first half of the first chapter which deals with European philosophy and cultural history rather than literature proper: Professors Jacques Maritain, Wallace Ferguson, Douglas Steere; the R. P. Pierre Golliet of the Université de Nimègue; Professor Victor Goldschmidt of the Université de Rennes; and Professors Majid Fahkry, Haig Khatchadourian, and Roland Puccetti of the Department of Philosophy at the American University of Beirut.

This book would never have been completed if it had not been for a generous grant from the Rockefeller Foundation, for which I wish to thank John Marshall of the Humanities Division of the Foundation, and Dean Farid Hanania and former Acting President Costi Zurayk of the American University of Beirut. I am equally indebted to Princeton University for making it possible for me to spend my year of sabbatical leave in the Department of English as a Visiting Fellow.

I wish to thank both my wife and my mother for invaluable assistance in the preparation of footnotes and the index. Finally I wish to thank those who have been in charge of the editorial work for the Princeton University Press: Mr. Ben Houston and, in particular, Mrs. Mathilde Finch, who had an attentive eye for textual defects. I cannot adequately thank her for her patient care in seeing the manuscript through all the stages of its preparation and for giving me advice as to ways in which the general presentation could be improved.

C.B.W.

9, Rue Chardin, Paris
June 1, 1960

ACKNOWLEDGMENTS

Acknowledgment is made to the following for permission to quote from copyrighted material:

Mme. Pierre Villey, for Pierre Villey, *Les Sources et l'Evolution des Essais de Montaigne*, 1908; Harcourt, Brace and Company, also Faber and Faber Ltd., for *Selected Essays 1917-1932* by T. S. Eliot, Copyright 1932, by Harcourt, Brace and Company, Inc.; Basil Blackwell and Mott Ltd., for Werner Jaeger, *Paideia*, 1945; Librairie Gallimard, for Paul Bénichou, *Morales du Grand Siècle*, Copyright 1948; American Book Company, for Karl Holzknecht, *The Backgrounds of Shakespeare's Plays*, 1950; Cambridge University Press, for Allardyce Nicoll, ed., *Shakespeare Survey 3*, 1950; University of Kentucky Press, for Robert B. Heilman, *Magic in the Web*, 1956; Charles Scribner's Sons, also Constable and Co., for *Essays in Literary Criticism of George Santayana*, Irving Singer, ed., 1956.

CONTENTS

PART II. SHAKESPEARE'S USE OF THE RENAISSANCE
CONCEPT OF HONOR

CONTENTS

CONTENTS

SHAKESPEARE

AND THE RENAISSANCE CONCEPT

OF HONOR

WE all covet this glory, as the first and lawful reward of our travell: and there is no man but is right glad to consecrate his name to immortalitie. For proofe whereof it is tolde that a certain writer published in print a little pamphlet of his own making, intituled, *The Contempt of Glory*, wherein by many notable reasons, hee indevoured to prove that it is a vanitie unseemely for a man to gape after glory, in consideration of his owne works. But that writer was afterwards charged to have committed the same fault, which hee found fault with in others, for that he had set his name in the first page and beginning of his booke.—M. S. GUAZZO, *The Civile Conversation*

INTRODUCTION

T HE first part of this book is a study of the moral values and the social and political convictions of the Elizabethans and Jacobeans; the second part, organized so that it will almost exactly parallel the first, deals with Shakespeare's use of these social and moral concepts in his poems and plays. The very first chapter, which serves as an introduction to both Parts I and II, attempts to telescope more than 2,000 years of European intellectual history into fewer than 100 pages in order to present the numerous facets of a single moral concept which has played a decisive role in shaping the cultural development of Western European civilization.

Although in the first chapter the concept of honor is presented as an idea with a "history," it will become increasingly apparent to the reader that I am more concerned with a comparison of the roles which have been assigned to honor in various moral systems than with the history of the idea itself. A chronological pattern is used so that the reader can more conveniently perceive the relationship of the concept to the major ethical systems of ancient and medieval times. This will, I hope, open the way to a better understanding of the manner in which the men of Shakespeare's age were influenced by both the Christian and pagan-humanist treatment of this concept in the Renaissance remolding of European values. When I speak of "pagan humanism," as I shall do repeatedly in this work, I am referring to those ethical concepts which the Renaissance moralists derived from the direct study of the pagan philosophers of classical antiquity. It is impossible to separate completely the Christian and classical heritages of the Renaissance, both of which were largely humanistic, but Renaissance moral philosophy in large part represents a secular morality based primarily on purely classical sources. I have arbitrarily labeled this secular morality "pagan humanism," having found no better name for it.

The survey in Chapter 1 of so many centuries must, of necessity, leave much fine historical detail out of the picture. But if much is lost, much is also gained by this cursory treatment of European intellectual history, since my main purpose is to make the reader as keenly aware as possible of the major alternative treatments of the concept of honor which would have been available to him if he were himself a man of Shakespeare's time.

Part I, the Renaissance background, examines at length the Elizabethan and Jacobean attitudes toward honor and related moral concepts. In this section of the book, the leading ideas are presented as directly as possible so that the reader can place himself in the position of the youth of the Renaissance who were poring over these formulations, in the various treatises to which I shall refer, as part of their formal study of moral philosophy. Very little attention is paid to the brilliant or the eccentric writers of the age (Christopher Marlowe, John Donne, and Francis Bacon, for example, are almost completely neglected), for we are concerned in Part I with the *typical*, not with the *original*. As E. M. W. Tillyard has observed, the job of the cultural historian is to discover "the commonplaces, the unargued presuppositions" of an age. Therefore he must always keep in mind "the imperative need, in any comparative discussions of epochs, first to decide what the norm of the epoch is."[1]

Part I is thus both a moral and sociological study of the ways in which the Renaissance rediscovered and revitalized certain earlier ethical formulations dealing with honor and related concepts. In this section I have endeavored to show that the sympathetic restatements in the 16th century of earlier definitions of these concepts are almost exclusively classical in origin. It is therefore my thesis in this book that Renaissance civilization can best be understood not as an age of a homogeneous Christian humanism—a "massive humanistic fusion of

---

[1] E. M. W. Tillyard, *The English Renaissance, Fact or Fiction?*, London, 1952, pp. 28, 27.

the glory of God with the glory of man," as Professor Herschel Baker of Harvard University has defined it—but as a period in which the attempt is made to weld together two distinct systems of value, Christianity and pagan humanism.[2] It is also my contention that, although Renaissance culture represents a profound interpenetration of Christian and classical elements, it is not a genuine fusion or synthesis comparable to the blending of Christian and humanist values in the age of Aquinas and Dante.

In the Middle Ages, with regard to formal philosophy, theology was always queen of the sciences and moral philosophy was never allowed to be independent of it. (Paradoxically, St. Thomas was free to incorporate a considerable body of pagan doctrine precisely because, as the man responsible for the synthesis—based on revelation and finding its center of gravity in theology—he could be sure that the pagan elements would play only a subordinate role.) In the Renaissance, on the other hand, ethics was no longer necessarily a handmaiden of theology. The men of the 16th century had available to them two integrated systems of ethics, two separate ideologies, which, as it turned out, were maintained almost on an equal footing. If it was a sacred duty to fulfill one's religious obligations, it was also a sacred duty to fulfill the ethical obligations which stemmed from the code of honor. Honor, indeed, was often considered inseparable from virtue itself.[3] Instead of being the loosely defined secular morality it had been for the medieval aristocracy, it was now a fully conceived, carefully

---

[2] In *The Dignity of Man*, Cambridge, Mass., 1947, p. 296.

[3] The Renaissance moralists cite endlessly this cardinal tenet of classical humanism: virtue is as inextricably connected with honor as the body is with its shadow. Thus Petrarch states that "Glory in a sense is the shadow of virtue." (Francis Petrarch, *Petrarch's Secret; or the Soul's Conflict with Passion: Three Dialogues between Himself and S. Augustine*, trans. William H. Draper, London, 1911, p. 182.) See also Robert Ashley, *Of Honour*, ed. Virgil Heltzel, San Marino, 1947, p. 34; Guillaume Du Vair, *The Moral Philosophie of the Stoicks*, trans. T[homas] J[ames], London, 1598, p. 78; Jacques Hurault, *Politicke, Moral and Martial Discourses*, trans. Arthur Golding, London, 1595, p. 63; Pierre de la Primaudaye, *The French Academie*, trans. T. B[owes], 4th ed., London, 1602-05, p. 296; Count Annibale Romei, *The Courtier's Academie*, trans. J[ohn] K[epers], London, 1598, p. 124.

3

rationalized and articulated, formal philosophical code. In the Renaissance, honor, basically a pagan idea, has become almost a religion. For example, while continuing to believe in Christian immortality, Shakespeare's contemporaries believed at the same time and just as passionately that "fame, in times to come, may canonize us," (*Troilus and Cressida*, II. ii. 202) and that, in the words of Cassio, to lose one's reputation is to lose "the immortal part" of oneself. (*Othello*, II. iii. 263-264).

Many of the Renaissance moralists whom we shall be examining were at least partially aware that they were worshiping at two altars at one and the same time, though few of them would have been willing to admit that, in deifying honor, fame, and glory, they were lesser Christians than the men of the Middle Ages. Indeed, they made every possible attempt to find a way to reconcile conflicts between the moral dicta of their two major ethical codes (Christianity and pagan humanism), even though they usually held that the medieval scholastic synthesis was inacceptable. Anyone troubling to read the numerous treatises on moral philosophy published in the Renaissance will find that every effort was made to emphasize the large area of agreement between the two codes and that, on many points, the interpenetration of Christian and pagan-humanist values resulted in a successful fusion, a new kind of Christian humanism. Pierre Villey has pointed out that Budé, Vivès, and Erasmus all held that there could be an "entente cordiale" between pagan morality and the Christian ethics, since the latter, presumably remaining master, could make a useful auxiliary of the former.[4] And so Erasmus could write that, since it is possible to do so, we should both remain good Christians and profit from ancient wisdom.

But if there were large areas of possible agreement in which Christian and Graeco-Roman concepts (as, for example, the ideals of honesty and personal integrity) could be harmoniously wedded, there were others in which cardinal tenets of the two systems of moral philosophy were bound to come into sharpest

[4] *Les Sources et l'Evolution des Essais de Montaigne*, Paris, 1908, I, 9.

conflict. Thus, on the question of the moral propriety of the duel or of taking private revenge, reconciliation between the Christian ethics and the code of honor was out of the question. The man of Shakespeare's time was torn by inner conflict on this issue because he was often heeding the moral imperatives of two separate moral systems which were expecting him to act according to diametrically opposite tenets. How could he extricate himself from the moral dilemma in which he was placed? Illogical as it may seem, he did so by heeding both. So we shall find him taking private revenge on a Thursday or fighting a duel on a Friday (in response to the call of honor and the imperative need to defend himself against any insult), and confessing his sins in church on the following Sunday, one of which sins has been his shedding of human blood in a private quarrel.[5] Many instances of this sort could be cited to show that the Renaissance was capable of maintaining consistently inconsistent ideals.

I should like to suggest, in other words, that the Renaissance was a complex age because of a basic duality, a deep-seated ambivalence, in values. The men of the Renaissance were Janus-faced and adhered to contradictory dogmas, just as in our time, in, say, Italy and Poland, there are many Christians who accept the validity of certain Marxist ideas and some Communists who marry and are buried in the church. Frequently in human history, cultures have existed which have had more than a single norm of ideal behavior—particularly if one of them is primarily religious and the other primarily secular in nature. To take another example from our own age, some of the Japanese soldiers who fought in the second world war for the glory of country and Emperor finally retired from their military careers in order to become Buddhist monks. Human social behavior has been, in many different epochs and many different societies, thoroughly inconsistent, or at least thoroughly ambivalent.[6]

---

[5] See section on revenge in Chapter 3, pp. 127-135.

[6] See Ralph Linton, *A Study of Man*, New York, 1936, p. 358. Linton points out that "Cultures, like personalities, are perfectly capable of including conflicting elements and logical inconsistencies. . . . Societies, like individuals, are capable of ambivalent attitudes."

While there was a basic ambivalence to the Renaissance ethos, I hope that Part I of this book will make it clear that the age was not, as has often been suggested, an age of moral chaos or confusion. The moral imperatives of the Christian and the pagan-humanist ethics were clearly and carefully defined, thanks to the painstaking endeavors of the numerous writers of Renaissance moral treatises whose works we shall be examining. *The Renaissance was as aware as any age in human history of the importance of values and of the need for a careful definition of them.*[7] Indeed, the age was often the more sensitive and alert to ethical considerations because it had to reconcile conflicts between two systems of value. The maxim or commonplace, for this reason, was not considered a mere platitude; it was instead a cardinal moral precept which could play a decisive role in determining human conduct.[8] As the letters and the journals of the period clearly indicate, such action was often on a heroic scale.

Part II of this book deals with the use Shakespeare made of the moral concepts considered in Part I. In this section, the major portion of the book, my second main thesis is presented: that Shakespeare was a man of his age and that his plays therefore reflect, with an inconsistency which has to be admitted and accepted, both the Christian and the pagan-humanist values of his period. Although I believe that Shakespeare, as a man of his time, makes use of both his Christian and his classical heritage, it is my conviction that in his writings he favors those definitions of good and evil which his age had inherited from the pagan humanists. If this is true, it is a mistake to suggest, as has often been done in recent studies of his plays, that Shakespeare in any single play consistently presented the essentials of Christian doctrine—although it would be a grotesque distortion of Shakespeare's meaning and of Shakespearean values to leave the Christian element out of

[7] See Part II, Foreword, for a discussion of the relation between art and moral belief in the Renaissance.
[8] See, for example, the definitions of ingratitude in Chapter I, pp. 64, 65.

6

the picture altogether, as has also been done all too frequently ever since George Santayana wrote his provocative essay "The Absence of Religion in Shakespeare." In certain scenes of a given play—for example, the sleepwalking scene in *Macbeth*—Shakespeare's values are profoundly Christian and the atmosphere of this, and many others of his plays, is saturated with a sense of the Christian supernatural. But the key to a sound interpretation of character and action lies in an understanding of those pagan-humanist values which were available to Shakespeare—values best exposed in his treatment of the Renaissance concept of honor.

Shakespeare, undoubtedly the greatest writer ever to use our tongue, certainly did not, by virtue of his genius, miraculously divorce himself from the preconceptions or even the prejudices of his fellow Elizabethans. Jonson's immortal phrase, "Not of an age, but for all time" is thus a dangerous half-truth. Shakespeare was very much of his age, and we can fully appreciate his meaning only if we endeavor to understand the Elizabethan and Jacobean sensibility. In making the assertion that we must place ourselves perseveringly in the shoes of a member of Shakespeare's audience if we are to interpret properly the meaning of his plays, I am running counter to much current opinion. On this subject R. B. Heilman has written, "One kind of pursuer of objectivity leaves us with a serious problem . . . when he tacitly identifies 'as it is' with 'as it was'; the real Shakespeare becomes an Elizabethan (or Jacobean) reality, and this reality is accessible to us only if we acquire an Elizabethan point of view. This conclusion rather begs the question of whether a completely historical attitude may be achieved, whether a sense of being Elizabethan in point of view does not contain something of the illusory."[9] Heilman then goes on to say that he doubts whether the person concerned with a complete historical restoration of a given age can do "entire justice" to the great literary monuments of the

[9] *Magic in the Web*, Lexington, Kentucky, 1956, pp. 14, 15.

7

past which he feels, quoting R. P. Blackmur, are "conformable to different cultures at different times" because of "the unity of the reality under all cultures at all times."[10]

Many of our modern literary critics are in substantial agreement with the point of view here expressed. The work of art, they would argue, is to be studied for its own sake; extraneous considerations, whether of a sociological, historical, philosophical, or psychological nature, should not be allowed to interfere with an attempt at full and sensitive aesthetic appreciation. Nor should the universality, the timelessness of the classic, they would add, be marred by irrelevant investigations of historical or biographical data. For these reasons, among others, G. Wilson Knight in his introduction to *The Imperial Theme* admits an open preference for "the imaginative and the intuitive" (which he labels "interpretation") to "the historical and the scholarly" (which he calls "criticism").[11] In much recent work on Shakespeare this intuitive approach has prevailed.

Is it not conceivable that a critic might want to be both "imaginative and intuitive" and "historical and scholarly"? Is it not possible that the proper kind of historical restoration, rather than smothering the living vitality of the classics under an avalanche of irrelevant historical detail, may bring to life a portion of the work's meaning buried from view simply because we did not possess the vantage point of the writer's contemporary audience? Is it not possible that Wilson Knight, in assuming as he does in *The Wheel of Fire* that our values are essentially the same as those of the Elizabethan audience (and that therefore we do not need to bother to attempt a definition of Renaissance values in order to be able to put ourselves in the shoes of a member of Shakespeare's audience), may be overlooking the three hundred years of European

[10] Quoted by Heilman in *ibid.*, p. 15.
[11] 3rd ed., London, 1951. See also G. Wilson Knight, *The Wheel of Fire*, 4th ed., London, 1949, Introduction (by T. S. Eliot) and Chapter 1, "On the Principles of Shakespearean Interpretation."

cultural history which lie between us and the man for whom Shakespeare was writing his plays?[12] Is there not perhaps what Heilman called "something of the illusory" in the modern critic's unwillingness to place the work of art in its historical context?

Many recent Shakespearean critics seem to me, as I shall attempt to show, to have been wearing historical blinders, with resultant grotesque distortion of Shakespeare's original meaning. And further, much modern Shakespeare criticism reveals, on many key points of "interpretation," not only historical ignorance but, even more important, a basic lack of sympathy with Renaissance pagan-humanist values in general and Shakespearean values in particular. This lack of sympathy seems to stem from the fact that our critics are often insufficiently aware of their own preconceptions and of the many respects in which our democratic ideals in the 20th century basically contradict the aristocratic assumptions of Elizabethan society.

Have not certain critics also perhaps allowed their Christian convictions to color their interpretations of the meaning of Shakespeare's plays? Since many of the values underlying Shakespeare's tragic vision are antipathetic to Christian values, to enter sympathetically into Shakespeare's tragic world his present-day reader must permit a momentary suspension of belief, just as another kind of reader must suspend his disbelief to appreciate fully *The Divine Comedy* or *Paradise Lost*. For, as Paul Bénichou has argued in his informative book on Corneille and Racine, *Morales du Grand Siècle*, "if pride is for the Christian the root of all sin, the essential characteristic of the aristocratic morality is that pride and the very notion of sublimity and grandeur are almost indistinguishable."[13] And so, Bénichou also points out, although the church, in the age of Louis the Thirteenth and Louis the Fourteenth, condemned aristocratic pride, to which it opposed the ideal of Christian humility, humility was "neither in theory nor in fact the virtue

---

[12] *The Wheel of Fire*, Chapter I.
[13] *Morales du Grand Siècle*, Paris, 1948, p. 33.

of the great [French aristocrats]. So likewise Corneille's heroes are never humble."[14]

The age of Shakespeare (1564-1616) held much in common with the age of Corneille (1606-1684) in its conception of honor and of tragic nobility. (Indeed, honor seems to be an essential ingredient of the tragic view of life; it was of cardinal importance in the first great age of European tragedy, the age of Aeschylus and Sophocles.) Both Shakespeare and Corneille were of bourgeois origin, writing for aristocratic audiences. The aristocratic ideals of honor, glory, magnanimity (aristocratic pride), and heroic sacrifice are tragic ideals which the two writers share. The question must be raised and faced with Shakespeare—as Bénichou has faced it with Corneille—whether we can properly interpret his plays if we start with the assumption that Christian pride is the key to an understanding of Shakespearean tragedy. Yet G. R. Elliott, in his study of *Othello*, observes that in recent Shakespeare studies the "general trend is towards the recognition of the tragedy of pride as central in the Shakespearean drama," that "pride is . . . not merely *a* sin; it may rightly be regarded as synonymous with sin itself," and that "Renaissance tragedy including Shakespearean tragedy is the tragedy of pride." As the result of his insistence that the Christian scale of values is consistently the proper scale of values by which to judge action, theme, and character in Shakespeare, he is led to make the following observations about Cassio's concern for honor: "[Cassio] is possessed of that resonant sense of honor, in certain respects excellent but always questionable and sometimes very wrong, that Shakespeare . . . took delight in dramatically criticizing."[15] Elliott also says of Cassio that "Infinitely worse than [his] transient insobriety is his fixed intoxication with his honor, his outward repute."[16]

It is my earnest hope that the following pages will provide

[14] *ibid.*, pp. 32-33.
[15] In *Flaming Minister*, Durham, N.C., 1953, pp. xvi, xiii, xix.
[16] *ibid.*, p. xxviii.

sure evidence that for the men of the Renaissance, including Shakespeare, a resonant sense of honor is in every respect excellent and never questionable. In Shakespeare's day, let it be repeated, virtue and honor were practically synonymous terms. As Du Vair observes, "True honour is the glittering and beaming brightnes of a good and vertuous action, which rebounds from our consciences unto the sight of them with whom wee live, and so by a reflexion in our selves, brings us a testimonie from others of the good opinion which they have of us, which makes us to enjoy great comfort of minde."[17] We are here considering an age in which men actually were possessed by a "fixed intoxication" with honor and with "outward repute." Whether we in the 20th century are also willing to place a high value on honor, reputation, glory, and fame, or not, should not prevent us from accepting the fact that these were the basic pagan-humanist values of the Elizabethan age and hence of Shakespeare's audience.

Throughout this discussion we should bear in mind that the concept of honor has two meanings which have to be distinguished from each other, even though Du Vair's definition shows that the two meanings were closely related. Honor, in one of its meanings, is an exclusively social virtue. Honor, in this sense, may refer to one's *reputation* in the community, to one's *credit* as a man of integrity, to the *honors* or *rewards* which are bestowed publicly as a testimony to one's virtue, to the *glory* and *fame* which one acquires as the result of exceptional or heroic accomplishments, or to the *good name* which is gained when one consistently behaves in a fashion which wins the *respect* and *esteem* of one's fellows. In recent years, honor in this public sense has tended to come into disrepute for a variety of reasons. Many of the most sensitive and intelligent men of our century have come to feel that honors are trivial and unreliable rewards and that too high a price may be paid for glory—or that glory may, particularly on the field of battle,

[17] p. 74.

be won for actions not really laudable. Thus Albert Camus writes, "Above all, I recognize my kinship with the average man. Tomorrow the world may be blown to pieces. In this threat that hangs over us there is a lesson of truth. Confronted with this future, hierarchy, titles, honors become again what they have always been: smoke that blows away."[18]

But honor also refers to one's *private* and *personal* judgment of one's *own* actions, one's *inner* conviction of *innate* moral rectitude. Honor, in other words, relates to *self-esteem* as much as to public approbation. Because this second meaning can be distinct from the first, it is possible that a man may paradoxically risk the loss of "honor" (i.e., may fail to conform to the norms established by a given society which will win him the praise and esteem of his fellows) in order to preserve his "honor" (i.e., avoid becoming dishonored in his own eyes). This second meaning of honor is the one most often equated with virtue. In sharp contradiction to public honor, honor in its private sense is an inalienable, priceless possession of which one cannot be deprived by any other person. Because of this basic ambiguity, Camus involves himself in what seems on the surface outrageous contradiction. For he proceeds, in the paragraph immediately following the one just quoted, to defend the preciousness of honor, which he had just dismissed as "smoke that blows away." He observes that "In the conflicts of this century, I have felt close to all obstinate men, particularly to those who have never been able to abandon their faith in honor. I have shared and I continue to share many contemporary hysterias. But I have never been able to make up my mind to spit, as so many have done, on the word 'honor'—no doubt because I was and continue to be aware of my human weaknesses and the injustices I have committed, and because I knew and continue to know instinctively that honor, like pity, is the irrational virtue that carries on after justice and reason have become powerless."[19]

[18] Quoted in Jean Bloch-Michel, "The Obstinate Confidence of a Pessimistic Man," *The Reporter*, 17, November 28, 1957, p. 37.
[19] *ibid.*, pp. 37-38.

It is essential to keep clearly in mind, in the pages which follow, the various senses in which the term honor can be used. (Fuller definitions are given at the beginning of Chapter 4.) The precise meaning can often be determined only by the context of a particular passage; sometimes the two meanings are both involved, as is the case when the signers of the American Declaration of Independence pledge "our lives, our fortunes, and our sacred honour." It is important to remember that the pejorative connotations now attached to honor, fame, and glory are not only the reverse of the favorable connotations which the words possessed in Elizabethan times, but that also the words had a fuller, richer, yet more precise meaning when they were used in England three and a half centuries ago. Some synonyms and related concepts like "good report" and "oblivion" today are archaic.

One final word on the relation of this study to the attempt to find a meaningful way of distinguishing between medieval and Renaissance culture. Our increased historical awareness has led many scholars to feel that the term "Renaissance" has meant so many different things to different men that it is no longer useful. It has even been labeled an "imaginary entity responsible for everything the speaker likes in the 15th and 16th century."[20] Wallace Ferguson's thorough study of the bewildering multiplicity of scholarly interpretations of this period (in *The Renaissance in Historical Thought*) leads to the same scholarly relativism. He admits that the word has lost the clarity of meaning it possessed when Burckhardt used it, and he raises the question whether we have any solid grounds for making distinctions between medieval and Renaissance culture. He suggests in his concluding pages that continuity between one age and another and a sense of evolutionary flow have practically destroyed any signposts which will permit us to state, without being guilty of naïveté, that we have crossed

---

[20] Quoted by C. S. Lewis, *English Literature in the Sixteenth Century*, Oxford, 1954, p. 55. See pp. 53-54 for a thoroughly unsympathetic presentation of Renaissance classical humanism. For an explanation of Lewis's bias against Renaissance pagan-humanist values, see Tillyard, pp. 10-19.

from one period into the other.[21] The same general conclusion is reached by Sidney Potter in his discussion of the problem in the opening pages of the Renaissance volume of *The New Cambridge Modern History* published in 1957.[22]

If some scholars are sceptical about the possibility of ever again distinguishing meaningfully between the two periods, others have become convinced that the two ages have a striking resemblance to each other. Traits which have conventionally been labeled "Renaissance" are, they feel, almost as characteristic of the Middle Ages, and features which have usually been designated "medieval," they believe, can frequently be found in the Renaissance. Thus Professor Herschel Baker of Harvard University suggests in *The Dignity of Man* that the secular concerns of medieval man and the spiritual concerns of the man of the Renaissance have been unduly minimized and he comes to the conclusion that "the Renaissance marks no radical new departure in man's habits of viewing himself and the world about him."[23] In the mid-century edition of the *Shakespeare Survey*, C. J. Sisson observes that this assumption has become general in recent studies of Shakespeare. He reaches the conclusion that it is impossible to find a dividing line between the two periods and that therefore "medieval England was implicit in Elizabethan England, and in Shakespeare's mind."[24]

In *The Elizabethan World Picture*, E. M. W. Tillyard seemed to be in substantial agreement with Baker and Sisson that one can "rail safely at the notion of a Chinese Wall" dividing the Middle Ages from the Renaissance.[25] More recently, in his thought-provoking book *The English Renaissance: Fact or Fiction?* Tillyard has warned against "exaggerating the continuity between the Middle Ages and the Renaissance."[26] Indeed, in his epilogue he acknowledges that "there were

[21] *The Renaissance in Historical Thought*, Cambridge, Mass., 1948, pp. 386-397.
[22] Sidney Potter, ed., Cambridge, Eng., 1957, I, 1-5.
[23] p. 296.
[24] *Shakespeare Survey*, III, ed. Allardyce Nicoll, Cambridge, Eng., 1950, p. 7.
[25] *ibid.*   [26] p. 95.

certain changes in England that could be called by the name of Renaissance," although he suggests that these changes came gradually.[27] It is my hope that the present study of the concept of honor will bear out his reconsidered later judgment. Although it is impossible to put a finger on the precise day, year, or even decade when the Renaissance began, I believe that this present study of medieval and Renaissance attitudes toward honor shows that the climate of moral opinion was radically different in Shakespeare's age from what it had been in the age of Dante. If the age did not, like the 13th century, represent a genuine synthesis of Christianity and classical values— Baker's "massive humanistic fusion of the glory of God with the glory of man"—it was nonetheless profoundly "aware of both these incompatibles," in Tillyard's words, and "to its glory succeeded in combining a measure of each."[28]

[27] p. 98.
[28] *The Dignity of Man*, p. 296; *The English Renaissance*, p. 23.

PART I
THE RENAISSANCE CONCEPT
OF HONOR

CHAPTER 1

THE CONCEPT OF HONOR FROM PLATO TO THE RENAISSANCE

T HE FOLLOWING brief survey of the varying attitudes toward honor from the 5th century in Athens to the early 17th century in England reveals a striking historical development from the generally favorable attitude toward honor found in Greek and Roman society to a sharply contrasting deprecation of it—a deprecation which occurred when Stoic and Christian values became popular at the time of St. Augustine, and which foreshadowed the typical medieval attitude. Finally in the high Renaissance (the 14th to 16th centuries) the classical attitude re-emerges into view, and becomes generally accepted, although the medieval Christian attitude also continues to hold widespread favor. The general cultural values of the Renaissance are in this regard largely derived from exclusively pagan sources. A particular 16th-century writer, however, may either share wholeheartedly the medieval Christian contempt for human fame and glory or reflect both the pagan-humanist and the Christian attitude at different times in his works.

Not only is it possible to establish a chronological pattern in the shifting degree of importance attached to honor by various ethical schools, but we can also determine a relationship between the nature of the ethical first principles of a particular philosophy and the extent to which exclusively human judgments of good and evil (i.e., human honor, praise, and esteem) will be considered of cardinal significance. Whenever a philosophy postulates the existence of some sort of transcendental being, divine essence, or cosmic first principle, the ultimate criterion by which human activity is judged will be likely to be its relative degree of approximation to a supra-human stand-

ard. Hence, the Christians, the Stoics, and Plato tend to minimize the importance of human praise and tend to consider it
a less reliable measure of rectitude than a judgment in terms
of their transcendental norms. Neo-Stoicism and Neo-Platonism
often merge with the Christian system of values, both in the
5th and in the 16th centuries, because of this emphasis on
transcendental values. Each of them assumes that man's good
lies in his adherence to the laws of the Eternal (whatever its
particular form), and that he should seek there, not in the
opinions of his fellow men, for permanent values and criteria
by which to judge his own behavior. Once one assumes a Cosmic
Being *superior to man in goodness* (not necessarily true of
Aristotle's conception of the Deity), in omniscience, in omnipotence, and in transcendence of time and morality, human values
which do not stem from Divine principles become inconsequential, since man's moral behavior is measured primarily by the
extent to which he lives up to a supra-human Ideal.[1] Pierre
Villey has come to a similar conclusion. He suggests that Plato's
philosophy, as the result of its idealism, can merge with Christianity more easily than any other philosophy, and that Stoicism, as the result of its moral elevation, of its belief in a
destiny or a providence which governs the universe, can also
adapt itself readily to the Christian metaphysics.[2]

If the gods are assumed to be purely intellectual concepts,
however, or mere shadowy figures, or subject to man's failings,
they may cease to be the standard of absolute perfection by
which man's shortcomings are to be judged. In this case, the
philosopher may use a predominantly human moral standard,
and the opinion of one's fellow men—the extent to which they

[1] See B. A. G. Fuller, *A History of Philosophy*, New York, 1955, p. 196. Fuller
may go too far when he states that "The Aristotelian God does not seem to be a
personal deity. He has no love, no hate, no will, no aim, no moral qualities or
activities." His interpretation, however, does point out the scientific bias in
Aristotle's conception of the Deity. This helps to explain why Christianity found
neo-Platonism and neo-Stoicism more congenial than modifications of Aristotle's
philosophy until St. Thomas Aquinas achieved his remarkable synthesis of Christianity and Aristotelianism in the 13th century. Of course, little was known of
Aristotle until the middle of the 12th century, but it is noteworthy that the
Church had forbidden the study of the Aristotelian texts that were available.
[2] *Les Sources et l'Evolution des Essais de Montaigne*, I, 30-31.

bestow honor and praise—may become of crucial importance. Thus, for Aristotle, the notion of deity, of an unmoved mover, at times seems to have only a tenuous theoretical relation to moral criteria. Cicero, although he frequently mentions the gods and apparently believed in the immortality of the soul, places these otherworldly, transcendental entities on the shadowy periphery of his moral universe. They bear little relation to his cardinal ethical principles. Hence both Aristotle and Cicero place more stress on the judgment of men—particularly men of the aristocratic elite, the judicious and discerning few—than do Plato and the neo-Stoics.

PLATO

Plato's treatment of the concept of honor, inaugurating our cursory historical study, is not to be found as a central topic in any particular work, so it is necessary to glean information from discussions which obliquely refer to some aspect of it. In *The Republic*, the question whether it is better to be just or unjust leads Socrates to define the good man as the man who is not influenced by the invidious motives of avarice and ambition. The avaricious man does good things because of his love of money; the ambitious man because of his love of fame.[3] Both motives are considered reprehensible compared to the disinterested love of virtue. The discussion which ensues about the nature of justice continually draws a sharp distinction between the man who seeks fame and other rewards and the more praiseworthy type of man who is solely concerned with the disinterested love of virtue.

The same idealistic and ascetic standards are upheld by Socrates in the *Phaedo*. Once again, the desire for fame is deprecated as an impure motive. Socrates tells his friends that "No one who has not been a philosopher and who is not wholly

[3] Paul Shorey, trans., Cambridge, Mass., 1943, I. 19; II. 4; II. 6. True, Plato gives the sense of honor (*philonikia*, perhaps best translated as ambition) an important role in his timocratic state, which he considers the most perfect of imperfect states. But in my remarks here I am concerned with Plato's notion of the *ideal republic*.

pure when he departs, is allowed to enter into the communion of the gods, but only the lover of knowledge. . . . Those who truly love wisdom refrain from all bodily desires and resist them firmly and do not give themselves up to them, not because they fear poverty or loss of property, as most men, in their love of money, do; nor is it because they fear the dishonour or disgrace of wickedness, like the lovers of honour and power, that they refrain from them."[4]

Plato, in his scorn for those who love fame and who fear dishonor, dissociates the love of fame from virtue. Hence his ethics stands in sharp contrast to the ethics of early Greek society and equally to Aristotle's morality. The Greece of Homer's time was preeminently a courtly and aristocratic society. It considered the quest for honor and fame as a primary duty of the nobleman, and one in which he was constantly placed in competition with his peers to prove that he was worthy of even greater honor than they.[5] Indeed, the conscience of the early Greek aristocrat was primarily a public conscience; it was by the expression of social approval and disapproval, honor and dishonor, that he could discover and measure the rightness or wrongness of his behavior. The individual private conscience of later times with which Socrates is concerned was for the most part unknown to him. Hence, honor was a central ethical criterion, completely praiseworthy.

But Plato, like the Christian, believed in higher and purer motives than the quest for fame and glory. This becomes particularly clear in the *Symposium*, where Socrates analyzes the tremendous craving of all humans for some sort of immortality.[6] In his discussion he presents the various methods of achieving this goal, including the immortality achieved by

---

[4] Plato *Phaedo* in *Euthyphro, Apology, Crito, Phaedo, Phaedrus*, trans. Harold North Fowler, Cambridge, Mass., 1953, 82. Elsewhere in the *Phaedrus* Plato, in speaking of the perfect lovers, who will be inspired by philosophy, suggests that if the love of wisdom has been replaced by the love of honor his lovers will be living in a rather gross manner.

[5] Werner Jaeger, *Paideia*, New York, 1945, I, 3-14.

[6] In *Lysis, Symposium, Gorgias*, trans. W. R. M. Lamb, Cambridge, Mass., 1953, 207-212.

begetting offspring, the eternal glory gained by memorable deeds of high virtue, the everlasting fame of the writer and poet, and finally the immortality achieved by the contemplation of absolute and universal beauty. Socrates, in this progression, goes from the baser and cruder methods of attaining immortality to the more pure, timeless, and absolute. Again, the acquisition of glory and renown is held in low esteem compared to Plato's transcendental goal, the philosopher's vision of the Ideal. It is this alone which really excites Socrates; the quest for human praise seems shabby indeed in comparison to it. "What if he could behold the divine beauty itself, in its unique form? Do you call it a pitiful life for a man to lead—looking that way, observing that vision by the proper means, and having it ever with him?"[7]

Plato's rapture over the possibility of contemplating the purely spiritual and transcendental bears resemblance to Dante's pilgrimage from the sullied and earthly to a progressively more purified, ethereal realm until his goal of contemplation of the Divine Essence is finally reached. For both, the satisfaction of their deepest yearnings depends on the fulfillment of a vision of something infinitely purer than this world will ever provide.

ARISTOTLE

If we turn abruptly to the *Nicomachean Ethics* after immersing ourselves for some time in the *Dialogues* of Plato, the striking temperamental and intellectual differences between the two great philosophers come almost as a shock. Plato seems usually to be striving to free himself from the concrete and earthly, to break loose from the prison of flesh and body. Aristotle, as a moralist at least, seems, on the contrary, to be neither capable nor desirous of mystical flights into the purer

---

[7] *ibid.*, 212. Plato is no mere mystic visionary, Socrates even less so. In the famous allegory of the cave, Plato points out that it is necessary to descend again into the cave, to mix in the affairs of the imperfect world of human society. But it is important to note that Plato regards this as a duty one must do for one's country and that, while he considers it an unavoidable task, he does not regard it as distinction.

regions of transcendental absolutes. Instead of rapturous contemplation of a Divine Beauty, he presents unemotionally the
postulate of an Unmoved Mover, whose relation to a supra-
human realm of goodness seems to be much more scientific and
intellectual than intuitive and emotional. Whereas Plato consistently held man's soul to be immortal, Aristotle can say, at
times, stolidly and conclusively, "Now the most terrible thing
of all is death, for it is the end, and when a man is dead, nothing, we think, either good or evil can befall him any more."[8]

The contrast between the two men is particularly evident
in their attitude toward human praise. For Aristotle, to gain
the respect of one's fellow men is a thoroughly worthy goal.
Indeed, the pursuit of honor is placed second only to the
summum bonum—the pursuit of happiness which results from
leading a good and virtuous life. Aristotle establishes the supremacy of virtue over honor at the very beginning of the
Nicomachean Ethics: ". . . we instinctively feel that the Good
must be something proper to its possessor and not easy to be
taken away from him."[9] Since honor depends on the opinion of
others, it is subordinate to this essential quality of virtue.

Aristotle views honor as reward. "Honor," he writes, "is the
prize of virtue, and the tribute that we pay to the good."[10] Honor
both in its private and public senses, is, in other words, a totally
praiseworthy objective, one which the Greek aristocrat passionately strives for and which he attains only by the accomplishment
of deeds of the highest nobility. Whereas Plato deprecated the
desire for glory (public honor) as a characteristic of ambition,
not of virtue, Aristotle considers it a logical consequence and
due reward for a life of great virtue. "Honor," he says in the
Rhetoric, "is the token of a reputation for doing good."[11]

Aristotle's concern for public recognition of outstanding merit
and nobility places him in the tradition of his age. The cultural

[8] *Nicomachean Ethics*, trans. H. Rackham, Cambridge, Mass., 1956, III. 6.
[9] *ibid.*, I. 5.
[10] *ibid.*, IV. 3.
[11] *The Art of Rhetoric*, trans. John Henry Freese, Cambridge, Mass., 1957,
I. 5.

values of Greek society of the 5th and 4th centuries B.C. accorded with the ethical formulations of the early Greeks of the time of Homer. In *Paideia*, Werner Jaeger writes of that earlier society and its ethos, and points out the great barrier which our own Christian values create to prevent a proper appreciation of its public morality:

"Nowadays we must find it difficult to imagine how entirely *public* was the conscience of a Greek. (In fact, the early Greeks never conceived anything like the personal conscience of modern times.) Yet we must strive to recognise that fact, before we can comprehend what they meant by honor. Christian sentiment will regard any claim to honor, any self-advancement, as an expression of sinful vanity. The Greeks, however, believed such ambition to be the aspiration of the individual towards that ideal and supra-personal sphere in which alone he can have real value. Thus it is true in some sense to say that the areté of a hero is completed only in his death. Areté exists in mortal man. Areté is mortal man. But it survives the mortal, and lives on in his glory, in that very ideal of his areté which accompanied and directed him throughout his life."[12]

CICERO

The moral philosophers of Rome, like those of the Renaissance, were not original thinkers, and present few ideas which are not derived from the great Greek schools which preceded them. Although Cicero admits his indebtedness to Plato as well as to the Peripatetics in the opening pages of the *Offices* (he was also influenced by Stoic doctrine), his attitude toward honor, reputation, and glory is, in all essentials, similar to that of Aristotle. He writes, for example, that no material reward, however great, can compare with the splendor of virtue, and the glory and reputation which result from it.[13] Whereas Plato, the

[12] I. 9-10.
[13] *De Officiis*, trans. Walter Miller, Cambridge, Mass., 1956, III. 20.

Stoics, and the Christians disparage fame and riches alike as mere earthly and transitory possessions, Aristotle and Cicero exalt the prize of honor to the skies and make a major ethical distinction between the mean and mercenary spirit of the trading classes, whose eye is on monetary gain, and the great nobility of the aristocrats, whose only measure of value is that of honor and who hold the acquisition of riches in the greatest contempt.

Cicero, in the development of his ethics, constantly has his eye on the "approbation of our fellowmen."[14] Indeed, he goes farther in this regard than Aristotle, who was primarily concerned with the opinion of the aristocratic elite. Cicero maintains that "We should, therefore, in our dealing with people show what I may almost call reverence toward all men—not only toward the men who are the best, but toward others as well. For indifference to public opinion implies not merely self-sufficiency, but even total lack of principle."[15] From this passage it is clear that the pagan humanist considers the indifference to public opinion of the Christian saint or the Stoic sage as mere vanity. The Christian, in turn, frequently disparages the Graeco-Roman concern for public approval and praise as manifestation of pride and self-esteem. Indeed, for the Christian, humility is the cardinal .virtue, since humility indicates man's recognition of his immeasurable inferiority, whenever he compares his own worth to the perfect goodness of God. But Aristotle and Cicero do not always judge men's actions by a Divine measure. Hence, they sometimes view humility (i.e., excessive indifference to the opinion of one's fellows), as an inverted sense of pride and they deplore it equally with boastfulness and arrogance as an inflated sense of one's own worth. The good man will avoid both extremes and possess a self-esteem proportionate to his worth, and look for honor as a just reward and testimony to his virtue. For Cicero, as for Aristotle, man's aim should be to deserve the reputation and glory which he seeks; provided that the ap-

---

[14] *ibid.*, I. 28.
[15] *ibid.* Cf. quotation facing introduction to this book.

plause and praise of the world accord with true worth, no limit
is set to the extent to which a man may seek public approbation. Aristotle's magnanimous man, who possesses all of the
virtues and to the fullest extent, becomes Cicero's high-minded,
great, and exalted soul. He may tower so far above the ordinary
mortal that men compare him in excellence to the Gods and
pay him equivalent honor (in the Christian ethics this is the
worst of sins; indeed, Satan was cast out of Heaven for just
such pride). As Cicero observes, "People admire in general
everything that is great or better than they expect, they admire
in particular the good qualities that they find unexpectedly in
individuals. And so they reverence and extol with the highest
praises those men in whom they see certain pre-eminent and
extraordinary talents."[16] When Scipio dies, Cicero pays him
just such tribute. To the modern reader his praise of Scipio
may seem extravagant, but for the pagan moralist it was strictly
in accord with his conception of man's potentialities for moral
greatness. Hence, as Cicero says of Scipio, the exalted hero
will be held in perpetual esteem by all posterity and his glory
and reputation will never die.[17] Cicero thus achieves permanence for his values; in place of Plato's abstract notion of a
Divine Beauty or the Christian belief in God and heaven, he
depends on succeeding generations of men to perpetuate the
fame of the great men of the past. Time and death are transcended, but not humanity. Cicero has no surer and more secure place in which these supra-personal values can repose.

THE STOICS

The Stoics, like the Christians and the neo-Platonists, hold
the desire for human praise in low esteem. Again, belief in
the existence of a transcendental force superior to man leads
to the disparagement of human opinion. The Stoic's aim was
to act in harmony with the principles of the Universe and therefore to be detached and aloof from mundane concerns. Hence,

[16] *ibid.*, I. 19.
[17] *De Amicitia* in *De Senectute, De Amicitia, De Divinatione*, trans. William A.
Falconer, Cambridge, Mass., 1953, 27.

as Cicero himself observes, "About good fame (that term being a better translation in this context than 'glory' of the Stoic
expression *eudoxia*) Chrysippus and Diogenes used to aver that,
apart from any practical value it may possess, it is not worth
stretching out a finger for."[18]

Seneca is not completely within the tradition of his fellow
philosophers in this regard. At times, he considers posthumous
reputation eminently desirable. Elsewhere, however, he contradicts himself and disparages the desire for honor with as
great zeal as any of his school. Thus in his *Letters* he writes,
"You say, again, that renown is the praise rendered to a good
man by good men. Praise means speech: now speech is utterance with a particular meaning; and utterance, even from the
lips of good men, is not a good in itself. For any act of a good
man is not necessarily a good; he shouts his applause and
hisses his disapproval, but one does not call the shouting or the
hissing good—although his entire conduct may be admired
and praised—any more than one would applaud a sneeze or
a cough."[19]

We have here reached a turning point in the historical development of this moral concept. The favorable opinion of
Aristotle and Cicero, and of their societies in general toward
public honor (fame, glory, renown), disappears in the late
Roman period as the Stoic philosophies and the Christian faith
gain popularity. Although there is a Carolingian Renaissance
in the 9th century and an even more significant rediscovery of
ancient wisdom in the 12th and 13th, the worldly spirit of
Aristotle and Cicero, reflected in this fervent espousal of human
reputation and glory, does not play a dominant role in any
medieval moral philosophy. Aquinas and Dante rely heavily
on both of the ancient philosophers, but not until Petrarch—
who marks the beginning of the true Renaissance, rediscovering
and recreating the spirit and values of the classical humanists—
can one say that the pagan ethics of Greece and Rome are gen-

[18] *De Finibus*, trans. H. Rackham, New York, 1921, III. 17.
[19] *Ad Lucilium Epistulae Morales*, trans. Richard M. Gummere, Cambridge,
Mass., 1943, III. 102.

uinely competing with Christianity for the philosophical allegiance of educated men.

For Marcus Aurelius, the need to disparage the things of this world becomes so great that an almost medieval mortification of the flesh results. Man becomes utterly insignificant; human things are as evanescent as smoke. Instead of exalting man's moral potentialities, Aurelius is constantly dwelling on man's insignificance: "How small a part of the boundless and unfathomable time is assigned to every man? For it is very soon swallowed up in the eternal! And how small a part of the whole substance? And how small a part of the universal soul? And on what a small clod of the whole earth thou creepest?"[20] Aurelius attacks vehemently, in accordance with this basic notion of man's trivial and inconsequential stature, all those illusions by which man seeks to create a better image of himself. Among these, his chief target is that love of fame which had so obsessed Cicero. Continually and systematically he belabors those who place any value on "the desire of empty fame."[21] Marcus Aurelius particularly desires to explode the notion that posthumous fame will give man immortality: "And consider too . . . how many know not even thy name, and how many will soon forget it, and how they who perhaps now are praising thee will very soon blame thee, and that neither a posthumous name is of any value, nor reputation, nor anything else."[22] Only fools, Aurelius says elsewhere, desire to have their virtuous deeds rewarded by the praise of men.

ST. AUGUSTINE

St. Augustine is in many ways the most significant figure of the late Roman era, since he was himself converted to Christianity and writes with a full awareness of the pagan values of Cicero. Many of his remarks in *The City of God* are a direct refutation of the Roman ethos; he continually contrasts to their

---

[20] *Meditations* in *Great Books of the Western World*, ed. Robert Maynard Hutchins, trans. George Long, Vol. 12, Chicago, 1952, XII, 32.
[21] *ibid.*, VIII, I.   [22] *ibid.*, IX, 30.

city of man his more glorious city of God. His opinions, moreover, are a foreshadowing of the typical medieval Christian attitudes. When he writes of honor and reputation, he apparently bears in mind that many of his readers, whom he is seeking to proselytize, are men whose allegiance to the pagan values has not been yet completely destroyed; hence, at times, he coaxes and persuades by suggesting that the Roman ethics is praiseworthy but somewhat inferior to the Christian. At other times, he blasts the opinions of his heathen opponents with all the fury and contempt of a zealous defender of the true faith.

Once again human praise is disparaged, primarily because of its inferiority to the divine measure of man's worth. Like Plato and the Stoics, Augustine believes that the ultimate source of goodness lies elsewhere than in the hearts of men, and that insofar as human beings are praiseworthy it is because they have been sanctified by God's grace. Hence, he admonishes his reader "to avoid this desire of human honour, the glory of the righteous being wholly in God."[23] Like all of the medieval philosophers, he insists on the supremacy of the Christian virtues: "But however much that virtue may be praised and cried up, which without true piety is the slave of human glory, it is not at all to be compared even to the feeble beginnings of the virtues of the saints, whose hope is placed in the grace and mercy of the true God."[24]

The Christian philosophers of the Middle Ages agreed with Augustine that all human glory was mere vainglory in the eyes of God, nor did the renaissances of the 9th and 12th centuries alter the general medieval philosophical attitudes, so predominantly Christian, however much certain medieval figures such as John of Salisbury may have read and revered the classical authors. Augustine expresses what was to become common medieval opinion concerning honor when he speaks of the trivial censures of mortal men and suggests that they are commonly beclouded in a mist of ignorance and error.

[23] Augustine, *The City of God* in *Great Books of the Western World*, ed. Robert Maynard Hutchins, trans. Marcus Dods, Vol. 18, Chicago, 1952, V, 14.
[24] *ibid.*, V, 19.

Whether one is dealing with the pessimistic view of man's nature held by St. Augustine or the optimistic attitude of St. Thomas, the desire for human glory is never considered a stable and reliable measure of human virtue. The two great masters of medieval philosophy disparage the desire for "vainglory" for exactly the same reason: piety and saintliness are man's goal and the zeal for human glory can only interfere with man's attainment of it. Man's relation to God is of paramount importance and hence contempt of glory is a great virtue. Augustine writes with a full awareness of the conflict between the Christian and the pagan-humanist ethics; he sees man's allegiance divided between the city of God and the city of man, and he completely rejects all worldly attachments:

"For so hostile is this vice to pious faith, if the love of glory be greater in the heart than the fear or love of God, that the Lord said, 'How can ye believe, who look for glory from one another, and do not seek the glory which is from God alone?' . . . But since these Romans were in an earthly city and had before them, as the end of all the offices undertaken in its behalf, its safety, and a kingdom, not in heaven, but in earth—not in the sphere of the eternal life, but in the sphere of demise and succession, where the dead are succeeded by the dying—what else but glory should they love, by which they wished even after death to live in the mouths of their admirers?"[25]

BOETHIUS

The Consolation of Philosophy by Boethius was influenced by both Platonic and Stoic philosophy. The extent to which Neo-Platonism and Neo-Stoicism could merge with Christianity is indicated by the fact that Boethius' book was frequently taken for a work of Christian philosophy. At the beginning of his treatise, Boethius laments the fact that he has been thrust in prison, "bereaved of my dignities, blemished in my good name."[26] The judgment of the world has been harsh and un-

[25] *ibid.*, V, 14.
[26] H. F. Stewart, trans., New York, 1926, I, 4.

31

fair and now he is subjected to the degradation of imprisonment. Lady Philosophy listens to Boethius' complaints about his
misfortunes and man's injustice to man, but, instead of ex-
tending sympathy to him, suggests that he examine more carefully the things which the world values so highly. She proceeds, in exactly the same manner as had Aurelius, systematically to expose and demolish the value of human fame. She
points out that if it had any intrinsic worth, honor would not
be bestowed on the most undeserving of men, as it commonly
is. She admits that virtuous minds which have not quite achieved
perfection may be attracted by "desire of glory, and fame of
best deserts toward their commonwealth."[27] But she repudiates
this Ciceronian concept.

She next explodes the notion that man can achieve immortality through posthumous reputation. Here the argument parallels Aurelius closely: "the fame of never so long time, if it be
compared with everlasting eternity, seemeth not little but none
at all."[28] Fame, anyway, is the mere "tattling" of men, "vain
rumours," and "popular blasts."[29]

Lady Philosophy presents a lengthy refutation of the pagan
notion of immortal fame: "But what have excellent men (for
of these I speak) who seek for glory by virtue, what have we,
I say, to expect for these by fame after final death hath dis-
solved the body? For if, contrary to our belief, men wholly
perish, there is no glory at all, since he to whom it is said to
belong is nowhere extant. But if a guiltless mind freed from
earthly imprisonment goeth forthwith to heaven, will she not
despise all earthly traffic who, enjoying heaven, rejoiceth to
see herself exempted from earthly affairs?"[30] Again it is evident
that those who believe in some moral power outside man and
superior to him find little need to worry about posthumous
reputation. Indeed, the degree to which a particular ethics
stresses the significance of immortal fame seems to vary almost
in direct proportion to the extent to which it is certain or un-

[27] *ibid.*, II, 7.   [28] *ibid.*
[29] *ibid.*   [30] *ibid.*

certain of a supra-mundane force in which its values repose eternally and to which the individual can attach himself after death. The Stoic unites with the Universe, the neo-Platonist strives to assimilate the spiritual part of himself to the Divine Beauty, and the Christian seeks union with God. In each case, posthumous reputation is considered of little importance, since men believe they have something greater than man to trust, to give security to their values, and to yield them immortality.

ST. FRANCIS AND THOMAS A KEMPIS

Medieval "contempt of the world," as we have seen, is a negation of those things which Aristotle and Cicero valued so highly—nobility, honor, friendship, and other human attachments—simply because there was something better to exalt. Whether it is the relatively pessimistic and otherworldly outlook of St. Augustine or the relatively optimistic and worldly emphasis of St. Thomas, the primary purpose of the medieval moralist is to exalt that which is not of this earth. Man's happiness lies principally in his love of God and his ultimate union with Him—although, as we shall see, Aquinas can and does place considerable emphasis on "thisworldly" values.

When the medieval saint carried this exaltation of God to its extreme, he not only spurned the favorable opinion of man but even hoped to be abused by his fellows. St. Francis writes that when he and his companions "were called of God and elect to bear in their hearts and in their deeds and preach with their tongues the cross of Christ, they seemed to be and were in very sooth men crucified. . . . Therefore they desired the more to suffer shame and contumely for the love of Christ, rather than honor of the world and reverence and praise of men: in insults they rejoiced and at honors they grew sad."[31] This is the antithesis of the Aristotelian ethics. Aristotle had held that honor (both in its private and its public sense) and virtue were practically synonymous. For St. Francis, on the

[31] *The Little Flowers of St. Francis of Assisi,* trans. T. W. Arnold, London, 1904, V.

other hand, "all virtue and all goodness come from Him, and not from the Creature, and . . . no man may glory in himself; but whoso will glory, may glory in the Lord, unto whom is honor and glory for ever and ever."[32]

The Imitation of Christ also goes to great lengths in its attempt to abase man and to exalt God. Thomas a Kempis, like Boethius' Lady Philosophy, exhorts his reader to lift up his eyes to the Heavens when he grieves that other men are unworthily honored while he is abused. The desire for human praise is considered vanity, since it is God, not man, who deserves praise for whatever good exists in man. Moreover, human glory is reprehensible because it diverts men from their ultimate good. "Verily vain glory is an evil plague, the greatest of vanities, because it draweth us away from the true glory, and robbeth us of heavenly grace. For whilst man pleaseth himself he displeaseth Thee; whilst he gapeth after the praises of man, he is deprived of true virtues."[33] Thomas a Kempis desired no worldly attachment to detract from man's passionate love of his Creator. Hence, "all human glory, all temporal honour, all worldly exaltation, compared to Thy eternal glory, is but vanity and folly."[34]

AQUINAS

St. Thomas Aquinas, by his synthesis of the Christian faith and the philosophy of Aristotle, widens considerably the medieval conception of man and of his place in the universe. Though he continues to exalt God and to insist on the supreme importance of the theological aspects of man's life ("the city of God"), he also emphasizes the significance of man's worldly life ("the city of man"). Whereas St. Augustine and St. Francis had tended to turn their eyes away from the things of this world, St. Thomas devotes much of his attention to the elaboration of a systematic ethics to guide man during the course of

[32] *ibid.*, x.
[33] Thomas a Kempis, *The Imitation of Christ*, trans. William Benham, in *The Harvard Classics*, ed. Charles W. Eliot, Vol. 7, New York, 1937, III, 40.
[34] *ibid.*

his mortal existence. In doing so, he relies on the Aristotelian ethics; as a result, the desire for temporal honor is once again admitted as a permissible goal. "Consequent to his life as a citizen, there are also certain goods that man needs for his civic actions. Such is *a position of honour*, through inordinate desire of which, men become proud and ambitious. . . . There is another desirable thing consequent to the civic life, and this is *to be well known*, through inordinate desire of which men are said to be desirous of vain glory."[35]

At first glance, it might seem that Aquinas has successfully merged Christ and Aristotle and that the 13th century ushers in a new era of genuine Christian humanism. But if one examines further Aquinas' attitude toward human praise, it becomes apparent that, though he tolerates it, he does so with many reservations. Indeed, in comparison to Divine measurements, Aquinas deprecates the desire for human praise as a standard of little reliability. His arguments echo Augustine's:

"The supreme good must needs be perfect, for it satisfies the appetite. But the knowledge of one's good name, wherein glory consists, is imperfect: for it is beset with much uncertainty and error. Therefore glory of this kind cannot be the supreme good. Furthermore. Man's supreme good must be supremely stable in human things: for it is natural to desire unfailing endurance in one's goods. Now glory, which consists in fame, is most unstable, since nothing is more changeable than human opinion and praise."[36]

This is a far cry from the *Nicomachean Ethics*, where Aristotle had suggested that the impulse toward honor and the dread of dishonor are the very qualities which distinguish the aristocrat from the commoner. Honor, for Aristotle, was central to his whole ethics; for Aquinas it plays a relatively minor role.

It is true that the Renaissance of the 12th and 13th centuries is responsible for the rediscovery of Aristotle and for his in-

[35] St. Thomas Aquinas, *The Summa Contra Gentiles*, trans. The English Dominican Fathers from the Latest Leonine Edition, London, 1928, III, I, 63.
[36] *ibid.*, III, I, 29.

corporation into Christian theology. But the pagan philosopher is Christianized in the process. Again and again, Aquinas stresses the precedence of faith over all other virtues. He also insists that the theological virtues of faith, hope, and charity, which define man's relation to God and which serve as guides to beatific union, are paramount, with Aristotelian virtues acceptable only in a subordinate position. Man's ultimate happiness is not to be found in this life, except for the rare person who like Aquinas or Dante has a Beatific vision before death, since it consists in the contemplation of God. In short, man's life should have one primary aim, man's supernatural last end. The desire for human honor is tolerated, but contempt of glory is praised as a sign of humility and higher virtue in accordance with the first Beatitude, "Blessed are the poor in spirit."[37]

If the 12th and 13th centuries are to be treated as a genuine renaissance of pagan values, and if St. Thomas Aquinas is to be considered the great philosopher who completely synthesized the Christian and the pagan-humanist ethics, then we must invent a new word for the Renaissance of the 15th and 16th centuries, for its resurrection of pagan values is of a wholly different order. Contrast, for example, Aquinas' omission of any reference to posthumous fame with the importance given to it by Bishop Guevara in the 16th century: "Onely the good and ill renoune of men aspire greatly to perpetuitie, for that they stande free from fortune, and prevaile even over the remembraunce of time: the persons determine, but their renoune lives ever."[38] Though both Aquinas and Guevara were influenced by the classical ethics, it is the Spanish bishop who is really treating honor in the spirit of the pagan humanists. Renown, honor, and posthumous fame receive again the major stress which pagan philosophy placed upon them; they are not, as with Aquinas, given a secondary role or damned with faint praise. Even though Aquinas relies much more heavily on other aspects

---

[37] *The Summa Theologica*, trans. the Fathers of the English Dominican Province, London, 1935, I, II, 69.
[38] Geoffrey Fenton, *Golden Epistles*, London, 1575, p. 142.

of the Aristotelian ethic, he has essentially but one all-consuming passion—the knowledge and love of God. Guevara, on the other hand, as a typical man of the Renaissance, emphasizes two distinct ethical systems, the one Christian and the other pagan, and his moral allegiance is divided between them.

DANTE

In the thirteenth canto of Dante's *Inferno*, Pier delle Vigne tells the poet that he committed suicide out of despair and asks him when he returns to the world to refresh his fame with his countrymen.[39] So, likewise, in the thirteenth canto of the *Purgatorio* the envious lady, Sapia, expresses a natural human yearning to have her fame restored with her kinsfolk.[40] Dante seems to pity these people who long so nostalgically for contact with their former homes. But in the eleventh canto of the *Purgatorio*, the miniature painter, Oderisi, is being purged of his pride, which consists largely in the importance which he attached to worldly reputation and the desire to excel his rivals. Humbled and penitent, he now realizes the emptiness of human fame:

"O empty glory of human powers! How short the time its green endures upon the top, if it be not overtaken by rude ages! . . . Earthly fame is naught but a breath of wind, which now cometh hence and now thence, and changes name because it changes direction.

"What greater fame shalt thou have, if thou strip thee of thy flesh when old, than if thou hadst died ere thou wert done with pap and chink,
before a thousand years are passed? which is shorter space to eternity than the twinkling of an eye to the circle which slowest is turned in heaven."[41]

These arguments are the time-worn commonplaces which we have been tracing ever since Augustine. It is an interesting

---

[39] *The Divine Comedy*, trans. Alan Howell and Philip Wicksteed, London, 1936, I, Canto 13.
[40] *ibid.*, II, Canto 13.   [41] *ibid.*, II, Canto 11.

commentary on Dante's own position as an artist that he replies to his fellow craftsman: "Thy true saying fills my heart with holy humility, and lowers my swollen pride."[42]

THE MEDIEVAL CHIVALRIC CODE

Desire for honor and glory was an obsession of the feudal nobility. The medieval attitudes toward honor just discussed have little relevance, therefore, to the aristocratic class. The typical medieval knight was not a deeply learned man and hence was not necessarily aware of what Augustine and St. Francis had to say about the transitory nature of fame and glory. It was most unlikely that he would understand the subtle, intricate way in which St. Thomas blended Christian principles and Aristotelian teaching in his treatment of honor. On the other hand, the knight was, by definition, a warrior. When he engaged in battle he was apt to be just as thirsty for fame and glory and just as keenly sensitive to public reproach and shame as his Renaissance counterpart. Honor, glory, reputation, and renown were an integral part of the medieval chivalric code, as were also the martial and heroic virtues of prowess, ambition (desire for fame), fealty, oathkeeping, loyalty to one's military leader, and generosity (largess) on his part in the distribution of rewards to his valiant soldiers. Indeed, kinship and clan ties were so strong, and sensitivity to insult was so acute, that blood revenge, as well as trial by combat, was quite common in the Middle Ages. These are pagan sentiments which came to the peoples of Western Europe from indigenous sources, largely from the tribal values of the Teutonic race. Hence, the heroes of the medieval epics and chronicles were often as warlike and bloodthirsty as the heroes of primitive folk epics in Anglo-Saxon, Teutonic, or Celtic literature.

Medieval culture was, in other words, a blending of Christian and pagan elements. Professor George Fenwick Jones of Goucher College has recently published a study of the concept

[42] *ibid.* See also Jacob Burckhardt, *The Civilization of the Renaissance*, Oxford, 1945, pp. 87-88.

of honor in medieval German literature. It is his conclusion, after tracing back to the purely Teutonic sources of this and related moral concepts, that medieval culture is profoundly ambivalent, since pagan values often had a more immediate and telling influence than the Christian (particularly for the aristocratic warrior class). This leads him to a conclusion that is implicit in Huizinga's study of aristocratic values in *The Waning of the Middle Ages*: the whole medieval world was a dualism, and man was expected to conform to two contradictory ideals.[43] One was that of Christ and the Virgin Mother; the other was that of the Sword.

Medieval man was not totally unaware that a basic ethical ambivalence existed as a result of the duality of his values. Joinville, for example, records some revealing comments of Philip of France in regard to a man who had been named after the Duke of Burgundy. King Philip said that he hoped "that God would make him as valiant (preux) a man as the duke. And they asked him why he had not said as right worthy a man (prud'-homme). 'Because,' said he, 'there is a great difference between a valiant man (preux-homme) and a right worthy man (prud'-homme). For there are many valiant knights in Christian lands, and in the lands of the Saracens, who never believed in God nor in His mother. Whence I tell you,' said he, 'that God grants a great gift, and a very special grace, to the Christian knight whom He suffers to be valiant of body, and at the same time keeps in His service, guarding him from mortal sin. And the knight who thus governs himself should be called right worthy (prud'-homme) because that prowess comes to him by the gift of God. And those of whom I spoke before may be called valiant (preux-homme) because they are valiant of their body, and yet neither fear God nor are afraid of sin.' "[44]

---

[43] This view is expressed in some detail in Chapter 6, *Honor in German Literature*, Chapel Hill, 1959, pp. 104-122.

[44] Joinville, *Chronicle of the Crusade of St. Lewis* in Villehardouin and de Joinville, *Memoirs of the Crusades*, trans. Sir Frank Marzials, London, 1955, p. 276.

Both the concept of "prud-homme" and that of "preux-homme" are, of course, integral parts of the medieval chivalric code. The pagan aspect of this code (i.e., preux-homme) had its roots both in Roman and Teutonic culture which blended together in the gradual development of medieval chivalry. For the aristocratic military class there is direct continuity of cultural ideals from the late Romans and the Teutons, through the Middle Ages, to the Renaisance. When Tacitus, for example, observes that the Teutons preferred death in battle to a life of shame, his observation may refer to the cultural behavior of the Germans but his remark is a Roman commonplace which was frequently cited both in the Middle Ages and in the Renaissance. For the warrior, whether Roman or Teuton, of the 13th or of the 16th century, was often eager to acquire glory and fame and was invariably sensitive to the possibility that he might disgrace himself publicly. Because he was so quick to resent an affront, trial by combat was common in the Middle Ages; indeed, this practice was the forerunner of the Renaissance duel. As we move from one age to another, the social institution may alter but the desire to preserve honor and avoid shame, to take justice into one's own hands, and even perhaps to take private revenge, remains in each case a fixed "ideal" of the military class.

But if there is much in common between the Middle Ages and the Renaissance in ambivalence of ideals, with a secular, aristocratic code on the one hand and the ideal of Christian perfection on the other, there is all the difference in the world between the two periods in their theoretical formulations of these ideals. Pagan commonplaces about honor and shame are to be found in abundance both in the medieval chronicles and in the medieval romances and epics, but these commonplaces are not part of a formal code of pagan moral philosophy since the Church did not permit ideal forms of life outside of its own moral realm. As George Jones has observed, the unlettered Teutons "were fighters rather than philosophers and therefore never formulated a definite moral dogma."[45] In his study of rationalism in the Renaissance, Henri Busson substantiates Jones's observation, stating that to the writers before 1533 "the idea had never occurred of constructing a system of metaphysics or of morality which would be independent of religious doctrines."[46] The typical medieval knight was obviously not a philosopher; more important, he did not even apparently feel the need for a philosophical rationalization of his pagan ideal of honor, however frequently he may have cited this or that pagan commonplace. In the Renaissance, on the other hand, the concept of honor was an integral part of a pagan-humanist ethics which was largely independent of Christian morality and was defined and elaborated with the greatest care.

If the medieval knight had no philosophical sanction for his pagan values, he was nonetheless tempted, like his Renaissance counterpart, to assert his independence of the Christian ethics. Not only is this indicated by King Philip's distinctions between "preux-homme" and "prud-homme" but also by the deathbed "confession" of William Marshal. His justification of his refusal to return booty he had acquired in his military campaigns is strongly revealing of medieval attitudes:

"Sir Henry said to him: 'Sir, you must think of your spiritual well-being: Death has no respect for any person whoever he may be and the clergy teaches us that no one will be saved if he does not return the booty which he has acquired.'

" 'Henry,' replied the earl, 'listen to me briefly: The clergy imposes too harsh conditions on us. They shave us too closely. I have captured 500 knights whose arms, whose horses and whose equipment I have appropriated. If for that the kingdom of God is denied me, there is nothing I can do about it, for I could not return them. I can do nothing more for God than to go to him repenting for all my sins. Unless the clergy wishes to ruin me completely they must abstain from hounding me

---

[45] *Honor in German Literature*, p. 40.
[46] *Les Sources et le Développement du Rationalisme dans la Littérature Française de la Renaissance*, Paris, 1922, p. xiv.

further. Either their argument is false, or no one can be saved.' "[47]

Not only does the medieval aristocracy assert a large measure of independence from Christian ideals by its adherence to its Roman and pre-Christian tribal values, but also it mingles its own ideals of military glory and renown with its ardent Christian passion for conquest over the infidels in the Holy Land. Count Thibaut of Champagne, for example, writes of the crusading knights: "All the worthless will stay here, those who love neither God nor the good, nor honor, nor worth. . . . Now they will go, the valiant bachelors who love God and the glory of this world, those who wisely wish to go to God, and the useless, the cowards will remain. Blind indeed is he who does not make once in his life an expedition to succor God and who for so little loses the praises of the world."[48] This statement obviously supports Huizinga's observation that the thirst for honor of the men of the Renaissance had its roots in the chivalric ideal.[49]

But as Huizinga also observes elsewhere, medieval Christianity did not permit moral ideals outside of its own realm of values.[50] Hence, the Church tried on the one hand to make chivalry into a Christian institution, on the other to denounce those aspects of it which did not conform to its own ideals. St. Bernard of Clairvaux, in his *De Laude Novae Militiae*, associates the desire for inane glory with anger and greed as the motives which cause unnecessary and morally unjustifiable wars. The Church spoke out with particular vehemence against the medieval tournament which represented, from its point of view, a totally unjustified form of homicide. A century after Bernard, the famous preacher Jacques de Vitry said that any knight who participated in a tournament was guilty of the sin of pride because he desired the praise of men and inane glory. Moreover, the Church instituted the truce of God, set periods in which

[47] Sidney Painter, *William Marshal*, Baltimore, 1933, pp. 285-286.
[48] Quoted by Sidney Painter, *French Chivalry*, Baltimore, 1940, p. 86.
[49] Johan Huizinga, *The Waning of the Middle Ages*, London, 1937, p. 59.
[50] *ibid.*, p. 58.

trial by combat was prohibited. If it could not completely sup-press the aristocratic love of combat, it hoped at least to ex-ercise a partial, restraining influence. Indeed, the Council of Clermont in 1130 prohibited tournaments altogether. The Catalan, Roman Lull, whose *Le Libre del Ordre de Cavayleria* was the standard work on chivalry in the 15th century (trans-lated into English by Caxton), held that the true knight would seek only after the honor and reputation of his order. To seek to acquire individual glory was, in Lull's opinion, a vicious and reprehensible individualism.

In addition to denouncing many aspects of feudal chivalry, the Church tried to make it into a thoroughly Christian insti-tution. This is particularly evident in the *Policraticus* of John of Salisbury. John claims that God has founded the military profession, and proceeds to compare the roles which he has ordained for his religious officers, the priests, and his military officers, the knights. John writes of the duty of Christian soldiery: "But what is the office of the duly ordained soldiery? To defend the Church, to assail infidelity, to venerate the priest-hood, to protect the poor from injuries, to pacify the province, to pour out their blood for their brothers (as the formula of their oaths instructs them), and, if need be, to lay down their lives. The high praises of God are in their throat, and two-edged swords are in their hands to execute punishment on the nations and rebuke upon the peoples."[51] In accordance with this Christian ideal, Salisbury denounces the behavior of the knights of his own day. He says that "It is nothing to the point if the men I have been speaking of walk crookedly, for such men are not under the military law because, if we speak accurately, none of them is a true soldier."[52]

In similar vein, in Langlois' fascinating book on life in the Middle Ages, Fauvel complains that all the princes, all of the chevaliers and Knights Templar of his time think only of ruin-

[51] *The Statesman's Book of John of Salisbury*, ed. and trans. John Dickinson, New York, 1927, p. 199.
[52] *ibid.*, p. 190.

ing the Church.[53] So, likewise, the Book of Manners laments
the degenerate ways of the knights and reminds them that when
they took their sacred vows in order to enter the chivalric orders,
they engaged themselves to be courageous, honest, loyal, and
devoted to the Church.[54] The moralist asks if it is not possible,
in front of the very altar where they took their vows, to chase
the wicked knights from the order. Of course, this vigorous de-
nunciation of the corruption of the Christian ideal of knighthood
did not destroy the validity of the ideal itself which was represented at its best by Chaucer's knight, by the saintly King
Louis or, at a more humble level, by the Earl Gaston of Foix
who "said many orisons every day, a nocturne of the psalter,
matins of our Lady, of the Holy Ghost, and of the Cross, and
dirige" and gave every day "five florins in small money at his
gate to poor folks for the love of God."[55]

In its attempt to transform chivalry from a secular institution
which exalted the pagan, warlike virtues of courage and military
prowess into a thoroughly Christian ideal, the Church had to
modify its own attitude toward honor and fame. In this regard,
the chivalric orders and the chivalric vows played an important role, for here the Church succeeded in sanctifying the
sentiment of honor which it had hitherto tended to deplore.
The honor with which it was concerned was largely synonymous
with the feeling of innate moral rectitude, with purity of heart,
with "noblesse de cœur." It involved an uncompromising refusal to perform any act which would make one unworthy either
in one's own eyes or in the eyes of God. Although in this sense
honor was synonymous with the Christian notion of the sanctity
of the private conscience, one cannot completely separate this
meaning of the word from the objective, external meaning. The
perfect Christian knight was apt likewise to wish to appear
"noble" and "glorious" in the eyes of others, in the eyes of the
world, as Joinville's description of St. Louis, the paragon of

[53] Charles Victor Langlois, *La Vie au Moyen Age d'après quelques Moralistes
du Temps*, Paris, 1908, p. 301.
[54] *ibid.*, p. 16.
[55] Quoted by Herbert Read, *The Sense of Glory*, Cambridge, Eng., 1929, p. 18.

Christian virtue, so fully attests. Just as Aquinas, in his moral formulations, at times could seem in strict accord with Augustine in regard to the impurity of those who considered the desire for honor a laudable motive and at other times could seem in strict accord with Aristotle in assigning to it a highly important role, so the chivalric code, in its Christianized form, fluctuated—at times seeming to reject pagan attitudes, at other times seeming to assimilate them without necessarily altering their basic meaning. As Bénichou observes in *Morales du Grand Siècle*:

"Without doubt there was a chronic conflict between Christian doctrine and the values which arose spontaneously from the individualism of the nobility. Christianity contained within itself both a principle of universality and one of constraint, a law, laid down from above, opposing itself to the pride of the aristocrat, which could permit the Church to play the role of a universal lawgiver. In fact, dominated by the force of events and careful of its interests, the Church has always been most prudent in its exercise of these functions. Its history has in part conformed to that of the secular world whose institutions and whose customs it has imitated. In the domain of ideas and of morality, the distinction between the sacred and the profane has not prevented their interpenetration, their adaptation to each other. . . .

"The entire idealism of chivalry is based on this compromise, and one can say that it is at one and the same time a conquest of Christianity over secular values and a retreat of Christianity before the values which sprang into existence from the conditions of aristocratic life. In the chivalric ideal, human glory and Christian charity are in accord with each other up to a certain point, or at least they cease to fight openly and become a unified hierarchy. They represent two points on a continuous chain. Without doubt the tradition of compromise was not all there was to Christianity; the Church remained something different and always kept the right to censure and to fulminate."[56]

[56] Paul Bénichou, pp. 81-82.

45

What conclusions are we to draw, then, about the medieval treatment of the concept of honor in the light of our study of the interpenetration of Christian and pagan values in Aquinas and in the chivalric ideal? First of all, it should by now be apparent that medieval chivalry was a social institution which was partially assimilated by the Church but which in large measure reflected the pagan values of the aristocracy and hence remained partially independent of it. Insofar as the nobility refused to subordinate the aristocratic thirst for glory (which could be considered only vainglory in the eyes of most medieval Christian moralists) to the glory and praise which should be given to God—or at least to justify the desire for glory as a manifestation of Christian virtue and righteousness—it was apt to be fiercely attacked by the moralists of the Church, who were always ready to point to the degeneracy or the worldliness of secular groups. As Villey points out, "medieval ethics rests essentially on the principle of authority; it is in the Divine Word that one finds the laws of human conduct. The Scriptures, mixed with a disfigured Aristotelianism, are the only authorized source of morality."[57]

If we turn to the moral ideas of the age, it can be stated that St. Thomas Aquinas comes closest of all the moral philosophers to approving the desire for glory, but even in his case its role in his ethics is subsidiary to more important religious concerns. It is true that he considers honor the greatest of external goods. It is also true that since he considers honor a natural good, like health, he holds malicious gossip and slander, which may destroy a man's reputation, to be a grave sin. Although he forbids man to take revenge on those who insult him, he does allow man to reprove an insolent person. But he adds that "the daring of the railing reviler should be checked with moderation, i.e., as a duty of charity, and not through *lust for one's own honour*.[58] [Italics mine.] Nor should it be forgotten that since for Aquinas honor is a natural good, it can have no lasting value.

[57] Pierre Villey, I, 6.
[58] *Summa Theologica*, II, II, 72.

One cannot achieve immortality through worldly fame and glory "since nothing is more changeable than human opinion and praise."[59] Finally, although Aquinas is willing to place a certain value on honor for the average man, still he stresses the counsels of perfection for the man aspiring to become a saint. So he reminds his reader that the first beatitude is "Blessed are the poor in spirit," which, he says, "may refer either to the contempt of riches or to the contempt of honors, which results from humility."[60]

In brief, honor at no time in the Middle Ages was considered in any formal ethical system as synonymous with virtue, as it frequently was in the moral philosophies of Greece, Rome, and the Renaissance. Apart from its incorporation into the framework of scholastic philosophy, the elaboration of an Aristotelian or a Ciceronian ethic was unthinkable, since ethics was the handmaiden of theology. As R. S. Rait observes, "the main point is the supremacy of Aristotle *as interpreted by the Schoolmen. Absurdem est dicere Aristotelem errasse.* ('It is absurd to say that Aristotle errs.')"[61] [Italics mine.] In the moral sphere the Church was the supreme authority, just as in the temporal realm it stood sentinel to secular rulers, reminding that the ecclesiastical authority had supremacy over the political authorities.[62]

For the Renaissance aristocrat, honor, glory, reputation, and renown were cardinal aspects of a system of pagan-humanist ethics which sprang from an independent study of Aristotle's *Nicomachean Ethics* and of Cicero's *Offices.* Instead of studying

[59] *Summa Contra Gentiles*, III, I, 29.
[60] *Summa Theologica*, I, II, 69.
[61] *Medieval England*, ed. H. W. C. Davis, Oxford, 1929, p. 443.
[62] Cf. the essay "Medieval Political Thought" by Ernest Baker, in F. J. C. Hearnshaw ed. *The Social and Political Ideas of Some Great Medieval Thinkers*, New York, 1923, pp. 12-13, in which he observes that: "The note of all medieval thought is its universalism. It assumes the existence of a single universal society, which, on its lay side, is the inheritance and continuance of the ancient Roman empire; and on its ecclesiastical side, the incarnation of Christ in a visible Church. . . . But the separation of the Church from the State was not the separation of the State from the Church. The sovereign Pope might exclude the temporal power from things spiritual: he could not, being sovereign, exclude the spiritual power from things temporal."

a "disfigured Aristotle" (Villey's phrase), the men of the Renaissance were studying the Greek and the Latin authors themselves because they were "eager to enlarge their horizons, to get back to the original sources, to read the text of the true Plato, of the actual Aristotle."[63] Thus, one year before Montaigne, stunned by the loss of his friend, Etienne de la Boétie, wrote his essay "On Friendship," Blaise de Vigenère translated three classical treatises on friendship into French—the *Lysis* of Plato, the *Laelius* of Cicero and the *Toxaris* of Lucien.[64] Does this not indicate that the Renaissance ethos is something rather more than "a medieval *Weltanschauung* masquerading in an ill-fitting toga"?[65]

The conclusion here reached that there are cultural differences in the medieval and Renaissance treatment of honor is not basically altered by acknowledging the chivalric thirst for glory and renown. These cultural values had no philosophical basis to support them outside of the moral formulations of medieval scholasticism, where the Aristotelian definitions of honor and related moral concepts were radically altered by Aquinas and approved only with elaborate qualification. Aris-

[63] Lucien Febvre, *Le Problème de l'Incroyance au xvie Siècle*, Paris, 1947, p. 403. The break with medieval scholasticism at Oxford is dramatically recorded by Layton: "Wee have set Dunce in Bocardo and have utterly banished him Oxford for ever, with all his blind glosses, and is now made a common servant to every man, fast nailed up upon posts in all common howses of easement, *id quod oculis meis vidi*. And the second time wee came to New College, after wee had declared your injunctions, wee fownd all the great Quadrant Court full of the Leaves of Dunce, the wind blowing them into every corner." (Quoted by Hastings Rashdall in *The Universities of Europe in the Middle Ages*, Oxford, 1895, II, 533.)

Ascham writes proudly of the renaissance of classical learning at Cambridge. He states that in place of "Duns, with all the rable of barbarous questionietes" Smith and Cheke had brought Aristotle, Plato, Tullie, and Demosthenes "to florishe as notable in Cambridge, as ever they did in Grece and in Italie: and for the doctrine of those fowre, the fowre pillers of learning, Cambridge than geving place to no universitie, neither in France, Spaine, Germanie, nor Italie." (Roger Ascham, *The Scholemaster*, ed. Edward Arber, London, 1923, p. 136.) See also Herschel Baker, *The Dignity of Man*, pp. 207-208. The Renaissance contempt for scholasticism is clearly reflected by the etymology of the word dunce (from Duns Scotus).

[64] Villey, I, 16.

[65] Quoted by Wallace K. Ferguson, "Italian Humanism: Hans Baron's Contribution," in *The Journal of the History of Ideas*, XIX, January, 1958, p. 17.

totle, for example, had said that men "covet being honoured by good men . . . because they are assured of their worth by their confidence in the judgement of those who assert it."[66] The vast gulf between the Aristotelian and the scholastic ethics is evident immediately if we compare the *Nicomachean Ethics* with the following passages from St. Thomas:

"Honour denotes reverence shown to a person in witness of his excellence. Now two things have to be considered with regard to man's honour. The first is that a man has not from himself the thing in which he excels, for this is, as it were, something Divine in him, wherefore on this count honour is due principally, not to him but to God."[67]

"It is true that some are heartened to do works of virtue, through the desire for human glory, as also through the desire for other earthly goods. Yet he is not truly virtuous who does virtuous deeds for the sake of human glory."[68]

"It is requisite for man's perfection that he should know himself; but not that he should be known by others, wherefore it is not to be desired in itself."[69]

"Again, it is incompatible with magnanimity for a man to glory in the testimony of human praise, as though he deemed this something great; wherefore it is said of the magnanimous man that he cares not to be praised."[70]

"Man's highest good must be supremely stable in human things, for it is natural to desire unfailing endurance in one's goods: Now glory, which consists in fame, is most unstable, since nothing is more changeable than human opinion and praise."[71]

Needless to say, these statements are a drastic modification of Aristotle's definitions of the concepts of honor and magna-

[66] *Nicomachean Ethics* VIII. 8.   [67] *Summa Theologica*, II, II, 129.
[68] *ibid.*, II, II, 132.   [69] *ibid.*   [70] *ibid.*
[71] *Summa Contra Gentiles*, III, I, 29.

nimity in the *Nicomachean Ethics*, which was closely studied by many a Renaissance prince but which was not available to his medieval counterpart.

PETRARCH

Petrarch has often been referred to as the first Renaissance man of letters. Recent scholarship has tended to deny this interpretation, as I have indicated in the introduction, since it has discovered that Christian humanism flowered in the Middle Ages (the "renaissances" of the age of Charlemagne, and the age of Dante and Aquinas) as well as in the high Renaissance. Thus C. J. Sisson, in his excellent "Studies in the Life and Environment of Shakespeare Since 1900," writes that "The general outlook of the Elizabethan intellectual world . . . has received much attention of late. The main trend of scholarship has been away from the simpler view which represents Shakespeare as the man of the Renaissance in the sense that a dividing line exists between the Renaissance and the Middle Ages, and in the direction of a view that presents continuity in a stream of thought merging the medieval world in the modern world."[72]

This is an admirable summary of the scholarly findings of much recent research on the Renaissance. That these findings are fallacious will, I trust, gradually become evident in the present evaluation of the concept of honor and its place in Shakespeare's work. At the moment, I wish merely to point out that as a result of these recent "discoveries," Burckhardt's *Civilization of the Renaissance in Italy* has been subjected to heavy criticism. Insofar as this criticism is leveled at Burckhardt's tendency to isolate single great figures from the total historical pattern and to make history consist of little more than the lives of great leaders, it is valid. But when we consider the relatively unsophisticated nature of historical interpretation in the 19th century, we can only be amazed at the extent to which Burckhardt does show an awareness of general cultural movements. Indeed, the imputation that Burckhardt was not aware

[72] *Shakespeare Survey*, III, Cambridge, Eng., 1950, p. 7.

of the Carolingian renaissance or of the renaissance of the 12th and 13th centuries does him serious injustice. He simply minimizes the significance of these movements in terms of the larger pattern of cultural development. Consider, for example, the following passages from *The Civilization of the Renaissance in Italy*:

The Carolingian Renaissance

The civilization of Greece and Rome, which ever since the fourteenth century, obtained so powerful a hold on Italian life, as the source and basis of culture, as the object and ideal of existence, partly also as an avowed reaction against preceding tendencies —this civilization had long been exerting a partial influence on medieval Europe, even beyond the boundaries of Italy. The culture of which Charlemagne was a representative was, in face of the barbarism of the seventh and eighth centuries, essentially a Renaissance, and could appear under no other form.[73]

The Renaissance of the 12th and 13th Centuries

In poetry, too, there will appear no want of similar analogies to those who hold that the greatest Latin poet of the twelfth century, the writer who struck the keynote of a whole class of Latin poems, was an Italian. We mean the author of the best pieces in the so-called 'Carmina Burana.' A frank enjoyment of life and its pleasures, as whose patrons the gods of heathendom are invoked, while Catos and Scipios hold the place of the saints and heroes of Christianity, flows in full current through the rhymed verses.[74]

The Third Renaissance (14th to 16th centuries)

The Renaissance is not a mere fragmentary imitation or compilation, but a new birth . . . the signs of this are visible in the poems of the unknown 'Clericus' of the twelfth century. But the great and general enthusiasm of the Italians for classical antiquity did not display itself before the fourteenth century.[75]

Burckhardt's final assertion is fully borne out by our study of the historical development of the concept of honor, reputation, and fame. Petrarch's *Secretum* is the first full philosophical discussion of the classical concept, after Augustine wrote *The*

---

[73] Jacob Burckhardt, p. 105.   [74] *ibid.*, p. 106.   [75] *ibid.*

City of God, which does not belittle the idea or subordinate it to the Christian idea of goodness. Instead, Petrarch debates with St. Augustine the conflicting views of Christianity and pagan humanism. The dialogue between them is of the greatest importance as a foreshadowing of the general Renaissance solution to the clashing views of its two major ethical traditions. Both the secular and the religious attitudes are tolerated even when they are antithetical. In the later development of the Renaissance, this becomes not mere toleration but a passionate defense of two different systems of value, even though they prove to be mutually contradictory on many important issues. The typical Renaissance nobleman, as I mentioned in the introduction, will defend his honor from the slightest affront and will even take private revenge against his enemies despite the teachings of his church. But he will also go to church on the Sabbath and listen to sermons on meekness, humility, and mercy; he will almost certainly die a Christian and seek forgiveness for his sins—which very likely will include his taking of private revenge.[76]

The pendulum may now be said to have swung too far away from the naïve view of the cultural historians of the late 19th century who saw medieval "night" suddenly replaced by Renaissance "day." In an attempt to counteract this naïveté, Herschel Baker suggests in *The Dignity of Man* that "such scholars as Dilthey, Gentile, and Cassirer have shown that the more we know about the late Middle Ages, the more shadowy becomes the line between them and the Renaissance," and that actually "what we have called the Renaissance began in the twelfth century."[77] This is the central thesis of his book; it is indeed a widely held view today. It is my hope that this present study of the concept of honor will provide evidence to indicate that the pendulum should now be allowed to come back in balance to the mean position, between these two extremes of historical interpretation, that is represented by E. M. W. Tillyard's concluding remarks in *The English Renaissance:*

[76] See discussion of Elizabethan attitudes toward revenge in Chapter 3.
[77] p. 220.

Fact or Fiction?, to which I alluded in the introduction to this book. Although the changes came slowly and almost imperceptibly, the cultural values of the Renaissance are radically different from those of the Middle Ages.

Let us here examine critically one of Herschel Baker's less sweeping judgments: that "Petrarch is traditionally called one of the first modern men, *yet emotionally he lies closer to Augustine than to Galileo*" [Italics mine], and that "he was convinced, as many notables of the Renaissance were, that man . . . was a guest in a strange house on this earth."[78] It is true that in the first part of Petrarch's argument with Augustine in *The Secretum*, the saint has an easy victory.[79] He tells Petrarch that his dreams of nobility make him forget his frailty. Augustine attacks these fumes of self-esteem and points out that "it is very prudent to despise oneself."[80] Petrarch comes to his own defense, but his opponent catches him again and again in inconsistency and demonstrates that he is simply rationalizing when he convinces himself that he has desisted from the pursuit of honor. Augustine then justly observes of himself: "I care as much for what the crowd thinks of me as I care what I am thought of by the beasts of the field."[81] The point is finally reached where Petrarch is forced to admit that he is defeated in the debate.

But then the discussion starts up once again. Augustine chastises Petrarch for still being influenced by ambition, by the desire for the praise of men, and by the hope of an undying name. The medieval commonplace is once more presented: "a false immortality of fame may shut for you the way that leads to the true immortality of life."[82] Petrarch at this point takes up cudgels in his own defense. His voice is the authentic voice of the pagan humanist of the true Renaissance: "I do not think to become as God, or to inhabit eternity, or embrace heaven and earth. Such glory as belongs to man is enough for me. That is all I sigh after. Mortal myself, it is but mortal blessings I

[78] *ibid.*, p. 222. [79] Francis Petrarch, p. 49.
[80] *ibid.*, p. 60. [81] *ibid.*, p. 91. [82] *ibid.*, p. 166.

desire."[83] This is an extreme statement. Petrarch soon qualifies it by the suggestion that man, during his earthly existence, can aspire to earthly rewards such as glory; at the time of his death, he can then put his thoughts on the eternal glory of heaven. This formulation, which almost reconciles Christian and pagan-humanist values, comes very close to defining what the Renaissance solution of the problem will be.

Near the close of the *Secretum*, Petrarch puts in the mouth of Augustine some of the cardinal axioms which *The City of God* had been written to refute. The medieval saint says, "I will never advise you to live without ambition; but I would always urge you to put virtue before glory. You know that glory is in a sense the shadow of virtue."[84] This precept becomes an integral part of Renaissance moral philosophy. It is antithetical to the medieval view that virtue (i.e., Christian virtue) has but the slightest of connections with human glory. So far as I know, since in the Middle Ages ethics was never treated as independent of Christian theology, it is a precept which will not be found in any formal philosophical writings between Augustine and Petrarch. If this is true, it surely will not do then, to find in "Vis Inertiae" the key to a sound interpretation of the nature of Renaissance man and of Renaissance values. Yet for Herschel Baker, the Renaissance "marks no radical departure in man's habit of viewing himself and the world about him," and he concludes that "in the subject that concerns us here—*man's estimation of himself* [Italics mine]— the sixteenth century anti-Scholastics coasted along quite comfortably on the same bland assumptions that had cheered the labors of Peter Lombard and Aquinas."[85]

THE CONCEPT OF HONOR IN THE
RENAISSANCE: ITS RELATION TO THE
MORAL PHILOSOPHY OF THE 16TH CENTURY

A proper appreciation of the pivotal role of the concept of honor in the Renaissance ethos depends upon an understanding

[83] *ibid.*, p. 172.
[84] *ibid.*, p. 182. See above, Chapter I, n. 3.
[85] *The Dignity of Man*, pp. 204-205.

of the nature of Renaissance moral philosophy. The writings of Castiglione, Guazzo, Della Casa, and Count Romei in Italy of Guevara in Spain, of La Primaudaye and Hurault in France and of Bryskett, Elyot, and Cleland in England, provide the Renaissance with a common core of religious and moral assumptions, and hence provide the modern scholar, if he is sufficiently curious to investigate these often dreary moral treatises, with excellent definitions of the general cultural values of the Renaissance aristocracy. The idea of gentility [courtesy] has been studied at great length by Ruth Kelso and Carroll Camden. But no one seems to have made a systematic study of Renaissance moral philosophy in general in order to attempt to define the secular values of Shakespeare's epoch.

For one thing, medieval scholasticism is so ignored by these scholars that they do not even bother to write against it at any great length; they almost never refer to any of the Schoolmen, though they often do inveigh against the kind of moralist who knots himself in subtle and complicated logical argument. The Renaissance moralist is trying to instill a simple set of moral precepts, and is forever mindful that "not Gnosis, but Praxis must be the fruit."[86] As Hardin Craig observes, "The Renaissance adopted the findings or principles of ancient ethics and neglected its methods. . . . Instead of a questioning and reasonable philosopher Aristotle becomes a lawgiver, and his ethical principles, which were once reasoned ideals, become precepts; and precepts so authenticated, called by social habit loudly for action, whether rejection or adoption. There was no room left for thought."[87] Most of the recent histories of philosophy leap quite rightly from scholasticism to such modern philosophers as Bacon, Descartes, and Hobbes without reference to the thoroughly derivative and unstimulating moral philosophy of the Renaissance. But the cultural historian who ignores it does so at grave risk; he is ignoring those very books which defined the values of the Renaissance aristocrat. No one

---

[86] Sir Philip Sidney, *Collected Works*, ed. Albert Feuillerat, Cambridge, 1923, III, 19.
[87] *The Enchanted Glass*, New York, 1936, pp. 199-200.

who has read widely in this literature will arrive at the conclusion either that the man of the Renaissance is a self-centered
individualist, or that he is living in a world not radically altered
from the Middle Ages. The typical Renaissance aristocrat is
a curious amalgam of two distinct cultures, Christianity and
pagan humanism. He ranges himself, in his moral allegiances,
all along the line between the two extremes of pure Christianity
and pure humanism. It would be hard to find a better summation
of the nature of Renaissance values, as defined in the writings
of the moral philosophers, than this of Pierre Villey:

"A truce is signed. These writings recognize the right for
moral philosophy to provide a code of behavior, but only after
imposing on it their own conditions. Alongside religious ethics,
and just subordinate to it, a way of life can develop according
to its own dictates. Revelation will continue to define the purpose
of human existence and will place a fine network of 'revealed'
morality over the whole of life. Reason will have to contain
itself within the interstices left free. Adopting the maxims of
the philosophers of antiquity, and creating new ones which
imitate them, reason will indicate the means by which the
sacred Christian principles can be carried out, and will dictate
the law in that portion of human activity which religion has
abandoned as a neutral zone.

"In such circumstances, then, what is likely to happen? Of
course, for true Christians, and for all those whose inmost
being is impregnated with an obsessive preoccupation with the
Beyond, with a deep sense of God's presence, and of faith in
Christ, the neutral zone will remain small and reason will be
strictly limited to a subordinate role. If reason nonetheless
manages to make morality evolve despite the immobility of the
sacred texts, it will do so secretly and without touching the
principle of authority, merely by modifying the sense of Scripture. The idea of the Eternal is too weighty and the word of
God is too powerful for those who are Christian in the full
sense of the word not to extend their jurisdiction over most of

life's actions or forbid positive reason (that is, reason based on facts) to encroach further on their province.

"But if the enticing game of giving free rein to reason in its unshackled form happens to catch men's attention and they turn their attention toward the realities of present human existence as toward a new pole, who does not see that moral philosophy, feeling hemmed in, will gnaw at the net, will extend the boundaries of the territory which has been conceded to it, will perhaps capture man's entire soul? In some cases, then, it will relegate religious faith to a back shop, where it will die out. In other cases religion, alive but completely enervated, will still be a part of life but actively participate in it only feebly and from a distance. Then the two roles will have been inverted; the pivot of human morality will have changed.

"Between these two extremes, an infinite number of intermediary positions offer themselves to Renaissance thinkers. Each man will place himself in the scale, more or less distant from the polar extremes, according to his intellectual temper— depending on whether positive reason has more or less power to organize his life and whether authority and metaphysics have more or less lost their hold on his conscience.

"Between 1550 and 1600 everybody is rushing headlong to the philosophies of antiquity. They are everywhere; it's a mass intoxication."[88]

Here is a complex statement of a complex problem, meriting extensive quotation since it enables our adjusting our telescopes so that a field of vision scattered and jumbled in kaleidoscopic fashion by an infinite number of possible individual configurations becomes, in its essential pattern, precise and clear. If we keep constantly in mind that a particular Renaissance writer may assume a position at almost an infinite number of points between the poles of Christian authority and "reason," we will not lump all Renaissance moralists together in an indistinguishable mass. Villey's clarification amends Herschel Baker's

---

[88] Pierre Villey, I, 12-13. Since it is impossible for me to convey all of Villey's subtle shades of meaning in English, the original French is given in an appendix, pp. 451, 452.

previously quoted description of the Renaissance as a "massive humanistic fusion of the glory of God with the glory of man,"[89] at the same time correcting Spencer's statement that "in the sixteenth century the combined elements of Aristotelianism, Platonism, Neo-Platonism, Stoicism, and Christianity were almost indistinguishably woven into a pattern which was universally agreed upon, and which, in its main outlines, was the same as that of the Middle Ages."[90]

Christianity was of great importance to the Italian, Spanish, French, and English moralists of the Renaissance, to whom I have just referred. But with obvious exceptions, such as *The French Academie* of Pierre de La Primaudaye and the writings of Bishop Guevara, these moralists do not concern themselves primarily with religious instruction. As Bryskett observes in the preface to his *Discourse*, the aim of the discourse in moral philosophy is the "well ordering and composing of thy mind, that through the knowledge and exercise of the vertues therein expressed, thou may frame thy self the better to attaine to that further perfection which the profession of a Christian requireth."[91] For Aquinas and other medieval scholastic philosophers to whom moral philosophy is the sustaining "handmaiden" of theology, this division between religious and moral teaching is unthinkable. Bryskett's remark, "I durst not presume to the study of Divinite," is nevertheless the typical attitude of many Renaissance moral philosophers.[92] Acknowledging their Christian faith in prefatory and concluding remarks, they frequently turn their attention primarily to the inculcation of precepts for daily living: "by study of Morall Philosophie to compasse . . . humane practicke felicite."[93]

In the fulfillment of this task, the Renaissance moralist draws on a thousand different sources, many of which are

[89] *The Dignity of Man*, p. 293.
[90] Theodore Spencer, *Shakespeare and the Nature of Man*, 2nd ed., New York, 1959, p. 1.
[91] Lodowick Bryskett, *A Discourse of Civil Life*, London, 1606.
[92] *ibid.*, p. 23.
[93] *ibid.*

Biblical, Greek, or Roman. Again the modern cultural historian is apt to see such bewildering multiplicity that he comes to feel that the job of defining the cultural values of the Renaissance is an impossible task. Actually, however, the Renaissance moralist is concerned primarily with the assimilation of two philosophical schools, the Academic and the Peripatetic, although he also frequently cites examples from Biblical history. (Biblical references occur much less frequently, however, in Italian moral treatises such as Castiglione's *The Courtier*, Della Casa's *Of Manners and Behaviour*, and Count Romei's *The Courtier's Academie*.) Sometimes the Stoic school is referred to as a third major school of classical philosophy, but none of the moralists we are discussing pay attention to those cardinal aspects of Stoic philosophy—as, for example, ascetic denial of pleasure, complete suppression of passion, or self-sufficient individualism—which contradict the teachings of the Academic and Peripatetic schools. Patriotic sentiments and civic obligations are rejected only in a specifically Stoic treatise such as the *Two Bookes of Constancie* of Lipsius. Otherwise these social concerns are of supreme importance not only for the Greeks and the Romans but equally for Renaissance Europe, which draws heavily on Aristotle and Cicero for authoritative and definitive statement of man's patriotic and civic duties. The notion of the Renaissance as an age of self-centered egoists and individualists, which dates back to Symonds but which has become particularly fashionable since the appearance of T. S. Eliot's essays on the nature of Renaissance values, springs from a disproportionate emphasis on the Stoic heroes of a Chapman. Lipsius' declaration that the bond "whereby we are linked thus to our countrie is but external and accidentall" runs counter to the pagan-humanist doctrines of antiquity and the Renaissance views alike.[94]

[94] Justus Lipsius, *Two Bookes of Constancie*, trans. John Stradling, London, 1595, p. 27. There were, as in every age, many famous egotists and even unprincipled individualists in the Renaissance. Moreover, Machiavelli, one of the prominent figures of the age, is sometimes considered the first modern political scientist because he divorced politics from ethical considerations. But the Renaissance moralists never considered unbridled individualism as an ideal and in England the Machiavellian villain was viewed with the utmost horror.

Because the Italian Renaissance preceded the English by more than a century, the Elizabethan moral philosopher often relies on the previous work of the Italian humanists to make his own task of popularization easier. Elyot, for example, borrows freely from the writings of Petrarch, Pontano, and Patrizzi. But when he relies upon Petrarch, he is using a work which is itself heavily indebted to Cicero's *Offices*. Toward the end of *The Gouernour*, Elyot goes directly to the original classical source. When I point here to the significance of Cicero's *Offices*, which was the grammar school textbook in Elizabethan moral philosophy, I do not intend to qualify my original statement as to the central position of Aristotle and Plato. Cicero states in the opening section of his treatise that he is simply following those two masters, though elsewhere he also acknowledges a debt to the Stoic school. (Medieval writers were primarily interested in the Stoic doctrines in Cicero's works and he was usually considered a Stoic philosopher in that period, but the eclectic Renaissance was influenced by various aspects of his moral philosophy.) Bryskett's remarks in the opening pages of his *Discourse of Civill Life* confirm that the English reliance on the Italian philosophers leads back to the two greatest of Greek thinkers. He writes that Piccolomini, Giraldi, and Guazzo have all "written upon the Ethick part of Morall Philosophy both exactly and perspicuously" and "taught all that which Plato or Aristotle have confusedly or obscurely left written."[95] Hence, he copies Piccolomini's presentation of the moral virtues where Piccolomini himself is but slightly altering the Aristotelian system.

The organization of most Renaissance books on moral philosophy is based, we might note, on the classical virtues presented systematically in the *Nicomachean Ethics* and Cicero's *Offices*. In this regard, the Renaissance moralist is much more heavily indebted to Aristotle and Cicero than to Plato. Elyot, for example, while preferring Plato to all other classical writers, depends in his presentation of the classical virtues and vices upon

[95] Bryskett, p. 24.

the systematic definitions of Cicero's *Offices* and the "warke of Aristotell called *Ethicae*, wherein is contained the definitions and propre significations of every vertue."[96] In an attempt to define the cultural values of the Renaissance, we can not stress sufficiently the importance for its moral philosophers of systematically formulated precepts—as, for example, the Aristotelian virtues—for they are repeated *ad nauseam*. When the Renaissance moralist searches for simple maxims and easily memorized definitions, the Platonic dialogues are much less influential. As Bryskett complains, "Plato hath couched his sense thereof so dispersedly in his dialogues, as I think he must be a man of great learning and exact judgment that shall picke them out, and sever them from the other parts of his Philosophie."[97] This is probably why Plato was not translated into English during the 16th century.

The shaping of the young mind of the Elizabethan prince confirms our recent generalization on the significance of Aristotle and Cicero. Cheke was tutor for the young Edward; he based the moral training of his protégé on Cicero's *Offices* and *Tusculan Questions*, and on Aristotle's *Ethics*. Ascham recounts Cheke's response to his query as to why the King should be reading the *Ethics* of Aristotle rather than the *Cyropaedia* of Xenophon. Cheke had said, "In order that his mind, first instructed in all those infinite examinations and dissections of the virtues and vices, may bring a sound judgment to each of those examples of character and conduct, that everywhere present themselves in history. . . . Still my endeavor is to give him no precept unaccompanied by some remarkable example."[98] Cheke's remarks parallel those of Sidney in *The Defense of Poesie* on the function of the historian, the philosopher, and the poet.

[96] Thomas Elyot, *The Boke Named The Gouernour*, ed. Ernest Rhys, London, 1937, I, 11. (These references are to book and chapter.)

[97] p. 24.

[98] Quoted by T. W. Baldwin, *William Shakspere's Small Latine and Lesse Greeke*, Urbana, Ill., 1944, I, 237.

These same classical works were of central importance in the moral training of the educated nobleman—as, for example, the young Sidney. Thomas Moffet writes in his biography of Sidney that he "lived through his adolescence in the Oxonian Athens" and that he eradicated the vices of his youth by a "proper care of his morals united with principles drawn from the *Ethics*."[99] (Note Moffet's casual assumption that his reader will immediately identify "the *Ethics*" as the "*Nicomachean Ethics*.") Baldwin, in *Small Latine and Lesse Greeke*, documents the fact that Sidney had earlier had the usual grammar school reading of Cicero's *Offices*. As part of his religious training, he also studied a catechism by Calvin.[100]

In short, both the moral training of the Renaissance aristocrat and the organization of the works of moral philosophy were based on the ethical writings of Aristotle and Cicero. This is especially evident in the presentation of the moral virtues by Hurault, La Primaudaye, Elyot, and Bryskett. Their tables of contents and their discussions of specific moral virtues are both derived from either or both of these writers. Sometimes the virtues are Christianized, as in La Primaudaye's presentation of the concept of magnanimity, but not once do these books refer to the Thomistic scheme of four cardinal virtues and three theological virtues, which are to be found as late as Caxton's 14th century translation, *The Book of the Ordre of Chyualry*. To a large extent, the classical vices also replace the medieval seven deadly sins, which are also to be found in that work; this change is particularly evident in Skelton's *Magnificence*, where Aristotelian vices are introduced into a dramatic form, the interlude, which had been hitherto almost wholly Christian.

What I am suggesting, in effect, is that Renaissance moral philosophy (a basic aspect of the training of the aristocrat in the Elizabethan school system) represents a cultural influence

[99] Nobilis, *A View of the Life and Death of a Sidney and* Lessus Lugubris, trans. and ed. Virgil Heltzel and Hoyt Hudson, San Marino, 1940, pp. 77-78.
[100] T. W. Baldwin, I, 390-391.

of profound significance in the shaping of the Elizabethan nobleman. I do not wish to imply that it is by any means the only factor to be considered; Christianity, though not in its scholastic form, continues to exert a widespread influence on all classes of English society. But a century of close scrutiny of the pagan ethics has drastically altered the nature of European man. Although this radical transformation did not take place overnight, Burckhardt's interpretation of the Renaissance is basically sounder and more balanced than that of certain modern scholars who find medieval England "implicit in Elizabethan England"[101] and who suggest that all of the objections of the Renaissance humanists to Scholasticism, "are, in the last analysis, superficial." It is both glib and unfair to Burckhardt to write that to Medievalists no writer is "so glib as the historian who bleats of man's emancipation in the dawn of a Burckhardtian Renaissance."[102]

The soundness of the earlier historians comes through best when we examine the concept of honor in the Renaissance. Almost every work of moral philosophy of the 16th century has a section on the twin concepts of honor and nobility; in each of these discussions we find the basic Aristotelian definitions systematically presented as the standard, authoritative definitions. As we have seen, honor was not a cardinal concept for either the Academic or Stoic schools, whereas for Aristotle "honour is a sort of measure of worth."[103] Here is a point of major philosophic significance in that it most clearly indicates the heavy debt Renaissance aristocratic values owe to the Peripatetic school. Medieval philosophy in general and St. Thomas Aquinas in particular could not accept such a radically unchristian definition of honor; hence, as we have already seen, Thomistic philosophy drastically modifies the Aristotelian notion of the relationship between honor and virtue. The sentiment of honor does exist in the medieval period as an aspect

---

[101] C. J. Sisson, *Shakespeare Survey*, III, Cambridge, Eng., 1950, p. 7.
[102] Herschel Baker, *The Dignity of Man*, pp. 207, 187. See p. 51 above.
[103] *Rhetoric*, I. 7.

of the chivalric code, but it completely lacks any formalized philosophic support.

For the Renaissance aristocracy, honor, good name, credit, reputation, and glory come close to the very center of their ethical values and receive expression almost wherever we look in the records of the nobility of that age. For this class, these values are so popular, so widespread, so trite, that they pass into its literature almost without definition, particularly into the drama of the age. Yet the precise definitions are at hand in almost any of the standard works of moral philosophy of that period. In 20th century American society, the assumption that in some important sense "all men are created equal" has similarly become trite; we accept it so completely that we seldom think of its origin in The Declaration of Independence, or of its philosophic roots in the writings of John Locke. Yet, when the values of our democratic society are challenged by world war, the deep-rooted emotional significance of the assertion is immediately obvious, not least of all in the intense hostility of the average American to the hierarchical caste system of his own army.

For this reason it is a mistake to speak of Renaissance commonplaces disparagingly, as commonplace. True, the Elizabethan school child himself spoke of his book of commonplaces —but these were not trite phrases, but cardinal moral precepts to be written down, memorized, and acted upon. The court audience, for example, which saw *King Lear* would not necessarily have consciously related Lear's remark, "Ingratitude, thou marble-hearted fiend," (I.iv.281) to Cicero's observation that there is no stronger obligation than that of gratitude, or to Seneca's, that there is no greater vice than ingratitude. But this audience could hardly have missed such a precept on ingratitude in some book of Renaissance moral philosophy. Let us look at several commonplaces:

"The most damnable vice . . . is ingratitude."[104]—ELYOT

[104] *The Gouernour*, II, 13.

"Everie gentle hart easily pardoneth all injuries, except unthankfulnes, which it hardly forgetteth."[105]—LA PRIMAUDAYE

"There can be no such injurie offered to a free mind and a bashfull face, then to be called unthankefull."[106]

"Vice for vice, and evill for evill, there is none in this world so evill as the ingratefull man. And of this it commeth that the humane and tender hart doth pardon all injuries, except ingratitude, the which he never forgetteth."[107]—GUEVARA

"Noe man can bee accused or blamed of a more shameful vice then of unthankefulnes."[108]—CLELAND

"For there is no obligation . . . so strong, as this of gratitude."[109]

"No vice laies a more foule aspersion upon man, then that of ingratitude."[110]—GUICCIARDINI

"Seneca was of opinion, that no vice was more contrary to humanitie . . . then ingratitude."[111]—BRYSKETT

"Ingratitude is the greatest faulte that may be."[112]—GASCOIGNE

No one can say whether Shakespeare had read these maxims; we can say that they are the moral values of the Renaissance aristocracy and that Shakespeare's treatment of ingratitude shows his awareness of these values. We can also safely assume that the use of Cicero's *Offices* as the standard textbook on ethics in the Elizabethan grammar schools (which Shakespeare probably attended) had a good deal to do with the absorption

---

[105] *The French Academie*, p. 401.

[106] Fenton, *The Golden Epistles*, p. 11.

[107] Edward Hellowes, *The Familiar Epistles of Sir Anthony of Guevara*, London, 1574, p. 71.

[108] James Cleland, *The Institution of a Nobleman*, facsimile reproduction of the 1607 ed., New York, 1948.

[109] Francisco Guicciardini, *Aphorismes Civill and Militarie*, trans. Robert Dallington, London, 1613, p. 200.

[110] *ibid.*, p. 112.

[111] *A Discourse*, p. 233.

[112] George Gascoigne, *The Complete Works*, ed. John W. Cunliffe, Cambridge, 1910, Vol. 2, p. 20.

of these moral concepts so that they became the cultural values of the ruling class of Elizabethan society.

How do such copy-book maxims on ingratitude or other subjects relate to any consideration of the Renaissance concept of honor? Honor as man's most precious possession, honor as the reward of virtue, honor as the ensign of virtue, honor as the testimony of the good opinion of others, and dishonor as a thing to be feared worse than death itself, are notions which are so all-pervasive in the 16th century that we hardly think of them as integral parts of a systematic philosophy. They do, however, mostly stem from Aristotelian definitions of honor in Renaissance textbooks on moral philosophy. The notion that honor is the reward of virtue is so general that we tend to think that any and every ethical system would say as much. Yet Plato in *The Republic* goes to great length to refute the notion that honor is virtue's true reward. Although Plato does not always condemn honor in his works, it is typical of Renaissance moral philosophy that Count Romei's courtiers are thoroughly Platonic in their discussion of love but their discourse on honor contains thirty-seven references to "the Philosopher" for authoritative definitions of this concept (to his *Rhetoric* and *Politics* as well as to the *Nicomachean Ethics*) and only six to Plato.

 If we isolate the concept of honor from the many other ethical issues discussed in Renaissance works of philosophy, we soon discover that Aristotle's original definitions are a hidden spring from which flow most of the ideas of the writers of the 16th century. We also discover that the code of honor becomes a remarkably consistent and integrated system and that this aspect of Renaissance morality reflects the Greek sense of public conscience (usually considered morally intolerable by Plato, the Stoics, and the Christians). As with Aristotle and Cicero, the Renaissance code of honor teaches that honor is a measure of value, and that it is one of man's primary obligations to act so that he wins the esteem and the praise of his fellow men. Both Guevara and Castiglione, for example, have one primary

goal in mind in their counsel to their courtier—that he attend
court to win honor, credit, reputation, and esteem. Count Romei
and Castiglione even go so far as to suggest, at times, that
he should be crafty and calculating in order to attain his goal.
This is not typical of their counsels, but their basic assumption
is that virtuous behavior will be rewarded by public esteem
(the Aristotelian notion that honor is the end, the reward, the
sign of virtue), and their emphasis is on the inextricable and
necessary connection between virtue and honor.

Robert Ashley is the voice of the Elizabethan nobility when
he argues, "For how can vertue stand if you take away honour?"[113] This is a characteristic Renaissance expression of the
close-knit alliance of honor and virtue which goes even beyond
Aristotle's precepts, standing in sharp contrast to the Thomistic
statement that "he is not truly virtuous, who does virtuous
deeds for the sake of human glory."[114] That Ashley is outdoing
Aristotle is particularly evident when he makes public testimony
a more reliable and trustworthy measure of a man's virtue than
his own private conscience. He argues that men desire honor
"that we may behold the Testimonie which good men and
wise have geven of our vertue and be delighted therwith, as
having not so much confidence in our selves herein as in the
judgement of others."[115] It is this stress on social approval
which made the Renaissance aristocrat so highly sensitive to
the opinion of others, so quick to resent a public affront, and so
ambitious to win high honors for himself. The whole code of
honor is a manifestation of an ethics which emphasizes the
moral importance of social approval in every aspect of man's
daily life. Della Casa's definition of pride, which inverts the
Thomistic notion that contempt of glory is a sign of great
humility, is but a logical extension of this Aristotelian social
ethics: "It is most sure, that he that refuseth that which every
man doth hunt for: sheweth therin, he reproveth or contemneth

[113] *Of Honour*, ed. Virgil Heltzel, San Marino, 1947, p. 28.
[114] Aquinas, *Summa Theologica*, II, II, 132.
[115] p. 59.

the common opinion of men. *And to contemne the honoure and renowne, which other men gape for so much, is but to glorie and magnifie himself above others.*"[116] [Italics mine.]

No statement could indicate more clearly the tremendous contribution the ethical philosophies of Greece and Rome made to the civilization of Europe in the 16th century. From Augustine to Petrarch, the European moral philosopher had persistently maintained the Christian view that "the common opinion of men" was an untrustworthy foundation for moral evaluations. In this quotation, however, the opinion of the community is an integral aspect of a humanist ethics, proclaiming the view of pagan antiquity that the man who ignores the public conscience—that collective judgment of his community—is asserting a reprehensible notion of the superiority of his personal conscience.

Let us here examine three key notions of Renaissance humanist philosophy which would have seemed heretical to medieval moral philosophers (for additional "heresies" see Chapter 3):

1. the virtuous individual must seek public approbation to confirm his belief in his own moral worth. This was expressed by two truisms:
   a. it is as impossible to separate honor from virtue as it is to separate the body from its shadow.
   b. honor is, or at least should be, the inevitable reward of virtue

2. the virtuous individual, indifferent to the opinions of others by inner conviction of his own righteousness, is lacking in humility because he is showing that he considers human praise, esteem and approbation an unreliable moral standard. To disparage the opinion of one's fellows is considered by the Renaissance moralists an indication of pride, not of humility. The difference between the Renaissance and medieval attitude on this matter is summed up by one word, vainglory, which

---

[116] Giovanni Della Casa, *Galateo: of Manners and Behaviour in Familiar Conversation*, trans. Robert Peterson, London, 1576, p. 38. Cf. quotation from Guazzo facing introduction to this book.

medieval writers used unvaryingly when referring to the meliorative "glory" so dear to the hearts of Renaissance moralists.

3. posthumous reputation (remembrance by the surviving community of men) can give the mortal individual a sense of permanence. Immortality for the Renaissance writers meant two things—Christian immortality and immortality through posthumous fame. Medieval philosophy had never given the idea of posthumous reputation serious consideration, holding nothing more evanescent and fickle than human opinion and praise.

Shakespeare may or may not have been acquainted with the numerous treatises on moral philosophy which provided the Renaissance with its standard definitions of the moral virtues, of honor and reputation, of posthumous fame, and of disgrace and ignominy—definitions of the code of honor which were primarily restatements of the basic definitions of Aristotle and Cicero. But he had probably read Cicero's *Offices* as a boy in grammar school, and he could not have missed numerous opportunities to observe the behavior of the Renaissance gentleman and man of honor whose actions were being so strongly conditioned by the formative influence of these works. The court of Queen Elizabeth was a living example of the classical virtue of magnificence, and the descriptions of this and other European courts by Sir William Segar and by Fynes Moryson are practically Aristotelian judgments in terms of the sumptuousness and magnificence of one monarch, of the parsimony or prodigality of others.

In addition, the informal accounts in biographies, journals and letters, which reveal how passionately the various Renaissance monarchs and aristocrats sought to guard and maintain their honor and reputation, correlate closely with the formalized exposition of the concept of honor in the books of etiquette and moral philosophy, and especially with the treatises on the dueling code. Shakespeare's acquaintance with this particular social practice of his age can not be doubted; consider, for example, the dueling scenes between Laertes and Hamlet or the imprisonment of Ben Jonson for killing a fellow actor. Indeed, dueling was a common practice in all the Renaissance courts around 1600. It had been banned in Italy by the Council of Trent in 1563, but had just reached the height of its popularity in France and England in the latter part of the century. Thus Henry the Fourth of France (1589-1610) commuted the sentences of seven thousand duelists. In England, dueling became particularly prevalent in the first years of the reign of James the First. It is of no inconsiderable significance, therefore, that the fifty works on honor and the duel which appeared in Italy in the 16th century rely constantly on Aristotle's definitions of honor as the authoritative explication of this concept.[117] Possevino's *Dialogo dell' honore*, for example, has fifty references to Aristotle and his various works in its first ten pages. In the same ten pages there is one reference to Plutarch; no other authority is mentioned. Aristotle, in other words, is being followed as closely by the Italian humanists as he had been by Aquinas three centuries earlier. But whereas the scholastic philosopher had modified the Aristotelian notion of honor so that it would accord with the Christian ethics, the Italian Renaissance moralists slavishly copy Aristotle's definitions. Thus Bernardi, Carbone, and Albergati all cite his definitions in the *Rhetoric* of contempt, spite, and insolence.[118] Though each writer presents an individual interpretation of his meaning, there is no alteration of Aristotle's general import. Albergati, for example, states that "contempt" brings disrepute because it indicates that one does not have a good opinion of another, whereas "spite" is a hindrance to that which another person desires, and "insolence" is apt to wound a person's honor.[119]

The Renaissance was well aware that in many important regards it was breaking away from the ethics of the Christian

[117] Frederick Bryson, *The Point of Honor in Sixteenth Century Italy: An Aspect of the Life of the Gentleman*, Chicago, 1935, Preface and p. 2.
[118] *ibid.*, pp. 27-30.
[119] *ibid.*, pp. 29-30.

Middle Ages. Patrizzi and Muzio, for example, thought of themselves as pioneering philosophers in their attempts to define points of honor in connection with the dueling code.[120] Indeed, although the code of dueling had its roots in the Middle Ages, all of these fifty works on honor and the duel go directly back to the *Nicomachean Ethics* for their basic definitions of honor, its relation to virtue, the precise meaning of contempt, spite, insolence, and for the reasons why dishonor and disgrace represent worse fates for the aristocrat than the loss of life itself. Bryson's *The Point of Honor in Sixteenth Century Italy: An Aspect of the Life of the Gentleman* makes this unmistakably clear; Aristotle, he finds, is the chief authority for the works of the Italian humanists on the code of honor and the duel. Antonio Possevino, for example, declared that Aristotle had been the first to discuss honor. In 1547 Antonio Bernardi, a cleric, gave a series of lectures on Aristotle's ethics in which he included a discussion of the concept of honor as related to the duel. Francesco Patrizzi begins his *Dialogo dell' honore* with the standard definitions of Aristotle.[121]

If the code of honor and the duel springs so directly from the moral notions of Aristotle, if this code is establishing terms of honor for every Renaissance aristocrat and every royal court of Europe, the question whether Shakespeare himself read Aristotle is a matter of little significance. We need only turn to Greville's life of Sidney, where the famous incident of the insult to Sidney by Oxford before the French ambassador on the tennis court is recounted at length, or to Robert Naunton's *Fragmenta Regalia*, which gives a vivid description of the life of Elizabeth's favorites, to see how directly the whole pattern of daily life of the typical Renaissance aristocrat was influenced by the diffusion of the Aristotelian notions of honor and disgrace into hundreds of different works of Renaissance ethics and etiquette. Every contemporary account of the courts of 16th century Europe indicates that the notion of honor, credit, good opinion, and reputation was as precious to the flesh-and-

[120] *ibid.*, pp. 1-2. [121] *ibid.*, p. 2.

blood aristocrat as it was theoretically cardinal in the treatises which defined honor. Lord Perrot, for example, was highly irritated when he lost public esteem because the Queen no longer treated him as one of her favorites. After she had expressed her contempt for him, she suddenly turned to him when she needed help in her wars against Spain. This led him to give vent to his anger by publicly insulting her. As Naunton recounts the episode: "He said publiquely in the great Chamber at Dublin: 'Lo, now she is ready to pisse her self for fear of the Spaniard; I am again one of her white-boyes.' "[122] But he could not endure the loss of the Queen's favor. The scorn she manifested towards him "brake in pieces the cords of his magnanimity."[123]

Public esteem was so closely related to self-esteem in the opinion of the Renaissance aristocrats that it was a cardinal moral imperative to maintain honor, reputation, and good opinion. Hence, Essex and Willoughby were just as quick as Perrot to take offense when their Queen slighted them. The mere fact that Elizabeth had favored another often led the English aristocrat to feel that his own honor was being slighted. Naunton recounts how Essex, on discovering that Elizabeth had given a Queen of chess of pure gold to Sir Charles Blunt, felt impelled to lower the prestige of his rival. He said, " 'Now I perceive every fool must have a favour.' This bitter and publike affront came to Sir Charles Blunt's ear, who sent him a challenge, which was accepted by my Lord."[124]

Many different cultures have placed a high value on honor, reputation, fame, and glory. The Anglo-Saxon chieftain and the medieval nobleman, for example, both felt honor and glory to be major goals of their military life. But the Renaissance aristocrat places an even greater emphasis on them. He considers honor and glory not merely goals to be pursued on the battlefield; they are as well an integral part of his life's goal—

[122] Robert Naunton, *Fragmenta Regalia*, ed. Edward Arber, London, 1870, p. 43.
[123] *ibid.*, p. 44.   [124] *ibid.*, pp. 52-53.

to be the epitome of all the classical virtues and thus win ever greater honor, the true reward of virtue.

The Renaissance aristocrat is, in other words, following a moral philosophy and a code of honor which affect every aspect of his life. Naunton's descriptions of the court of Queen Elizabeth are a direct reflection of a formalized ethics which was part of the training of every one of her favorites. Della Casa's *Galateo of Manners and Behaviour*, one of the most popular of the Italian treatises on ethics and etiquette translated into English during Elizabeth's reign, presents succinctly the cardinal moral precepts carried into practice in Greville's and Naunton's accounts of the life of the English nobility. "I doe not allow, that a man should scorne or scoffe at any man, what so ever he be; no not his very enimy, what displeasure so ever he beare him: for, it is a greater signe of contempt and disdaine, to scorne a man, then to do him an open wrong."[125] And he adds that "He that is familiarly mockte in pastime" interprets it otherwise, "to be done to his shame and dishonour, and thereat he takes a disdaine."[126] These statements reflect the spirit of the typical Renaissance aristocrat, for they are part of the code of honor of his age. Their roots are neither in early Christian philosophy, medieval scholasticism, nor primarily in the writings of either Plato or the Stoics.

Shakespeare's heroes, like the great lords of Elizabeth's court, feel an allegiance to Christian as well as to Greek and Roman ideals, but Shakespeare reflects a concept of honor—of moral esteem dependent on the public recognition of virtue—whose philosophic roots lead directly back to Aristotle and Cicero. That there is only one reference to Aristotelian moral philosophy in Shakespeare's works is irrelevant. As I have already stated, in its definitions of honor, the *Nicomachean Ethics* was the hidden spring from which an endless number of Renaissance ethical treatises and literary works flowed. Shakespeare would have known the thoughts, if not their source.

[125] Della Casa, p. 62.   [126] *ibid.*, p. 65.

73

To be held in low esteem, to fail to receive due public recognition of one's worth, is as morally intolerable for Shakespeare's heroes as it is for the aristocrats of his age. There are no better reflections of the almost obsessive moral concern for public esteem of the Greek, Roman, and Renaissance nobility than the following passages from Shakespeare's major plays:

Othello

CASSIO: Reputation, reputation, reputation! O, I have lost my reputation! I have lost the immortal part of myself, and what remains is bestial. My reputation, Iago, my reputation! (II. iii. 262-265)

Hamlet

HAMLET: O good Horatio, what a wounded name
(Things standing thus unknown) shall live behind
me! (V. ii. 355-356)

King Lear

LEAR: 'Tis worse than murther
To do upon respect such violent outrage.
(II. iv. 23-24)

Macbeth

MACBETH: My way of life
Is fall'n into the sere, the yellow leaf;
And that which should accompany old age,
As honour, love, obedience, troops of friends,
I must not look to have; but, in their stead,
Curses not loud but deep, mouth-honour, breath,
Which the poor heart would fain deny, and dare
not. (V. iii. 22-28)

Julius Caesar

BRUTUS: If it be aught toward the general good,
Set honour in one eye and death i' th' other,
For I will look on both indifferently;
For let the gods so speed me as I love

The name of honour more than I fear death.
            (I. ii. 85-89)

Antony and Cleopatra

ANTONY: If I lose mine honour,
    I lose myself. (III. iv. 22-23)

ANTONY: I have offended reputation—
    A most unnoble swerving. (III. xi. 49-50)

Troilus and Cressida

ULYSSES: The great Achilles, whom opinion crowns
    The sinew and the forehand of our host,
    Having his ear full of his airy fame,
    Grows dainty of his worth and in his tent
    Lies mocking our designs. (I. iii. 142-146)

ULYSSES: Perseverance, dear my lord,
    Keeps honour bright.

            The cry went once on thee,
    And still it might, and yet it may again,
    If thou wouldst not entomb thyself alive
    And case thy reputation in thy tent,
    Whose glorious deeds, but in these fields of late,
    Made emulous missions 'mongst the gods
            themselves
    And drave great Mars to faction.
            (III. iii. 150-151, 184-190)

HECTOR: Mine honour holds the weather of my fate.
    Life every man holds dear, but the dear man
    Holds honour far more precious-dear than
        life. (V. iii. 26-28)

We shall later be examining these famous speeches in their proper contexts. But, upon even so cursory a glance at them, is it not possible to state unequivocally that Shakespeare reflects in his plays the favorable attitude toward honor of Renaissance pagan humanism, and that certainly here Shakespeare is of his age, if also "for all time"?

CHAPTER 2

PART 1: THE ARISTOCRATIC
CLASS STRUCTURE OF THE RENAISSANCE

THE DEFINITION OF NOBILITY

"I GRANT that not only in respect of our beginning, but of our ending too, we are all equals without difference or superioritie of degrees, all tending alike to the same earth from whence we sprong . . . but in the middle course . . . we are over-runne by our betters and . . . must needes confesse that some excell and are more noble than others."[1] The basic aristocratic assumptions of Renaissance society are admirably summed up by this passage from James Cleland's *The Institution of a Nobleman*, which so clearly indicates the vast gulf separating the democratic ideals of Western European civilization in the 20th century from the aristocratic ideals of that same civilization in the 16th century. The inequality of men, the fundamental superiority of some and inferiority of others, and the acquiescence of the vast majority of Elizabethans in being "over-runne by their betters" are as basically the political and social assumptions of Renaissance society as the notions of a social and political equality of all men, of a classless society—with consequent resentment of any attempt to assert class superiority—are the fundamental ideals of our own democratic society.

Despite the fact that Renaissance Europe represents one of the strongest influences in our own cultural heritage, we must recognize our profound antagonism toward many of its basic moral, social, and political assumptions fully to comprehend its concepts and its sensibility. Particularly when we examine political and social ideas of aristocratic superiority, of degrees of moral "nobility" and of social worth, must we recognize deeply rooted beliefs totally alien to us, for it is in just these aristo-

[1] p. 2.

cratic assumptions that the Renaissance concept of honor is rooted. Hence, an adequate analysis of this concept depends on a thorough comprehension of the aristocratic, hierarchical structure of Elizabethan society, and, in particular, a clear idea of the meanings it assigned the concept of nobility.

A central problem of every Renaissance work on moral philosophy was to define the nature of true nobility. An abundance of material on nobility exists which has been studied with painstaking thoroughness by Ruth Kelso in her able and informative book, *The Doctrine of the Elizabethan Gentleman*. Although there is bewildering complexity and sometimes even outright contradiction in the definitions of the concept, they can be reduced to three essential notions. The first of these is based on the idea of virtue and moral worth, but it places its emphasis particularly on outstanding and preeminent virtue, superior moral excellence, manifested by undertaking lofty enterprises, civil or military, in the service of the state. The second results from the inheritance of noble blood from a long line of aristocratic ancestors. Finally, there is "nobility dative"—the particular titles of nobility which could be acquired by the accomplishment of deeds of outstanding public service.

Each of these was an aspect of the Renaissance concept of nobility. The apparent complexity of discussions of them results from a given writer's stressing one at the expense of another, usually for the didactic effect an exaggerated emphasis would produce. Thus Sidney writes in his *Aphorisms*: "I am no herald to inquire of men's pedigrees; it sufficeth me, if I know their virtues."[2] Montaigne makes a sharper distinction between personal worth and inherited nobility, placing a higher value on the first. Nobility and virtue, he says, "have affinitie; but therewithall great difference: their names and titiles should not thus be commixt: both are wronged so to be confounded. Nobilitie is a worthy, goodly quality, and introduced with good reason, but in as much as it dependeth on others, and may fall to the share of any vicious and worthlesse fellowe, it is in estimation

---

[2] Sir Philip Sidney, *Aphorisms*, London, 1807, I, 3.

farre shorte of vertue."[3] The two men are not as indifferent to aristocratic ancestry as they appear to be. The tendency of the Renaissance moralists, culling eclectically from the pagan moralists, to involve themselves in paradox, contradiction, and outright inconsistency, should be recognized from the start.

Yet, although Renaissance moral ideas were seldom original and lacked the systematic integration and logical consistency which a single man, Aquinas, could give to 13th century thought, we find remarkable agreement on many essential points. The problems discussed so exhaustively in the books of moral philosophy were also receiving attention in the literature and drama of the Renaissance, were shaping the ideas and opinions of the men of the age, and hence were reflected in the social customs of the time. The extent to which central ethical concerns were unified in moral theory, literature, and life, is revealed in Renaissance discussions of true nobility. Henry Medwall's *A Goodly Interlude of Fulgens . . . and Lucrece* (1497) is nothing more than the presentation of such nobility in dramatic form. To trace its sources is rewarding as an indication of the truly international nature of humanist ideas and of the many links in the chain which connect the English manifestation of them with their classical sources in Italy. The original document was a dull treatise on the nature of true nobility, *De Vera Nobilitate*, written by Bonaccorso in 1428. Jean Mielot composed a French version of the book which was in turn translated into English by John Tiptoft, Earl of Worcester, and printed by William Caxton. Medwall makes use of the English translation.

The central moral and social issue of the play is simple enough. Lucrece, daughter of a noble senator of Rome, has to choose between two suitors. The one, Gaius Flaminius, is of common stock but great moral worth; the other, Publius Cornelius, although of aristocratic origin, is morally corrupt and ill-mannered. In Tiptoft's version, the daughter refers the

[3] *The Essayes of Michael Lord of Montaigne*, trans. John Florio, London, 1910, III, 5. (These references are to book and chapter.)

suitors to her father, who in turn appeals to the Roman senate to decide which of the two men is the worthier suitor. The story ends inconclusively without any resolution of the dilemma. In Medwall's version, on the other hand, although Lucrece hesitates for some time before arriving at a decision, her final choice is unequivocally in favor of the plebeian but virtuous Flaminius. She decides,

> As the more noble man sith he this wise
> By means of his virtue to honor doth arise.

> I said this before
> That a man of excellent vertuouse conditions
> All though he be of a pore stoke bore
> Yet I will honour and comende him more
> Than one that is descendide of right noble kin
> Whose liffe is all dissolute and rotide in sin.[4]

The conflict between simple virtue and inherited nobility is revealed with even greater dramatic force in the account of the trial of Lord Essex. During the trial Essex saw fit to mention that Cecil's grandfather had been an innkeeper, while Essex himself could boast of a pure and illustrious aristocratic heritage. Whereupon Cecil arose with great indignation and replied: "My Lord of Essex . . . the difference between you and me is great. For wit I give you the preeminence, you have it abundantly; for nobility also I give you the place—I am not noble, yet a gentleman; I am no swordsman—there also you have the odds; but I have innocence, conscience, truth, and honesty, to defend me against the scandal and sting of slanderous tongues, and in this Court I stand as an upright man, and your Lordship as a delinquent."[5]

Although Cecil suggests that he is a more virtuous man than Essex, he nonetheless defers to no inconsiderable extent to Essex, since Elizabeth's erstwhile favorite could boast of aristo-

---

[4] Henry Medwall, *Fulgens and Lucres*, New York, 1920, fol. g. i.
[5] *The Life and Death of Robert Devereux Earl of Essex*, ed. G. B. Harrison, New York, 1937, p. 307.

cratic lineage. Indeed, as Johan Huizinga points out in his informative book *The Waning of the Middle Ages*, even when the nobleman was sentenced to death, he was still accorded all the respect to which his rank entitled him. The cloth placed over his eyes and the cushion on which he knelt were of crimson velvet as symbols of his high station.[6]

The basic assumption of aristocratic theory was, further, that the nobleman would be less likely to be vicious than the common man. As *The Courtier's Academie* suggests, "the noble seemeth borne with a better inclination, and disposition unto vertue, then a plebeian, or one extracted from the common sorte."[7] Several arguments were advanced to support this idea. One of them bears a striking resemblance to racial doctrines of our own 20th century, although the purity of blood desired was that of a class elite rather than one of race. In the words of Cornwallis, "since Time hath distild our bloods and separated us from the crowde, I holde nobility bound not to commit any action tasting of a degenerate humor."[8]

Another argument stressed that a noble line of ancestors provided an incentive to emulate their renowned and preeminent virtues. The aristocrat had not only his own reputation to consider, but also the good name of his family. Castiglione, for example, insists that his ideal courtier must be born of noble stock: "For it is a great deale less dispraise for him that is not borne a gentleman to faile in the actes of vertue, then for a gentleman. If he swerve from the steps of his ancestors, hee staineth the name of his familie."[9] Conversely, as *The Courtier's Academie* points out, the plebeian inherits a predisposition to lesser virtue and can only convince the world of his unusual worth and merit by the greatest effort: "As it is knowne that the one is nobly borne, and the other not, with every one he ignoble shal be lesse esteemed, than the other noble; and it is necessary, that one ignoble, by many endeavours,

[6] London, 1937, p. 34.   [7] p. 185.
[8] William Cornwallis, *Essayes*, ed. D. C. Allen, Baltimore, 1946, p. 39.
[9] Baldassare Castiglione, *The Book of the Courtier*, trans. Thomas Hoby, London, 1928, pp. 31-32.

and in long time, imprint in the minde of men, a good opinion of himselfe."[10]

The third major argument used by the aristocratic theorist to support his notion that the sons of the aristocracy were, almost inevitably, superior to the sons of the middle or working class, was that of breeding and education. Thus La Primaudaye observes: "The Nobilitie is the ornament of everie Commonwealth. For commonly the Nobles are of greater abilitie, of better behaviour and more civill than the common people, than artificers, and men of base estate, because they have beene brought up from their infancie in all civilitie and amongst men of honor."[11] As this passage indicates, honor and nobility were restricted to the aristocratic class largely because that class had sufficient leisure for a humanistic education in the liberal arts and the moral disciplines. "To acquire vertue, quiet, and leasure is requisit."[12] This leads Count Romei, in *The Courtier's Academie*, to make a sharp distinction between the education of the gentleman in the liberal arts and the training of the lower classes in the mechanical arts.

Nobility, then, could mean exalted moral worth or it could mean exalted class position. As the above quotation from *The French Academie* suggests, the two were usually closely linked —a man of noble blood would, presumably, receive the proper training in morals and manners, and hence would, in all likelihood, be noble and worthy of honor because of both his rank and his character. Even though the moral philosophers made due allowance for nobility without virtue, and for virtue without nobility, the ideal gentleman would be able to boast both of his noble lineage and of his virtue. Mulcaster agrees, noting that if he adds "desert in his own person . . . [he] doth well deserve double honour among men, as bearing the true coate of right and best nobilitie, where desert for vertue is quartered with discent in blood, seeing aunciencie of linage, and derivation of nobilitie is in such credit among us and alwaye

[10] p. 224.   [11] *The French Academie*, p. 687.
[12] Count Romei, p. 199.

81

hath bene."[13] Every Renaissance work on moral philosophy reaches this conclusion when it discusses the nature of true nobility. Each kind of nobility is desirable, but as an ideal neither is sufficient by itself. The more exalted one's rank or one's virtuous qualities, the more one is deserving of receiving honor. In the words of Elyot, "Severitie ... Magnanimitie ... Constance ... Honour ... Sapience ... Continence. ... These qualities ... do expresse or sette out the figures of very nobilitie; whiche in the higher astate it is contained, the more excellent is the vertue in estimation."[14]

THE POLITICAL HIERARCHY

The Renaissance moralists, in accordance with their pyramidal and hierarchical view of degrees of superiority in the social body, found an especial correlation between the exalted elite of heroic and magnanimous men of outstanding virtue and those who belonged to the highest political ranks. The monarch, in theory at least, was both politically and morally supreme, and the great lords of the realm were presumably the high-minded, great-hearted souls whose preeminent virtue made them the heroes of the age. Count Romei sums up this ideal correlation when he suggests that political degrees "have amongst themselves like proportion of nobilitie, as in them of vertue there is supposed."[15]

For the aristocratic society of the Renaissance, the positions of the greatest social importance were the "seven degrees of superioritie" described by Segar in *Honor Military and Civill*, "Of Gentlemen, the first and principal is the King, Prince, Dukes, Marquesses, Earls, Viscounts, and Barons. These are the Nobilitie, and be called Lords, or Nobleman. Next to these be Knights, Esquiers, and simple gentlemen, which last number may be called *Nobilitas minor*."[16] This classification includes all the groups which could rightly consider themselves

---

[13] Richard Mulcaster, *Positions*, London, 1581, p. 200.
[14] Thomas Elyot, I, 21.
[15] p. 227.
[16] William Segar, *Honor Military and Civill*, London, 1602, II, 51.

members of the aristocracy. The sharp line the Elizabethans drew to distinguish the upper from the lower classes appears in Markham's remarks on gentility. "*Honor* or *Nobilitie* which the Grecians doe call *Eugenia,* and signifieth liberal and good Birth, is nothing else but *Gentrie,* or the true title of Gentleman; which, howsoever it alter by multiplication of Titles, yet that is the first and most auncient; as being the only Groundworke or Base, from whence is raised and built up the goodly Pyramed or Collosses of all other great denominations, for it can Support and beare up it selfe of it selfe, when without it all other Titles fall, vanish, and are nothing. And whether we derive it from *Generosus,* or *Gentilis,* that is, from *Honor* or good familie, yet it is the first witnesse of Vertue, and makes the person in whom it dwels capable (by merit) of all other Honors whatsoever."[17] The famous incident of Sidney's challenge to Oxford on the tennis court in front of the French ambassador indicates how important it was to Queen Elizabeth to maintain degrees of rank. She rebuked Sidney as an inferior challenging a superior; obviously she was more concerned with a proper and due respect for superior rank than she was with the propriety of a challenge to a duel, though, as we shall see, the Renaissance monarch was opposed to that particular Renaissance ritual.

The Monarch. The monarch stood at the apex of Renaissance society. His position became more and more exalted as the national states took shape and, directly or indirectly, challenged the supreme power of the medieval church. At this point, Christian and pagan-humanist theory coalesce, both bestowing on the regal position an almost divine character. In Christian theory, the king was the direct representative of God on earth, hence his position was sacrosanct. A challenge to the king's authority was a challenge of the divine order of things; sedition and atheism were often linked by the political philos-

[17] Francis Markham, *The Booke of Honour or Five Decads of Epistles of Honour,* London, 1625, p. 44.

ophers of the 16th century. Indeed, it was sometimes assumed that even a wicked monarch was to be given unquestioned obedience since many Renaissance Protestants took it for granted that God could have selected an evil tyrant only if he wished to scourge a nation for its sins. Guazzo gives apt expression to the religious injunction which lay behind the political abso-lutism of the age. "I have alwayes blamed in my minde, those which will appoint lawes and orders of life to Princes, who are Lordes over Lawes, and injoyne them to others. And therefore by my will we will not apply the humilitie of our Philosophie to the Majestie of Princes: for that beeing Gods on earth, it is to bee thought, that all which they doe is done well; and that to reason of and call into question their dooinges, is noth-ing else but with the Giants, to lay siege to heaven."[18] Guazzo therefore admonishes his Courtier to give the Prince "the love, fidelitie, diligence, and reverence, whiche is due to Princes"; the Prince being "a God on earth, it behoveth him to doe him honoure as to a sacred thing."[19]

Pagan-humanist theory likewise held that the monarch de-served the highest esteem since monarchy and aristocracy were the two forms of government which received the fullest ap-proval of the pagan philosophers. According to the ideal theory of pagan-humanist philosophy, the prince excelled in virtue and valor to the same extent as he was preeminent in social rank. He was, as Hurault said, "the chiefe and most excellent of all."[20] Hence he should be the first to be admitted to that select circle of heroes and demigods who surmount all other men in virtue. In the words of Count Romei, "Seeing honours and preroga-tives, are imparted to nobilitie correspondent to the vertue, which in their kind is presumed to bee . . . the last, wherin vertue heroicall is supposed, being that of Kings . . . is most superior."[21] Hurault in like manner quotes from Aristotle's

---

[18] M. S. Guazzo, *The Civile Conversation*, trans. George Pettie, London, 1581, II, 47.
[19] *ibid.*, III, 55.
[20] Jacques Hurault, *Politicke, Moral and Martial Discourses*, p. 5.
[21] p. 227.

Politics to support his admonition that a king "ought to be esteemed as a God among men."[22]

To justify this exaltation of the monarch, the pagan philosophers argued that the first men to become kings were selected for their goodness and virtue. Hurault, quoting from the *Offices* of Cicero, states that "the first chusings of Kings, was for the estimation which men had of them, that they were good and just men."[23] This, of course, gave added sanction to the monarch's position, since it suggested that the royal families passed on their superior virtue from generation to generation. In their political theory, the pagan humanists made a sharp distinction between the king, who by his very title was a good man, and the tyrant, whose government was among the worst. Tyrannicide had its place in the ethics of the Greek and Roman philosophers. In the Renaissance, certain Calvinist writers (Philip Mornay, Bishop Pynet, and George Buchanan, for example), and the Jesuits supported it; the majority of political theorists, however, accepted the Christian view for which La Primaudaye speaks in the following passage: "whatsoever they are, they have their authoritie from God onely: the good as mirrors of his goodnes, the bad, as scourges of his wrath to punish the iniquitie of the people. . . . Therefore in respect of obedience and reverence, we owe as much to the unjust, as the just prince."[24]

The exalted position of the Renaissance sovereign, in short, entitled him to the utmost respect, even to a semi-divine reverence. It is easy for us to read our own cultural values into this matter and to view the zealous concern with which the Renaissance monarch guarded his high prestige as but the expression of haughty pride. But both the Christian and the pagan-humanist ethics assumed that the monarch would display an imperial dignity. When Queen Elizabeth writes, for example, that "as a Queen Sovereign" she expects to have "our royal superiority preserved," she is only giving expression to

[22] p. 5.   [23] *ibid.*, p. 187.   [24] p. 576.

85

the cultural values of her age.[25] Because the great lords of the realm felt themselves similarly entitled to the highest respect and esteem, it is in the clashes of will between Queen Elizabeth and her great lords that we can observe the high aristocratic dignity of the Renaissance leaders presented in its most colorful and dramatic form.

Some of her most powerful favorites, particularly Essex, dared at times to resent her claim that even the greatest lord was a "creature of her own."[26] It is not merely the fiery temperament of Elizabeth which leads her into a high rage at Essex's conduct. When she rebukes Essex, either by a slap or by written rebuke, she speaks for the political supremacy which her age allowed her. Thus she writes Essex, "Can you imagine that the softness of my sex deprives me of the courage to resent a public affront? The royal blood I boast could not brook, from the mightiest Prince in Christendom, such treatment as you have within the last three months offered to me."[27] Elizabeth felt that she was being presented to the world as the "spectacle of a despised princess" and she would not tolerate such treatment.[28]

The Great Nobles. The extent to which the great nobles were aware of their own lofty stature has been indicated; Essex and Peregrine Bertie, in particular, refused to accept an affront from anyone, not excepting the Queen. The French Ambassador, De Maisse, was urged by Essex to call on Burleigh, Essex's great enemy. De Maisse was tremendously impressed by this display of magnanimity and wrote of the great English nobles, "They have great respect for each other."[29] These nobles, unless attending court, lived on large country estates in a magnificent style appropriate to their high position. The Earl of Pembroke, for example, had more than a thousand servants all clad in his livery. Indeed, even at the end of the 16th cen-

[25] *Letters of Queen Elizabeth*, ed. G. B. Harrison, London, 1935, p. 243.
[26] *ibid.*, p. 170.   [27] *ibid.*, p. 218.   [28] *ibid.*, p. 219.
[29] André Hurault Sieur de Maisse, *Journal*, ed. G. B. Harrison and R. A. Jones, London, 1931, p. 114.

tury, a few of the feudal families remained who were treated with a deferential respect almost equal to that shown the English monarch. The crown, of course, did not meekly accept this haughty independence of the old nobility, for it threatened the unity of the nation and contradicted the patriotic spirit of the first great age of European nationalism. Nonetheless, the lord's retainers often felt a greater loyalty to their own master than to their Queen.

The Professions and the Merchant Class. In the Renaissance the profession of learning in general, and the practice of law in particular, were held in the highest repute, even though the scholar was not necessarily of noble blood. Indeed, the final chapter of *The Courtier's Academie* presents a debate on whether the military profession or the profession of letters is entitled to the higher prestige. The resolution of the debate is as convenient and happy as the ending of a Shakespearean comedy. The soldier, it is decided, is more deserving of honor; the scholar should be revered, rather than honored, but held in equal esteem.[30]

Whether the mercantile class could also consider itself worthy of respect was a question of great importance. Fynes Moryson points out how greatly the French and the Italians differed on this matter. Speaking of the French, he says, "The Nobility high and lowe, I meane lordes and gentlemen, are altogether free from Impositions or Tributes because they serve the king in his Warrs (as well in person as with a cer-taine number of horsemen according to their quality) without taking any pay. And this Immunity little diminisheth the kings profitt, because the Nobility scornes to be Marchants, thincking such traffique ignoble, according to the Heraults rules, howsoever the Italians even the very Princes disdaine not traffique by the great, leaving only the gaine of Retailing to the people."[31]

[30] Count Romei, p. 295.
[31] *Shakespeare's Europe: Unpublished Chapters of Fynes Moryson's Itinerary,* ed. Charles Hughes, London, 1903, pp. 171-172.

It will be seen that here ideals are being brought into conformity with the realities of the social structure of a particular country. Italy was not primarily a nation of warriors, but rather of learning and trade, as is indicated by the influential role of the Medici family. Therefore the scholar and merchant acquire greater prestige than in other European countries. True, Castiglione does adhere to the humanist dictum that anyone who worked for gain was ignoble: "You know in great matters and adventures in wars the true provocation is glory: and who so for lucres sake or for any other consideration taketh it in hande (beside that hee never doth any thing worthie praise) deserveth not the name of a gentleman, but is a most vile marchant."[32] Count Romei also admits that "the Philosopher affirmeth, that the life of marchants is base, and contrary to vertue."[33] Yet he is confronted by the fact that the Venetian Republic was held in the highest esteem throughout Renaissance Europe. He ponders the gulf between theory and reality: "I would willingly understand, if to practice marchandise wer any obstacle of Nobility: For if that should be true, the Venetian nobility so highly esteemed of, wold be nothing worth, in that there be seldome any of their nobles, which are not also marchants."[34]

The resolution of this dilemma involves an interesting compromise. The motives of the particular merchant are scrutinized; insofar as public service, benefit to the state, can be ascribed to him, he is exonerated from the charge of baseness since the humanist philosophers had always exalted patriotism. "For marchandise may be practised two manner of waies, the one, by causing to be brought out of farre countries, those commodities which are not in their own, to their own gaine, and for benefit also of the common-wealth, the other, by not respecting publike benefit, but onely to enrich himselfe."[35] The conclusion is obvious. The merchant motivated by a desire to serve the state is to be considered noble and worthy of praise,

---

[32] p. 70.　　[33] p. 204.　　[34] *ibid.*　　[35] *ibid.*, p. 205.

but he who is motivated simply by self-interest is utterly ignoble, "this being grounded upon avarice, and a sordide gaine, as it is from vertue farre remote."[36]

The Working Class. A close correlation exists in pagan-humanist writings between baseness, as a description of one's low social standing, and baseness in its moral sense. Here again, the Renaissance moralists use Aristotle as their authority.[37] In the *Politics* he had observed, "it is therefore clear from these considerations that in the most nobly constituted state, and the one that possesses men that are absolutely just, not merely just relatively to the principle that is the basis of the constitution, the citizens must not lead a mechanic or a mercantile life (for such a life is ignoble and inimical to virtue)."[38] In accordance with this social theory, Count Romei makes a sharp distinction between the upper and lower classes and argues that virtue belongs almost solely to the aristocracy. "The practice of mechanicall and vile trade, is proper to him ignoble," he observes, and hastens to add "that the life of mechanicall artificers is base, degenerating from vertue, and unworthy a civill man."[39] Elsewhere he is even more sweeping in his indictment of the lower classes. "He which is employed in base practises cannot exercise vertue: and there is no doubt, but all common wealths, as well ancient, as moderne, distinguish by this caracter, the noble from the vulgar sort."[40] Again and again, the Renaissance moralists emphasize this major social theme: that the greatest gulf exists between the aristocratic and the lower classes, and that this is as it should be. Our use today of such insulting epithets as "boor," "rustic," and "farmer" indicates

---

[36] *ibid.*

[37] Aristotle is "the Philosopher" in both the 13th and 16th centuries. That he is the authority (the "moral pilot" of Europe, in Eliot's phrase) in both centuries does not mean that there is any necessary parallel in interpretation of Aristotle by Dante's and by Shakespeare's contemporaries. As Henri Busson points out "the greatest enemy of the Christian faith in the 16th century is precisely the person who had been its main support in the 13th—Aristotle." Henri Busson, *Les Sources et le Développement du Rationalisme*, p. 9.

[38] H. Rackham, trans., Cambridge, Mass., 1944, VII, 8.

[39] p. 195.   [40] *ibid.*, p. 202.

the extent to which our terms of opprobrium in a democratic society had their origin in the aristocratic and hierarchical class distinctions of the Renaissance.

It would overstate Renaissance attitudes, however, to suggest that no allowances were made for the possibility that the lower classes might be virtuous. One of the three definitions of nobility was purely in terms of virtue, per se, as has been indicated. The aristocrat might have a greater inclination to lead a virtuous life, and he might possess the virtues more abundantly, but no Renaissance moralist would completely deny that a peasant or artisan could at least possess the simple virtues. As Cornwallis says, "I am not so precise to call no Actions noble that carry not with them a rumour or a glittering. To my meaning, nobility and honesty meane al one; and thus may a paineful Artisan be noble, if he follows his vocation painefully and constantly, he is honest, and so noble, being a Limme of a state though no maine Organ."[41] Similarly, in *The Steel Glas* Gascoigne exalts the virtues of the simple plowman. Indeed, he warns that Peerce Plowman may climb to heaven before the priest since he may possess greater humility. Hence he admonishes: "Behold him, priests, & though he stink of sweat/ Disdaine him not."[42]

Whatever the allowances of this sort, no book or treatise on ethical and political philosophy concealed the tone of disdain and contempt with which the aristocrat referred to his social inferiors. For Plato, Aristotle, and Cicero, democracy rivaled tyranny as an example of the worst of governments precisely because the lower classes, viewed as a whole, were considered ignorant, irresponsible, and hence utterly incapable of self-government. The masses were to be feared, distrusted, held in scorn, and kept in their place. They were usually described in such derogatory terms as "base," "vulgar," "fickle," and "foolish." Insofar as they knew their proper station, respected their betters, and were true and loyal subjects of their sovereign,

[41] p. 198.
[42] George Gascoigne, *Complete Works*, Vol. 2, p. 170.

they were entitled to his love. But in an age in which such a great Lord as Leicester was referred to by his Queen as a "creature of her own," the common people could hardly expect the monarch to display anything more than the condescending and paternalistic love of a father for an infant child.[43] On this issue the Graeco-Roman philosophers had been in complete agreement. Whether Academic, Peripatetic, or Stoic, the writer of antiquity had held that the multitude would be deficient in the rational faculties on which all the classical virtues were based. Bryskett's reference to the "vulgar sort, whose judgement is so corrupt and crooked, that they cannot discerne what true honor and dignity is," is but reiteration of the view of antiquity.[44]

PART 2: THE RENAISSANCE CONCEPT OF HONOR

DEFINITION OF THE CONCEPT OF HONOR

THE best definition of the Renaissance concept of honor, as it affected the individual, comes from Rabelais. In speaking of the order of free will in his Thelemite monastery, he describes the simplicity of its rules of virtuous behavior: "In all their rule, and strictest tie of their order, there was but this one clause to be observed:

DO WHAT THOU WILT

Because men that are free, well-borne, well-bred, and conversant in honest companies, have naturally an instinct and spur that prompteth them unto virtuous actions, and withdraws them from vice, which is called honour."[45] As is so often the case, we are here confronted with a contradiction in the ethos of the

---

[43] *Letters of Queen Elizabeth*, ed. G. B. Harrison, p. 170.
[44] p. 191.
[45] François Rabelais, *Gargantua and Pantagruel*, trans. Sir Thomas Urquhart and Peter Motteux in *Great Books of the Western World*, Vol. 24, Chicago, 1952, I, 57. (These references are to book and chapter.)

pagan humanists. It is suggested on the one hand that the desire for virtue is innate, but on the other hand it is pointed out that the Renaissance aristocrat is carefully instructed in the moral disciplines and refrains from intercourse with any who is not of a like virtue. Virtue is hereditary and in the blood, but it will not, apparently, bear wholesome fruit if the soil is not as carefully selected as the seed.

The sense of honor, the desire for virtue, is then deeply implanted in the soul of the Renaissance gentleman. He is not concerned primarily with the opinion of others, but with his own conscience, his own inner sense of integrity. Insofar as Renaissance moral treatises followed the humanist philosophers of antiquity, first emphasis was placed on the individual's acquisition of a sense of his own value and moral worth. Both Aristotle and Cicero placed major stress on the fact that virtue was not implanted by the gods but resulted largely from a man's own inclination and training. Stoic philosophy developed this theory of individualism and self-reliance to its extreme, but Epictetus is uttering a mere truism of pagan philosophy when he says, "Fidelity is your own, virtuous shame is your own."[46]

According to pagan-humanist theory, however, the sentiment of honor was to be found only in the aristocratic classes. Aristotle had said that arguments: "are powerless to stimulate the mass of mankind to moral nobility. For it is the nature of the many to be amenable to fear but not to a sense of honour, and to abstain from evil not because of its baseness but because of the penalties it entails."[47] This remark becomes a Renaissance commonplace. Repeatedly a distinction is made between those who are motivated "for vertues sake, for feare of reproch, for love and reverence to honestie" to lead upright and virtuous lives, and those who are compelled to goodness and virtue "for feare of punishment to be inflicted on them by the magistrates."[48]

To the modern mind, confronted by three centuries of egali-

[46] *The Discourses of Epictetus*, trans. George Long in *Great Books of the Western World*, Chicago, 1952, Vol. 12, p. 25.
[47] *Nicomachean Ethics* x. 9.
[48] Bryskett, p. 138.

tarianism and scientific scepticism, Renaissance concepts of virtue, conscience, and honor not only tend to have a fuzzy vagueness because they are so abstract, but also fail to evoke any passionate emotional response because our values are, in theory at least, largely democratic. For the man of the Renaissance, on the other hand, they involved his whole being. Honor was related to the intellectual faculties, but was equally an "ardent heate which enflameth the minde of man, to glorious enterprise, making him audacious against enemies, and to vices timerous."[49]

The Renaissance has often been described as an age of exuberant Falstaffian licentiousness and of Marlovian immorality —an age in which the lust for power and the love of sensual delights overflowed all ethical restraints and justified itself simply in terms of animal vitality and emotional intensity. To deny these aspects of the Renaissance spirit would be folly, but they should be subjected to a rarely made qualification. The intensity of Renaissance feeling, while it overflowed with torrential energy the banks of its two main ethical streams, was to a large extent held within the channels of these two rivers. Indeed, the very fact that Renaissance emotion was so channeled, and so directed, gave it much of its intensity. The death of More as a Christian martyr and of Sidney as a soldier fighting for country and honor were as typical as the death of Marlowe in a tavern brawl. Even Montaigne, who at times seems the very embodiment of the sceptical attitude toward life, highly esteems this sort of moral integration: "The reputation and worth of a man consisteth in his heart and will: therein consists true honour: Constancie is valour, not of armes and legs, but of minde and courage."[50] Only an age which, generally speaking, had an unquestioned faith in the reality of good and evil—be it Christian, or pagan-humanist, or most frequently a mixture of the two—could mold its elite to such a single-minded, intense devotion to virtue and honor.

[49] Count Romei, p. 78.   [50] III, 6.

Honor, as an inner quality, was then first of all a sentiment and passion; it is only when we exhume its corpse from the dreary pages of Elizabethan ethical treatises and breathe into it the living fire with which it possessed the heart, soul, and mind of the English gentleman that we can appreciate its real significance. But the definition of the ethical concept is also important. Honor results from the pursuit of virtue and is inextricably connected with it. A favorite metaphor endlessly quoted by the eclectic Renaissance moralists compared the inseparability of virtue and honor with that of the body and its shadow.[51] It was often suggested that one should seek virtue, and honor will follow like a shadow, whereas it would be folly to pursue honor for its own sake. An equally popular description of the inseparable connection between honor and virtue is that of La Primaudaye: "For this cause the auncient Romans built two Temples joined together, the one being dedicated to Vertue, and the other to Honor: but yet in such sort, that no man could enter into that of Honor, except that he passed through the other of Vertue."[52]

Robert Ashley's *Of Honour*, which was produced sometime between 1596 and 1603, the period in which Shakespeare was writing many of his greatest plays, is the most compact work on the subject to appear during the English Renaissance. In this work is to be found one of the fullest definitions of honor (one almost identical with the definition in Du Vair's *Moral Philosophy of the Stoicks*, to which I have already referred in the Introduction). Ashley observes that "neither to be praised, nor to be reverenced, nor to be esteemed is for it self to be desired; but that we may behold the Testimonie which good men and wise have geven of our vertue and be delighted therwith, as having not so much confidence in our selves herein as in the judgement of others."[53] The excellence of this definition lies in its close and precise distinction between honor as an inner quality and honor as a sign of public respect. The opinion of

[51] See Introduction, n. 3.   [52] La Primaudaye, p. 233.
[53] *Of Honour*, p. 59.

94

others is not to be ignored as in the ancient Stoic or medieval Christian scheme, but is to give satisfaction by confirming one's inner sense of honor.

THE INDIVIDUAL VIRTUES

Since most of the Renaissance moralists were agreed that honor results from the pursuit of virtue, they felt it essential to define virtue itself. For Renaissance moral philosophy, as for the philosophers of antiquity from whom they drew their inspiration, four cardinal virtues were of primary importance— prudence or wisdom, justice, fortitude, and temperance. Cicero's statement in the widely quoted *Offices* demonstrates why these were considered "cardinal" virtues: "For, since all moral rectitude springs from four sources (one of which is prudence; the second, social instinct; the third, courage; the fourth temperance), it is often necessary in deciding a question of duty that these virtues be weighed against one another."[54] These four virtues were the keystones of every Renaissance book on moral philosophy. The Aristotelian virtues expanded beyond them, but largely by building on them. Thus, the virtue of magnanimity arises out of that of fortitude. For the Renaissance moralist, extensions beyond the cardinal four were rarely systematic; he was seldom concerned to copy exactly the twelve Aristotelian virtues. Often, as in *The Faerie Queene*, Christian virtues are mixed with classical. But, as T. S. Eliot has observed, there is an overtone of Christian piety and pity in medieval literature not usually to be found in Elizabethan verse.[55] Hurault and La Primaudaye, however, closely identify magnanimity with the Christian virtue of patience. Almost invariably a Renaissance work on moral philosophy included magnanimity or greatness of soul, liberality, magnificence, modesty, and courtesy, in addition to the four cardinal virtues. Whether or not Christian values were also discussed depended on the extent to which the author was concerned with religious as well as

---

[54] I. 43.
[55] "Seneca in Elizabethan Translation," *Selected Essays*, New York, 1932, pp. 87-88.

secular morality. La Primaudaye's *French Academie* is largely religious in tone; Count Romei's *Courtier's Academie* is, like so many Italian treatises, primarily secular.

PATRIOTISM AS AN ASPECT OF FORTITUDE

Patriotism was usually considered one of the essential aspects of the cardinal virtue of valor or fortitude which was also often linked with the all-embracing virtue of magnanimity. The warlike and patriotic spirit of the Elizabethan age is fully delineated in Raleigh's account of *The Last Fight of the Revenge*. Not only does the courageous behavior of the English sailor illuminate his pages, but equally Raleigh's intense patriotic zeal and concern for the reputation of England.

The rise of nationalism in the sixteenth century is a historical truism; the change in sensibility which resulted from an exaltation of national sentiment in wars between Christian nations has often been overlooked. The spirit of Renaissance nationalism is a far cry from medieval attitudes, where, whatever the military realities, war was often justified as a crusade against the infidel or heretic. Loyalty to country and to one's monarch replaces, to no inconsiderable extent, loyalty to the one universal (Catholic) church. The Elizabethan attitude toward the Papists was as much the result of fear of their political might as it was of a distaste for their dogma. Elizabeth might sympathize from the religious point of view with the French Huguenots, but her sympathies did not interfere with her more central concern that the principle of royal supremacy and of the iniquity of rebellion be fully recognized throughout Europe. Her remonstrance to the French King about the massacre of her fellow Protestants was but a mild rebuke.

The patriotic sentiment of the Renaissance drew great moral support from the humanist philosophy of antiquity. The intense patriotic fervor of the Roman writers in particular was rapidly picked up by the 16th century moralists. Cicero's definition of glory in *The Philippics* as "praise won by honourable deeds, and great services toward the state" reveals the close correlation between individual achievement and social obligation, the twin poles of Renaissance morality.[56]

HONOR AS HONESTY, INTEGRITY

The ideal Renaissance gentleman was a man of absolute honesty and integrity. Hence, one of the traditional privileges of the aristocrat had been his right to testify in court without bond and without witnesses. The mere word of a gentleman was, presumably, as trustworthy as the sworn testimony of a man of the lower classes. From this belief arose the conventional form of insult—to give a man the lie—which was a part of the etiquette of the dueling code. The sense of honor and of honesty were equally involved in these cardinal aspects of the dueling code.

Indeed, honor and honesty were practically interchangeable in the Renaissance, although the shading of meaning which distinguishes the two words today had begun to differentiate them. The Latin word *honestas* meant worth, virtue, honorable character, probity. As Guirino, one of Count Romei's courtiers, observes, "by the definition of honour . . . it seemeth that honour and honestie are inseparable."[57] Hurault also maintains that the man who has lost his credit (i.e., honesty, integrity) "hath no more to lose, because the whole welfare and honour of a man dependeth thereupon."[58]

The emphasis on honesty was so great that the pagan philosophers seemed to prefer an honest simpleton to a man who proved to be even slightly deceitful, however brilliant he might be. The humanist philosophers held nothing in greater abhorrence than the feigning of emotions not felt; open enmity is infinitely preferable to pretended love. Cleland is expressing one of the fundamental Renaissance precepts when he says that a friend is "such in his hart as hee appeareth in action, without al dissumulation or deceit, loving nothing but honest, faithful,

[56] Walter C. A. Ker trans., Cambridge, Mass., 1957, I. 12.
[57] p. 117.   [58] p. 93.

plain, and simple dealing."[59] Montaigne suggests that nothing shows greater ignobility than deceit: "Of all vices, I finde none that so much witnesseth demissenesse and basenesse of heart. It is a coward and servile humour, for a man to disguise and hide himselfe under a maske, and not dare to shew himselfe as he is. . . . A generous minde ought not to belie his thoughts, but make shew of his inmost parts: There al is good, or at least all is humane. Aristotle thinkes it an office of magnanimitie to hate and love openly, to judge and speake with all libertie."[60] In this passage, the close integration of various Renaissance virtues is indicated; openness and lack of all pretense are considered indispensable attributes of the magnanimous man. In Renaissance England simplicity may have possessed the pejorative meaning which the word now has but it meant equally a quality of the highest nobility. "In vertue may be nothing fucate or counterfayte. But therein is onlely the image of veritie, called simplicitie."[61]

In no aspect of its creed is humanism more dogmatic than in its concern for absolute truthfulness. Anything short of perfect honesty is viewed with dismay; "an honest man . . . never crackt his credit, but is wel known for such an one, and this man is truely worthy of honor, and deservedly honored."[62] Bryskett designates "the bright-shining vertue of truth" a moral virtue, and adds that "this is that excellent vertue that is of al others the best fitting a Gentleman, and maketh him respected and welcom in all companies."[63] Ben Jonson lays particular emphasis on this quality in his description of Shakespeare, finding him "(indeed) honest, and of an open, and free nature."[64]

If one feels unquestioned confidence in the honesty of others, then a sense of loyalty and fidelity is but a logical concomitant and accessory virtue. For if one accepts the assumption of the human-

---

[59] p. 195.
[60] *Essayes*, III, 13.   [61] *Elyot*, IV, 4.
[62] Count Romei, p. 108.   [63] p. 243.
[64] *Works*, ed. C. H. Herford and Percy and Evelyn Simpson, Oxford, 1943, Vol. 8, p. 584.

ist moral philosophers that the aristocrats will be guided by a creed of honorable righteousness, then one can rely on the complete confidence of their followers who will have absolute trust in them. Elyot, indeed, insists that trust and loyalty are one and the same virtue: "That which in latine is called *Fides*, is a parte of justice and may diversely be interpreted, and yet finally it tendeth to one purpose in effecte. Some time it may be called faithe, some time credence, other whiles truste. Also in a frenche terme it is named loyaltie. And to the imitation of latine it is often called fidelitie. All which wordes, if they be intierly and (as I mought saye) exactly understanden, shall appere to a studious reder to signifie one vertue or qualitie, all thoughe they seme to have some diversitie."[65]

In a world which of necessity involved much unpredictable mishap, brought on by fickle Fortune or callous Fate, which contained a relatively small proportion of virtuous men and a multitude who were ignorant, deceitful, treacherous, malicious, and vicious, the pagan humanist depended on the mutual integrity which he felt could exist between men of honor and good will. This was the cord which held human society firmly knit. Thus Hurault asks, "How could mans frailtie be upheld among so many waves and storms, if there were no firmnesse in the doings and saiengs of princes? Among fellowes, faithfulnesse maintaineth friendship. It maketh servants to obey their maisters with all integritie."[66] Loyalty, integrity, and trustworthiness were indeed the primary virtues of the servant class. Since they were people of low birth, one could not expect them to be heroic—not even honorable in the full sense of the word. Guazzo observes that, though one's servants be "not all of the civillest, yet they are faithfull and trustie, which is a thing more to bee set by, then civilitie, finenesse, or bravery."[67]

If simple honesty and faithfulness are such cardinal virtues in the pagan-humanist ethics, it is not surprising that the greatest attention is paid to the vice of fraud and deceit. Elyot defines fraud as "an evill disceite, craftely imagined and devised,

[65] III, 6.   [66] p. 90.   [67] III, 53.

whiche, under a colour of trouthe and simplicitie, indomageth him that nothing mistrusteth."[68] The fear of this vice led classical moralists to write endless pages of advice as to how the true friend could be distinguished from the flatterer and false one. Cleland, in his *Institution of a Nobleman*, lines up the qualities of the two side by side, so that they can be compared with the greatest ease:

A freind is such in his hart as hee appeareth in action, without al dissimulation or deceit, loving nothing but honest, faithful, plain, and simple dealing.	Where your flatterer under the appearance of a modest grave, and holy countenance, and under the skin of a gentle lambe, shal be ful of fraude and falshood like the foxe.[69]

The Renaissance moralist labored no theme with greater emphasis than that of the disaster which lay in store for the man who could not distinguish between these two types. Since integrity and faithfulness between men of honor were the bonds which cemented human society, the man who masked his self-interest and viciousness under the pretense of good will was considered particularly dangerous. The English admired and distrusted Italy, a land which to them symbolized both the link with a classical past which was becoming more and more meaningful to Northern Europe, and the source of all the sophisticated vices of a pleasure-loving, epicurean civilization. Fynes Moryson, for example, praises the Italians for their good breeding and courtesy on the one hand, but damns them on the other for their lack of integrity. His is a typically English view which finds its most eloquent expression in his *Itinerary*. "Touching the manners of the Italians. They are for the out side by natures guift excellently composed. By sweetnes of language, and singular Art in seasoning their talke and behaviour with great ostentation of Courtesy, they make their Conversation sweete and pleasing to all men, easily gaining the good will of those with

[68] III, 4.   [69] p. 195.

whome they live. But no trust is to be reposed in their wordes, the flattering tounge having small acquaintance with a sincere heart, espetially among the Italians."[70] Ironically, this is the country which first rediscovered the classical heritage of European civilization and whose books on the humanist ethics, etiquette, and moral philosophy were constantly being translated, and whose civilizing influence on England in the late 16th century was much greater than that of France.

[70] p. 415.

CHAPTER 3

POINTS OF CONFLICT BETWEEN CHRISTIANITY AND THE PAGAN-HUMANIST ETHICS

I. THE NOTION OF GODLIKE EXCELLENCE

THE social and moral distinctions which stemmed from the Renaissance definitions of nobility led to a pyramidal view of human society—a pyramid whose extensive base represented the plebeian class and whose pinnacle was restricted to the monarch and great lords of the realm because they presumably possessed superior and preeminent virtues. Pagan-humanist moral philosophy was primarily concerned with the small elite of leaders who topped the pyramid, for these leaders could presumably achieve a moral excellence close to the pagan-humanist ideal of complete moral perfection. Indeed, the idea that man "was capable of attaining such excellence that he might even challenge comparison with the gods" was, according to Lecky, common to most schools of Roman moralists.[1] Even the Aristotelian golden mean did not preclude this ideal. Count Romei writes, for example, "For I did not thinke that in vertue there could have beene any defect, mediocritie, or excesse, the Philosopher having tolde me, that there can never be too vertuous a man."[2]

To excel in virtue, to aspire after a moral perfection which ignored the cardinal Christian virtues of piety and humility and the cardinal Christian doctrine of man's sinful and fallen nature, was the chief goal of Renaissance pagan-humanist ideals. Nor were the writers of that age unaware that they were trying to reconcile two moral systems fundamentally irreconcil-

[1] William E. H. Lecky, *A History of European Morals*, 3rd ed., London, 1877, I, 196.
[2] p. 200.

able. Thus Cornelius Agrippa writes, "Ye have harde howe some Philosophers have placed felicitie or blessednesse . . . in honour, fame, and greatnesse of name, but Christe in sclaunder, and hatred of men . . . some in glorie of warre and subduinge of countries, but Christe in peace: some in honour and pompe, but Christe in humilitie, calling the meke blessed. . . . Christe teacheth that perfect vertue is not gotten but by grace geven from above, the Philosophers saie, that it is gotten by our owne strength and exercise. . . . Christe teacheth . . . not to take revengment of any, that we ought to geve to every one that asketh: contrary-wise the Philosophers saie, that we should geve to none but them onely, which doe requite benefite for benefite, moreover it is lawfull to be angrie, to hate, to fighte, to make warre, and to practice usurie."[3]

In theory, at least, the aristocratic elite could reach so near perfection that a more than human goodness seemed involved. Thus was created a race of heroes: "The excesse then of vertue, according to the Philosopher, is after this maner expressed: the which excesse is of such a nature, as it cannot passe into vice, but rather is properly that which maketh a man magnanimous, and it is called vertue heroicall, as that which participateth both of humanitie and divinitie."[4] Castiglione admits his ideal courtier to this select race of magnanimous and perfect heroes, holding that he can "attaine unto that heroicall and noble vertue, that shall make him passe the boundes of the nature of man, and shall rather be called a demy God, than a man mortall."[5]

Cicero writes of the sudden disappearance of Romulus in an eclipse of the sun; after this event occurred, the Romans held that he "had been added to the number of the gods, indeed such an opinion could never have gotten abroad about any human being save a man preeminently renowned for virtue."[6]

---

[3] Henry Cornelius von Nottesheim Agrippa, *Of the Vanitie and Uncertaintie of Artes and Sciences*, trans. Ja[mes] San[ford], London, 1569, LIV, 75a, 75b.

[4] Count Romei, p. 201.   [5] p. 276.

[6] *De Re Publica* in *De Re Publica, De Legibus*, trans. Clinton Walker Keyes, Cambridge, Mass., 1951, II, 10.

It was an easy jump for the Renaissance pagan humanist from the semi-deification of his moral elite to the creation of a fictitious, pagan heaven in which to ensconce his heroes after death. Coluccio Salutati's *Labours of Hercules* gave the man of valor, who had performed great and noble deeds, a dwelling among the stars. Often however, while a Renaissance moralist would accept the pagan notion of an excellence of virtue which transcended human limitations, his devotion to the Christian ethics would cause him to stop short of the heretical notion that this quality could be godlike. The Christian ethics could not tolerate the idea that man could compare with God in excellence; man was, howsoever great his moral stature, a creature made by God, dependent on Him, and inferior to Him.[7]

One easy solution to the conflict between Christian and pagan-humanist values was to suggest that the pagan-humanist inclination to ascribe godlike qualities to man was no more than a convenient poetic fiction. Thus Bryskett writes that the valiant man will despise the terrors of adversity; he "feeleth them not in respect of justice and honestie, wherby such men became equall to the Gods, as poets fained."[8] Sidney likewise suggests that the poet has licence to create a race of heroes; "in making things either better than Nature bringeth foorth, or, quite a new, formes such as never were in nature: as the *Heroes, Demigods, Cyclops.*"[9]

But frequently the Christian moralist bitterly attacked the pagan-humanist notion that man could rival the Gods in excellence. La Primaudaye, for example, singles out as his target the Greek Dion, esteemed by his countrymen as "no lesse vertuous than his God Jupiter, to whom they attributed perfect divinitie."[10] Although *The French Academie* faces two ways about many important ethical issues (at times, for example, condemning suicide as sinful; at times citing with approval

[7] See Etienne Gilson, *The Spirit of Medieval Philosophy*, trans. A. H. C. Downes, London, 1950, pp. 128-147.

[8] p. 87.

[9] *Collected Works*, ed. Albert Feuillerat, Cambridge, 1923, III, 8.

[10] p. 15.

tales of suicide as examples of pagan fidelity), in this instance, La Primaudaye's Christian values lead him completely to reject the pagan-humanist concept. Dion is subjected to merciless scorn and ridicule and treated as an example of human vanity.[11] Montaigne also, whether because of his Christian faith or his sceptical temperament, finds such notions of near-divinity ridiculous. He complains about "that fond title which Aristotle gives us of mortal gods, and that rash judgement of Chrysippus, that Dion was as vertuous as God: And my Seneca saith, he acknowledgeth that God hath given him life, but how to live well, that he hath of himselfe. Like unto this other . . . We rightly vaunt us of vertue, which we should not doe, if we had it of God, not of our selves."[12] Montaigne is shocked and appalled that man should display such inordinate vanity. He invokes the Christian idea of man's dependence on God in order to refute the pagan-humanist notion of man's self-sufficiency. "So long as man shall be persuaded to have meanes or power of himselfe, so long wil he denie, and never acknowledge what he oweth unto his Master."[13] The passage ends with the famous quotation, "He must be stripped into his shirt," which Montaigne proceeds to do in the longest essay he ever wrote, the "Apology for Raimond Sébond."[14]

Pagan-humanist philosophy did not place its major emphasis on heroes of godlike proportions; they were altogether too exceptional and extraordinary. But it did focus on that relatively small group of individuals who would display a moral superiority and preeminence of which the vast majority of men would be incapable. Indeed, Aristotle argues in his *Politics* that the man who excels in virtue has the most right to rebel (although he will be least likely to do so) since he is morally superior.[15] Poggio, in his treatise *On Nobility*, expresses a preference for the Latin root of the word over the Greek, because the Latin suggests that to be noble is to be remarkable, outstanding, preeminent.

[11] *ibid.*   [12] *Essayes*, II, 12.   [13] *ibid.*
[14] *ibid.*   [15] v. 1.

Of course, every age has tended to exalt its heroes, the men who live up to the ideals of the age to an extraordinary degree. But it is of the utmost importance to discern what the particular heroic type is—whether it be the great warrior and tribal chief of the Anglo-Saxons, the saints and chivalric knights of the Middle Ages, or the heroes of antiquity (Epaminondas, Brutus, Cato, and the like) so often admired in the Renaissance. Here, as elsewhere, we must give due recognition to the continuation of medieval Christian ideals. Philip Sidney was described by Fulke Greville as the prince of chivalry, and Edmund Spenser's description of the gentleman involved the Christian virtues equally with the classical. But the Renaissance man of honor was not adhering to the medieval chivalric code; he did not go on crusades or wander endlessly around the world in the hope of discovering forlorn damsels in distress. The ideal gentleman—courtier, scholar, and soldier—of the Renaissance was as much concerned with reputation as with salvation; insofar as he sought to gain and maintain his honor and reputation he was adhering to the ideals and social code of pagan Rome. Huizinga's description is accurate: "The thirst for honor and glory proper to the men of the Renaissance is essentially the same as the chivalrous ambition of earlier times, and of French origin. Only it has shaken off the feudal form and assumed an antique garb."[16]

2. MAGNANIMITY

"Magnanimity," "high-mindedness," "noble courage," and "greatness of heart" were synonymous terms for the virtue which Aristotle had designated as *megalopsychia*. A courageous man would attempt noble deeds for the sake of honor but the magnanimous man aspired to even a higher degree of honor. As Aristotle had said: "He will not compete for the common objects of admiration, or go where other people take the first place; and he will be idle and slow to act, except when pursuing some high honour or achievement; and will not engage in

[16] p. 59. Cf. Chapter 1, n. 65.

many undertakings, but only in such as are important and distinguished."[17] Cicero's definition of the same concept includes the Aristotelian definition, but goes beyond it. "The soul that is altogether courageous and great is marked above all by two characteristics: one of these is indifference to outward circumstances; for such a person cherishes the conviction that nothing but moral goodness and propriety deserves to be either admired or wished for or striven after, and that he ought not to be subject to any man or any passion or any accident of fortune."[18] Elsewhere Cicero speaks of "the greatness and strength of a noble and invincible spirit."[19] Once again the Renaissance moralists took their formulations from Aristotle and Cicero. Their definitions included the following: first, greatness and heroic stature in performing deeds of unusual difficulty; second, contempt for fortune and external influences since the magnanimous man feels self-sufficient and superior to them because of his innate virtue; and third, unshaken resolution and constancy in the performance of one's duties.

Renaissance moralists did not slavishly follow Aristotle in their description of this virtue, but what they lacked in systematization they made up for by the profusion of references to it. Count Romei, for one, points out how essential it is to the military profession: "Magnanimitie is no lesse an adjunct of military profession, then is whitenes of snowe: for that warrior who hath not a loftie and magnanimous mind, shall never accomplish glorious enterprises."[20] Hurault plàces the same emphasis on great deeds and suggests that magnanimity should be primarily a virtue of princes since they alone can be majestic enough to be truly magnanimous.[21] Bryskett follows Aristotle in asserting that only the man endowed with all the virtues will be capable of true magnanimity and that he will be "among vertuous men . . . esteemed in the highest degree."[22] By 1627 the heroic ideals and aspirations of the Renaissance had lost much of their sparkle; Drayton therefore dedicates his poems

---

[17] *Nicomachean Ethics* IV. 3.   [18] *De Officiis* I. 20.   [19] *ibid.*, I. 5.
[20] pp. 276-277.   [21] p. 286.   [22] p. 231.

to those who "in these declining times have yet in your brave bosoms the sparks of that sprightly fire of your courageous ancestors; and to this hour retain the seeds of their magnanimity and greatness."[23] But the great lords of the Court of Elizabeth were indeed high-minded, lofty, and proud (in the Aristotelian sense). Willoughby, for example, stayed away from court and deliberately slighted Elizabeth. "It was his saying, (and it did him no good) that he was none of the *Reptilia*, intimating, that he could not creep on the ground, and that the Court was not in his Element; for indeed, as he was a great Souldier, so was he of a suitable magnanimity."[24] The quality of virtue of the great Lord was not different in kind, but in degree, from that of the mere gentleman. Essex's description of his own soldiers reveals a cavalier disdain for picayune and trivial displays of virtue: "I love them for their virtue's sake, for their greatness of mind,—for little minds tho' never so full of virtue, can be but a little virtuous."[25]

The second attribute of magnanimity, its superiority to the trials and afflictions which confront it, stems from a feeling of self-sufficiency and of justified pride in one's own noble stature. Virtue, and the sense of honor which went with it, were superior to fortune and could not be removed by it; the malignancy of others could cause adversity and suffering, the chance occurrences of an indifferent fortune could ruin one's material position or even jeopardize one's life itself. But all of the pagan-humanist philosophers—not alone the Stoics, who carried the sense of self-sufficiency and sheer brute endurance to an individualistic extreme—emphasized that man was capable of surmounting external difficulties by his sense of innate nobility. Hurault, for example, finds that "Magnanimitie is an ornament to all vertues, because it maketh them the greater, in that the honor whereon the nobleminded man setteth his eye, surmount-

---

[23] Michael Drayton, *Works*, London, 1753, Vol. 1, p. 27.
[24] Robert Naunton, *Fragmenta Regalia*, pp. 37-38.
[25] W. B. Devereux, ed., *Lives and Letters of the Devereux Earls of Essex in the Reigns of Elizabeth, James I, and Charles I, 1540-1646*, London, 1853, I, 487.

eth all things."[26] The magnanimous man could be crushed, but his spirit could not be broken by misfortune. It could remain upright, staunch and unflinching, however great the maladies and afflictions to which it had been subjected. Not even the physical weakness of the body was viewed as an obstacle, in comparison to strength of heart and soul. La Primaudaye, for example, exalts the heroic qualities of generals who, "especially such as were placed in offices of captains and conductors of armies, have executed infinite great and glorious exploits, surmounting all weaknes of their bodies, through the magnanimitie of their hart."[27]

3. MAGNANIMITY AND SELF-RELIANCE

The conflict between Christian and pagan-humanist values in the Renaissance is the more evident in this stress on the self-reliance of the magnanimous man. According to Christian teaching, one relies in moments of adversity on the solace and spiritual strength provided by one's faith in God and the sense of intimate communion with Him. "Confidence in one's self," which Sir Philip Sidney calls the "chief nurse of magnanimity," violates the cardinal Christian notions of dependence on God and a sense of His omnipotence, compared to which man's strength is utterly trivial.[28] Yet most Renaissance moralists, discussing magnanimity, follow pagan-humanist dogma by placing total emphasis on the capabilities and inner strength of the natural man of virtuous endowments. "He is always higher then his fortune, be it never so great, and be she never so contrary, she cannot overthrow him."[29] The medieval moralists had repeatedly warned that man should put no trust in the capabilities of frail human nature, cursed by sin, radical imperfection, and human weakness. There was, to be sure, a great difference between the pessimism of an Augustine and the relative optimism of a St. Thomas. But, as Gilson points out, no Christian philosophy could support the notion of man's

[26] p. 287.   [27] p. 256.   [28] Sidney, *Aphorisms*, I, 47.
[29] Bryskett, p. 232.

individual self-reliance and independence of God.[30] To a considerable extent, the Christian humanist solved this dilemma by a probably unconscious alteration of the pagan-humanist view to fit it into the Christian scheme. Yet the concept of magnanimity, discussed in almost all the books on moral philosophy written during the Renaissance, can never be brought into a true reconciliation with the Christian virtue of humility and the Christian sense of dependence on God; its major stress, the tone which always predominates, is one of exultation in man's self-sufficiency and self-reliance. As Hurault puts it, "if a man bend himselfe to despise the things that are commonly had in estimation, as strength, beautie, health, riches and honor, and regardeth not their contraries; he may go with his head upright, and make his boast, that neither the frowardnes of fortune, nor the opinion of the comon people, nor sorrow, nor povertie, shall be able to put him in feare, but all things are in his hand, and nothing is out of his power."[31] This contempt of grief and death has a Stoic ring to the modern ear. Actually, however, it is basic to much pagan-humanist philosophy, and is a natural corollary to the pagan-humanist view that man's sense of inner virtue bestows on him a dignity and genuine source of self-satisfaction that no external misfortune can eradicate. The death of Socrates, as recounted in *The Apology*, constitutes one of the most moving expressions of this pagan-humanist conviction that man's dignity can make him superior to his particular predicament, even if his virtue fails to receive a reward in an afterlife.

Heroic endurance, derived from an unshakable sense of one's personal worth, provided the pagan humanist with his answer to the problems of adversity, of pain, death, and grief. Since the magnanimous man set his ideals so high, daily events, trivial actions and common human behavior could be regarded disdainfully. The contempt the proud Renaissance aristocrat felt toward "the world" had an altogether different meaning from the medieval "contemptus mundi." It was rooted in a

[30] pp. 128-134.   [31] pp. 287-288.

profound faith in the virtuous capabilities of the natural man, who could possess all of the virtues and in the highest degree. Piccolomini, for example, notes that the magnanimous man will not utterly despise his fellow men but will refuse to show respect for those who lack virtue, since virtue is the only thing in life which he really values. The individualistic emphasis, the sense of self-complacency and of virtuous superiority, suggested by this attitude, has been a source of irritation to critics of the pagan-humanist ethics for many centuries. Thus Montaigne, when exhibiting the sceptical or the Christian, rather than the pagan-humanist, facet of his personality, could only be annoyed by claims of almost godlike perfectibility for the mere human creature. Thoroughgoing Christians would only be the more enraged, since a sense of self-sufficiency, of self-bestowed virtue, and of capability to cope with the dilemmas of earthly existence without turning to God for comfort and solace, were to them the worst of heresies. As has already been pointed out, the greatest danger confronting Christianity has always been the notion that man can be independent of God. This sense of independence, rather than mere vanity, constitutes the real sin of pride for which Satan was expelled. Yet self-reliance based on this sense of one's own independent virtue is the pagan-humanist answer to the uncontrollable and unforeseeable nature of worldly events. In the words of H. O. Taylor: "The Greek, as well as the Roman, was self-reliant; he looked to himself for his own strength. The gods might provide opportunity, or they might thwart men or enmesh the self-reliant doer in nets of fate. But the man himself and the quality of his own accomplishment were the work of his own strength—of his *virtus* and *prudentia*, his valiant energies and the mind which informed and guided them."[32]

4. HONOR AND SELF-ESTEEM

The classical virtues which we have been discussing—justice, temperance, prudence, valor, honesty, and magna-

[32] Henry Osborne Taylor, *The Classical Heritage of the Middle Ages*, New York, 1901, p. 19.

nimity—constituted the inner qualities which permitted the Renaissance aristocrat to feel such a strong sense of rectitude. As a result of his possession of these virtues, he acquired a sense of personal worth and value which resulted in a self-esteem of no inconsiderable proportions. Here Aristotle's distinctions are of the utmost importance, since so many of the Roman writers derive their notions from him. In his definition of *megalopsychia*—the concept of highmindedness, loftiness, greatness of heart—Aristotle states that a just sense of pride in one's own virtue is highly desirable and that aristocratic pride is a proper mean between the extremes of vanity, an exaggerated sense of one's own worth, and undue humility, an exaggerated sense of one's inferiority. This Aristotelian sense of pride runs into direct conflict with two fundamental Christian dogmas: first, it suggests that humility is an extreme and an exaggeration, and second, it denies the Christian view that man's virtue comes from God, whom he should thank for whatever virtue he may possess. T. S. Eliot, writing on Shakespeare, discusses the "Senecan attitude of pride," which he feels reveals itself in the self-satisfaction of Othello and Hamlet at the end of the plays in question. In the course of his essay he states that "humility is the most difficult of all virtues to achieve; nothing dies harder than the desire to think well of oneself."[33] As is evident here, Eliot's attack, reflecting his Christian values, should be made, like Augustine's attack in *The City of God*, against the whole pagan-humanist tradition, not simply against the Stoics who carry the pagan sense of pride to a ridiculous extreme and do lend themselves to caricature. The desire to think well of oneself, in the pagan-humanist view, is an entirely worthy desire, as long as one is taking a justified pride in one's own possession of virtue. Cicero speaks for the classical tradition in his *On Friendship* when he observes, "I grant that Virtue loves herself; for she best knows herself and realizes how lovable she is."[34] (The Christian moral

[33] "Shakespeare and the Stoicism of Seneca," *Selected Essays*, pp. 111-112.
[34] p. 26.

tradition, incidentally, has not always insisted that one be totally self-effacing—Christ states that one should love one's neighbor *as oneself*. [Italics mine])

The Renaissance reflects this pagan-humanist tradition of self-congratulation for one's good qualities side by side with the Christian ethics of humility and self-abasement. Thus, Spenser's Sir Guyon, who personifies the classical virtue of temperance, wanders alone across the plains in the second book of *The Faerie Queene*, feeling thoroughly satisfied with himself: "And evermore himselfe with comfort feeds,/ Of his owne vertues, and praise-worthy deedes."[35] On the other hand, the Red Cross Knight, a symbol of Christian virtue, in the first Canto of the same book, had rejected the notion that he deserved "everlasting fame" and a "glorious name" for his achievements. He tells the Palmer:

> His be the praise, that this atchiev'ment wrought,
>   Who made my hand the organ of his might;
> More than goodwill to me attribute nought:
>   For all I did, I did but as I ought.[36]

Montaigne's combination of scepticism and Christianity, leads him, as I have already mentioned, to his famous attack on the dignity of man in "The Apology for Raimond Sébond": "So long as man shall be perswaded to have meanes or power of himselfe, so long wil he denie, and never acknowledge what he oweth unto his Master. . . . He must be stripped into his shirt."[37] Here is the spirit of self-abnegation. But we find elsewhere in his writings a pagan-humanist note which utterly contradicts it. "I am of opinion that we should be cautious in forming an estimate of ourselves, and equally conscientious in expressing it impartially, whether it be high or low. If I thought myself good or wise, or nearly so, I should shout it at the top of my voice. To make ourselves out worse than we are, is foolishness, not mod-

---

[35] In *The Poetical Works*, ed. J. C. Smith and E. de Sélincourt, London, 1937, II, vii, 2, ll. 4-5.
[36] *ibid.*, II, i, 33, ll. 2-5.
[37] II, 12.

esty. To be content with less than we are worth is want of spirit and pusillanimity, according to Aristotle."[38]

If we choose to attack a particular instance of this attitude of satisfaction with one's own dignity and nobility, we must attack the pagan-humanist tradition in general—with the notable exception of Plato's Socrates. Aristotle, Cicero, and the Stoics are as one here; for all of them, to be unduly humble is nothing but inverted pride and just as bad as conceit. In the words of Della Casa: "And you may be sure, they that embase themselves thus beyond measure, refusing that worship and honour that is but duely their owne of very right; shewe more pride in this contempte then they that usurpe those things, that are not so due unto them."[39]

If the pagan humanists believed strongly in the propriety of a justified sense of self-esteem, they nonetheless insisted that modesty should accompany it. They did not, however, equate modesty with humility. To believe in one's own worth was entirely fitting; to be ostentatious or pushing in making others aware of this was the height of ill-manners. Thus Castiglione admonishes his Courtier to be "in everie place . . . lowly, sober, and circumspect, fleeing above all things, bragging and unshamefull praising himselfe: for therewith a man alwaies purchaseth himselfe the hatred of the hearers."[40] Castiglione is careful to point out, however, that a virtuous man should not let his virtue pass unnoticed by the world. Lord Gasper immediately protests that he has "known few men excellent in any thing whatsoever it be, but they praise themselves. And me thinke it may wel be borne in them: for he that is of skill, when he seeth that hee is not knowne for his workes of the ignorante hath a disdaine, that his cunning should be buried, and needes must he open it one way, least he should bee defrauded of the estimation that belongeth to it, which is the true rewarde of vertuous travailes."[41]

[38] *ibid.*, II, 6.
[39] *Galateo*, p. 38. Cf. quotation facing Introduction, above.
[40] p. 37.   [41] *ibid.*

The pagan-humanist consensus, nevertheless, holds self-praise unnecessary. Modesty is considered an indication of one's gentility. The pagan humanist does not deny that men should wish for public approbation, but suggests that noble deeds will be their own trumpet and will not require accompanying self-advertisement. Thus, Castiglione's Sir Frederick suggests that modesty and great worth go together. "Though [modesty] of it selfe lie still, the worthie deedes speake at large, and are much more to be wondred at, than if they were accompanied with presumption or rashnesse."[42] Montaigne, in the passage quoted above, had justified self-praise, suggesting, if rhetorically, that if he felt himself great, he would shout it from the housetops. But elsewhere he admits that "Custome hath made a mans speech of himselfe vicious. And obstinately forbids it in hatred of boasting, which ever seemeth closely to follow ones self witnesses."[43]

5. THE HONORABLE DEATH

No aspect of life revealed more completely the qualities of valor, magnanimity, and constancy than the way in which the Renaissance man of honor faced death, for here lay the proof of his greatness of heart and of his contempt for his most precious material possessions. Hurault speaks for the classical tradition when he says, quoting Aristotle: "It is the dutie of Prowesse to be utterlie undismaied with the feare of death, to be constant in suffering adversitie, to be void of dread of danger, to chuse rather for to die with honour, than to live with dishonour, or to be conquered in battell."[44] For the Renaissance man of honor the only admissible fear was that of infamy. Pagan-humanist idealism did not prevent a realistic awareness that "few men resolve themselves to die the death that lieth in them to eschew."[45] Yet, "the state of Prowesse consisteth chiefly in the contempt of greef and death. And that man is counted a man of noble courage, which when an honest or honourable

---

[42] *ibid.*, p. 111.   [43] II, 6.
[44] pp. 275-276.   [45] *ibid.*, p. 281.

death is offered unto him, is nothing afraid of it."[46] The motives for which one died were of no inconsiderable importance. Christian martyrdom was extolled, but along with it, and of equal merit, were love of honor, of country, or affection for a particular person. To die in the service of one's country was especially honorable since patriotism was extolled by almost all Renaissance moralists as it had been by their Greek and Roman predecessors. As *The French Academie* suggests, "They that die . . . in the defence of their Common-wealth, live alwayes by glorie."[47]

Raleigh's *The Last Fight of the Revenge* reveals how closely the arguments presented by the Renaissance moralists were followed in actual battle. When Sir Richard Grenville realizes that his tiny ship can fight no longer against the mighty Spanish Armada he "commanded the maister Gunner, whom he knew to be a most resolute man, to split and sinke the shippe; that thereby nothing might remaine of glorie or victorie to the Spaniards . . . and perswaded the companie, or as manie as he could induce, to yeelde themselves unto God, and to the mercie of none els; but as they had like valiant resolute men, repulsed so manie enemies, they should not now shorten the honour of their nation by prolonging their owne lives for a few houres, or a few daies."[48] Many of the crew agreed that an honorable death was infinitely preferable to dishonorable surrender. But the captain of the ship suggested that it would be more patriotic to live on since there were "diverse sufficient and valiant men yet living, and whose woundes were not mortall, they might doe their countrie and prince acceptable service hereafter."[49] When the Spanish Admiral offered honorable conditions of surrender, most of the men agreed to the captain's suggestion and his decision was carried out.

Renaissance history abounds with examples of heroic deaths— even of criminals who died nobly and magnificently. From

[46] *ibid.*, p. 282.
[47] La Primaudaye, p. 687.
[48] Sir Walter Raleigh, *Selections*, ed. G. E. Hadow, Oxford, 1926, pp. 152-153.
[49] *ibid.*, p. 153.

More's final words, "Plucke upp thie spirittes, man, and be not affrayed to do thine office, my necke is verye short"[50] in 1534 to Raleigh's in 1611, "So the heart be right, it is no matter which way the head lies," the spirit is one and the same.[51] A detailed description of the death of Mary Queen of Scots confirms this fact. Woman she might be, but the account of her death is the portrayal of a regal dignity completely befitting an Elizabethan queen: "She passed out of the entery into the great Hall, with her countenance carelesse, imparting thereby rather mirth then mournfull cheare, and so she willingly stepped up to the scaffold which was prepared for her in the Hall."[52] All through the proceedings leading up to the execution, she maintained this cheerful calm. Two of her maids removed her apparel: "All this time they were pulling off her apparell, she never chaunged her countenaunce, but with smiling cheere she uttered thes wordes, 'that she never had such groomes to make her unready, and that she never put off her clothes before such a company.' "[53] Finally, when all the preparations were finished, "the two women departed from her, and kneeling downe upon the cusshion most resolutely, and without any token or fear of death," she prepared for the fatal blow.[54]

6. SUICIDE

The Renaissance attitude toward suicide is a particularly revealing one, for here, too, we may note the divergence between the Christian and the classical ethics which led to a divided allegiance. The Christian taboo against suicide encompassed all sects and creeds, for, as has been frequently pointed out, "though there are many crimes of a deeper dye than suicide, there is no other by which men appear so formally to renounce the protection of God."[55] Even the classical philosophers often protested against it and stated that true courage was shown in en-

---

[50] *Source Book of English History*, ed. Elizabeth K. Kendall, New York, 1900, p. 143.

[51] Sir Walter Ralegh, *Works*, London, 1751, I, lxxxv.

[52] Kendall, p. 175.   [53] *ibid.*, p. 177.   [54] *ibid.*, p. 175.

[55] Mme. La Baronne de Staël-Holstein, *Réflexions sur le Suicide Suivies de la Défense de la Reine, et des Lettres sur J. J. Rousseau*, Paris, 1814, p. 21.

during life. The prohibition of suicide in Cicero's *Republic* sounds amazingly Christian: "All good men must leave that soul in the custody of the body, and must not abandon human life except at the behest of him by whom it was given you, lest you appear to have shirked the duty imposed upon man by God."[56]

Yet Cicero also presents the Stoic point of view in the third book of *De Finibus*. Since the Renaissance depended largely on Roman moralists for their interpretation of classical ethics, it would be surprising if they completely ignored this Stoic view. For, as Lecky observes, suicide was much more popular during the Roman period than it had ever been in Greece, particularly among the Roman Stoics who took Cato for their model.[57]

Eisinger's *Das Problem des Selbst-mordes in der Literatur der Englischen Renaissance* is an exhaustive, painstaking study of the growing tolerance of suicide in the literature of the Renaissance.[58] The Christian taboo was strong against it, but as the 16th century progresses Christianity has less and less of a hold, and increasing approval is demonstrated, at least for the literary expression of it. Lecky substantiates this view. "We find many facts," he writes, "exhibiting a startling increase of deliberate suicide, and a no less startling modification of the sentiments with which it was regarded. The revival of classical learning, and the growing custom of regarding Greek and Roman heroes as ideals, necessarily brought the subject into prominence. The Catholic casuists, and at a later period philosophers of the school of Grotius and Puffendorf, began to distinguish certain cases of legitimate suicide, such as that committed to avoid dishonour or probable sin . . . or that of a man who offers himself to death for his friend."[59]

Montaigne's essay "A Custom of the Island of Cea" presents a multitude of arguments both for and against suicide.

---

[56] VI. 15.
[57] I, 216.
[58] Fritz Eisinger, *Das Problem des Selbst-mordes in der Literatur der Englischen Renaissance*, Überlingen/Bodensee, 1925, IX.
[59] II, 55.

Two of the most pertinent of those against it are the Christian injunction and the patriotic argument that one owes one's life to one's country. Montaigne also suggests that more courage is shown in enduring adversity. Thus he recounts a conversation between the Stoic Therycion and the Stoic Cleomenes. Therycion exhorts Cleomenes to kill himself, considering this preferable to the death in battle he had just escaped. But Cleomenes argues: "That to live, is sometimes constancie and valour; That he will have his very death serve his Countrie, and by it, shew an act of honour and of vertue."[60] Even the Biblical example is presented of the good elder Razis who attempted suicide unsuccessfully in order to avoid ignoble surrender, and finally, after capture, managed it by plucking out his bowels. The extensiveness of Montaigne's reading is indicated by his recounting of an incident concerning Minachetuen, an Indian lord, and the Portuguese viceroy of Malacca who wanted to depose him. The motives—particularly the desire to avoid ridicule—which lead to suicide in this story of the Far East, are similar to those of Shakespeare's Roman heroes and their actual counterparts in pagan Rome. The Portuguese lord told his people "that having so often witnessed, armed at all assayes for others; that his honour was much dearer unto him than life, he was not to forsake the care of it for himselfe; that fortune refusing him all meanes to oppose himselfe against the injurie intended against him, his courage, at the least willed him to remove the feeling thereof, and not become a laughing stocke unto the people and a triumphe to men of lesse worth: which words as he was speaking, he cast himselfe into the fire."[60] Montaigne's conclusions as to valid reasons for suicide are somewhat less glorious than the motives described in this account. His practical nature responds favorably only to the inducements provided by intolerable pain and the fear of a worse death. But elsewhere, in his essay "Three Good Wives," he recounts tales of pagan fidelity and it is obvious that he approves of the heroic actions of three Roman ladies who commit suicide as

[60] II, 3.

proof of their love for their husbands.[61] His account of the
story of Seneca's death is noteworthy as an indication of the
willingness of Renaissance moralists to view suicide as an honorable act, incidentally reminding us of the deaths of Shakespeare's
Antony and Cleopatra. Seneca, deciding that the time has come
to end his life, admonishes his wife, Paulina, not to grieve since
"he embraced death, not only without griefe but with exceeding joy. Wherefore my deere-deere heart, do not dishonor it
by thy teares, lest thou seeme to love thy selfe more than my
reputation. . . . To whom *Paulina*, having somwhat rouzed
her drooping spirits, and by a thrice-noble affection awakened
the magnanimitie of her high-setled courage, answered thus:
No *Seneca*, thinke not that in this necessitie I will leave you
without my company.

"I would not have you imagin that the vertuous examples of
your life have not also taught me to die: And when shal I be
able to do it or better, or more honestly, or more to mine own
liking, then with your selfe? And be resolved I wil go with
you and be partaker of your fortune. *Seneca* taking so generous
a resolve, and glorious a determination of his wife in good
part, and to free himselfe from the feare he had to leave her
after his death, to his enemies mercie and cruelty: Oh my deare
Paulina, I had (quoth he) perswaded thee what I thought was
convenient, to leade thy life more happily, and doost thou then
rather choose the honour of a glorious death? Assuredly I will
not envy thee: Be the constancie and resolution answerable to
our common end, but be the beautie and glory greater on thy
side."[62]

Renaissance moral philosophy ordinarily adhered to the
Christian position that suicide was not permissible, but few books
fail to acknowledge that it was condoned by certain pagan philosophers. *The Courtier's Academie* presents the Stoic justification of suicide. Gualinguo argues: "This is not a doubt of small
importance: and the opinions of famous and learned men be

[61] *ibid.*, II, 35.
[62] *ibid.*

120

in this point divers: the greater part affirming that the combatant ought rather to die, than yeeld: for in any case, a man of honor shuld alwaies preferre death, before infamous safetie. And this the philosopher testifieth in the 3 of his morals saying, A valiant man ought much more to feare infamy then death: and also in another place in his Morals: that an honourable man, should rather choose a short life honourable, then a long life, but contumelious. And upon this foundation the Stoikes in some cases permitted the violent killing of one's selfe to avoide a dishonorable life."[63]

La Primaudaye, after inveighing against suicide at some length, recounts the story of the son of Scaurus who slew himself out of shame.[64] Whetstone and Bryskett mention the Roman opinion that "it is the part of a stout heart, for a man to kill himselfe rather then to suffer shame or servitude, as we reade that Cato did, and Cassius, and Brutus."[65] North's *Plutarch*, in its account of the lives of Brutus and Antony, presented many an Elizabethan, including Shakespeare, with the pagan view.

Indeed, despite legal and religious injunctions against it, suicide was not altogether unknown in Renaissance England. Whetstone's *The Honourable Reputation of a Souldier* presents an interesting case where the pagan ethics challenges the Christian, even though the author hedges sufficiently to avoid appearing unchristian.

"The Earle of Shrewsbury . . . was beset with a great power of french men, beyonde all possibilitie, for his strength to overcome. . . yet hee courageously abode their incounter, and upon this resolution, he thus said unto his sonne.

"Sonne, (quot he) thou art yong, and mayst with honour flye. But I am old, and have had my life honored with many victories, all of which I should loose, if I should deferre my death . . . by a timerous flight. Therefore I am bounde to staye.

---

[63] Count Romei, p. 101.   [64] p. 249.   [65] Bryskett, p. 183.

"What should his sonne doe, but even which he did: followe the fortune of his father, and so like as they lived died valiant men. This precise preservation of honor, neither the devines, nor many politick Martialistes, do allowe: the one absolutely reproving desperate ende; the other forbidding a man willfully to die, when by his death, hee neither benefiteth his frend, nor hurteth his enimie. And yet, the greatnes of these mens courages, are to be honored, although not necessary to be followed. But necessitie many times approveth resolute bouldnesse, to be honorable, profitable, and necessarie."[66]

Raleigh likewise quibbles with the Christian taboo. "I knowe it is forbidden to destroye ourselves," he says, "but I trust it is forbidden in this sorte, that we destroye not our selves dispairinge of gods mercie."[67]

Raleigh also refers casually to suicide in his account of *The Fight of the Revenge*. Sir Richard Grenville's suggestion, mentioned earlier, that the English sink their ship in order to deprive the Spaniards of the glory of conquest is quite in accordance with the Roman attitude. When the crew finally decides to accept honorable conditions of surrender, "The maister Gunner finding him selfe and Sir Richard thus prevented and and maistered by the greater number, would have slaine himselfe with a sword, had he not been by force withheld and locked into his Cabben."[68] Raleigh's narration of the voyage to Virginia in one of his letters contains another reference to an Elizabethan who imitated the Roman practice as a means to escape disgrace. Raleigh's Captain Kemishes was sent to attack a Spanish mine and failed in his mission. Whereupon Raleigh recounts in offhand manner: "But at Kemishes returne from Orenoque, when I rejected his Counsell and his course, and told him, that he had undone me, and wounded my credite with the King past recoverie, he slew himself. For I told him, that seing my sonne w[as] lost, I cared not, if he had lost a hundred

[66] George Whetstone, London, 1585, cii.
[67] Sir Walter Raleigh, *Selections*, p. 179.
[68] *ibid.*, p. 154.

more in opening the Min[e,] so my credite had bene saved."[69] Donne's *Bianthanatos* is probably the most famous of all the Renaissance treatises which discuss suicide. But since Donne is in some respects an eccentric figure, his favorable attitude toward suicide should perhaps be considered primarily as one aspect of his personal scepticism and therefore not given much weight as evidence of currents of opinion in the early 17th century.

7. EMULATION AND AMBITION

To hunt after honors by striving to excel others in performing heroic deeds was the most legitimate of aspirations for the great Renaissance noblemen. This leads to a curious ambiguity in Renaissance discussions of ambition. On the one hand, the man who deliberately seeks honor "incurreth suspect of ambition, which ought to be abhorred of an honest man"; on the other, by "not laboring and suing after it, he is in danger to be thereof deprived, and consequently, not to be known for vertuous."[70] Ben Jonson plays with this paradox in his *Discoveries*. Speaking of the bringing up of children, he observes, "I would send them where their industry should be daily increa'd by praise; and that kindled by emulation. It is a good thing to inflame the mind; And though Ambition it selfe be a vice, it often is the cause of great virtue. Give me that wit, whom praise excites, glory puts on, or disgrace grieves: hee is to bee nourish'd with Ambition, prick'd forward with honour."[71] Hurault is careful to make the same distinction between legitimate aspiration and illegitimate greed. In his discussion of pride and ambition, he protests that he does not mean "to take from a yoong man the desire of honour, and a vertuous emulation that may make him to glorie and delight in his weldoing."[72]

Here again the fundamental definitions are to be found in Aristotle. In seeking honor, Aristotle holds that a legitimate

[69] *ibid.*, p. 190.
[70] Count Romei, p. 114.
[71] In *Works*, Vol. 8, p. 615. This is a Renaissance commonplace.
[72] p. 265.

aspiration is a mean between two undesirable extremes. La Primaudaye, making use of this Aristotelian definition, states that "ambition is an unreasonable desire to enjoy honours, estates, and great places. . . . For that man . . . is modest who desireth honour as he ought, and so far foorth as it becommeth him."[73] As Hardin Craig, Willard Farnham, and Roy Battenhouse have all observed, ambition comes more and more to be the major vice for the men of the Renaissance and for their dramatic counterparts, although Marlowe's heroes are a significant exception. Sometimes ambition is linked with pride, as when Hurault announces that "a desire to be great" and "to be had in honor" proceeds from pride.[74] But the Italian humanists, who were perhaps closest to the spirit of pagan humanism, can find no reason to link ambition with the Christian sin of pride, since they do not consider it a major vice. They state quite simply: "If wee do but thinke upon the examples, as well of the ancientes, as men of these times, we will conclude, that valiant men ought to seek, and hunt after honors, that they may be known to be the men they are."[75]

8 . ANGER

Anger seemed to involve the Renaissance moralist in even more inconsistency than suicide or ambition. Here we are confronted with contradictions resulting from divisions of opinion both among the Christians and the pagan moralists. Thus, Hurault considers anger a short madness and presents a graphic description of the angry man which is in full accord with the Christian view that anger is one of the seven deadly sins: "Ye shall see his eyes sparckling, his face red and fierie, his mouth writhed, all his lims trembling, and as it were in a palsie, his tongue stammering, his words misplaced, and without discourse of reason, like the words of a foole, or a drunken man, or of a man out of his wits."[76] La Primaudaye also considers anger a passion unworthy of man even though he admits that he

[73] p. 212.   [74] p. 265.   [75] Count Romei, p. 115.
[76] p. 363.

is contradicting the opinion of Aristotle and his followers."[77] It is necessary to trace back to the original discussions of the classical philosophers to discover what moral views the Renaissance would be likely to hold on this matter. Aristotle treats righteous anger as a mean between two extremes, one of which is spiritlessness, the other irascibility (unreasonable anger). His definition suggests that anger in itself is not blameworthy: "Now we praise a man who feels anger on the right grounds and against the right persons, and also in the right manner and at the right moment and for the right length of time. He may then be called gentle-tempered, if we take gentleness to be a praiseworthy quality (for 'gentle' really denotes a calm temper), not led by emotion but only becoming angry in such a manner, for such causes and for such a length of time as principle may ordain."[78] Of course, not all the pagan philosophers took such a favorable view of the passions. The Stoics are famous for an almost impossible suppression of all emotion, and so we find Seneca protesting against Aristotle's opinion since he considers anger an undignified and useless passion.

On the fundamental issue at stake here, whether the affections should be suppressed completely or merely checked by the bridle of reason, we find the Stoics in accord with the popular medieval condemnation of anger and the Aristotelians, together with their scholastic disciples in the Middle Ages, drawing a sharp distinction between a reasonable and unreasonable anger and approving a just anger. Much has been made of the Stoic influence on the Renaissance, which was great indeed. But their doctrines were treated primarily as a counsel for adversity; that is, for the suppression of the emotions of pain and grief. Stoic and medieval Christian asceticism were alike rejected when such asceticism meant a suppression of positive, active emotions. Thus, Castiglione's courtiers present the Aristotelian view in an almost literal rendering of Plutarch: "Then the Lorde Cesar Gonzaga, I wot not (quoth he) what vertues requisit for princes may arise of this temperance, if it

---

[77] p. 295.   [78] *Nicomachean Ethics* IV. 5.

be she that riddeth the minde of affections (as you say) which perhaps were meete for some Monke, or Heremite, but I can not see how it should be requisite for a Prince that is couragious, freeharted, and of prowesse in martiall feats, for whatsoever is done to him, never to have anger, hatred, good will, disdaine, lust, nor any affection in him: nor how without this he can get him authoritie among the people."[79] To which the Lord Octavian adds: "The affections therefore that be cleansed and tried by temperance are assistant to vertue, as anger, that helpeth manlinesse: hatred against the wicked helpeth justice, and likewise the other vertues are aided by affections, which in case they were clean taken away, they woulde leave reason very feeble and faint, so that it shoulde litle prevaile, like a shipmaister that is without winde in a great calme."[80]

Hurault likewise follows Aristotle in relating the passion of anger to the virtue of fortitude: "Aristotle saith, That anger must be used as a souldier: he meaneth a certaine . . . princely coragiousnes. . . . For such a boiling forwardnesse, favoreth more of noblenesse of mind, than of wrath."[81] The distinction between anger and wrath is typical and leaves room for a reconciliation of the Aristotelian and Christian virtues. Yet the Christian virtues of charity, humility, patience, and forgiveness come out second. "And yet notwithstanding he that is meeld and mercifull, faileth not to be angry. For else he should be blockish and without any feeling. But he is angry with reason."[82] To be "blockish," "senseless as a stone," is a recurrent Renaissance criticism of the Stoics; most Renaissance moralists are Aristotelian in this regard and label Stoic lack of feeling the vice of pusillanimity.

The passages just quoted suggest that, except for the Stoics, the pagan moralists consistently approved of the emotion of anger. But no moralist fails to warn his reader against the dangers of unreasonable anger and most of them present a negative view side by side with the positive one. Indeed, the

[79] pp. 271-272.   [80] *ibid.*, p. 272.
[81] p. 360.   [82] *ibid.*, p. 354.

Golden Epistles of Antonio de Guevara presents both views in a single sentence. His observation that "Anger is then somewhat tollerable, when the occasion is juste" leads immediately to the consideration of it as "a vice so imperious in man."[83] Hurault, who fully approved of a just and reasonable anger, immediately passes on to warn his reader: "Let him read histeries, and consider the blame that hath lighted upon irefull persons. I will not speake of Coriolane, and others, who through that onely vice have defaced great vertues, and misguided their affaires."[84] La Primaudaye completely denies his pagan-humanist self to present the Christian injunctions against anger. Yet he realizes that he is in opposition to the Aristotelian view: "Neither doth it make against our saying, to alledge the opinion of Aristotle, and of all the Peripeteticks, who maintained that we ought to moderate the affections and passions of the soul: but otherwise that they were necessarie to pricke men forward to vertue."[85]

9. REVENGE

The duality of Renaissance ethics is striking in any discussion of revenge—a subject closely akin to that of anger. Here Christian teaching is completely clear and dogmatic, so here the divided soul of the Renaissance most clearly reveals itself. The law of the land of course accorded with the teachings of the church. But the powerful hold of the pagan-humanist ethics, and of the code of honor which resulted from it, led to sharp cleavage between religious theory and the civil law on the one hand and actual Elizabethan practice on the other. Thus Cornwallis confesses, "About nothing doe I suffer greater conflicts in my selfe then about induring wrongs; for other duties—though perhaps I seldome performe them, yet am I resolved they should be done; and it is not the fault of my meditation but of my negligent flesh. But heere is set up Reputation as the Garland appointed, and he that revengeth not is not capable of this glorie."[86] What do the workers for salvation and the

---

[83] Fenton, p. 147.   [84] p. 368.   [85] p. 295.   [86] p. 14.

workers for reputation have in common? Cornelius Agrippa
had asked this question, although in fact it was the major task
of every Renaissance moralist to reconcile the two systems of
ethics. But on such a fundamental issue as this, reconciliation
was impossible—the Christian injunction was definite, but so,
too, was the passionate concern of the Renaissance gentleman
to defend his honor, good name, and reputation. Montaigne
muses on this dilemma, "By the law and right of armes he
that putteth up an injurie shall be degraded of honour and
nobilitie and he that revengeth himselfe of it, shall by the civill
Law incurre a capitall punishment."[87] The contradiction is so
striking that one could hardly believe it possible to hold a
divided allegiance—yet this is precisely the Renaissance solution.

Elizabethan Revenge Tragedy, a scholarly and comprehen-
sive investigation of this subject as it applied to the tragedy of
the age, contains an excellent introductory chapter in which
F. T. Bowers goes exhaustively into the moral and legal
theory of both the Christian and pagan traditions and also into
the sociological and anthropological aspects of the question as
revealed by the customs of Anglo-Saxon England and the actual
practice of the Elizabethans. His conclusions have great significance for our study. He says:

"There can be little question that many an Elizabethan
gentleman disregarded without a qualm the ethical and religious opinion of his day which condemned private revenge,
and felt obliged by the more powerful code of honor to revenge personally any injury offered him. The ordinary Englishman did not abjure revenge as such, especially when the duel
was the means of action. It was only when the more treacherous
and Italianate features were added (as in the murder of Over-
bury) or when accomplices were hired to revenge (as by Sanquire) that he considers revenge despicable. The frequency
with which open assaults, even with disparity of numbers, and
"honorable" duels were pardoned by the rulers of England in

[87] I, 22.

the seventeenth century indicates strongly that no matter what the position of the law—it was the method and not the act itself which was largely called in question."[88]

Such moral dualism was not restricted to England; the whole of Renaissance Europe was affected by this conflict between two ethical systems held to be equally valid. Bryson, in *The Sixteenth Century Italian Duel*, points out any number of instances in which the Christian injunction was not strong enough to hold against the floodtide of aristocratic sentiment . against it. Muzio, the chief authority of the century on the code of honor, admitted that the duel was contrary to both Christian and imperial law but felt that the princes would be powerless to prevent it, no matter how great their authority. Even theologians defended the duel of honor. "Bishop Guevara, although he asserted that as a gentleman, a Christian, and a cleric he would rather forget offenses than avenge them, said that questions . . . concerning . . . affairs of honor [must be handled] by the lance or the sword."[89] Others argued that even New Testament ethics permitted the duel. "According to the Bible, 'let none of you suffer as a murderer, or as a thief, or as an evildoer, or as a busybody' in other men's matter, this was explained as meaning that a man must not suffer an insult if he did not deserve it; he must put aside hatred but not the regard for honor."[90] The issue was clearly drawn between the meekness, humility, and charity stressed by the Christian ethics, and the highmindedness and loftiness of the Renaissance man of honor. Fantastic contortions were involved in the attempt to rationalize the two:

"Some, moreover, at least before the time of the Council of Trent, with regard to the duel ignored the teachings of religion or even defied them. One writer said that, although the duel was opposed by Christianity, lofty souls could not endure offenses; hence, the most noble knights defended their honor,

---

[88] Fredson T. Bowers, *Elizabethan Revenge Tragedy*, Princeton, 1940, p. 37.
[89] Frederick Bryson, *The Sixteenth Century Italian Duel*, Chicago, 1938, p. 123.
[90] *ibid.*, p. 121.

which was more valuable than all the treasures of the world. Yet he expressed the hope that his book, written to satisfy their martial souls, would attain this purpose by the help of God. The duel was tolerated, furthermore, by the emperor and other secular princes, who permitted such combats for causes which they regarded as just. Although it was admitted that, since the forgiveness of enemies was enjoined by Christ, the law should compel reconciliation, yet there was an exception for those who professed the *religione* of honor."[91]

Elizabethan attitudes toward revenge were a direct parallel to those on the Continent. According to legal theory, the administration of justice was the concern of the state and the taking of private revenge was a usurpation by the individual of those powers which belonged to the state alone. The Christian argument against revenge intertwined with the legal, since monarch and magistrate were representatives of God, his earthly legal agents. In the words of Thomas Becon: "to desire to be revenged, when all vengeance pertaineth to God, as he saith, 'Vengeance is mine, and I will reward' . . . this to do ye are forbidden."[92] To take revenge into one's own hands was to challenge divine authority: "God would never have assumed the power of revenge as a parcell of his owne prerogative in case his purpos had bene to leave all men to the revenge of their owne particularities."[93] To challenge divine authority meant, of course, to risk damnation. Cleaver, for example, warned the revenger that he stripped himself of divine protection and that God would not heed his prayers for a blessing. Bishop Hall predicted that the man who sought vengeance would suffer a double death, of body and soul, for ignoring the Christian law. In striking contrast to Cicero's careful distinctions between a just and an unjust revenge, the religious moralists denounced all those who thought that God would view their private vengeance with favor simply because they had been unworthily abused. Private revenge was absolutely wrong; for the Christian,

[91] *ibid.*, pp. 119-120.   [92] Quoted by Bowers, p. 13.
[93] *ibid.*, p. 23.

Cicero's definitions of just grounds for revenge were meaningless.

Elizabeth considered herself a Christian sovereign and an absolute one. Hence, it is not surprising to find that courtiers were jailed (as were, for example, John Hollys and Jarvis Markham) when they fought against the Queen's express command. At the Queen's request, the Privy Council in 1600 forbade a fight between Southhampton and Wilton.[94] Such evidence as this leads Lily Campbell to conclude: "there was a persistent condemnation of revenge in the ethical teaching of Shakespeare's England."[95] Here, as everywhere, when a particular critic insists on the consistency of Renaissance ethics, whether it be a Christian or pagan-humanist consistency that he seeks, he becomes involved in the defense of an untenable position. The moralists were equally busy and equally fervent in defending and condemning revenge; sometimes the same moralist will express on one page a Christian abhorrence, and a few pages later a pagan-humanist approval, of it. Such was the ethical inconsistency of that eclectic age. The only real common denominator was the moral passion with which the ethical imperatives of both systems were defended.

Consider, for example, Segar's *Booke of Honor and Armes* which begins with the assertion that "vertue alloweth just revenge."[96] True, Segar cautions the reader that "this booke doth not incite men to unadvised fight, or needles revenge . . . but enformeth the true meanes how to shunne all offences." Yet he adds immediately that "being offended, [it] sheweth the order of revenge and repulse, *according unto Christian knowledge* and due respect of Honor."[97] [Italics mine] Indeed, Segar finds "that al humaine lawes have permitted the triall of Armes, and that everie injurious action not repulsed, is by

[94] *ibid.*, p. 35.
[95] Lily B. Campbell, "Theories of Revenge in Renaissance England," *Modern Philology*, XXVIII, 1931, p. 281.
[96] Sir William Segar, *The Booke of Honor and Armes*, London, 1590, The Epistle Dedicatorie.
[97] *ibid.*, fol. A3.

common consent of all Martiall mindes holden a thing dishonorable, infamous, and reproachfull; it cannot be, but at some times and occasions such questions and quarrels shall arise, as necessarilie must receive triall by the Sword."[98]

In his *Discourse of Civill Life*, Bryskett presents both Christian and pagan-humanist arguments against the taking of private revenge. He argues, for example, "that the magnanimous or great minded man, utterly despiseth all injuries" and hence will be incapable of offence, sure in his inner knowledge of virtue.[99] But Bryskett goes on to "say (as before) that if the injury be done unto a man of magnanimitie; the way to shake it off, is to despise it, because the excellencie of his vertue is greater than any injury that can be done unto him: and if it be done to him that is not come to that degree of vertue as to be magnanimous, he may perchance at the instant repulse the same, or revenge himself in hot bloud without any great reproch."[100]

The convenience of the dialogue as a form by which ethical contradictions and ambiguities could be easily handled, if not resolved, is illustrated in the presentation of the same argument in *The Courtier's Academie*. There Gualinguo argues that "it was never by any common wealth accepted, or approved of, neither by any auncient State, that for cause of honor . . . they should have recourse to combate: nor Aristotle, Plato, or any other philosopher, or Law-giver, did ever approve or so much as know this monstrous maner of conflict."[101] Earlier, however, the same courtier had argued: "The Peripatetike . . . doth not spoile a man of affections, like the Stoike, for man being partaker of the sensitive facultie, can not be insensible; but woulde, that with reason moderating them, he might reduce them to the state of mediocritie: it is therefore necessary, that a man in the same instant hee is offended, should be angry, and therefore at the same time it shall be lawfull for him to make that re-

[98] *ibid.*, fol. A2. [99] p. 76.
[100] *ibid.*, p. 77. [101] Count Romei, p. 148.

venge he can, and which honestie permitteth: when not doing, he runneth into the vice of stupiditie, or pusillanimitie."[102]

In the discussion of Renaissance attitudes toward suicide, I pointed out not only that suicide was sometimes viewed with the greatest sympathy but also that the fight of the *Revenge* and the suicide of Raleigh's lieutenant in Guiana show that the Renaissance sailor and soldier could act on this theory, whatever the Christian injunctions against such behavior. Here, with revenge, the same correlation exists between pagan-humanist doctrine and the actual practice of the Elizabethan nobleman. Bowers cites an illuminating illustration of English aristocratic behavior. Lord Sanquire was reproved by James the First of Scotland for having suffered the loss of an eye and not having avenged the injury. Sanquire, stung by the king's remark, proceeded to hire two ruffians who murdered Turner, the man who had put out his sight in a fencing bout. James himself saw to it that Sanquire was brought to trial for this murder which he had instigated. The words of the condemned man in his own defense are a dramatic presentation of the conflict between Christian and pagan-humanist values in the Renaissance: "I must confess I ever kept a grudge in my soul against him, but had no purpose to take so high a revenge: yet in the course of my revenge, I considered not my wrongs upon terms of Christianity . . . but being trained up in the courts of princes and in arms, I stood upon the terms of honour. . . . Another aspersion is laid on me, that I was an ill-natured fellowe, ever revengeful, and delighted in blood. To the first I confes I was never willing to put up a wrong, where upon terms of honour I might right myself, nor never willing to pardon where I had the power to revenge."[103]

10. THE DUEL

However far a particular Renaissance moralist may have gone in defense of private revenge, he would take the greatest care to make the qualification that "a quarrel must not be under-

---

[102] *ibid.*, p. 144.   [103] Quoted by Bowers, p. 29.

taken by a private man without just cause."[104] Indeed, the duel, according to Bryson, demonstrated the two cardinal virtues of justice and valor which constituted one of the favorite pagan-humanist definitions of honor. "The cause of all Quarrell," Segar states, "is Injurie and reproach, but the matter of content, is Justice and Honor."[105] Presumably the winner of the duel thus demonstrated the justice of his cause, and by so doing, as well as by displaying his courage, proved that he was a man of honor.

The customs associated with the duel varied with the individual country, but the ideal of honor and the laws of the duel formed a common code for all Renaissance Europe. Thus, the cause for a duel could not be a matter of property, but only one in which a man's character was slurred. The duel was permitted especially when there was an absence of proof and the legal penalty would be death or public infamy. Indeed, whether a quarrel was decided privately or taken to court, the punishment of the loser was public disgrace, the worst of penalties for the Renaissance man of honor. *The Courtier's Academie* outlines the legal procedures in the following manner: "Whereupon the Magistrates and lawes enforce the injurer, to restore honor with his tongue to him injuried, which is no other, but to confesse himselfe culpable, and the injured innocent . . . that hee injurying acknowledge, that hee injured is not woorthie of contempt, and that hee is a man of valour. . . . The Magistrates compell them who impeach other mens honor to make restitution thereof . . . to the end that for penaltie of their offence, they may receive infamie."[106]

The etiquette of the challenge was worked out with detailed concern for proper form. An insult to a man, the defamation of his character, led to the response suggested by Sir William Segar in the *Book of Honor and Armes*: "Thou hast spoken in prejudice of mine honor, honestie and credite, and therefore doest lie."[107] As Bryson points out, the emphasis placed on the

[104] Cornwallis, p. 124.   [105] *The Booke of Honor and Armes*, fol. A2.
[106] pp. 165-166.   [107] p. 6.

134

lie as a form of insult has lasted down to this day, though twentieth century society has put the duel far behind it. Even today the suggestion that a man is a liar is an accepted provocation to a blow even more than the suggestion that he is a murderer. This was the etiquette of the sixteenth century. Thus *The Court of Civill Courtesie* states:

"If I give one occasion of offence that toucheth but his profit, and he give me reprochful name for it, as the Lie, or knave: I must for my credit sake, not only requite these words with like words, but count the wrong mine and either offer the first blow (if the place serve for it) or els challenge him into the field: unlesse I can (for pollicies sake) drive him to challenge me, to save my self from the danger of the law. For fighting quarels never are made for profit, but for honor. . . . If I offer the first reproch, disdain or dispight, the quarrel is the others. . . . But if the other give me the first lie, or like disgrace, it is not ynough to say he lieth again: but I must needs offer a blow, or chalenge the field."[108]

Injury of words is compensated for by injury of deed; a lie is answered by a box on the ear.

The etiquette which follows—the sending of a challenge, the appointing of seconds, the meeting on the field of honor— is not pertinent to our discussion. The whole affair was, of course, surrounded by elaborate ritual. As *The Court of Civill Courtesie* says, "if any man bee called by any reprochfull names, they must needes be requited, both in termes and deedes, but after sundrie maners according to the person, the cause and the place."[109] *The Courtier's Academie* gives an excellent definition of the ethical purpose of the combat itself: "Combate is a battaile betwixt twoo of equall interest, in some point of honor, in the end whereof the vanquished incurreth infamy, and the victor remaineth possessed of Honor."[110]

---

[108] S[imon] R[obson] Gent, *The Court of Civill Courtesie*, London, 1591, fol. c3.
[109] *ibid.*, fol. c2.   [110] p. 131.

CHAPTER 4

HONOR AS PUBLIC ESTEEM

WE turn now from the consideration of honor in its private sense, as an instinct toward righteousness which dwells in the breast of the Renaissance aristocrat, to a consideration of honor in its public sense, as an outward sign and token of that righteousness. It may be helpful at this point to summarize the basic meanings of the concept as they are given in the *New English Dictionary*.[1]

DEFINITIONS OF HONOR

Honor as self-esteem. Personal title to high respect or esteem; honourableness; elevation of character; nobleness of mind, scorn of meanness; magnanimity. A fine sense of strict allegiance to what is due or right.

"Noble" as a synonym for "honorable." Having high moral qualities or ideals; of a great or lofty character. Proceeding from, characteristic of, indicating or displaying, greatness of character. Characterized by moral superiority or dignity; elevated, lofty.

Honor as public esteem. High respect, esteem, or reverence accorded to exalted worth or rank; deferential admiration or approbation.

As rendered or shown: The expression of high estimation.

As received, gained, held, or enjoyed: Glory, renown, fame; credit, reputation, good name.

As reward: Something conferred or done as a token of respect or distinction; a mark or manifestation of high regard; esp. a position or title of rank, a degree of nobility, a dignity.

---

[1] These definitions are taken from the *New English Dictionary*. I have rearranged the order of presentation to accord with the divisions in the table of contents of this book.

Honor as chastity. (Of a woman) Chastity, purity, as a virtue of the highest consideration; reputation for this virtue, good name.

THE DUTY OF SHOWING PROPER RESPECT
AND ESTEEM

The public display of honor, respect, and esteem, as an expression of high regard for those superior in rank or virtue, was generally considered by the Renaissance moralists as one of the most important aspects of one's "duties" to God, one's country, and one's fellow men. It is perhaps for this reason that Cicero's "*Offices*" (i.e., book of "duties") was the standard textbook on Renaissance ethics. But every Renaissance textbook on moral philosophy also contained definitions of "duty." It is defined in *The French Academie* as "that which bindeth the soule, cheerefully and willingly without force or constraint to give to everie one that which belongeth unto him; honor, to whom honor; reverence to whom reverence."[2] In every relationship between two individuals, the superiority or inferiority of the men in question must be delimited. Since these relationships involved family, social, and political ties, the Renaissance moralist had to busy himself with considering which obligations deserved preference. Thus Cleland discusses the problem of the son who is king to his own father; the conflict of duties must be examined and resolved. He speaks of "the royal act of the worthie Statesman Don John King of Arragon, father unto Don Ferdinando King of Castile: who . . . would not suffer his sonne to kisse his hand, nor yet to give him the upper hand at their going through the Cittie. . . . Sonne, (said he) you who are the cheife and Lord of Castile, whereof we are descended, should accept of us that honour, reverence, and service, which appertaineth unto you: in respect that our duty towards you, as our King and superior, is farre above that, of the sonne unto the father."[3] How essential it was to manifest

---

[2] La Primaudaye, p. 88. Cf. Count Romei, p. 113.
[3] *The Institution of a Nobleman*, p. 182.

respect and deference in a hierarchical aristocratic society is all too evident from Della Casa's warning that "many times it chaunceth that men come to daggers drawing, even for this occasion alone, that one man hath not done the other, that worship and honour uppon the way, that he ought."[4]

The sense of reverent respect for a titled nobility—a categorical imperative in the Renaissance, both in the Christian and the pagan-humanist ethics—has become almost meaningless in a democratic society such as ours. The American, French, and Russian Revolutions (not to mention the beheading of King Charles in 1649 and the Bloodless Revolution in 1688) have largely destroyed the notion that any man is deserving of respect simply because he can assert class superiority over another man. Because of our democratic values we are more than sceptical of the aristocratic concept that exalted rank gives one a hereditary predisposition to greater virtue than that of the man born in the log cabin. Yet if we are to enter vicariously the Elizabethan social world, we must momentarily set aside our own values and accept the idea that noble blood implies moral stature and dignity. This is difficult for most Americans, despite our vicarious enjoyment of the glittering spectacle provided by a British coronation. Our notion of the monarch includes the bungling King George the Third; our idea of the true hero is likely to be Andrew Jackson or Abraham Lincoln. It is a long leap backward from our cultural values to those of the Renaissance.

Both in the Christian and in the classical ethics, respect and reverence for one's parents were moral imperatives. To honor one's father and one's mother was not only one of the ten commandments, but equally one of the first laws of nature. Plato and Plutarch both suggest that filial disrespect is the surest sign of impiety and atheism. Cicero, reflecting the importance which the Romans attached to patriotism, places the obligation to one's parents second only to the obligation to one's country. As Lecky observes, "In Rome the absolute authority of the head of the

[4] p. 45.

family was the centre and archetype of that whole system of discipline and subordination which it was the object of the legislator to sustain. Filial reverence was enforced as the first of the duties."[5]

To honor and to revere one's parents were among the first obligations of the Renaissance child. Even when the parents were mean and cruel, the admonition to respect them should override any imperfections they might show. Thus Guazzo states, "If the father bee churlish, and curst unto them, let the manifold benefites received of him, countervaile that crueltye, and continue them in their duetye."[6] Here, too, the need for sincerity is stressed; in the words of Cleland, "This dutiful honour is not performed by an outward behaviour of the countenance in uncovering the head, in bowing the knee, or in naming them, father and mother (which I thinke the most honorable style or title that children can give to their Parents) but requireth also that you reverence them, in hart, and minde."[7]

It was just as important to honor one's elders as it was to honor one's parents. Here again the Roman moralists establish an ethical precedent for the moralists of the Renaissance. Over and over, Cicero stresses the obligation to show a proper respect to age. In *The Republic*, for example, he refers to the mutual esteem which Laelius and Scipio felt for each other. "Laelius honoured Scipio like a god in the field, on account of his unexcelled glory in war, while at home Scipio in his turn revered Laelius like a father, on account of his greater age."[8] In his essay "On Old Age," he refers frequently to the crowning glory which the aged deserve.[9] The attitude of the Renaissance moralists again is in agreement with that of the writers of antiquity. In his *Golden Epistles*, Guevara equates respect for old age with a nation's right to consider itself civilized. The Spanish bishop suggests "that there hath bene no nation of such barbarous rudenesse, nor any people so intractable, whiche have . . . withholden reverence from olde age."[10]

[5] *A History of European Morals*, I, 298.   [6] III, 36.   [7] p. 127.
[8] I. XII.   [9] XVII.   [10] Fenton, p. 137.

In this connection, it is interesting to hear what Bernard Shaw, one of our modern prophets, has to say about the modern family. In the preface to "Getting Married" he describes the ideal of family life as the aspiration of a group of people to stew "in love continuously from the cradle to the grave," and then refers to the realities of family living in our century as "an unnatural packing into little brick boxes of little parcels of humanity of ill-assorted ages, with the old scolding and beating the young for behaving like young people, and the young hating and thwarting the old for behaving like old people."[11]

REPUTATION

However much the Romans may seem to have gone to obsessive lengths in their concern for honor and reputation, they could hardly have outdone the eagerness with which the Renaissance gentleman sought and guarded it. Hurault is representative of Renaissance judgment on the value of "opinion": "the pleasure then of every gentlemanly heart, and especially of a prince, tendeth to honor, to glory, to reputation, that his name may be spread abroad with renowne over all the earth, and that he may be esteemed wise and vertuous."[12] Reputation was a matter of especial concern for the Elizabethan soldier. The rivalry between Raleigh and the other English nobles in the Cadiz action indicates the extent to which the military leaders were vying for the honors of battle. At Fayal, Raleigh and Essex were also in conflict. Essex was highly indignant, for he felt that Raleigh had deliberately disobeyed his command to deprive him of credit for taking the town. Raleigh went to Essex and explained that, on the day in question, his intention had been only to take on water, but that when the Spanish showed

[11] George Bernard Shaw, Preface to *On Getting Married* in *The Works of Bernard Shaw*, London, 1931, Vol. 12, pp. 195-196. Shaw's iconoclastic treatment of Victorian sentimentality toward honor, love, the family, and patriotism may have been a healthy breath of fresh air at the time he was writing, but it scarcely assists our sympathetic understanding of Elizabethan sensibility. This is particularly evident in modern critics' false assessment of the aged Lear, as I show in Part II, below. See especially pp. 375, 376.
[12] p. 52.

themselves so impudently before him, he felt his reputation at stake and proceeded to engage the enemy. Raleigh himself felt slighted because so little attention was paid to his actions. Writing of the incident in an essay "Concerning Naval Transport," he lets it be known that "I landed those English in Fayal, my-selfe, and therefore ought to take notice of this instance. For whereas I finde an action of mine cited, with omission of my name; I may, by a civill interpretation, thinke, that there was no purpose to defraud me of any honour . . . to reserve the title of such an exploit . . . for a greater person."[13]

POSTHUMOUS REPUTATION

The desire for posthumous reputation was possibly even greater than that for reputation during one's lifetime. For the Romans, posthumous fame was the chief means by which man's values could outlast the life of the individual. Although Cicero and Seneca spoke at times of immortality of the soul, the greater portion of the Roman moralists were wavering and uncertain in their belief in it, and some of the Stoics, such as Epictetus, completely denied it. The hereafter described in Cicero's account of Scipio's dream is related to the Roman conception of nobility—heaven was reserved for those who achieved heroic stature by their greatness. Hence, in accordance with classical mythology, great heroes such as Hercules became deified after their deaths.

Here again the Roman attitudes have a profound effect on Renaissance thought. Uncertainty as to man's future existence, and consequent emphasis on the importance of posthumous fame, are related themes of 16th century writers. Most Elizabethans undoubtedly clung to the belief in immortality; Raleigh, we noted, dismissing the Christian injunction against suicide, qualifies his position by suggesting that self-slaughter is permissible if we do not die despairing of God's mercy. Yet the agnosticism of some of the classical philosophers had a profoundly disturbing influence, as Buckley has pointed out in

[13] *Selections*, p. 111.

his study entitled *Atheism in the English Renaissance*.[14] From the beginning of the 16th century, a controversy over the immortality of the soul took place in the philosophical schools of Northern Italy. Pompanazzi, for example, denied immortality and suggested that one could be idealistic on purely humanistic grounds. His work was not unknown in England. After the middle of the 16th century, there was fairly widespread disbelief in certain intellectual circles in Italy and France. The English were aware of the spreading atheism on the continent although they tended to identify atheism with Machiavellianism, viewing both with horror. Atheism, however, was not always equated with the destruction of ethical values. Etienne Dolet, humanist and moralist, "was certainly incredulous about many points of Christian dogma. In his poems he spoke doubtfully of immortality, referring to death as a quiet sleep . . . and even advanced the opinion that there was no immortality except glory or renown, a lasting name, such as Cicero's or Caesar's."[15] A remark by Philip Stubbes indicates that such attitudes were not isolated; in 1583 he writes that there are those who consider hell but a mere fable or a metaphorical way of speaking and who ridicule the idea of future rewards and punishments. Marlowe's *Faustus* also suggests that the Elizabethans were aware of the current of religious scepticism of the age—although none of the heroes of Marlowe's plays, any more than the hero, "the Senecan superman," in most of Chapman's plays, is in any sense representative of general Elizabethan attitudes.

Whatever the degree of uncertainty about Christian immortality, the passion for some sort of earthly immortality became increasingly strong and by the end of the century had become a substantive concern of the Renaissance moralists. (This concern was already apparent in Petrarch's *Secretum*, discussed in chapter 1.) George Whetstone, explaining why posthumous reputation was so meaningful to the men of antiquity, throws light on the Elizabethan sensibility which was so imitative of

[14] George Buckley, *Atheism in the English Renaissance*, Chicago, 1932, pp. 20-26.
[15] *ibid.*, p. 14.

that former, golden age. "In auncient times the lives and vertues of honorable and worthy personages were published for three especiall causes. The first, that oblivion should not bury the vertues with their bodies. The second, that the trompe of fame might encourage a number to the like adventures. The third, and chief cause, was—that the auncestors noble monuments might be precedents of honour to their posterities: and, therefore, it was not unproperly said, that the histories of the time were a second life, and tooke away a great part of our fears to die."[16]

The solace provided the pagan humanist by immortality of good name was no mere rationalization of the ugly fact of death. Emotionally he had wholly surrendered himself to the love and pursuit of virtue; this devotion had become more important than life itself, hence he could derive great satisfaction from the knowledge that his reputation as a man of noble character would live on after he died. A sudden and violent death, to be expected at any time in an age of war, famine, plague, and medical ignorance, could be largely compensated in the assurance that noble deeds would be remembered. Hurault writes, for example, that noble achievements would be "flowne through all the worlde, and . . . commended and honoured of posteritie."[17] Guevara points out that "in true honour and good renoume are laid up monuments of perpetuitie and fame so long as we live, and after our death they lift us to immortalitie."[18] Honor and reputation are spiritual possessions, infinitely superior to wealth or political and military might. Thus, as La Primaudaye shows, the virtuous Brutus wins a spiritual victory, even when defeated by Octavius and Antony, because he leaves after him the memory and praise of his virtues, "which praise our conquering enemies neither by might nor monie can obtaine, and leave to posteritie."[19]

The immortal reputation of the great men of antiquity was

[16] *A Mirror of Treue Honnour and Christian Nobilitie*, London, 1585, Dedication (p. d.).
[17] p. 297.   [18] Fenton, pp. 122-123.   [19] La Primaudaye, p. 276.

so real for their Renaissance followers that a spiritual communion existed between them. Montaigne writes that he has
"undergone a hundred quarrels for the defence of Pompey
and Brutus his cause. This acquaintance continueth to this day
betweene us. . . . I ruminate those glorious names betweene my
teeth, and make mine eares to ring with the sound of them. . . .
I do reverence them, and at their names I do rise and make
curtesie. (Seneca)"[20] From the Christian point of view, nothing in this world could be viewed as eternal; the most permanent
monuments of man were doomed to ultimate destruction. For
the pagan humanist, however, as keenly aware as the Christian of the transitory nature of human values, the just reward
of virtue should be "honour and perpetuall memory."[21] And,
indeed, the memory of the heroes of antiquity had seemed to be
durable and lasting. Sidney, writing of posthumous reputation,
asks, "See we not . . . Rebell Caesar so advanced, that his name
yet after 1600 yeares, lasteth in the highest honor?"[22]

The Renaissance moralist not only had a substitute for Christian immortality; he also could threaten the vicious with a fate
just as horrible, for the non-believer, as the Christian hell. Again
and again, the pagan moralists had warned evil men that the
consequence of their behavior would be an abominable memory
among men, or that they might even be completely forgotten
by their contemporaries and posterity. Thus the gentle Elyot
warns his reader: "that man which in childehode is brought
up in sondry vertues, if either by nature, or els by custome, he
be nat induced to be all way constant and stable, so that he
meve nat for any affection, griefe, or displeasure, all his vertues
will shortely decaye, and, in the estimation of men, be but as a
shadowe, and be soone forgotten,"[23] Cornwallis, in his essay "Of
Estimation and Reputation," reiterates this warning. Personify-
ing reputation, he writes that "who imbraceth vertue, she comes
after and kisseth him. Baseness and sensualitie, shee gives in

[20] III, 9.   [21] Elyot, *The Gouernour*, III, 8.
[22] Sir Philip Sidney, *Complete Works*, III, 18.
[23] III, 19.

pray to her opposite, the most abhorred thing of Nature, Oblivion.''[24]

Renaissance biographies, chronicles, and poetic eulogies assumed tremendous importance since they were the vehicles by which a man's reputation could be passed on to succeeding generations. Thus, in *Honour in his Perfection*, Markham suggests that man should perform noble and valiant deeds in order to seek "the glory of Eternitie, that is, famous Cronicles, to keep his Name and Reputation to eternall memorie.''[25] The title page of Whetstone's *A Mirror of Treue Honnour and Christian Nobilitie* shows something of the extent to which biographies took the form of eulogistic reports of the virtuous character of their subject:[26]

A Mirror of Treue Honnour and Christian Nobilitie

Whereunto is adjoined
A Report of the vertues
of the
Right Valiant and Worthy Knight
S. Frauncis, Lord Russell.

The Report of George Whetstone, Gent.
A faithful servaunt of the said right honourable earle.

Imprinted at London, by Richard Jones
1585.

HONOR AS THE REWARD OF VIRTUE

Honor, in the sense of reward, is most frequently referred to as "dignity" by the Elizabethans. It was particularly by the bestowal of title and office that the Renaissance aristocrat was rewarded for his virtuous endeavors, whether on the field of battle, in the civil government of men, or in the court of princes. We have seen that every moralist was anxious to portray virtue

---

[24] p. 93.
[25] Gervase Markham, *Honour in his Perfection*, London, 1624, p. 2.
[26] George Whetstone, London, 1585, title page.

as so precious a possession that no material compensation should be needed as an added incentive to make men virtuous.

The moralists, however, hastened as usual to contradict themselves and to emphasize the importance of rewarding deserving men with honors. Thus, *The Courtier's Academie* defines true and perfect honor as that which "is knowne by exterior action" and adds that "the honorer by rewarding, giveth some signe thereof, as also the honored, by receiving it."[27] Elsewhere in the same book Count Romei's courtiers decide that "publike stipend [is] in a number of things honorable, and honor of an honest man desired, as an ensigne of vertue."[28] In Chapman's *The Revenge of Bussy d'Ambois*, Clermont resolves the seeming contradiction between these two points of view, when he tells Renel:

> Honour never
> Should be esteemed with wise men, as the price
> And value of their virtuous services,
> But as their sign and badge.[29]

In *The Gouernour*, Elyot insists that rewards are needed as an incentive to virtue. "Where honeste and virtuous parsonages be advaunced, and well rewarded, it sterith the courages of men, whiche have any sparke of vertue, to encrease therein, with all their force and endevour."[30] This remark may strike the modern reader as philistine, but that it was a common Renaissance view is unquestionable. Hurault asserts that "the state of a kingdom or common weale cannot stand where vertue is not honoured and recompenced, and vice punished."[31] Elsewhere he designates rewarding as that which "most holdeth the noble and gentlemanly hearts in their duties."[32] The moralists seem to be saying that virtue is its own reward because the delight one feels in being virtuous is sufficient pleasure in itself, and then, turning their backs on their idealistic selves, seem

[27] Count Romei, p. 84.
[28] *ibid.*, p. 204. This is a Renaissance commonplace.
[29] George Chapman, *The Revenge of Bussy d'Ambois*, III, ii, 29-32 in *The Plays and Poems of George Chapman*, ed. Thomas Marc Parrott, New York, 1910.
[30] II, 10.   [31] p. 191.   [32] *ibid.*, p. 206.

to be adding the canny bit of worldly advice that rewards are a necessary additional incentive. That the Renaissance monarch concurred with the moral philosophers of the age is apparent in the advice given by James of Scotland to his son: "Use trew Liberalitie in rewarding the good, and bestowing frankly for your honour and weale: but with that proportionall discretion, that every man may be served according to his measure."[33]

To seek preferment was an altogether laudable ambition for Renaissance man; thousands of gentlemen's sons flocked to court for just this purpose. As we have seen, however, such ambition had to be held in moral check; an inordinate desire for glory and dignities was among the most reprehensible of vices. Moreover, the motivation involved was carefully scrutinized by the moralists. La Primaudaye, for one, stipulates that "onely wee must seeke, without pride and envie, after excellencie and preferment in that which is vertuous, and profitable for human societie."[34] Spenser states, in *The Teares of the Muses*, that the ideal courtier whose mind is fixed on honor spends his days in his Prince's service,

> Not so much for to gaine, or for to raise
> Himselfe to high degree, as for his grace,
> And in his liking to winne worthie place;
> Through due deserts and comely carriage.[35]

Unlike his medieval counterpart, the Renaissance aristocrat was supposed to be highly contemptuous of gifts of money. This attitude is an integral aspect of the pagan-humanist ethics which held honor and reputation in such high esteem that the desire for monetary gain was considered the sign of a cheap and mercenary spirit. Thus, Montaigne writes that people of quality were more jealous of rewards of honor than of those

[33] Charles Howard McIlwain, *The Political Works of James I*, reprinted from the 1616 ed., Cambridge, Mass., 1918, p. 42.
[34] p. 219.
[35] Edmund Spenser, "Mother Hubberd's Tale," in *The Poetical Works*, p. 502, ll. 774-777.

which were profitable. For "if to the prize, which ought simply to be of honour, there be other commodities and riches joined, this kind of commixing, in stead of encreasing the estimation thereof, doth empaire, dissipate, and abridge it."[36] *The Courtier's Academie* cites the case of the ancient Romans, whose most virtuous leaders were often poor, yet despised wealth. In the Renaissance, as in most historical epochs, there was often a vast discrepancy between the ideal and the reality. Queen Elizabeth showed not the slightest sign of hesitation about receiving gifts of money from her subjects. But her "thrifty" behavior does not negate the importance of the Renaissance ideal or its tremendous influence on the writers of heroic drama.

If money was viewed as a contemptible reward for services rendered, title, on the other hand, was seized upon with the greatest eagerness. It was within the power of the sovereign to lift a man from low station to high degree; in an aristocratic society, this was no picayune matter. No aspiration counted more with the Renaissance aristocrat than the opportunity to rise from gentleman to knight, from knight to baron, and so on, up the social ladder. This was not viewed as social climbing, but rather as the legitimate aspiration of men of worth to have their merit recognized. For, as Markham wrote, "It is not a matter of mean and indifferent regard, for a vulgar or mean person to be raised to honor or nobility, to have his posterity forever distinguished, to be made capable (without disparagement) to match in noble families, to draw from the common people respect, with whom before he was but equal; to walk hand in hand with the noble, to whom before he was inferior; to be liable to many places and honors in the commonwealth, whereof before he had nor hope nor likelihood; to enter into the princes house with privilege, whence before he was secluded, to display his ensign in the face of the enemy, and at his death, to enjoy the rites of noble and solemn funeral."[37]

Not only would the bestowal of title enable a man to move

[36] II, 7.   [37] *The Booke of Honour*, II, 3.

up the social ladder; it would also give his descendants a hereditary right to title. In fact, to a considerable extent, there was
rivalry between the hereditary nobility and those who were
granted titles of nobility by action of the king. Selden points out
this distinction between the two with typical exclamatory effect:
"The king cannot make a gentleman of blood; (what have you
said) nor God almighty; but he can make a gentleman by creation. If you ask which is the better of these two; civilly, the
gentleman of blood; morally the gentleman by creation may
be the better; for the other may be a debauched man, this is
a person of worth."[38]

Despite the eclectic "rag-bag" nature of Renaissance moral
philosophy—to borrow T. S. Eliot's adjective—it should by
now be apparent that there is an underlying consistency to its
central moral concepts.[39] However much a particular Renaissance moralist picked a bit here and a bit there, giving the impression, as, again, Eliot describes it, of "broken fragments of
systems," and however many intermediaries stood between him
and the original classical sources, the central notions remain
recognizable and organized. Aristotle and Cicero were sufficiently systematic to impose order and discipline on their Renaissance disciples. Thus, Renaissance definitions of "justice distributive" clearly follow the *Nicomachean Ethics* which describes it as justice "exercised in the distribution of honour,
wealth, and the other divisible assets of the community."[40]
Almost every book of moral philosophy refers to this Aristotelian definition. Thus Elyot's *The Gouernour* makes use of
the Aristotelian distinction between "justice distributive" and
"justice commutative," as do also La Primaudaye, Gelli, Count
Romei, and Hurault, in their discussions of justice.[41]

The bestowal of honors and rewards was a question not only
of justice, but also of liberality. Again, the Renaissance moralists were relying on basic Aristotelian concepts. To be just in

[38] John Selden, *Table Talk*, ed. Frederick Pollack, London, 1927, p. 50.
[39] "Shakespeare and the Stoicism of Seneca," *Selected Essays*, p. 118.
[40] V. 2.   [41] Elyot, III, 1.

the conferring of honors and dignities indicates that a prince is fair-minded; to be liberal shows that he is neither stingy nor parsimonious, two puritan virtues which the great-hearted aristocrat thoroughly despised as signs of small-mindedness and niggardliness. Hurault admonishes his Prince to be liberal and magnificent in rewarding honorable deeds of arms. Liberality was, of course, the mean between the two equally deplorable extremes of parsimony and prodigality. The prince who was reckless and extravagant in his expenditures was censured as sharply as the one who refused to spend his wealth in a manner befitting his position and income.

MAGNIFICENCE — ACCOUTREMENTS OF HONOR

Middle-class Puritanism, which, in the early 17th century, had come increasingly into conflict with the aristocracy, leading finally to the civil war between Cavaliers and Roundheads, clashed violently with Aristotelian humanism on the issue of magnificence, pomp, and ceremony. Questions of the propriety of sumptuous and gaudy apparel, of stately and expensive ceremony, of magnificent buildings and homes, and of large and well equipped retinues may appear to be unrelated to the concept of honor since they are partially a demonstration of the aesthetic taste of the period. Actually, however, the taste of the aristocratic class was shaped largely by the central Aristotelian concept of magnificence; sumptuousness and pomp were integral to the whole concept of honor. As Elyot says, "Lette it be also considered that we be men and nat aungels, wherfore we knowe nothinge but by outwarde significations. Honour, wherto reverence pertaineth, is (as I have said) the rewarde of vertue, which honour is but the estimation of people, which estimation is nat every where perceived, but by some exterior signe, and that is either by laudable reporte, or excellencie in vesture, or other thinge semblable."[42]

The values of our own middle-class society are so strongly

[42] III, 2.

opposed to the aristocratic values of the Renaissance in this particular respect that it is difficult for us to sympathize with the taste of the Elizabethan nobleman. Our values, or prejudices, are reflected in the word pompous. Pomp to us suggests pride and an over-emphasis on form. It seems almost incredible to us today that the word had a favorable connotation in the Renaissance. The roots of our attitude are revealed in the Puritan "protest" (i.e., the Protestant reformation) in the 16th and 17th centuries; Stubbes, for example, in *The Anatomie of Abuses*, tells his reader that the "externe efficient cause of pride, is gorgeous attire."[43]

The vast majority of Renaissance aristocrats held an altogether different view of the matter. (It should not be forgotten that some aristocrats were Puritans—among others, John Milton.) To understand their attitude properly, we must go back to Aristotle's discusssion of magnificence in the *Nicomachean Ethics*. Magnificence, he announces, "consists in suitable expenditure on a great scale."[44] He continues: "So the magnificent man's expenditures is suitable as well as great. And consequently the objects he produces must also be great and suitable; for so only will a great expenditure be suitable [to the result] as well. . . . Again, the motive of the munificent man in such expenditure will be the nobility of the action, this motive being characteristic of all the virtues. Moreover he will spend gladly and lavishly, since nice calculation is shabby; and he will think how he can carry out his project most nobly and splendidly, rather than how much it will cost and how it can be done most cheaply."[45]

Aristotle's values are almost exactly the reverse of middle class Puritan values; whether superior or inferior, they are nonetheless an integral part of the humanist ethics of the Renaissance aristocracy. To comprehend the extent to which they were accepted by the men of the age, we need only turn to descriptions of the courts of kings in that period. Consider, for example,

[43] Philip Stubbes, *The Anatomie of Abuses*, London, 1595, pp. 19-20.
[44] IV. 2.   [45] *ibid.*

Segar's eye-witness report of a combat at the court of Queen Elizabeth: "Trulie, this action was mervailouslie magnificent, and appeared a sight exceeding glorious to those that wer below looking upward to the Tarrace, wher her Majestie, the Lords and Ladies stood, so pompously apparailed, Jewelled and furnished as hardly can bee seene the like in anie Christian Court; as my selfe and other the Actors . . . with great admiration did behold and thinke."[46]

Apparel. Renaissance etiquette in regard to dress paralleled the etiquette of pomp and court ceremony. Again, the two extremes of parsimony and stinginess and of a gaudy showiness and prodigality are to be avoided. Guevara advises his courtier to "use rather a certain mean and measure in his apparel (wearing that is comely and gentlemanlike) than others of most cost and worship."[47] Yet he assumes that a man's worth will be indicated by the sumptuousness of his apparel, as in the following:

"Also the young Courtier that commeth newly to the Court, must of necessity be very well apparelled, according to his degree and calling, and his servants that follow him well appointed. For in Courte men regard not onely the House and familie hee commeth of, but marke also his Apparel and servants that follow him.

"And I mislike one thing very much, that about the Court they doe rather honour and reverence a man, brave and sumptuous in apparel being vicious, then they doe a man that is grave, wise, and vertuous. And yet nevertheless, the Courtier may assure himselfe of this, that few will esteeme of him, either for that hee is vertuous or nobly borne, if hee be not also sumptuously apparelled and well accompanied; for then onely will every man account and esteeme of him."[48]

The extent to which the Elizabethan nobleman was conscious during every moment of his existence here on earth of his place

[46] *The Booke of Honor and Armes,* p. 97.
[47] Guevara, *The Diall of Princes,* trans. Thomas North, 3rd ed., London, 1619, p. 626.
[48] *ibid.,* p. 626.

in the social hierarchy and the extent to which the question of proper apparel was directly related to the aristocrat's position in the social caste becomes apparent from the following table, which appeared in 1574 in one of the homilies against gorgeous apparel:

MEN'S APPAREL [49]

None shall wear in his apparel any:

Silk of the color of purple, cloth of gold tissued, nor fur of sables — but only the — King, Queen, King's — Mother, Children, Brethren and Sisters, Uncles and Aunts, — and except — Dukes, Marquesses, and Earls, who may wear the same in doublets, jerkins, linings. . . .

Cloth of { gold, silver, tinseled satin, } Silk, or cloth mixed or embroidered with any gold or silver, — except — all degrees above Viscounts. . . .

Woolen cloth made out of the realm. . . . Velvet, crimson or scarlet, Furs, black jenets, lucernes, Embroidery of tailor's work having gold or silver or pearl therein — except — Dukes, Marquesses, Earls, Viscounts, Barons. . . .

Satin, damask, silk chamlet, or taffeta, in gown, coat, hose, or uppermost garments. Fur, whereof the kind groweth not within the Queen's dominions . . . — except — the degrees and persons above mentioned, and men that may dispend £100 by the year, and so valued in the subsidy book. . . .

Hat, bonnet, girdle, scabbards of swords, daggers, etc., shoes and pantofles of velvet. — except — the degrees and persons above named, and the son and heir apparent of a knight. . . .

Spurs, swords, rapiers, daggers, skaynes, wood-knives, or hangers, buckles of girdles, { gilt, silvered, or damasked } — except — Knights' and barons' sons, and other of higher degree or place.

[49] Cited in Karl Holzknecht, *The Backgrounds of Shakespeare's Plays*, New York, 1950, p. 44.

Retinue. The number of servants the Renaissance aristocrat had in his train, and the fact that these "servants" were well appointed, counted heavily in the world's estimation of him. Guazzo compares the poor gentleman scholar who lacks servants with his more fortunate confreres who possess a retinue: "so those gentlemen which keepe open householde, which have a great train after them, and which spend much and freely, are much more esteemed of the other comon scholers, who are gentlemen to, and yet those former are honored and courted of them."[50]

If mere scholars and gentlemen considered the number of servants in their retinue an important symbol, the Elizabethan nobleman could only take it as a matter of course that, both at home and when traveling, he would be accompanied by a large number of retainers. Consider, for example, the remarks of Giacomo Soranzo, Venetian ambassador under Edward the Sixth and Queen Mary: "The nobility, save such as are employed at Court, do not habitually reside in the cities, but in their own country mansions, where they keep up very grand establishments, both with regard to the great abundance of eatables consumed by them, as also by reason of their numerous attendants, in which they exceed all other nations, so that the Earl of Pembroke has upward of a 1000 clad in his own livery."[51]

In the case of the great lord, many of these servants were themselves gentlemen by birth. It is reported of Burghley, for example, that most of the principal gentlemen in England sought to prefer their sons and heirs to his service, and that he had attending on his table twenty gentlemen, each of whom had £1000 a year.[52] Harrison, in his colorful essay "The Social Background of Shakespeare's Age," provides detailed proof that a lord's "servant" was no mere servant:

"The treasurer of the Household to Edward Earl of Derby, who died in 1572, was a knight, Sir Richard Shierborn: the

[50] II, 41. [51] Kendall, p. 200.
[52] *A Companion to Shakespeare Studies,* ed. G. B. Harrison and Harley Granville-Barker, New York, 1937, p. 203.

House Steward of Gilbert Talbot, seventh Earl of Shrewsbury, who died in 1592, had previously been senior Fellow of St. John's College, Cambridge. The Steward of the fifth Earl of Northumberland, in Henry VIII's time, had three personal servants to attend him. The Steward of the Earl of Derby ruled an establishment of eighty gentlemen and five hundred yeomen. The Steward of even the most modest household, such as that of Katharine Willoughby, Dowager Duchess of Suffolk, would have at least eighty to a hundred persons in his charge."[53]

DISHONOR AND SHAME

If the Renaissance aristocrat loved and pursued honor intensely and with his whole being, it follows logically that dishonor was the one thing in life which could not be tolerated. Aristotle's distinction between the aristocracy and the plebeian class is frequently referred to by the Renaissance moralists. Aristotle had said that it is "the nature of the many to be amenable to fear but not to a sense of honour, and to abstain from evil not because of its baseness but because of the penalties it entails."[54]

In *The French Academie*, La Primaudaye elaborates on this basic theme; his remarks include some of the most commonplace of Renaissance maxims. Thus he states:

"For the more we love glory and honor, the more we feare, and labor to eschew shame and dishonor."[55]

"Virtuous shame beseemeth youth."[56]

"A wicked man . . . hath no shame in him."[57]

"I looke for small goodnes of a yoong man (saith Seneca) except of such a one as blusheth after he hath offended."[58]

Hurault expounds another favorite precept of the humanist ethic. The man of fortitude, he says, is not totally without fear:

[53] *ibid.*, pp. 203-204.   [54] *Nicomachean Ethics* x. 9.
[55] La Primaudaye, p. 242.   [56] *ibid.*, p. 243.
[57] *ibid.*   [58] *ibid.*

"As Plutarch saith in the life of Agis, It seemeth that the men
of old time, tooke prowesse to be not an utter privation of feare,
but rather a feare of blame and reproch, and a dread of dishonor."[59] The strength of the sense of shame as a moral check
in an age which saw all problems in terms of absolute moral
imperatives is put forth in the sayings and anecdotes of the
various Renaissance moralists. Thus, Guicciardini's *Aphorisms*
recounts the tale of Barnardino da Corte, an old Servitor of an
Italian Duke, who had been "promoted" by the Duke and put in
charge of the impregnable castle of Milan. Barnardino turned
traitor and sold out to the French: "An act so infamous and hate-
ful, as even the French themselves to whom he betraid it, abhorred him and shunned his company and fellowship, as if he
had bin some venomous serpent. In so much as playing at cards,
they wold call him Barnardino da Corte, when they were to pul
for a traitor (a sort in their pack, as Knaves are in ours) to his
perpetual reproach. With the shame hereof, and sting of a
guilty conscience, he was so tormented, as within few daies
he languished and died."[60]

No crime was of a worse hue, in the eyes of the pagan humanists, than that which robbed another man of his honor. To deprive a man of his life would not ruin his reputation and credit
among men, but to stain his honor in any way might affect the
opinion of the community towards him. Thus Hurault cites the
opinion of Alexander Severus: "That princes ought to esteeme
liers and slaunderers, as great enemies unto them, as those that
enter upon their lands by force. For these do but seize upon
their grounds and lordships, but the others do rob them of their
reputation and renowne."[61] In similar vein, Count Romei's
courtiers decide that adultery is a much worse crime than theft
because the adulterer is a "greevous injurier or destroyer of an
other mans honour."[62]

Essex and Raleigh provide dramatic flesh and blood proof
of the extent to which the great Elizabethan nobles lived in

[59] pp. 283-284.   [60] Guicciardini, p. 276.
[61] p. 346.   [62] p. 96.

fear of disgrace and infamy. Essex, for example, pleads with Elizabeth to take his life rather than destroy his reputation. He writes, as the general in command of the English troops at the siege of Rouen: "If her Majesty would now revoke me with disgrace, when Rouen were to be won, I would humbly beseech her that she would take from me my life, and not my poor reputation, which I cannot lose, the place I hold considered, without some dishonour to her Majesty."[63] Later, when Essex had procured the extreme disfavor of the Queen, he writes to her pleadingly, "[I] saw my poor reputation not suffered to die with me, but buried and I alive."[64] He goes on to complain that he feels "as if I were thrown into a corner like a dead carcase, I am gnawed on and torn by the basest creatures upon earth. The prating tavern haunter speaks of me what he lists; they print me and make me speak to the world, and shortly they will play me upon the stage."[65] The aristocrat was particularly upset by the contempt of the populace. To be mocked in ballads and ridiculed on the stage were the worst of fates, for the most baseborn of men would be sitting in judgment, feeling morally superior.

The final conflict between Elizabeth and Essex followed the incident in which the Lord had his ears boxed by his Queen because of his petulancy. Essex never forgot this affront which, he said, he would not have accepted at the hands of King Henry the Eighth himself. Elizabeth was determined to "break him of his will and pull down his great heart."[66] When Essex disobeyed her explicit orders and returned to London, she exclaimed, "By God's son, I am no Queen. That man is above me. Who gave him command to come here so soon? I did send him on other business."[67] But Essex would not bow to the will of his sovereign. As a result of his humiliation, despair overcame him, followed by uncontrollable rage. According to Har-

---

[63] Devereux, ed., *Lives and Letters of the Devereux*, I, 240.
[64] *Essex*, ed. Harrison, p. 261.
[65] *ibid.*
[66] Quoted by J. B. Black, *The Reign of Elizabeth*, Oxford, 1936, p. 370.
[67] *ibid.*, p. 371.

ington he became a person "devoid of good reason as of right mind."[68]

Raleigh's lamentation, when accused by Cobham of having betrayed his country to the Spanish, is as eloquent as Essex's frantic pleas to his Queen to restore his wounded reputation. Raleigh in 1603 writes to his wife from prison, thinking he is to be executed for his presumed treachery. Again fear of death is inconsequential compared to the fear of being despised by contemporaries and by posterity. Raleigh writes: "that I can live to thinke howe you shal be both left a spoile to my enimies, and that my name shal be a dishonour to my child, I cannot, I cannot, indure the memorie thereof."[69] That his services to his country will be forgotten causes as much dismay as the fate of his child. The torture of such infamy leads him to wish for death as a blessed release from torment; in the oblivion of forgetfulness and extinction, his frenzies will be stilled: "Oh what will my poore servannts thinke at their retourne," he exclaims, "when they heare I am accused to be Spanish, whoe sent them to my great Charge to plant and discover upon his territorie, Oh intollerable infamie, Oh God I cannot resiste theis thoughts, I cannot live to thinke how I am derided, to thinke of the expectation of my enimies, the scornes I shall receive, the crewell words of lawyers, the infamous tauntes and dispights, to be made a wonder and a spectacle. O death hasten the unto me, that thowe maiste destroye . . . my memorie which is my Tormentour, my thoughts and my life cannot dwell in one body."[70]

Both the Renaissance dueling code and the practice of taking private revenge stemmed from the imperative need to preserve one's honor from insult. Even Bacon, who was hardly a model of honorable virtue and whose cynicism at times matched that of Machiavelli, warns that "contempt is that which putteth an edge upon anger, as much or more than the hurt itself."[71]

[68] *ibid.*   [69] Raleigh, *Selections*, pp. 177-178.   [70] *ibid.*, p. 180.
[71] Francis Bacon, *The Essays or Counsels, Civil and Moral*, ed. Samuel Harvey Reynolds, Oxford, 1890, p. 379.

Guazzo advises that "it is not good to mocke any man in any maner of wise. For if hee bee our better, or equall, hee will by no meanes abide that wee shoulde abjectly esteeme of him."[72] In fact, the nerve of the Renaissance aristocrat was highly sensitized to the least suggestion of lack of esteem. The petulant manner in which Essex reacted to an affront from his Queen is not merely the manifestation of his personal sensitivity. His behavior is typical of the aristocrat of his age.

CHASTITY AND WOMAN'S HONOR

A woman's "honor" and "honesty," in the 16th century, consisted almost exclusively in the preservation of her virginity as long as she was unmarried and in her faithfulness to her husband after marriage. *The Courtier's Academie* defines "honor feminine" as a quality which "is preserved by not failing onely in one of their proper particular vertues, which is honestie."[73] The continuity of certain ethical values from the Renaissance to the present day is thus demonstrated, for a man's honor would not be affected to the same degree by lack of sexual purity. The double standard already prevailed; nor was the age without its reformers who were happy to point out man's hypocrisy in this matter.

Although woman's honor was almost exclusively a question of sexual purity, the moralists stressed the same incentives as in their discussion of a man's honor. Castiglione states that "generally a great bridle to women, is the zeale of true vertue, and the desire of good name, which many that I have knowne in my dayes more esteeme, than their own life."[74] La Primaudaye emphasizes the sense of shame which is merely the reverse side of the coin. He tells his reader that "the fortresse and defence that nature hath given to a woman for the preservation of hir reputation, chastitie, and honour, is shame."[75]

Revenge for adultery, by the murder of both wife and adulterer, was tolerated in the early laws of every European

[72] II, 29.   [73] Count Romei, p. 126.
[74] p. 223.   [75] p. 487.

country. Here again, the obsessive concern of Renaissance man to preserve his honor at no matter what cost is apparent. In the words of Bowers, "the Renaissance spirit of vengeance on an erring wife was not so much sexual jealousy (although this is a broad statement) as the desire to spoil the triumph of others, and to vindicate oneself publicly."[76] In Italy, in particular, the betrayal of a husband's honor by an erring wife was a justified cause for murder, accepted by public opinion and condoned by the law. The English view was somewhat more temperate; the high sensitivity of the Latin temperament did not meet with complete approval nor did the tendency of the Italians to resort to secret means of homicide. Thus, Moryson observes, "In Italy as Adultry seldome or never falls within the punishment of the lawe, because the Italians nature carries them to such an high degree of private revenge as the lawe cannot inflict greater (which private revenge by murther upon just groundes of jeloyse is Commonly taken secretely, and if knowne, yet wincked at and favoured by the Magistrate, in his owne nature approving as well the revenge as the secrecy thereof, for avoiding shame)."[77] Yet Moryson is willing to admit the possibility of "murther upon just grounds of jeloyse."[78] Since honor was dearer than life, the taking of the wife's life for bringing dishonor on her husband was considered a lesser wrong than the injury which she had done to him.

Woman's relative inferiority to man was an accepted commonplace of the humanist tradition. Here, once again, Aristotle was the authority: "The relation of husband to wife seems to be in the nature of an aristocracy: the husband rules in virtue of fitness, and in matters that belong to a man's sphere; matters suited to a woman he hands over to his wife."[79] Since the Renaissance assumed that man was superior, the second most important virtue for a woman was that of obedience. In Aristotle's words, "the temperance of a woman and that of a man are not the same, nor their courage and justice, as Socrates

[76] p. 49.   [77] p. 411.   [78] *ibid.*   [79] *Nicomachean Ethics* VIII. 10.

thought, but the one is the courage of command, and the other that of subordination."[80] Elsewhere he states cavalierly that "a man would be thought a coward if he were only as brave as a brave woman."[81] The Renaissance moralists echoed Aristotle and usually accepted his generalizations without reservation. *The Courtier's Academie* assumes that woman "have not mortal vertues in that perfection as hath a man."[82] Gelli's *Circe* emphasizes woman's incapacity to comprehend great and important matters.

If the Renaissance often viewed woman as a basically inferior creature, it would be an exaggeration to say that she was never considered capable of heroic actions. Elyot's *Defence of Good Women* insists that women have great moral potentialities. The lengthy discussion of the position of woman in Castiglione's *The Courtier* leads to a heated argument in which she is not without defenders. The range of attitudes possible for the Renaissance gentleman included both extremes and also a middle position which would neither stress her inferiority exclusively nor give her complete equality with men. One of Count Romei's courtiers presents this more balanced, if by no means emancipated, outlook: "And a little afterwards, he addeth that though a woman have not morall vertues in that perfection as hath a man, yet notwithstanding, that shee also is indued with fortitude, justice, temperance, and with that prudence, which of it self is sufficient to obey well, towardes him that knoweth as well howe to commaunde."[83] Camden's study of *The Elizabethan Woman* is an excellent presentation of the complexity of Elizabethan attitudes on this matter.[84]

It should not be forgotten that Shakespeare's monarch was a woman who has been revered as one of the most glorious sovereigns in British history, and that her rival, Mary, Queen of Scots, went to the executioner's block without the slightest sign of fear. In the Renaissance, as in every other age of Euro-

[80] *Politics* I. 5.   [81] *ibid.*, III. 2.   [82] Count Romei, p. 235.
[83] *ibid.*
[84] Carroll Camden, *The Elizabethan Woman*, London, 1952.

pean social history, women were at one and the same time revered and hated, admired and held in contempt. Shakespeare had available to him, then, a wide range of attitudes. His portrayal of women on the stage shows that his attitudes were as variegated as those of any of the writers of his age.

PART II

SHAKESPEARE'S USE OF THE RENAISSANCE CONCEPT OF HONOR

DOES DRAMA HAVE A MORAL FUNCTION?

T HE 20th century has been an age of brilliant and perceptive Shakespeare criticism—at least as great as the age of Dryden, of Pope, of Johnson, of Coleridge, or of Bradley. Thanks to the work of Granville-Barker, Muriel Bradbrook, and Arthur Colby Sprague, our appreciation of Shakespearean stagecraft and of Elizabethan dramatic conventions is greater than it has ever been; thanks to the work of Clemens, Wilson Knight, and Caroline Spurgeon, we are much more sensitive than any previous age to the subtle effects Shakespeare achieved through his imagery; thanks to the work of Robertson, Ernest Jones, and T. S. Eliot, we are now aware of the many respects in which Shakespeare anticipated modern psychological discoveries; thanks to Hardin Craig, Theodore Spencer, and E. M. W. Tillyard, we have a much greater awareness of the theological and cosmological background which Shakespeare shared with his audience; and thanks to the work of Heilman and Danby, we are much more open than any previous age to the possibility that Shakespeare's plays contain a rich multiplicity of meanings, some of which may be of a symbolical or even allegorical nature.

In my opinion, however, we are far behind the critics of the 18th and 19th centuries in one important respect. We have allowed our ever-increasing knowledge about the details of Renaissance social history in general and of the Elizabethan mores in particular to blur and confuse our perception of the values of the age. As Janet Spens has remarked: "the inner life of the age of Elizabeth, only three centuries distant, and the experience of men of our own race, is far less intelligible to us [than the cultural life of Greece, Rome, and the Middle Ages]. Scholars have done much to elucidate a mass of allusions to the minutiae of daily life; we can make a picture of that life, but we do not understand how a true Elizabethan felt in the inner chambers of his heart."[1] With similar feelings of scholarly frustration, Hardin Craig, who has studied the intellectual background of the Renaissance as exhaustively as any man, admits that "it does little good to learn the kind of houses the Elizabethans inhabited" if it is impossible to discover "how people thought and felt while they were living in those houses."[2]

The cultural historians themselves, in other words, are admitting that the work of historical restoration of a given age may be held back if we permit ourselves to be buried under an avalanche of historical detail so that we are never free to get sufficient perspective to perceive the essential values of the age. The wealth of our accumulated knowledge may be preventing us from understanding how an Elizabethan felt in the inner chambers of his heart.

But is there not a more serious reason for our defective vision when we try to perceive Shakespeare's relation to his age? We live in an age in which didactic literature is not in fashion. We resent the artist who tries to make us better men. Indeed, we sometimes refuse to admit that moral evaluations can do anything but distort our aesthetic response to the work of art.

The current tendency to avoid all "value judgments" (in such disparate realms as art and sociology) has become so fashionable that such evasion has sometimes come to be considered an irrefutable canon of critical good taste. In my opinion, this tendency is preventing us from properly interpreting Shakespeare's plays. In his "naïve" willingness to speak in moral terms, the 18th century critic is often closer than we are to an understanding of the text, even though our 20th century critics have much greater historical awareness. Shakespeare usually rises above crude didactic effects, yet each of his plays is basically organized as a conflict between good and evil. This being true, we must employ the finest scales to de-

[1] "Chapman's Ethical Thought," *Essays and Studies*, XI, Oxford, 1925.
[2] *The Enchanted Glass*, New York, 1936, p. 239.

tect the precise values relevant to our judgment of character and action. As Arthur Sewell has pointed out, in reading Shakespeare "character and moral vision must be apprehended together."[3]

The remaining pages of this book will have little or no meaning for the reader who fails to perceive that the greatness of the classics stems essentially from the clarity and grandeur of their moral vision, and that, in Shakespeare particularly, there is profound interpenetration of moral and aesthetic values.

Below are cited some representative opinions on the question, "Does Drama Have a Moral Function?" The reader is asked to judge which critical position seems to have the greatest relevance to an understanding of Shakespearean drama.

THE RENAISSANCE VIEW

"Anger the Stoikes said, was a short madnesse: let but *Sophocles* bring you *Ajax* on a stage, killing and whipping sheepe and oxen, thinking them the Army of Greekes, with their Chieftaines *Agamemnon*, and *Menelaus*: and tell me if you have not a more familiar insight into Anger, then finding in the schoolemen his *Genus* and *Difference*. See whether wisdom and temperance in *Ulysses* and *Diomedes*, valure in Achilles, friendship in *Nisus* and *Euryalus*, even to an ignorant man carry not an apparent shining: and contrarily, the remorse of conscience in *Oedipus*; the soone repenting pride in Agamemnon; the selfe devouring crueltie in his father *Atreus*; the violence of ambition in the two *Theban* brothers; the sower sweetnesse of revenge in *Medea*; and to fall lower, the *Terentian Gnato*, and our *Chawcers Pander* so exprest, that we now use their names to signifie their Trades: And finally, all vertues, vices, and passions, so in their owne naturall states, laide to the view, that we seeme not to heare of them, but clearly to see through them."—SIR PHILIP SIDNEY, *The Defence of Poesie*[4]

---

[3] *Character and Society in Shakespeare*, Oxford, 1951, p. 59.
[4] In *Collected Works*, ed. Albert Feuillerat, Cambridge, England, 1923, III, 14-15.

"Now therein of all Sciences (I speake still of humane and according to the humane conceit) is our *Poet* the *Monarch*. For hee doth not onely shew the way, but giveth so sweete a prospect into the way, as will entice anie man to enter into it. . . . Hee beginneth not with obscure definitions, which must blurre the margent with interpretations, and loade the memorie with doubtfulnesse: but hee commeth to you with words set in delightfull proportion . . . and with a tale, which holdeth children from play, and olde men from the Chimney corner; and pretending no more, doth intend the winning of the minde from wickednes to vertue."—SIR PHILIP SIDNEY, *The Defence of Poesie*[5]

"Excitation of virtue and deflection from her contrary are the soul, body and limbs of an authentical tragedy."—GEORGE CHAPMAN[6]

"For anything so overdone is from the purpose of playing, whose end, both at the first and now, was and is, to hold, as 'twere, the mirror up to nature; to show virtue her own feature, scorn her own image, and the very age and body of the time his form and pressure."—SHAKESPEARE, *Hamlet* (III. ii. 22-28.)

SOME REPRESENTATIVE MODERN VIEWS

1. *Shakespeare was an objective dramatist who tried to describe every aspect of the human scene without committing himself to the point of view of any of his dramatic creations.*

"To dramatize a doctrine is not necessarily to believe in it."—ELIZABETH POPE[7]

"In Shakespeare [there is] no prepossession, no prejudice, no theory."—UNA ELLIS-FERMOR[8]

[5] *ibid.*, pp. 19-20.
[6] *The Revenge of Bussy d'Ambois*, Dedication, in *The Plays and Poems of George Chapman*, ed. Thomas Marc Parrott, New York, 1910.
[7] *Shakespeare Survey*, II, ed. Allardyce Nicoll, Cambridge, England, 1949, p. 80.
[8] *ibid.*, III, ed. Allardyce Nicoll, Cambridge, England, 1950, p. 142.

"Like an honest miscellaneous dramatist [Shakespeare] was putting into the mouths of his different characters the sentiments that, for the moment, were suggested to him by their predicament."—GEORGE SANTAYANA, "Tragic Philosophy"[9]

"Each of them, from the kings to the clowns, has indeed a philosophy, which he makes singularly clear. Each judges life in his own way, from his own angle, whence he may utter a remark strikingly true; and profound also, in many instances. But all this is the emanation of a vigorous dramatic genius. . . . Their number is commensurate only with the diversity of human judgments, and reveals only the playwright's marvellous versatility and his consciousness of the relative nature of all things."—EMILE LEGOUIS[10]

2. *Since Shakespeare was not a philosopher, he was not concerned with questions of value.*

"The Renaissance needed no mastering living religion, no mastering living philosophy. Life was gayer without them. . . . Even in a Hamlet, a Prospero or a Jacques, in a Henry the Sixth or an Isabella, the poet feels no inner loyalty to the convictions he rehearses; they are like the cap and bells of his fools; and possibly if he had been pressed by some tiresome friend to propound a personal philosophy, he might have found in his irritation nothing else to fall back upon than the animal despair of Macbeth. Fortunately we may presume that burgherly comfort and official orthodoxy saved him from being unreasonably pressed."—GEORGE SANTAYANA, *"Tragic Philosophy"*[11]

"There are, of course, a number of . . . current interpretations of Shakespeare: that is, of the *conscious opinions* of Shakespeare: interpretations of category, so to speak; which make him either a Tory journalist or a Liberal journalist or a Socialist journalist. . . . We have also a Protestant Shakespeare, and a

---

[9] In *Essays in Literary Criticism of George Santayana*, ed. Irving Singer, New York, 1956, p. 288.
[10] Emile Legouis and Louis Cazamian, *A History of English Literature*, New York, 1939, pp. 448-449.
[11] *Essays in Literary Criticism of George Santayana*, p. 269.

sceptical Shakespeare, and some case may be made out for an Anglo-Catholic, or even a Papist Shakespeare. My own frivolous opinion is that Shakespeare may have held in private life very different views from what we extract from his extremely varied public works."—T. S. ELIOT, "Shakespeare and the Stoicism of Seneca"[12]

"I would suggest that none of the plays of Shakespeare has a 'meaning,' although it would be equally false to say that a play of Shakespeare is meaningless. All great poetry gives the illusion of a view of life."—T. S. ELIOT[13]

"I can see no reason for believing that either Dante or Shakespeare did any thinking on his own."—T. S. ELIOT[14]

"I doubt whether belief proper enters into the activity of a great poet."—T. S. ELIOT[15]

"The end of the sixteenth century is an epoch when it is particularly difficult to associate poetry with systems of thought or reasoned views of life."—T. S. ELIOT[16]

3. *The Renaissance was a Christian age. Therefore Shakespeare, like every other writer of his age, must have been profoundly influenced by Christianity.*

"Whether we wish it or not, the character of our western societies is always, profoundly, Christian. . . . Today one may choose to be a Christian or not. In the 16th century, there was no possibility of choice."—LUCIEN FEBVRE[17]

"Renaissance tragedy, including Shakespearean tragedy, is the tragedy of pride."—G. R. ELLIOTT[18]

"Christianity had greatly emphasized just and merciful charity, the human need of humility and conversion, the invidious power of pride, and the mystery of grace, i.e., the divine will

---

[12] *Selected Essays*, New York, 1932, p. 108.
[13] *ibid.*, p. 115.   [14] *ibid.*, p. 116.   [15] *ibid.*, p. 118.   [16] *ibid.*
[17] *Le Problème de l'Incroyance au XVIe Siècle*, Paris, 1947, p. 362.
[18] *Flaming Minister*, Durham, N.C., 1953, p. xix.

at work through and with the human will. Not one of those things was entirely foreign to the classic pagan humanism upon which Occidental culture was founded and which was very much alive in the Renaissance mind; but Christianity had stressed them in a revolutionary manner: thus they were strong strands in the very texture of the secular, as well as the religious imagination of the time."—G. R. ELLIOTT[19]

"Shakespeare [lived] in a pre-Cartesian world. . . . [His fellow Elizabethans were] children of God and they knew it."—HARDIN CRAIG[20]

4. *Religious values are absent from Shakespearean tragedy since the tragic view and the religious view are incompatible.*

"Now Christianity is dramatic, but it is not tragic, for, as historians from Raleigh to Hegel have realized, Christian teleology robs death of its sting."—SYLVAN BARNET, "Some Limitations of a Christian Approach to Shakespeare"[21]

"The Elizabethan drama was almost wholly secular; and while Shakespeare was writing he practically confined his view to the world of non-theological observation and thought, so that he represents it substantially in one and the same way whether the period of the story is pre-Christian or Christian."—A. C. BRADLEY[22]

"The tragic picture is incompatible with the Christian faith [or] with any form of religious belief that assumes the existence of a personal and kindly God."—CLIFFORD LEECH[23]

5. *The "meaning" of Shakespeare's plays changes in accordance with the preconceptions and bias of each new generation of readers. The "meaning" is subjective, not objective.*

---

[19] *ibid.*, p. xxvi.
[20] *Shakespeare Survey*, III, 107 and 114.
[21] *A Journal of English Literary History*, Vol. 22, Baltimore, 1955, p. 85.
[22] *Shakespearean Tragedy*, London, 1932, p. 25.
[23] *Shakespeare's Tragedies and Other Studies in 17th Century Drama*, London, 1950, p. 18.

[Shakespearean tragedy is] "a creature of its time, and yet a free agent, communicating with other ages even in their own different idioms."—ROBERT HEILMAN[24]

[In Iago] "Shakespeare produces a character so full and flexible that it can accommodate itself to the psychological habits of different generations."—ROBERT HEILMAN[25]

6. *Part of Shakespeare's greatness lies in his ambiguity. Therefore we can consider his plays a rich mine for a wide variety of interpretation of "meaning" or "pattern." The critic should seek for allegory and symbolism and thus discover meanings which will be suggestive, though not necessarily definitive or final.*

"It is axiomatic that the poem is symbolic, whether or not the poet consciously calls attention to the second dimensions of meaning. The burden of proof [for restricting the meaning to its literal sense] rests on the literalist. . . . The symbolic quality is an almost inevitable consequence of the use of poetic language. . . . We might say that Iago is 'original evil'. It would then not be difficult to regard him as the devil incarnate and to turn the play into a parable echoing Genesis. . . . Or we might picture Satan as attacking a specifically Christian community. . . . Othello would then be the wavering Christian and Desdemona the embodiment of Christian virtue. . . .

"The Magic in the Web produces a character so full and flexible that it can accommodate itself to the psychological habits of different generations. Iago may be understood as Invidia or as the Machiavel or as the Jealous Man or as the False Friend: he can be sensed at his narrowest as the villain of melodrama or at his widest as Satan—a projection of 'the forces within and without us that threaten our supreme values.' "
—ROBERT HEILMAN[26]

[24] *Magic in the Web*, Lexington, Kentucky, 1956, p. 15.
[25] *ibid.*, p. 44.
[26] *ibid.*, pp. 41-44.

7. *It is impossible to understand Shakespeare if one does not consider the moral values which give his plays their structure and meaning. In Shakespeare there is a profound interpenetration of moral and of aesthetic values.*

"When we have studied Shakespeare in the light of all this we shall agree that there could be no greater error than to mistake his breadth of understanding and receptivity of mind for lack of moral conviction. His judgments are not suspended but complex. . . . His dominating themes are integrity, loyalty, patience, love, forgiveness, humility, and his work is a final answer to those who would assert the radical dissociation of art from the good life."—DONALD STAUFFER[27]

My own judgment, from the evidence presented, is that Stauffer, closest among recent critics to the Elizabethan point of view, has best perceived and underscored the moral conviction of Shakespeare which the modern reader will do well to consider seriously in each of the plays. This is not to minimize the importance of modern critical works dealing with Shakespeare primarily as poet or dramatist. Shakespeare is the greatest of English writers precisely because we must follow so many different avenues to begin to comprehend and appreciate his many-faceted genius.

[27] *Shakespeare's World of Images*, New York, 1949, Epilogue.

CHAPTER 5

SHAKESPEARE AND THE ARISTOCRATIC CLASS STRUCTURE OF HIS AGE

THE DEFINITION OF NOBILITY

NOBILITY as Exalted Virtue. The Renaissance concept of nobility, defined at the beginning of Chapter 4, is most clearly exemplified in Shakespeare's plays by his characterization of Brutus, "the noblest Roman of them all." (V. v. 68) For Brutus, whose very perfection of character makes him less subtle and less dramatically interesting than the later tragic heroes, is as much the epitome of the hero of antiquity for the Renaissance as Scipio, Epaminondas, or Alexander. Chapman's hero, Clermont, for example, whose "virtues [rank] with the best of th' ancient Romans," is succinctly described by the statement, "In all, Rome's Brutus is revived in him."[1] Pompey, in *Antony and Cleopatra*, speaks in no less glowing terms of the "all-honour'd honest Roman, Brutus." (II. vi. 16)

Almost every page of *Julius Caesar* attests to the lofty character of this flawless hero. Even though the play leaves the spectator with divided sympathies, and even though its ending suggests that Caesar's murderers have received an inevitable, if not totally fitting, punishment, Brutus' action is generally presented as beyond reproach. The high repute in which Brutus is held by all of the Romans is evident not only in the repeated references to "the noble Brutus" but is likewise explicitly stated:

No man here
But honours you; and every one doth wish
You had but that opinion of yourself
Which every noble Roman bears of you. (II. i. 90-93)

[1] *The Revenge of Bussy d'Ambois,* II, 1, 259, and II, 1, 103.

Brutus also is continually presenting self-testimony to his own nobility and frequently comments on the idealistic motivation of his own actions. When Cassius first approaches him to join his cause, Brutus indicates his willingness to act in any honorable enterprise which will further the general good, but never for merely selfish ends. Caesar's famous accusation of betrayal by a dear friend, "Et tu, Brute," is quite simply answered by Brutus' remark to the common people, "Not that I lov'd Caesar less, but that I lov'd Rome more."[2] (III. ii. 22, 23) Antony's more eloquent peroration makes telling sarcastic use of the phrase, "For Brutus is an honourable man," (III. ii. 88) yet his final eulogy indicates clearly that this is Antony's actual opinion. By the moving testimony of this closing eulogy, Brutus' high nobility during the course of the play—his willingness to risk his life for the common good, his unwillingness to be spiteful or vengeful, his scorn of the other conspirators for their desire to bind each other by oath, and his contempt for Cassius for his dishonorable selling of offices—is given a fitting coda in an eloquent expression of the Renaissance concept of nobility as exalted and outstanding virtue.

> This was the noblest Roman of them all,
> All the conspirators save only he
> Did that they did in envy of great Caesar;
> He, only in a general honest thought
> And common good to all, made one of them.
> His life was gentle, and the elements
> So mix'd in him that Nature might stand up
> And say to all the world, 'This was a man!'
>
> (V. v. 68-75)

Nobility as Exalted Rank. Shakespeare's characterization of Brutus seems to fit Sidney's aphorism, "I am no herald to in-

---

[2] Vyvyan speaks deprecatingly of the patriotic spirit of the Renaissance. (Once again, the critic is distorting Shakespeare because of a modern bias.) He observes that the "fatal flaw in the soul of Brutus . . . is that he puts politics before humanity," and adds that his weak point is that "he sets what we now call an ideology higher than love." (John Vyvyan, *The Shakespearean Ethic*, London, 1959, p. 19.)

quire of men's pedigrees; it sufficeth me, if I know their virtues."[3] While Brutus is referred to as a Roman lord, the high esteem in which he is held, as the noble Brutus, suggests primarily his superior moral qualities. But the importance for Shakespeare of pedigree, of nobility in the sense of exalted rank, is not therefore to be minimized. In every other tragedy—and it is in the tragedies that the definition of nobility is of greatest importance—Shakespeare either presents a hero who comes from a noble family or else takes pains to document the fact that the hero has aristocratic ancestry. Hamlet is a prince, Macbeth a kinsman of the King, Lear a king, Antony one of the three rulers of the Roman Empire, and Cleopatra a royal queen. Othello's black skin, which so much enhances the bitterness of Brabantio toward the man who has eloped with his daughter, does not prevent Shakespeare from presenting him as a man of the highest moral calibre. Yet it probably demanded, for the Jacobean audience, a careful documentation of his aristocratic pedigree, which Shakespeare artfully weaves into the dramatic action almost at the beginning of the play. In answer to Iago's warning that Brabantio is enraged over the loss of his daughter and will appeal to the court of Venice with all the influence he can command, Othello calmly asserts,

> Let him do his spite.
> My services which I have done the signiory
> Shall outtongue his complaints. 'Tis yet to know—
> Which, when I know that boasting is an honour,
> I shall promulgate—I fetch my life and being
> From men of royal siege. (I. ii. 17-22)

Shakespeare, in his presentation of the noble tragic hero, could not overlook the sentiments of an audience which would read in a typical Renaissance moral treatise, *The French Academie*, that "Nobilitie (as Aristotle saieth) is a glittering excellencie proceeding from ancestours, and an honour that commeth

---

[3] Sir Philip Sidney, *Aphorisms*, London, 1807, I, 3.

from an ancient linage and stocke."[4] In *Othello*, he manages to establish the hero's pedigree with great dramatic economy; in *Coriolanus*, establishing such lineage involves a lengthy description which would probably be cut from a modern production as tedious and of little consequence. Shakespeare has Junius Brutus, one of the tribunes of the people, attest to Coriolanus' noble pedigree:

What stock he springs of,
The noble house o' th' Marcians; from whence came
That Ancus Marcius, Numa's daughter's son,
Who after great Hostilius here was King;
Of the same house Publius and Quintus were,
That our best water brought by conduits hither;
And [Censorinus, who was] nobly nam'd so,
Twice being [by the people chosen] Censor,
Was his great ancestor. (II. iii. 245-253)

Although Shakespeare suggests that both Othello and Coriolanus have royal blood in their veins, their royalty is not stressed. His chief concern is to imply that their "derivation was from ancestors/ Who stood equivalent with mighty kings"—Marina's answer to Lysimachus in *Pericles*, when he questions her as to her stock. (V. i. 91-92) All Shakespeare's tragic heroes meet the Aristotelian requirement that the hero be from a family of note. Whether Shakespeare had read the *Poetics* or not, it is only too evident that he desired his hero to be noble in rank, since this would enhance his stature in the eyes of the Elizabethan audience.

The Dual Concepts of Nobility. The nobility of the Shakespearean tragic hero, we have seen, corresponds to the dual concepts of nobility—exalted rank and exalted virtue—which constituted the full definition of this concept in the Renaissance treatises on moral philosophy. Except in the case of Brutus, the hero's possession of exceptional moral qualities does not obliterate certain fundamental faults in his character,

---

[4] La Primaudaye, p. 694.

but his noble stature is nonetheless evident. They make him, ethically speaking, more impressive than a flawless character of lesser grandeur. Indeed, the faults of Shakespeare's greatest tragic heroes seem inconsequential in any final assessment of their tragic stature. When Octavius Caesar is told that Antony is dead, his response reflects our own: "The breaking of so great a thing should make/ A greater crack." (V. i. 14-15) Caesar has shown fewer faults throughout the play than Antony, and he does evoke a sort of cold admiration. Antony's faults are freely admitted in the eulogies which follow. How inconsequential they seem in comparison to the tribute of admiration bestowed on him!

> MAECENAS   His taints and honours
> Wag'd equal with him.
>
> AGRIPPA   A rarer spirit never
> Did steer humanity; but you gods will give us
> Some faults to make us men. Caesar is touch'd.
>
> MAEC. When such a spacious mirror's set before him,
> He needs must see himself. (V. i. 30-35)

It is not an easy matter to define moral qualities in Shakespeare since, as Santayana remarks, "The medium is rich and thick, and more important than the idea."[5] This is particularly evident in *King Lear*. Nowhere in the play is Lear referred to as noble; yet if we think of the 16th century definition of nobility as the possession of a great or lofty character, we might well be tempted to defend the assertion that he is the noblest of Shakespeare's heroes. Pitiable, old, and downtrodden he may be, yet, after his initial arrogance in the opening scene, his nobility and greatness of mind illuminate his every appearance in the play. As Segar observes, "Seneca saith, that who so will trulie judge what worthines is in man, must consider of him naked, laying aside his livings and titles of honor . . . and

⁵ *Essays in Literary Criticism of George Santayana*, ed. Irving Singer, New York, 1956, p. 270.

then weigh of what value or excellencie he is in minde, because nobilitie is placed in the minde."[6]

To speak of Macbeth as a noble hero seems, on the face of it, utterly absurd. In place of the conventional eulogy of the tragic hero, Macduff cuts off his head and brings it to Malcolm who then refers to "this dead butcher." (V. viii. 69) Yet if we turn to the *Offices*, or to references to this treatise by La Primaudaye and Elyot, we discover that Renaissance moral philosophy presents as a fundamental humanist commonplace the very notion which Shakespeare dramatically embodies in the character of Macbeth. Cicero warns in the *Offices* that "it is in the greatest souls and in the most brilliant geniuses that we usually find ambitions for civil and military authority, for power, and for glory."[7] Elsewhere he adds that "from this exaltation and greatness of spirit spring all too readily self-will and excessive lust for power. . . . The more notable a man is for his greatness of spirit, the more ambitious he is to be the foremost citizen, or, I should say rather, to be sole ruler."[8] This paradox, that the very greatness of a man's character may cause him to become too ambitious, is reiterated by Elyot. Elyot maintains that "Every noble hart desireth [glorie]," but a few pages later, in discussing magnanimity, he warns that "the more higher of courage that a man is . . . the soner [is] he meved to do thinges againe right."[9]

Out of this paradox, with a subtlety that eludes easy or precise definition, Shakespeare draws the character of Macbeth. Despite Macbeth's unspeakable crimes, his conscience does not rest easy until he passes into a mood of fatalistic indifference near the end of the play. Even then, he continues to display that exalted courage and high sensitivity to disgrace which characterized the Renaissance man of honor. Malcolm's observation that "a good and virtuous nature may recoil/ In an imperial charge" serves as an accurate choral commentary. (IV. iii. 19-20) Indeed, the essence of Macbeth's tragedy lies in that nobler self

---

[6] *The Booke of Honor and Armes*, p. 35.
[7] I. 8.   [8] *ibid.*, I. 19.   [9] *The Gouernour*, III, 13 and 16.

which never entirely vanishes and which is constantly evaluating
and condemning those acts which his ambition, and his wife's
accusations of cowardice, lead him to commit. So, near the end
of the play, we are given a brief glimpse, in the penultimate
soliloquy, of the changes which have been taking place in Macbeth's heart and discover that he has lost all taste for life
since mere power, without "honour, love, obedience, troops of
friends," provides no lasting satisfaction.

THE POLITICAL HIERARCHY

The Concept of Order and Degree. At the beginning of
King Henry the Fifth appears the following passage:

> Therefore doth heaven divide
> The state of man in divers functions,
> Setting endeavour in continual motion;
> To which is fixed as an aim or butt
> Obedience; for so work the honeybees,
> Creatures that by a rule in nature teach
> The act of order to a peopled kingdom.
> They have a king, and officers of sorts,
> Where some like magistrates correct at home,
> Others like merchants venture trade abroad,
> Others like soldiers armed in their stings
> Make boot upon the summer's velvet buds,
> Which pillage they with merry march bring home
> To the tent-royal of their emperor,
> Who, busied in his majesty, surveys
> The singing masons building roofs of gold,
> The civil citizens kneading up the honey,
> The poor mechanic porters crowding in
> Their heavy burthens at his narrow gate,
> The sad-ey'd justice, with his surly hum,
> Delivering o'er to executors pale
> The lazy yawning drone. (I. ii. 183-204)

This speech, delivered by the Archbishop of Canterbury, is a compact and idealized description of Shakespeare's England. If it places somewhat less emphasis on the high degrees of Elizabethan society than the famous speech on order in *Troilus and Cressida*, it nevertheless merits scrutiny for its suggestion, by tone and image, that the lower classes of Elizabethan society can find as much contentment in their position of social and political inferiority as the king and his officers in their august positions at the head of the state. Although a poetic justification of the typically conservative, hierarchical, and ordered view of society which manifests itself wherever we look as the Elizabethan's notion of his own society, it is colored by the gentle warmth and humanity so frequently to be found in Shakespeare's dramatic presentation of the various classes of Elizabethan society in his plays. It is this tone of acceptance and of affection which leads so many casual readers of Shakespeare to protest whenever anyone tries to prove that Shakespeare was aristocratic, or a bourgeois gentleman, or as a conservative looked down on the working classes of his society. There is an element of justice in this protest; Shakespeare does seem to sympathize with many diverse characters as they come to life in his hands. At times, as in Shylock's famous speech of protest about the persecution of his race, Shakespeare's humanity seems even to get the better of his dramatic intent. His ability to identify with Shylock's predicament suggests an allegiance to all humanity, above the prejudices of a particular age or class or race.

It would be highly unfair to attempt to deny this aspect of Shakespeare's art. It was commented upon as early as 1664 when Margaret Cavendish suggested that Shakespeare's powers of empathy were so great that one might think he had been metamorphosed from a man into a woman. Keats made this view ever more popular when he wrote of Shakespeare's negative capability (which he related to his own chameleon-like qualities), which meant that all points of view could be espoused with equal fervor. But the admission that these qualities exist in Shakespeare should not lead, as it so often does, to the view that he is completely cut off, or completely divorced, from the moral convictions and the social and political ideas of his age. Legouis, we remember from the foreword to Part II, states that each of Shakespeare's characters, "from the kings to the clowns, has indeed a philosophy, which he makes singularly clear. Each judges life in his own way, from his own angle, whence he may utter a remark strikingly true, and profound also, in many instances."[10] Legouis reaches the conclusion, however, that these philosophies in no manner reveal Shakespeare's personal judgment of life.

The fallacy here is indicated by the way in which Shakespeare reflects the hierarchical and aristocratic ordering of Elizabethan society in his presentation of character. Shakespeare's clowns, fools, and rogues may be lovable in a simple way but they are not ordinarily portrayed as worthy of high esteem (Lear's fool is a notable exception). In this regard, the ordering of the Shakespearean dramatic world in terms of degrees of superiority reflects the idea of order in such a typical Elizabethan work as Elyot's *The Gouernour*. Elyot observes, "in every thing is ordre, and without ordre may be nothing stable or permanent; and it may nat be called ordre, excepte it do containe in it degrees, high and base, accordinge to the merite or estimation of the thing that is ordred."[11] Essentially, there is no questioning of this view of the social hierarchy in Shakespeare. Posthumus, the son of a poor but worthy gentleman, may gain more of the audience's esteem than Cloten, the son of a Queen. But Posthumus' prestige is carefully enhanced by the emphasis placed on his father's honorable service and the title which he has earned. Rank is equally important for the hero's servants whom one tends, mistakenly, to think of as mere servants. Kent is a Lord, Paulina a gentlewoman. When the attendant is not of noble birth, as is the case with Juliet's nurse, a comic portrayal is at once demanded. Touches of pro-

---

[10] Legouis and Cazamian, *A History of English Literature*, pp. 448-449.
[11] I, I.

test exist, as in the gravediggers' conversation in *Hamlet*. One clown states, "Will you ha' the truth an't? If this had not been a gentlewoman, she should have been buried out o' Christian burial." To which the other clown replies, "Why, there thou say'st! And the more pity that great folk should have count'nance in this world to drown or hang themselves more than their even-Christen. Come, my spade! There is no ancient gentlemen but gard'ners, ditchers, and grave-makers." (V. i. 26-34) But such protest, when it becomes effective and wide-scale, as in Cade's rebellion, is given short shrift. And Belarius' remarks about the burial of the villain Cloten in *Cymbeline* are more typical than those of the clowns:

> He was a queen's son, boys;
> And though he came our enemy, remember
> He was paid for that. Though mean and mighty rotting
> Together have one dust, yet reverence
> (That angel of the world) doth make distinction
> Of place, 'tween high and low. Our foe was princely;
> And though you took his life as being our foe,
> Yet bury him as a prince. (IV. ii. 244-251)

The importance of class distinctions is particularly evident when we consider how frequently inferior class position is used as a barrier to romantic involvements between Shakespeare's heroes and heroines. Posthumus is banished in *Cymbeline* because of his effrontery in marrying a Queen's daughter, Florizel draws the ire of his father in *The Winter's Tale* for wishing to marry a "sheephook," and Helena in *All's Well That Ends Well* despairs of marital happiness because Count Bertram disdains a poor physician's daughter for a wife, even though the King promises to promote her. In this last instance, the King's speech stresses the fact that mere virtue is a sounder basis for distinguishing worth than social status; but, as has been indicated, the notion that nobility could be equated with mere virtue did not fundamentally alter the social basis of Renaissance society, however often it may have been referred to in the books of moral philosophy. Helena's service to the King, which would entitle her to "nobility dative" (the granting of title for services rendered the state), would have been more important to the Elizabethan audience, in making her acceptable as the wife of a Count, than the King's speech which emphasizes to an unusual degree the importance of mere virtue. The King argues,   Strange is it that our bloods,

Of colour, weight, and heat, pour'd all together,
Would quite confound distinction, yet stand off
In differences so mighty.

From lowest place when virtuous things proceed,
The place is dignified by th' doer's deed.
Where great additions swell's, and virtue none,
It is a dropsied honour. (II. iii. 125-128, 132-135)

The more typical attitude is that of Florizel in *The Winter's Tale*. When asked by Leontes whether he is married to Perdita, his discouraged response reflects the Elizabethan fondness for finding correspondences in the ordering of human society and the ordering of the physical universe. Florizel says sadly,

We are not, sir, nor are we like to be.
The stars, I see, will kiss the valleys first.
The odds for high and low's alike. (V. i. 205-207)

The ramifications of this concept of superiority of degree extend like a fine network through all aspects of Elizabethan social life and equally through Shakespeare's dramatic world. The etiquette of his entire society was a manifestation, more often than not, of the relative superiority of some, the relative inferiority of others. Occasionally equal rank demands equal esteem, as when Antony and Octavius Caesar meet for the first time in *Antony and Cleopatra*. Each politely suggests that the other sit first—and then they sit down at the same time. Sometimes a superior can show courtesy to an inferior by foregoing his superior position, as when Hamlet graciously suggests

to his friend Horatio at the end of the first act that they leave
the stage together. But more frequently social conventions rigidly
defined the relationship of superior to inferior. Needless to
say, these conventions were strictly observed. The popularity
of translations of Italian books on manners and social behavior
is an indication of how seriously the English Renaissance took
to its newly acquired gentility. To be ill-mannered was to be
barbaric, as is indicated by Leontes' remarks to Hermione,
when he believes her to be false.

                                          O thou thing!
     Which I'll not call a creature of thy place,
     Lest barbarism, making me the precedent,
     Should a like language use to all degrees
     And mannerly distinguishment leave out
     Betwixt the prince and beggar. (I. i. 82-87)

Nothing indicates more clearly the security which the Elizabethan felt by having a defined place in an ordered society—
ordered by a strict definition of the relationship between the
individuals of every social unit, whether it be the greatest
political body or humblest family household—than the dismay
felt toward the only seeming alternative, disorder, chaos, or
confusion. Thus Elyot, writing of the "discrepance of degrees,
whereof procedeth ordre," conjectures, "More over take away
ordre from all thinges what shulde than remaine? Certes
nothinge finally, except some man wolde imagine eftsones
Chaos: whiche of some is expounde a confuse mixture. Also
where there is any lack of ordre nedes must be perpetuall con-
flicte: and in thinges subjecte to Nature nothinge of him selfe
onely may be norisshed; but when he hath distroyed that where
with he dothe participate by the ordre of his creation, he him
selfe of necessite muste than perisshe, whereof ensuethe univer-
sall dissolution."[12] As Theodore Spencer has pointed out in
Shakespeare and the Nature of Man, the Elizabethan fondness
for correspondences meant that an introduction of confusion
into one aspect of the ordered structure tended immediately

---

[12] *ibid.*

to throw the whole system out of kilter.[13] Thus, Donne discovers that Copernicus may upset the ordered Ptolemaic universe and immediately questions the validity of the hierarchical, ordered relation of king and subject, father and son. The parallel between the organization of the physical universe and the organization of human society (especially the analogy between sun and king) was extremely popular throughout Elizabethan society and is referred to frequently in Shakespeare.

The upsetting of order and degree is particularly the theme of *King Lear*, since both in the main plot and in the subplot the father's superiority over his children is challenged, as is also the superiority of the elder. At the end of the first act of *King Lear*, Cordelia leaves the stage with the admonition to her sisters. "Use well our father." (I. i. 274) They curtly reply, "Prescribe not us our duties." (I. i. 279) But as soon as they are alone on the stage, their cunning is revealed; despite all their professions of devotion to their father, they are planning to destroy what little authority he has left. The Jacobean audience would view their plot as monstrous, since it involves not only deceit, the worst of all vices, but also the upsetting of the accepted order of society. This is fully disclosed at the end of the scene:

> GON.   If our father carry authority with such
> dispositions as he bears, this last surrender
> of his will but offend us.
> REG.   We shall further think on't.
> GON.   We must do something, and i' the heat.
>
> (I. i. 308-312)

They have hardly left the stage when the second scene opens with Edmund complaining about the plague of custom which gives an older brother precedence over a younger and a legitimate son precedence over a bastard. To the Jacobean audience, this first soliloquy of Edmund's is equally an indication of monstrous villainy, for it is a direct challenging of the hierarchical ordering of its society, even more so than the machinations

---

[13] p. 31.

of a Claudius or an Iago. Goneril, Regan, and Edmund are in this sense more akin to Cade than to the other tragic villains. They seem to be justifying the upsetting of order and degree in a way which almost makes *King Lear* into a dramatic presentation of Ulysses' speech on order in *Troilus and Cressida*. (Goneril and Regan are challenging the prerogative of age, Edmund primogeniture.) Ulysses asks rhetorically how could

> The primogenity and due of birth,
> Prerogative of age, crowns, sceptres, laurels,
> But by degree, stand in authentic place?
> Take but degree away, untune that string,
> And hark what discord follows! Each thing meets
> In mere oppugnancy. The bounded waters
> Should lift their bosoms higher than the shores
> And make a sop of all this solid globe;
> Strength should be lord of imbecility,
> And the rude son should strike his father dead.
>
> (I. iii. 106-115)

Shakespeare is thinking in just such terms of corresponding disruption in the physical universe in *King Lear*. The two revolutionary speeches, first of the two disloyal daughters, then of the disloyal Edmund, are almost immediately followed by Gloucester's lament that "these late eclipses of the sun and moon portend no good to us." (I. ii. 112-113) Gloucester finds the same sort of correspondence between eclipses (disorder in the heavens) and ensuing mutinies (disorder in human society) as is to be found in the general thinking of Elizabethan society. His fear that one disorder may spread until there is complete confusion, dissension, and division throughout society parallels Elyot's remarks on order and chaos already quoted. He tells Edmund that "Love cools, friendship falls off, brothers divide. In cities mutinies; in countries, discord; in palaces, treason; and the bond crack'd 'twixt son and father. This villain of mine comes under the prediction; there's son against father: the King falls from bias of nature; there's father against child. We have seen the best of our time. Machinations, hollowness, treachery, and all ruinous disorders follow us disquietly to our graves." (I. ii. 115-125)

This theme constitutes the plot of the rest of the play (Gloucester's speech occurs in the second scene of the first act). In the very next scene Goneril calls her father an "idle old man" and tells Oswald to be deliberately discourteous to the old king. (I. iii. 16) So when Lear and the steward next meet, and Lear asks Oswald, "Who am I, sir?" he responds with the deliberate insult, "My lady's father." (I. iv. 86-87) A modern audience can easily miss the full implications of this insult—that by suggesting that Lear is his daughter's father, her position is given preeminence over his. The superiority of degree basic to the Elizabethan and Jacobean conception of an ordered, hierarchical society is completely ignored. In the eyes of the Renaissance audience, this is not only a monstrous personal insult but also a dangerous challenging of their most cherished social convictions. Lear responds to the insult by calling Oswald a "whoreson dog" and, when the steward bandies looks with him, strikes him. Of this incident Mr. Granville-Barker writes, "Lear's striking Oswald really was an outrage; after due complaint Goneril would doubtless have reproved his impertinence—for all that she had prompted it."[14] This show of faith in the goodness of Goneril's intentions makes us wonder what meaning to give to Goneril's line in the previous scene when she says to Oswald, "Put on what weary negligence you please/ You and your fellows." (I. iii. 12-13)

Would the Renaissance audience, which for the first performance of *King Lear* was a court audience, consider Lear's striking the insulting steward an outrage? Granville-Barker's suggestion that the outrage is Lear's quite overlooks both the superiority of his position in the social hierarchy and the immense prestige which attached to the position of a king. In the words of Cleland, "There is no man I thinke of what qualitie, estate, condition, or profession soever, but he would

---

[14] *Prefaces to Shakespeare*, I, 286.

be honoured and respected in his owne rancke, if hee bee not more dul and senselesse, then a blocke. If wee should suffer ourselves to be dishonoured by anie whosoever, except it bee by his Majestie, who maie dispose of our lives at his pleasure, our state was miserable."[15] The Jacobean audience would consider Lear's response to such an insult to his kingly position but mild. They would applaud Kent's tripping Oswald to teach him differences in degree and the respect an inferior should show a superior.

When Goneril lectures her father later in the scene, the same essential issue is involved—the complete upsetting of the whole hierarchy of relationships which Elizabethan society took for granted. The modern critic, unaware of the immense superiority which the father possessed in the patriarchical society of Elizabethan England, tends to see in Lear's anger and curses just cause for his daughter's behavior. But this is a topsy-turvy view of the play. Not only do the daughters provoke Lear's righteous indignation, but also, according to the Jacobean social code, they would be expected to "suffer pacientlie, and indure willinglie their [father's] imperfection, choller, or fro-wardnes."[16] In this case, the prerogative of age is equally involved. Hence, the Renaissance audience would not have shown the least sympathy for the two daughters at any time after they had revealed their true intentions at the end of the first scene.

The climax to this inversion of the natural order of preeminence is reached when Lear leaves Goneril and visits Regan but is refused hospitality. Regan tells him to return to her sister and to confess that he has wronged her! So finally the king kneels, with utmost irony, to beg hospitality. This situation is an exact parallel to the scene in *Coriolanus* where the mother, wife, and child come in supplication to ask their son to spare Rome. But there the son feels a conflict of loyalties and so he utters what is left unspoken in *King Lear*. His words serve as choral commentary and demonstrate that the audience, in the parallel situation in *King Lear*, would have felt no sym-

---

[15] p. 235.   [16] *ibid.*, p. 128.

pathy whatever for the two daughters, who so many modern critics feel are unhappily burdened with a choleric old father. As Volumnia enters the stage, she bows to Coriolanus and he comments:

> My mother bows,
> As if Olympus to a molehill should
> In supplication nod. (V. iii. 29-31)

When she finally kneels to her son, his response again indicates the analogy which the Elizabethan felt existed between superiority in human relationships and superiority in the realm of nature.

> What is this?
> Your knees to me? To your corrected son?
> Then let the pebbles on the hungry beach
> Fillop the stars! Then let the mutinous winds
> Strike the proud cedars, 'gainst the fiery sun,
> Murd'ring impossibility, to make
> What cannot be, slight work! (V. iii. 56-62)

No aspect of Elizabethan society was untouched by these differences of degrees and rank. Democratic equality is not, in short, a dominant social attitude in Shakespeare's world. Where there seem to be suggestions of it, as in the conversation between the two clowns in *Hamlet*, we have only to wait a few lines to hear the aristocratic hero of the play complaining, "the age is grown so picked that the toe of the peasant comes so near the heel of the courtier he galls his kibe." (V. i. 151-153) The Elizabethan assumption of the inequality of man was the basis for the hierarchical, pyramidal view of society which resulted both in gradations of moral esteem and in class distinction. The king, theoretically at least, topped both these pyramids; his tremendous prestige made him a man apart.

The King. In his many allusions to kingship, Shakespeare frequently refers to the traditional Christian notion that the king was God's divine representative on earth. But in the great tragedies, only *Macbeth* presents a leading figure who is the

epitome of all the Christian virtues. Macbeth's characterization
of Duncan has strong Christian overtones:

> Besides, this Duncan
> Hath borne his faculties so meek, hath been
> So clear in his great office, that his virtues
> Will plead like angels, trumpet-tongu'd, against
> The deep damnation of his taking off. (I. vii. 16-20)

When Macduff enters in the second act to bring the news of
Duncan's murder, his comments support this characterization:

> Confusion now hath made his masterpiece!
> Most sacrilegious murther hath broke ope
> The Lord's anointed temple and stole thence
> The life of the building. (II. 3. 71-74)

In *King Richard the Second*, that chronicle history which so
frequently verges on the tragic, the Christian idea of kingship
is fully presented. At the beginning of the fourth act, when
Bolingbroke lays claim to the throne "in God's name," the
Bishop of Carlisle protests most emphatically against anyone
who dares judge Richard as an unworthy king, for Richard is
"the figure of God's majesty,/ His captain, steward, deputy
elect." (IV. i. 125-126) When the Bishop prophesies the dire
events to follow if Bolingbroke usurps the throne, he, too,
refers to the concept of order and unity central to all Elizabethan social thinking:

> My lord of Hereford here, whom you call king,
> Is a foul traitor to proud Hereford's king;
> And if you crown him, let me prophesy,
>
> Peace shall go sleep with Turks and infidels,
> And in this seat of peace tumultuous wars
> Shall kin with kin and kind with kind confound;
> Disorder, horror, fear, and mutiny
> Shall here inhabit. (IV. i. 134-136, 139-143)

Carlisle's prophecy of "wofullest division" finally comes true in the Wars of the Roses. But the real significance of the speech lies in that it points to the king as the symbol of unity of the whole state. Precisely at this point Renaissance individualism merges with its social philosophy—the king's prestige is paramount both because of his presumably exalted moral character and because, as head of the state, he is the fountainhead of all its powers.

When King Henry the Fourth pardons the Duchess of York's son for his treason at the end of *King Richard the Second*, the Duchess calls him "a god on earth." (V. iii. 136) This sort of adulation was conventional court flattery in the Renaissance, but that it was conventional should not lead the modern reader to forget that many Elizabethan subjects reverenced their monarch almost as a divine being. Both Christian and pagan-humanist social philosophy spoke of kings as gods on earth—the Christian implication being that the king, as God's agent on earth, was sacrosanct.

The Renaissance monarch was the sovereign ruler of a sovereign state. Shakespeare's presentation of the royal monarch accords in most instances with the preconceptions of his age. At the beginning of the fifth act of *King John*, however, the king, in accordance with medieval views of kingship, hands his crown to Pandulph, the Pope's representative, who returns it to him with the comment:

> Take again
> From this my hand, as holding of the Pope
> Your sovereign greatness and authority. (V. i. 2-4)

In most cases, the Shakespearean king assumes that his position is absolute and acts in accordance with Elizabeth's dictum to Leicester, "As we have authority to rule, so we look to be obeyed."[17] The slightest sign of disobedience on the part of a subject is considered a great insult to the royal position. The conflict between King Henry the Fifth and the French King involved an English claim to feudal possessions acquired by

---

[17] *The Letters of Queen Elizabeth*, ed. G. B. Harrison, p. 198.

Edward the Black Prince. But *King Henry the Fifth* ends with an accord between the two nations which preserves the sovereignty of each. In a similar conflict between England and France in *King John*, the Dauphin voices the spirit of Renaissance nationalism when he responds to the news that the English king has made his peace with Rome with the contemptuous exclamation, "Am I Rome's slave?" (V. ii. 97) As the sovereign monarch of a national state, he likewise rejects Pandulph's request that he cease warring against the English. Both his position as the head of a sovereign state and his preeminence within his own nation are indicated by his reply:

> I am too high born to be propertied,
> To be a secondary at control,
> Or useful servingman and instrument
> To any sovereign throughout the world.
>   (V. ii. 79-82)

In similar spirit, Cymbeline refuses to yield to the Roman emperor; he tells his emissary "Our subjects, sir,/ Will not endure his yoke," and adds that for himself "to show less sovereignty than they, must needs/ Appear unkinglike." (III. v. 4-5, 6-7)

The Renaissance sovereign never accepts orders from a foreign nation. His authority is often just as unchallenged within the boundaries of his own kingdom. King Henry the Fourth, for example, warns Worcester that "majesty might never yet endure/ The moody frontier of a servant brow." (I. iii. 18-19) Nothing was more infuriating to the Renaissance monarch than the feeling that his commands were being ignored. Shakespeare does not overlook the dramatic possibilities implicit in such situations where a great leader suddenly finds his power and authority slipping from his hands. Thus, after the first fight with Caesar, Antony admits that he has lost command. He is "unqualitied with very shame." (III. xi. 44) But gradually he regains composure and decides to challenge Caesar to single fight. When he returns to the stage he finds Cleopatra dealing with Caesar's emissary and allowing him to kiss her hand:

ANT.   Favours, by Jove that thunders!
        What art thou, fellow?
THYR.   One that but performs
        The bidding of the fullest man, and worthiest
        To have command obey'd.
ENO.   [aside] You will be whipp'd
ANT.   Approach there!—Ah, you kite!—Now, gods and
            devils!
        Authority melts from me. Of late, when I cried 'Ho!'
        Like boys unto a muss, kings would start forth
        And cry 'Your will?' Have you no ears? I am Antony
            yet.
                [Enter Servants]
        Take hence this Jack and whip him.
ENO.   [aside] 'Tis better playing with a lion's whelp
        Than with an old one dying. (III. xiii. 85-95)

If we invoke the democratic and humanitarian values of the present century, Antony must seem both tyrannical and cruel. But for the Jacobean audience, his indignation over his loss of command would have been thoroughly understandable.

Loss of kingly authority is one of the central issues in *King Lear*. At the end of the first scene, the two daughters are plotting to remove his last remnants of power. In the third scene Goneril makes another attempt to reduce his authority. She tells Oswald to be deliberately insulting:

        If he distaste it, let him to our sister,
        Whose mind and mine I know in that are one,
        Not to be overrul'd. Idle old man,
        That still would manage those authorities
        That he hath given away. (I. iii. 14-18)

Lear becomes aware of what is happening. When Kent offers his services and observes that he is "as poor as the king," Lear replies, "If thou be'st as poor for a subject as he's for a king, thou art poor enough." (I. iv. 22-23) But even after Oswald humiliates him deliberately by departing without answering the king's direct question as to the whereabouts of his daughter, Lear is willing to overlook the humiliation being heaped upon him. He answers his knight's observations that his Highness is being wronged by stating: "Thou but rememb'rest me of mine own conception. I have perceived a most faint neglect of late, which I have rather blamed as mine own jealous curiosity than as a very pretence and purpose of unkindness." (I. iv. 72-76) These are not the remarks of a proud, haughty man.

When Kent offers his services to Lear, Shakespeare again takes pains to emphasize the fact that Lear is worthy of command, not the "idle old fool" that Goneril makes him out, nor the "puerile intellect" that Wilson Knight and other eminent Shakespearean critics find him. Kent's remarks are testimonial:

LEAR. Dost thou know me, fellow?
KENT. No, sir; but you have that in your countenance which
       I would fain call master.
LEAR. What's that?
KENT. Authority. (I. iv. 28-32)

When Lear leaves Goneril, under the illusion that he will receive better treatment from Regan, the question whether he has any right to authority is again raised. Once more, Lear is deliberately insulted; Regan and Cornwall use the pretext of fatigue to explain their failure to greet Lear when he arrives at their castle. Lear is compelled to make a request to Gloucester that he be allowed to speak with his daughter and son-in-law. Lear's loss of prestige is stressed in the lines which follow:

GLOU. Well, my good lord, I have inform'd them so.
LEAR. Inform'd them? Dost thou understand me, man?
GLOU. Ay, my good lord.
LEAR. The King would speak with Cornwall; the dear father
       would with his daughter speak, commands her serv-
       ice. (II. iv. 99-103)

Lear's kingly authority here merges with his authority as a father. In the textbooks of moral philosophy, an analogy was often drawn between the power of the king and the power of the father. Thus La Primaudaye observes, "this commandment over children, is called royall, bicause he that begetteth, commandeth by love, and by the prerogative of age, which is a kind of kingly commanding."[18]

Goneril and Regan persist in their intentions of destroying Lear's remaining authority. As they whittle down the size of his retinue, the thought occurs to Regan that two separate commands are unnecessary and that Lear can be attended by her servants. The old king feels that he is being stripped of his last vestige of power. Lear's madness ensues. Yet during the second storm scene, in the midst of all his indignities, we still hear Lear insisting, "I am the King himself," (IV. vi. 84) and later, when the blind Gloucester asks, "Is't not the King?" the ringing response is given, "Ay, every inch a King!" (IV. vi. 108-109) Shortly thereafter, when Lear is rescued by Cordelia's attendants, Shakespeare continues to dwell on the contrast between Lear's present predicament and his innate royalty. Lear cries,

> Come, come, I am a king;
> My masters, know you that?
> GENT. You are a royal one, and we obey you. (IV. vi. 203-
> 205)

Cordelia's attendants dress him again in royal garb and when he is restored to sanity, humble and repentant of the wrongs he has done Cordelia, she addresses him as "my royal lord," "your Majesty," and "your Highness"—titles of dignity which Cordelia's sisters had rarely bothered to employ in addressing Lear. Finally, at the end of the play, Lear's authority is restored. Albany tries to make Lear feel once again fully the king:

> You lords and noble friends, know our intent.
> What comfort to this great decay may come
> Shall be applied. For us, we will resign,

[18] p. 501.

> During the life of this old Majesty,
> To him our absolute power. (V. iii. 296-300)

Of course, it is too late. Lear has suffered too much to appreciate these well-intentioned but trivial compensations for all that he has endured.

In stressing the importance of Lear's claim to power, it should be made clear that the issue is primarily that of Lear's authority over his hundred knights. Lear's initial surrender of his power is not a matter of vague generalities; he precisely stipulates what he wishes to keep and what he is giving away. He says to Albany and Cornwall:

> I do invest you jointly in my power,
> Preeminence, and all the large effects
> That troop with majesty. Ourself, by monthly course,
> With reservation of an hundred knights,
> By you to be sustain'd, shall our abode
> Make with you by due turns. Only we still retain
> The name, and all th'additions to a king. The sway,
> Revenue, execution of the rest,
> Beloved sons, be yours; which to confirm,
> This coronet part betwixt you. (I. i. 132-141)

It is apparent from this passage that Lear is surrendering his power to his two sons-in-law, but that he wishes to retain the name and the title of king. Can there be any doubt that the preservation of this symbol of high moral and social rank would have been considered by the Jacobean audience a matter of great importance? When Lear insists in the storm scenes that he *is* the king, he is clearly primarily concerned about the name and title of king.

The importance of mere name in itself for princes of royal blood is indicated when King Henry the Fifth lists the French dead after the battle of Agincourt. The high nobility, those of unusual prominence, are mentioned by name; the great aristocrats are so famous that their very names are sufficient indications of their position and prestige. Percy tells Bolingbroke in *King Richard the Second* that the nearby castle is manned by three hundred men; "And in it are the Lords of York, Berkeley, and Seymour,/ None else of name and noble estimate." (II. iii. 55-56) In the same scene, when Berkeley addresses Bolingbroke as "My Lord of Hereford," Bolingbroke replies:

> My lord, my answer is—'to Lancaster';
> And I am come to seek that name in England;
> And I must find that title in your tongue
> Before I make reply to aught you say. (II. iii. 70-73)

Berkeley thereupon assures him, "'Tis not my meaning/ To rase one title of your honour out." (II. iii. 74-75)

If the name of a great lord was in itself indicative of his high rank and prestige, the name of the king was an almost sacred symbol. *King Richard the Second* is a veritable study in Renaissance attitudes toward kingship, since Shakespeare makes such frequent dramatic use of the ironic contrast between the high dignity of Richard's position and his actual weakness as a man. On hearing of Bolingbroke's success, Richard advises his followers to desert him. When Aumerle admonishes him, "Comfort, my liege. Remember who you are," Richard replies,

> I had forgot myself. Am I not King?
> Awake, thou coward majesty! thou sleepest.
> Is not the King's name twenty thousand names?
> Arm, arm, my name! A puny subject strikes
> At thy great glory. (III. ii. 83-87)

In the next scene, as Bolingbroke's power grows, he exclaims, "O that I were as great/ As is my grief, or lesser than my name!" (III. iii. 136, 137)

Richard provides the appropriate chorus on the reasons for his own decline. In the celebrated mirror scene, Northumberland addresses him as "my lord." Richard replies,

> No lord of thine, thou haught insulting man,
> Nor no man's lord. I have no name, no title—

No, not that name was given me at the font—
But 'tis usurp'd. (IV. i. 254-257)

The situation in *King Lear* is in many respects markedly similar to that in *King Richard the Second*. In both plays the protagonist first loses his power and authority, then is brought to realize that, without them, too great a disparity exists between his sense of what he was and his sense of what he is for him to maintain his own integrity. His greatness was an essential part of his very character; without it, he has, in a sense, ceased to exist. Lear, for example, exclaims,

Doth any here know me? This is not Lear.
Doth Lear walk thus? Speak thus? Where are his eyes?
Either his notion weakens, his discernings
Are lethargied—Ha! waking? 'Tis not so!
Who is it that can tell me who I am? (I. iv. 246-250)

The fool replies cryptically: "Lear's shadow." Shakespeare frequently uses the mere name of the protagonist in this fashion to symbolize every aspect of his great dignity. Thus Hamlet, awakened from his melancholy musings, resolute, and strong in passion, leaps into the grave with the exclamation, "This is I,/ Hamlet the Dane." (V. i. 280-281) When Antony believes that Cleopatra has betrayed him, he indicates his great disgust at her behavior by demanding, "What's her name,/ Since she was Cleopatra." (III. xiii. 98-99) Othello responds to Lodovico's query, "Where is this rash and most unfortunate man?" with the brief comment, "That's he that was Othello." (V. ii. 283, 284) Antony, too, shows that his own self-confidence has returned, after his first defeat of Caesar, by exclaiming, "I am/ Antony yet." (III. xiii. 92-93) In other words, the mere name of the great protagonist conveys a sense of the majesty of his personality precisely because that name is so renowned. As Octavius Caesar observes,   The death of Antony
Is not a single doom; in the name lay
A moiety of the world. (V. i. 17-19)

The Death of Princes. Calpurnia's famous words of warning to Caesar are known by every schoolboy: "When beggars die there are no comets seen;/ The heavens themselves blaze forth the death of princes." (II. ii. 30-31) These lines refer not only to the imminent death of her husband; she is iterating the common Renaissance belief, mentioned earlier, that disasters in the human realm are reflected by great disturbances in the natural realm. The death of one of Shakespeare's great kings, whether it be Julius Caesar, the elder Hamlet, Duncan, or Lear, is considered truly catastrophic. Hence even the heavens seem to be disturbed by the event.

The allusions to natural disorders accompanying the deaths of great Princes are of a varied nature. Gloucester, in the first act of *King Lear*, refers to the late eclipses of the sun which he feels portend disorder and confusion. Horatio, in the first scene of *Hamlet*, compares the recent disturbances of heaven and earth to the ones which occurred at the time of Julius Caesar's death. In both these cases, the omen is treated as a portent of national disunity and confusion. Similarly, *The First Part of King Henry the Sixth* opens with Bedford's invocation:

> Hung be the heavens with black, yield day to night!
> Comets, importing change of times and states,
> Brandish your crystal tresses in the sky. (I. i. 1-3)

In *Macbeth*, on the other hand, the main emphasis lies on the upsetting of Nature, with the implication that the upsetting of the normal hierarchy in human society is being accompanied by a similar upsetting of the natural hierarchy in the animal world. The old man tells Ross that "A falcon, tow'ring in her pride of place,/ Was by a mousing owl hawk'd at and kill'd." (II. iv. 12-13) He also reports that Duncan's horses have broken loose from their stalls as if to defy mankind. These reversals of the normal provide an amplification of Macduff's first remark when he brings the news of Duncan's death: "Confusion now hath made his masterpiece." (II. iii. 71) In all these instances, Shakespeare is emphasizing the effect on the kingdom of the death of the mighty prince—which in *King Lear, Hamlet,* and *Macbeth* become particularly disruptive and terrifying by hinting that the death itself has been unnatural and that there are evil agents working to overthrow the social order and usurp the ruler's position.

At other times, Shakespeare ignores the social implications of the downfall of a preeminent individual. Thus, when Antony dies, we do not think particularly of confusion in the social realm, since Antony never seemed to be a central unifying force, much as he was esteemed throughout the play as a great general. Octavius Caesar remains, at the end of the play, not only a victorious opponent but also the symbol of order and unity. Hence Caesar's response to the news of Antony's death, like Cleopatra's, focuses primarily on the heroic qualities of a great individual.

Shakespeare manages to raise Desdemona to the stature of a great queen by suggesting that her death should have been followed by earth-shaking phenomena. But again the emphasis is on her qualities as an individual, in this case, largely on the effect which Desdemona's death has on Othello. He exclaims:

> My wife! my wife! what wife! I have no wife.
> O, insupportable! O heavy hour!
> Methinks it should be now a huge eclipse
> Of sun and moon, and that th' affrighted globe
> Should yawn at alteration. (V. ii. 97-101)

This speech had been foreshadowed much earlier in the play. Just as Iago began to spin his devilish web around Othello, the hero had exclaimed:

> Excellent wretch! Perdition catch my soul
> But I do love thee! and when I love thee not,
> Chaos is come again. (III. iii. 90-92)

By such far-reaching metaphors, Shakespeare makes his audience feel that Desdemona's murder is almost as catastrophic as the downfall of a great prince. Shakespeare is not really concerned with what happens to the state on the heroine's death, but by giving her such tragic grandeur he raises the play far above the level of mere domestic tragedy. And by making Othello's emotional responses of such colossal proportions, he manages to convey the impression that the hero is, indeed, great of heart.

The almost superhuman proportions of Shakespeare's tragic protagonists are also indicated by the grief and distraction felt by their associates at the time of their death. Thus, the intensity of Hamlet's grief is directly proportionate to the admiration which he feels for his father, to Hamlet the one consistently heroic figure in Denmark. Hamlet's grief is greatly enhanced by the fact that it is he alone who mourns—the rest of Denmark is celebrating the coronation and marriage of a new king. For a court audience which worshiped Sidney so intensely that it was considered unseemly to appear at court in gaudy apparel for a long time after his death, the vivid contrast between the melancholy, black-suited Hamlet and the gorgeous, festive costumes of the rest of the court would not have been missed.

Dekker's comments on the death of Elizabeth indicate how widespread the reactions to the death of a great monarch could be: "never did the English Nation behold so much black worne as there was at her Funerall . . . her Herse . . . seemed to be an Iland swimming in water."[19] Similarly, when Lear dies, Albany observes, "Our present business/ Is general woe." (V. iii. 318-319) Kent goes even further; the depth of his loyalty and devotion is indicated by the comment: "I have a journey, sir, shortly to go./ My master calls me; I must not say no." (V. iii. 321-322) Just as Mary Queen of Scots was surrounded by devoted, weeping followers, so likewise, as Cleopatra dies, the weeping Charmian exclaims: "Dissolve, thick cloud, and rain, that I may say/ The gods themselves do weep!" (V. ii. 302-303) Like Kent in *King Lear*, Cleopatra's ladies wish to die with their mistress. In similar fashion, Horatio seizes the

[19] Thomas Dekker, *The Wonderfull Yeare*, New York, 1924, p. 20. Cf. Thomas Moffet, *Nobilis*, p. 69.

poisoned cup so that he may follow Hamlet even in death. His comment underlines the extent to which the pagan-humanist values of friendship and fidelity can at times establish their supremacy over supernatural values. Loyalty to God has at least momentarily been replaced by worship of the hero; certainly this is the meaning of Horatio's cry, "I am more an antique Roman than a Dane." (V. ii. 352) Though Desdemona is not a queen, Emilia's devotion is as great as though she were. When Othello threatens her, she exclaims, "Thou hast not half the power to do me harm/ As I have to be hurt." (V. ii. 162-163) Shortly thereafter she adds, "I'll kill myself for grief." (V. ii. 192) The intensity of love, admiration, and consequent grief felt on the death of a single individual may seem fantastic and unrealistic to the sceptical youth of the 20th century. Yet within the context of the work of art it is completely convincing to thousands of modern theatre-goers.

The social upheaval which follows a great King's death in Shakespeare's plays is truly cataclysmic. Thus, after Julius Caesar is killed, Trebonius reports a state of general distraction among the people. In this play not grief, but alarm, terror, and amazement are the predominant emotions since the stability of the state is at stake. Trebonius observes that "Men, wives, and children stare, cry out, and run,/ As it were doomsday." (III. i. 97-98) This remark accords with Dekker's description of the reaction of the Elizabethan people to the death of Queen Elizabeth. Dekker writes "Oh what an Earthquake is the alteration of a state! Look from the Chamber of Presence, to the Farmers cottage, and you shall finde nothing but distraction: the whole Kingdome seemes a wildernes, and the people in it are transformed to wild men."[20] Troilus anticipates similar emotions when Troy shall hear the news of Hector's death. He tells Aeneas:

> Go into Troy and say there 'Hector's dead';
> There is a word will Priam turn to stone;

[20] p. 20.

> Make wells and Niobes of the maids and wives,
> Cold statues of the youth, and in a word
> Scare Troy out of itself. (V. x. 17-21)

Although many of Shakespeare's tragedies end with the death of the hero, the final note is not one of grief, anxiety, or distraction. In every case, except that of *Troilus and Cressida*, the characters who remain alive undertake to restore order to the state. When questions are raised as to who will inherit the throne, as in *Hamlet, Macbeth*, and *Lear*, the audience is provided with the necessary information. When the villain, who has been the cause of so much suffering and social disruption, remains alive, the audience is assured that he will receive due punishment. When the closing summary seems to leave room for further explanations, as in *Hamlet*, the audience is assured that a full accounting will be made after the close of the play so that any ambiguities which remain can be cleared up. Almost invariably (*King Lear* is the exception) the feelings of grief and sadness are counterbalanced by a eulogy which sets before us those qualities of the dead protagonist which call for admiration. The attempt is made, in short, to end the play with a coda which will somewhat diminish the turmoil of the catastrophe and lighten the ensuing gloom. As the curtain falls, we are led to feel that the great stature of the protagonist has been given due recognition and that some order and stability have been restored to the state. The need for such restoration of order and stability, when a king or prince has fallen, is made evident by Rosencrantz's observation:

> The single and peculiar life is bound
> With all the strength and armour of the mind
> To keep itself from noyance; but much more
> That spirit upon whose weal depends and rests
> The lives of many. The cesse of majesty
> Dies not alone, but like a gulf doth draw
> What's near it with it. It is a massy wheel,
> Fix'd on the summit of the highest mount,

To whose huge spokes ten thousand lesser things
Are mortis'd and adjoin'd; which when it falls,
Each small annexment, petty consequence,
Attends the boist'rous ruin. Never alone
Did the king sigh, but with a general groan. (III. iii. 11-23)

CHAPTER 6

SHAKESPEARE AND THE
RENAISSANCE CONCEPT OF HONOR

THE CONCEPT OF HONOR

BRUTUS is just as much the prototype of the Renaissance man of honor as he is the dramatic personification of Shakespeare's conception of nobility. (See the definition of honor at the beginning of Chapter 4, p. 136.) Throughout the play, all Brutus' actions are motivated by his strong sense of honor. When he quarrels with Cassius and is finally threatened by him, he replies with the calm serenity of one who is so sure of his innate rectitude that he cannot be ruffled. Brutus says,

> There is no terror, Cassius, in your threats;
> For I am arm'd so strong in honesty
> That they pass by me as the idle wind,
> Which I respect not. (IV. iii. 66-69)

With similar integrity and loftiness of sentiment, he scolds Cassius for his selling of offices. To Brutus it is almost inconceivable that anyone would allow the temptation of a mere monetary reward to destroy his honorable character. Again Brutus speaks with the firmness of one so possessed by a sense of honor that he can not grasp the motivation and behavior of those less idealistic than himself. He tells the erring Cassius, "I had rather be a dog and bay the moon/ Than such a Roman." (IV. iii. 27-28)

That the hero of a play based on *Plutarch's Lives* should be possessed of a strong sense of honor is not surprising. Values such as this one are not, however, peculiar to the Roman plays; as with many of the ethical issues to be discussed, the values of a particular play are common to all the plays and are often the general cultural values of Shakespeare's age. Thus, Brutus is described as "the all-honoured honest Roman" in *Antony and Cleopatra*, (II. vi. 16) and Portia in *The Merchant of Venice* is compared for her great worth "To Cato's daughter, Brutus' Portia," (I. ii. 166) who, in *Julius Caesar* stands out, in the few scenes in which she appears, as a wife as honorable as her famous husband. To bestow consummate praise on Antonio, Bassanio tells Portia that his friend is one in whom "The ancient Roman honour more appears/ Than any that draws breath in Italy." (III. ii. 295-296)

As we have seen, the sentiment of honor was regarded by the men of the Renaissance as something innate, an instinct toward virtue and an almost instinctive shrinking from vice. In its stress on self-reliance, it is distinct from the Christian conscience, since it is not a God-given attribute but one which results primarily from an aristocratic lineage and from early training in the moral disciplines. Indeed, the sentiment of honor is so closely associated with the hero's sense of personal identity that the two become almost completely fused. Thus Antony tells Octavia when he prepares to war against her brother that "If I lose mine honour,/ I lose myself." (III. iv. 22-23) On this issue, W. C. Curry's *Shakespeare's Philosophical Patterns* presents an interpretation of *Macbeth* which does not hold together under examination. Curry suggests that Shakespeare's portrayal of Macbeth is influenced by the ethics of St. Thomas Aquinas, specifically in Macbeth's "inordinate desire for worldly honors."[1] For Curry, following St. Thomas and the medieval view, honor is a temporal, a mutable, a worldly good. But for Shakespeare, and for Renaissance aristocratic society in general, the pagan-humanist attitudes toward honor are usually completely accepted. Honor is rarely deprecated as something temporal or worldly; on the contrary, most Renaissance moralists believed that through honor one achieved immortality. As Montaigne points out, Julius Caesar and other great men of antiquity con-

[1] Baton Rouge, 1937, p. 113.

tinued to live through the honor of their names more than
sixteen hundred years after their death.

The great cultural changes which took place, however slowly,
between the 13th and the 16th centuries, are clearly revealed
by the fact that the attitude of the Renaissance, apart from
purely Christian writings, reflects the Ciceronian antithesis between honor and riches. Shakespeare's King Henry the Fifth
seems to speak for his whole age in answer to the medieval
Christian attitude toward honor when he says to his men before
the battle of Agincourt:

> By Jove, I am not covetous for gold,
>
> But if it be a sin to covet honour,
> I am the most offending soul alive.
>   (IV. iii. 24, 28-29)

In the Renaissance merging of Christian and classical values,
Christian values have not maintained the dominant position
they held in the Middle Ages. In this speech, honor is being
viewed in the Roman manner as the most precious of man's
possessions; the medieval Christian attitude is being ignored.
This does not mean that King Henry the Fifth ceases to be a
Christian monarch; it simply means that he is adhering to a
dual system of values. That this is the typical Renaissance
solution appears in James the First's taking as his two major
concerns his conscience in the eyes of God and his reputation in
the eyes of the whole world. Shakespeare, reflecting the attitudes prevalent in his age, never refers to honor as worldly
honor, as something temporal and mutable. A great and fundamental shift of attitude is evident here if we consider the extent
to which Aquinas and Shakespeare differ in their attitudes
toward the permanence of honor. For Aquinas: "Man's highest
good must be supremely stable in human things: for it is natural
to desire unfailing endurance in one's goods. Now glory, which
consists in fame, is most unstable; since nothing is more change-

able than human opinion and praise."[2] For the Romans, for the Renaissance, and for Shakespeare, the typical attitude is one which associates honor and the idea of permanence. *The Sonnets* attempt to convey immortality through the praise bestowed by the poet. Likewise, in *Measure for Measure*, Isabella, who had been a novice at the beginning of the play, says to her brother, Claudio:

> O, I do fear thee, Claudio, and I quake,
> Lest thou a feverous life shouldst entertain,
> And six or seven winters more respect
> Than a perpetual honour. (III. i. 74-77)

There are relatively few lengthy references to the sentiment of honor in Shakespeare. But if we think of the Aristotelian definition of it—as an instinct which leads men to virtue and away from vice, as Rabelais rephrases it, or as the doing "the things uncommaunded which other folkes doe for fear of lawes," as Hurault restates it—then the sentiment of honor is manifested on almost every page of the Shakespearean text.[3] In the tragedies, in particular, the hero is frequently guided by a concern for his honor and by fear of shame. Hamlet, Lear, Antony, and even Macbeth do not seem to be guided primarily by the law. They obey the dictates of their own conscience and when they fail to adhere to their own ideals, they tend to rebuke themselves. Othello, especially, from the moment he first appears on the stage, seems to rise above the dictates of the law. When the concern to preserve honor and the passion of jealousy obliterate Othello's self-control, it is a cause for shocked comment, so great is the ironic contrast:

> Is this the noble Moor whom our full Senate
> Call all in all sufficient? Is this the nature
> Whom passion could not shake? Whose solid virtue
> The shot of accident nor dart of chance
> Could neither graze nor pierce? (IV. i. 275-279)

---

[2] *Summa Contra Gentiles*, III, 1, 29.
[3] *Gargantua and Pantagruel*, I, 57; *Discourses*, p. 64.

When Othello enters the bedroom to kill Desdemona, he displays once again the majestic poise and dignity he had manifested at the very beginning of the play. Without a trace of apparent jealousy, he asserts, "It is the cause, it is the cause, my soul." (V. ii. 1) But his passions are once again aroused when his innocent wife insists on defending Cassio. After the savage murder, when Othello discovers how terribly he has erred, he observes in regard to his own predicament:

> I am not valiant neither;
> But every puny whipster gets my sword.
> But why should honour outlive honesty?
> Let it go all. (V. ii. 243-246)

Othello is no longer the noble Moor, the all-in-all sufficient Renaissance man of honor. From here until the end of the play, his character fluctuates rapidly. The dignified, noble, courageous Othello of the opening scenes is replaced by the Othello who completely loses self-control in the great tide of remorse and anguish which overwhelms him. Then we have the Othello who reasserts his former prowess and dignity, and finally the Othello who, by taking his own life heroically, denies the right of the Venetian state to subject him to its laws. By this rapid contrasting of the dignified and honorable hero with the man who is but a hollow shell of his former self, Shakespeare makes us vividly conscious of all that is involved in the Renaissance concept of honor.

Othello is not the Senecan superman.[4] This great hero, whose every action had been motivated by his innate sense of righteousness, is a supreme dramatic embodiment of the pagan-humanist notion of man's potentialities for moral grandeur and dignity—a notion which the Renaissance had inherited from the whole pagan-humanist tradition, from Plato, Aristotle, Cicero, and the Stoics. Much as Shakespeare may circumscribe

---

[4] Ever since T. S. Eliot criticized Othello for his "Bovarysme," modern critics have been most harsh in their final judgment of Othello. Again and again, he has been criticized for his "egotism" and "theatrical gestures."

pagan-humanist ideals by giving his great tragic heroes flesh and blood, emotional warmth, and a unique personality, he is nonetheless through his realistic medium attempting to say something universal about man's inherent nobility and grandeur. Othello's every action, every motive, and every emotion are a direct expression of positive (generally speaking, pagan-humanist) values; when he becomes a man mad with savage jealousy, our reaction to this fact loses most of its meaning if it is dissociated from our image of what he was. ("That's he that was Othello.") (V. ii. 284)

Even when the Shakespearean tragic hero gives way to vice, the primary ethical criterion involved is his innate sense of honor and shame. The character of Antony is a particularly clear illustration of this point. Early in the play, when he is completely ensnared by his passion for Cleopatra and so obviously an example of the cardinal humanist vices of intemperance, of sensuality, and of epicureanism, he indicates by his behavior his awareness of his misconduct. As he embraces Cleopatra, he exclaims, "The nobleness of life/ Is to do thus." (I. i. 36-37) Humanist ideals are just as consciously defied here as Christian ideals are deliberately rejected when Faustus, in Marlowe's play, aspires after worldly pleasure. Antony is torn by inner conflict because his involvement in licentious pleasure forces him to act against his own keen sense of honor. Thus Cleopatra complains, "He was dispos'd to mirth; but on the sudden/ A Roman thought hath struck him." (I. ii. 86-87) When Antony hears what is happening in Rome in his absence, he decides to obey the call to duty, and remarks, "These strong Egyptian fetters I must break/ Or lose myself in dotage." (I. ii. 120-121) Later in the play Antony is to say: "If I lose mine honour,/ I lose myself." (III. iv. 22-23) In fact, the dramatic conflict is largely a conflict between the dual aspects of his personality, his honorable self and his epicurean, erotic self. Throughout the early scenes of the play, Cleopatra tries to persuade him not to leave her. The inner conflict taking place becomes evident in the ensuing dialogue:

ANT.   My precious queen, forbear,
And give true evidence to his love, which stands
An honourable trial.

CLEO.   So Fulvia told me.
I prithee turn aside and weep for her;
Then bid adieu to me, and say the tears
Belong to Egypt. Good now, play one scene
Of excellent dissembling, and let it look
Like perfect honour.

ANT.   You'll heat my blood. No more.

                            (I. iii. 73-80)

In the next scene, Caesar eulogizes the man who had once been the epitome of the Roman ideal of spartan austerity:

                          Antony,
Leave thy lascivious wassails. When thou once
Was beaten from Modena, where thou slew'st
Hirtius and Pansa, consuls, at thy heel
Did famine follow; whom thou fought'st against
(Though daintily brought up) with patience more
Than savages could suffer. Thou didst drink
The stale of horses and the gilded puddle
Which beasts would cough at.

                    On the Alps
It is reported thou didst eat strange flesh,
Which some did die to look on. And all this
(It wounds thine honour that I speak it now)
Was borne so like a soldier that thy cheek
So much as lank'd not. (I. iv. 55-63, 66-71)

This description, like that of Othello of his former life as a soldier, lays great stress on the spartan qualities of willing endurance of that discomfort which inevitably goes with the military life. Othello and Antony are both esteemed for their great soldiership; but whereas Othello, requesting permission to bring his love with him to Cyprus, can assert without reservation that the temptations of amorous desires will never interfere with his performance of his duties as a soldier, Antony has to tear himself from the lap of Egypt's widow. But to point out this major distinction between the love of Othello and Desdemona on the one hand and of Antony and Cleopatra on the other is not to deny Antony's strong sense of honor. Throughout the play he is torn by his conflicting desires, until at the end his lustful attachment is transformed into an honorable, constant fidelity. There is nothing of the epicurean and fickle and sensuous in the final scenes of the play; romantic love it may be, but it is as noble and enduring as the links which bind any of Shakespeare's lovers. At the conclusion, every speech is so composed as to emphasize the great transformations which have taken place in the hero and the heroine. The shameful aspect of Antony's passion for Cleopatra has disappeared; the heroic suicides of the lovers attest as much to the nobility of their attachment as to their determination to preserve their honor by evading Caesar's triumphs. And so, as in *Othello*, the hero's final action evinces that Aristotelian sense of honor which does things "uncommaunded which other folke doe for fear of lawes."[5] In Dercetas' words, informing Caesar of Antony's death:

> He is dead, Caesar,
> Not by a public minister of justice
> Nor by a hired knife; but that self hand
> Which writ his honour in the acts it did
> Hath, with the courage which the heart did lend it,
> Splitted the heart. (V. i. 19-24)

Although Aristotle had not looked with favor on suicide, the motivation here accords almost precisely with the fundamental Aristotelian distinction between the aristocrats and the masses. The distinction, which was one of the commonest of Renaissance humanist maxims and therefore possibly a part of Shakespeare's reading even if he knew "small Latine and lesse Greeke," argued that the aristocrat would be self-motivated by

[5] Hurault, p. 64.

213

his innate sense of honor and by his desire to avoid shame and reproach; whereas "theories . . . are powerless to stimulate the mass of mankind to moral nobility. For it is the nature of the many to be amenable to fear but not to a sense of honour, and to abstain from evil not because of its baseness but because of the penalties it entails."[6]

Hamlet's last soliloquy, in which he ponders his own indecisiveness and contrasts it with the resolution of Fortinbras, dwells on the same sentiment of honor and shame. It is shame, not fear, which finally drives Lear to madness. Brutus, like Hamlet, ponders the pros and cons of suicide; at first, he decides against such "cowardly" and "base" action, but then he reverses his decision because he feels he could not endure the shame of going bound to Rome. When Juliet berates Romeo for his slaying of her kinsman, her nurse adds her own invective, and finally says, "Shame come to Romeo!" Juliet abruptly replies,

> Blister'd be thy tongue
> For such a wish! He was not born to shame
> Upon his brow shame is asham'd to sit;
> For 'tis a throne where honour may be crowned
> Sole monarch of the universal earth.
>
> (III. ii. 90-94)

Even Macbeth—even at the very end of the play—is still motivated by the sense of honor and shame. When he discovers that Macduff is not born of woman, as Thomas Whately observes in his excellent comparison of *King Richard the Third* and *Macbeth*, the hero feels "his sense of honour being touched by the threat, to be made the shew and the gaze of the time"; and as "he disdains the thought of disgrace" so he dies as becomes a soldier.[7] Whately is a good example of how much closer some of the critics of the 18th century are to the basic values and psychological motivation of the plays than is such a scholarly 20th century critic as Curry, whose greater historical

---

[6] *Nicomachean Ethics* x. 9.
[7] *Shakespeare Criticism*, ed. D. Nicoll Smith, Oxford World Classics, p. 83.

awareness leads him farther from, rather than closer to, the text.

In *The Courtier's Academie,* one of the courtiers states: "Universally therefore wee will affirme that honour is the most precious of all goods externall."[8] This commonplace, which can be found in any of the books on moral philosophy written in the Renaissance, is frequently echoed in Shakespeare. Hector, for example, tells Cassandra when she tries to prevent him from going forth into battle, that

> Mine honour keeps the weather of my fate.
> Life every man holds dear, but the dear man
> Holds honour far more precious-dear than life.
> (V. iii. 26-28)

Brutus, holding the same view, consents to join in Cassius' cause, as long as it leads to the common good; "for let the gods so speed me as I love/ The name of honour more than I fear death." (I. ii. 88-89) Hermione courageously defends herself against her husband's accusation that she is an adulteress by asserting to the court audience:

> For behold me—
> A fellow of the royal bed, which owe
> A moiety of the throne, a great king's daughter,
> The mother to a hopeful prince—here standing
> To prate and talk for life and honour fore
> Who please to come and hear. For life, I prize it
> As I weigh grief, which I would spare. For honour,
> 'Tis a derivative from me to mine,
> And only that I stand for. (III. ii. 38-46)

Since honor was so highly esteemed, not only one's own life, but also the lives of those close and dear to oneself, might be sacrificed in order to maintain one's reputation. This conflict

---

[8] Count Romei, p. 79. One should compare carefully this quotation with that following, from *Troilus and Cressida*. Undeniably the former is an echo of Aristotle, although it is impossible to know where Shakespeare picked up his restatement of the same idea. Shakespeare's formulations are rarely, in any formal sense, philosophical. The contrast to Dante in this respect is striking.

between love and honor, a source of major conflict in some of Corneille's tragedies, provides Shakespeare with minor scenes of great dramatic intensity. In the last act of *King Richard the Second*, for example, the Duke of York discovers that his son has plotted against King Henry's life. The duke prepares to disclose his treachery to the king; his wife pleads with him to "hide the trespass of thine own." (V. ii. 89) York ignores the mother's pleas, but finds that Aumerle has preceded him to court and extracted a promise of pardon from the king. York asks the king to retract his promise—indeed, implores him to take his own son's life. Such behavior may be incomprehensible to the modern mind, but this is simply because we dismiss the commonplace that honor is the most precious of man's goods as a mere commonplace, and fail to realize that an Elizabethan would plead to have his own son killed in order to restore the honor of his family. As York says,

> And he shall spend mine honour with his shame,
> As thriftless sons their scraping father's gold,
> Mine honour lives when his dishonour dies,
> Or my sham'd life in his dishonour dies,
> Thou kill'st me in his life. (V. iii. 68-72)

Aristotle had said that the good man "will face danger in a great cause, and when so doing will be ready to sacrifice his life, since he holds that life is not worth having at every price."[9] It is in this spirit that Shakespeare's characters place their love of honor before their love of life. Coriolanus, for example, appeals to those patricians who prefer "a noble life before a long" to take sides with him against the people. (III. i. 153) Antony completely identifies life and honor in the previously cited lines: "If I lose mine honour/ I lose myself." (III. iv. 22-23) Later in the play, after he has met defeat at Caesar's hands, he prepares to fight him again and exclaims,

> Or I will live,
> Or bathe my dying honour in the blood
> Shall make it live again. (IV. ii. 5-7)

[9] *Nicomachean Ethics* IV. 3.

Mowbray tells Richard the Second that he must fight Bolingbroke in order to prove that Bolingbroke is a slanderer since
"Mine honour is my life. Both grow in one;/ Take honour
from me, and my life is done." (I. i. 182-183)

In no single play is it more important for the modern reader
to remind himself constantly of the tremendous importance the
Renaissance attached to honor than in *King Lear*. Although
the word is seldom mentioned, the Jacobean audience would
have considered every slighting of Lear's royal dignity by his
daughters a direct attack upon his honor. When Lear finally
arrives before Gloucester's castle and finds his messenger in the
stocks, it is obviously his honor which is at stake. Hence, from
the Jacobean point of view his indignation is completely justified. Indeed, Kent had remarked as they placed him in the
stocks:

> "You shall do small respect, show too bold malice
> Against the grace and person of my master,
> Stocking his messenger." (II. ii. 137-139)

To Lear it is incredible that his daughters should place him
so repeatedly in an ignominious position. The enormity of this
particular indignity provokes a comment which expresses not
simply his own high indignation, but also the precise attitude
of an Elizabethan or Jacobean audience. Lear exclaims: " 'Tis
worse than murther/ To do upon respect such violent outrage."
(II. iv. 23-24) For the men of the Renaissance, loss of esteem
was often considered a greater injury than loss of life—certainly greater than a bodily injury. Granville-Barker's previ-
ously-mentioned suggestion that Lear's slapping of Oswald,
after the steward had insulted him, was an outrage reflects our
modern point of view, which tends to consider physical violence
much more aggressive than the mere hurling of insults. To
appreciate *King Lear* properly, we should think of the Jacobean
audience shuddering with horror and indignation each time his
daughters heap a new insult on his head. Shakespeare's audience
would not have had the least sympathy with the wicked daugh-

ters. Yet modern critics can find cause for great sympathy with Goneril and Regan. Granville-Barker writes, "If the quarrel between King Lear and his two daughters had been brought into the law courts, counsels' speeches for Regan and Goneril would have been interesting. . . . A jury of men and women of common sense might well give their verdict against Lear; and we can hear the judge ruling upon the one point of law in his favor with grave misgiving that he is doing him no good."[10] Granville-Barker goes on to say that the daughters do become fiendishly cruel in the later part of the play. But his suggestion that Lear errs as grievously as they do in the first two acts is hardly the judgment a Jacobean audience would have made. The insults which they heap on their king, their father, their benefactor, would have been considered just as cruel, just as fiendish, as their plucking out of Gloucester's eyes. Lear's protest that their insults are worse than murder means just that.

The sentiment of honor was not a passive sentiment. *The Courtier's Academie* had defined it as an "ardent heate which enflameth the minde of man to glorious enterprises."[11] It is true that in Shakespeare's tragedies the hero is not usually searching for glory and renown; the central concerns reflect more mature considerations and more complex definitions of the term honor. Nonetheless, in the character of Hotspur, we sense the youthful, impassioned enthusiasm of the seeker after glory. Here, as in so many other instances, Cicero's *Offices* provides suggestive definitions which may help us comprehend Shakespeare's characters. Cicero comments: "but the more a man is endowed with these finer virtues—temperance, self-control, and that very justice about which so much has already been said—the more he deserves to be favored. I do not mention fortitude, for a courageous spirit in a man who has not attained perfection and ideal wisdom is generally too impetuous."[12] Hotspur's character is so well known as to need little discussion. His impatience with the temporizing of his fellow conspirators, his

[10] *Prefaces to Shakespeare*, I, 301-302.
[11] Count Romei, p. 78.
[12] I. 15.

itching eagerness to meet the Prince of Wales expressed in "I am on fire/ To hear this rich reprisal is so nigh," (IV. i. 117-118) and his final remarks at the time of his death, "I better brook the loss of brittle life/ Than those proud titles thou hast won of me," (V. iv. 78-79) all suggest the impetuous quality of one so inflamed by the desire for honor that nothing else in life matters. Particularly in the famous speech, "By heaven, methinks it were an easy leap/ To pluck bright honour from the pale-fac'd moon," (I. iii. 201-202) we feel the youthful ardor with which many an English nobleman's son sought honor fighting for king and country in battles on the continent or in the great sea fights with the Spanish.

In the discussion of honor as the most precious of man's possessions, it was suggested that the Renaissance man of honor was completely without fear of death if he felt his honor was at stake. Indeed, if one rigidly followed the pagan-humanist ethics, no fear was permissible except the fear of disgrace. How, then, can we account for Shakespeare's sympathetic treatment of Claudio's apprehensions of death in *Measure for Measure*?

To understand this matter properly, let us consider the attitude toward death found in Shakespeare's plays. Aristotle had said that death "is the end, and when a man is dead, nothing, we think, either good or evil can befall him any more."[13] From this typically classical point of view had arisen the frequent comparison of death with sleep, with "peaceful oblivion." This is the attitude reflected in Hamlet's famous soliloquy on suicide. But Hamlet in his musings passes on to the observation that "the dread of something after death . . . puzzles the will." (III. i. 78, 80) A similar ambivalence is apparent in the Duke's speech in *Measure for Measure*. The Duke, disguised as a friar, tells Claudio that man is

by no means valiant;
For thou dost fear the soft and tender fork
Of a poor worm. Thy best of rest is sleep,
And that thou oft provok'st; yet grossly fear'st
Thy death, which is no more. (III. i. 15-19)

[13] *Nicomachean Ethics* III. 5.

Shakespeare's most poetic passages on death seem to involve two attitudes; one in which death is accepted as something soothing and restful, a balm from the worries and anguish of life, and another in which the quality of the poetry suggests that the poet's imagination has been deeply stirred by fear of the decay of the body and by uncertainty as to the fate of the soul.[14] As Willard Farnham points out in *The Medieval Heritage of Elizabethan Tragedy*, this second attitude is not to be discovered in the writings of antiquity for it is peculiar to the Gothic imagination.

In the third act of *Measure for Measure* a debate takes place between Claudio and Isabella as to whether he is to lose his life or she is to lose her virginity to Angelo in order to obtain pardon for Claudio. The second act closes with Isabella's assurance to Angelo that her brother has such "a mind of honour" that he will gladly sacrifice his life to preserve his sister's chastity. (II. iv. 179) Yet in the next act Claudio, at first assenting to his own death, gradually weakens and finally pleads with his sister:

> Sweet sister, let me live!
> What sin you do to save a brother's life,
> Nature dispenses with the deed so far
> That it becomes a virtue. (III. i. 133-136)

Isabella promptly calls her brother a faithless coward. And so he is, by all the ethical canons of our recent discussion. He has shown himself to be ignoble, craven, and timorous. Yet somehow this is not our reaction, for Claudio wins our sympathy as much as his sister. In the realm of heroic ideals, Isabella is quite right to tell her brother that for him to consent to the sacrifice "would bark your honour from that trunk you bear/ And leave you naked." (III. i. 72-73)

But Shakespeare also appeals to us on a naturalistic, amoral plane. Even Aristotle, in his insistence that the truly brave man would not fear death, had admitted that "the most terrible

---

[14] Willard Farnham, *The Medieval Heritage of Elizabethan Tragedy*, Berkeley, 1936, p. 422.

thing of all is death."[15] In giving expression to man's natural
love of life and fear of death, Shakespeare has written some of
his most magnificent poetry. With the Isabella-Claudio episode,
as in Hamlet's famous soliloquy, he awakens the fear of death
latent in all of us; the Duke, for example, in enumerating the
reasons why man should not fear death, arouses precisely those
emotions he thinks to allay. To say, as he does, that men fear
the tender fork of a worm is to stir up in us that fear. When
Isabella tells Claudio that she fears "Lest thou a feverous life
shouldst entertain,/ And six or seven winters more respect/
Than a perpetual honour," (III. i. 75-77) Shakespeare is again
arousing our great love of that feverish life. Moreover, further
to stir up these feelings in us, he has Isabella herself unkindly
point out to her brother that the "sense of death is most in
apprehension" and speak of the pang that every living creature
feels at having its life snuffed out. (III. i. 78-81) Shakespeare,
poetically and imaginatively, is here working on the fear of
death which exists in every man. References to "a perpetual
honour" seem ironically cold in comparison. By the time of
Claudio's great speech, we are at least half persuaded in
Claudio's favor. And then one hears those terrible lines:

> Ay, but to die, and go we know not where;
> To lie in cold obstruction and to rot;
> This sensible warm motion to become
> A kneaded clod; and the delighted spirit
> To bathe in fiery floods, or to reside
> In thrilling region of thick-ribbed ice. (III. i. 118-123)

Shakespeare has seized hold of deep-seated fears in each and
every member of the audience; honor and nobility become,
momentarily, meaningless abstractions. By now we are fully
involved in Claudio's predicament, since it is our predicament,
too. So we set aside our high moral convictions and allow our
natural, instinctive emotions full sway. Now we are ready to
accept Claudio's conclusion (Hamlet's as well):

[15] *Nicomachean Ethics* III. 6.

> 'Tis too horrible
> The weariest and most loathed worldly life
> That age, ache, penury, and imprisonment
> Can lay on nature is a paradise
> To what we fear of death. (III. i. 128-132)

Shakespeare in this scene arouses our sympathy both for Claudio's predicament and for Isabella's. Elsewhere he presents heroes who are utterly contemptuous of those who fear death; here he presents a hero who gives way to his apprehension of its terrors and whose refusal to be heroic seems natural and inevitable. Instead of a burning desire for honor, there is a passionate attachment to life. Does not this mean that Shakespeare is an objective dramatist, who is aware of the relative nature of all things, and who can present a great number of points of view with equal sympathy?

Any dogmatic, absolute answer to this question would be rash. But it can be safely pointed out that Shakespeare does not champion all points of view with equal enthusiasm. In *Measure for Measure*, as in *Twelfth Night*, the hypocritical Puritan is presented without the least suggestion of sympathy. Sir Toby Belch's retort, "Dost thou think, because thou art virtuous, there shall be no more cakes and ale?" (II. iii. 123-125) is precisely the attitude of the lower class characters toward Angelo in *Measure for Measure*, and becomes our attitude toward the excessively self-righteous and ascetic character. Shakespeare never shows great sympathy for the person whose "blood is very snow-broth," whether it be Angelo, or on another level, the cold and efficient Caesar pronouncing judgment on Antony's failings. Definite Shakespearean values exist which, while difficult to define, are still similar to those in the works on moral philosophy of his age. In particular, we find a definite idea of the nature of evil. As in the Renaissance treatises on ethics, malicious deceit, ingratitude, envy, and excessive ambition are clearly viewed as vicious traits, and their viciousness is never condoned, or approved. Nor are the faults which many of the tragic heroes possess equated with them. There is a very definite hierarchy of values, of virtues and vices; it is essential to gain as clear a view of them as possible, or else we shall be arguing, with Granville-Barker, that the malicious deceit, the ingratitude, the lack of respect for an aged parent—the multiple vices which Goneril and Regan display in the first two acts of *King Lear*—are no greater faults than those Lear commits. Granville-Barker argues, "They played the hypocrite for a kingdom; but which of us might not?"[16] With this light dismissal of evil, Lear's indignation loses its point and he becomes a senile old man. But the whole of Renaissance ethics rested solidly on Cicero's definition: "While wrong may be done, then, in either of two ways, that is, by force or by fraud, both are bestial: fraud seems to belong to the cunning fox, force to the lion; both are wholly unworthy of man, but fraud is the more contemptible. But of all forms of injustice, none is more flagrant than that of the hypocrite who, at the very moment when he is most false, makes it his business to appear virtuous."[17] This is the situation at the end of the first scene of *King Lear*. To the Jacobean audience, Goneril and Regan were practising this "greatest of villainies." However difficult it may be to define fully the Shakespearean notion of good and evil, it can be said that there is not the least tolerance for this sort of hypocrisy—it is clearly to be considered vicious, and adequate justification for Lear's righteous indignation, his "barbaric" cursing, and his even more "barbaric" disowning of his daughters. The Shakespearean audience's attitude of profound sympathy for Lear and of hatred for his two daughters can be clearly discerned, since it is reflected in the above passage from Cicero, and can be seen, too, in Guevara's typically Renaissance and humanist definition of ingratitude: "Vice for vice, and evill for evill, there is none in this world so evill as the ingratefull man. And of this it commeth that the humane and tender hart doth pardon all injuries, except ingratitude, the which he never forgetteth."[18]

[16] *Prefaces to Shakespeare*, I, 302.   [17] *De Officiis*, I. 13.
[18] *The Familiar Epistles*, p. 71. Cf. Chapter 1, pp. 64, 65.

Shakespeare's characters are, then, to be judged on two planes: the one involving the definitions of the classical virtues and vices which constituted Renaissance moral philosophy; the other involving an amoral, naturalistic attitude, which views man's human emotions, his love of life, his yielding to the pleasures of the flesh, his shrinking from his deep-seated fears of old age and death, with sympathy and tolerance. It is on this second plane, in large part, that we judge Claudio—and then his reluctance to give up life, like his initial fault of lechery, becomes a minor aberration almost to be condoned. On this level, Angelo, like Malvolio, becomes an object of scorn, exasperation, and ridicule. By magnifying man's petty weaknesses so that they become major vices, Shakespeare's self-righteous Philistines reveal a basic lack of humanity so that instinctively we side with Claudio, Lucio, Pompey, Sir Toby Belch, and Maria against them.

These attitudes come particularly into play in our judgment of Sir John Falstaff as he appears in *King Henry the Fourth, Part I*. He seems to be Shakespeare's summation of this natural view of life and defense of it. Sir John gains our sympathy from the start; indeed, we admire him for his irony and wit, his sanity and common sense. But it should be noted that when we first become acquainted with him he is not really malicious. He does not defy Shakespeare's general conception of good and evil; he ignores it. Liar and hypocrite he is, but not with malicious intent. As he is first presented to us, we lay aside our usual moral judgment. He seems a necessary counterbalance to Shakespeare's idealized conception of what man can be, for he says, in effect, that all of us have foibles and weaknesses which have to be recognized and freely admitted. Yet he exists side by side with characters who embody Shakespeare's conception of our nobler capabilities. Falstaff's existence, and our liking for him, does not negate this other view. He epitomizes the Chaucerian side of Shakespeare—but to emphasize him at the expense of Shakespeare's other great figures would be to deny the extent to which Shakespeare's view of life surpasses Chaucer's.

Falstaff exists in a sequence of chronicle histories which includes such diverse characters as Richard the Second, Bolingbroke, Prince Hal, and Hotspur, all of whom, in varying degrees, evoke feelings of sympathy, liking, and admiration. This means that there is diversity and breadth to Shakespeare's view of life; he does indeed seem to be championing many different points of view. But this does not mean that Shakespeare's attitude is relativistic or neutral. Certain basic moral assumptions are involved in our judgment of Richard the Second and Bolingbroke: insofar as Richard the Second is a weakling, we do not feel admiration; insofar as he shows the capacity for imagination, perspective, and great inward suffering, a sort of admiration is aroused. But it is not the same degree or quality of emotion as is involved in our response to Hamlet, Lear, or Othello, who, in different ways, are comparable with Richard because they, too, are much-imposed-upon heroes.

Our response to Falstaff as he first appears to us eschews moral approval or disapproval. When he says to Hal before the battle, "I would 'twere bedtime, Hal, and all well," we do not ask whether or not this statement is cowardly. (V. i. 125-126) It appeals instinctively to a response within ourselves, which empathically is in complete accord. When Falstaff soliloquizes on honor, our reaction is similar to that toward Claudio in *Measure for Measure*. If the Renaissance code of honor were the only criterion by which to judge, such attitudes could only be considered ignoble, craven, and dishonorable. But these attitudes—the amoral responses of our natural human passions—appeal to us on an instinctive level which precedes the formulation of moral judgments. If they involved a cynical denial of ethical values, as in Iago's cool and contemptuous dismissal of Cassio's concern about loss of reputation, our response would be quite different. Iago's statement hurls a direct challenge to any moral view of life and leads us immediately to form a judgment for or against him. But when Falstaff looks at the corpse of Sir Walter Blunt or Hotspur, there is no such cynicism. The response is natural, spontaneous, human. The audience shares his involuntary shudder as he looks at the corpses and a part of ourselves concurs inevitably with his sentiments: "I like not such grinning honour, as Sir Walter hath. Give me life; which if I can save, so; if not, honour comes unlook'd for, and there's an end." (V. iii. 62-65) A moral evaluation of life, and an amoral, naturalistic acceptance of it exist side by side in Shakespeare. Neither by itself would be a fair, or a complete, description of his *Weltanschauung*.

THE INDIVIDUAL VIRTUES

According to one of the most popular of Elizabethan commonplaces, as we have seen, virtue and honor were as one, as inseparable as the body and its shadow. Hence, in discussing Shakespeare's concept of honor, it is essential also to examine his notion of virtue. Once again let it be said that the Christian element in Shakespeare is not the dominant one. The scale here is tipped as much in favor of pagan humanism as it is tipped in favor of Christianity in the case of Dante or Milton. The cardinal Christian virtues of piety and humility are rarely referred to by name in the five great tragedies, and the central religious concepts of holiness, saintliness, and salvation are relegated to the "back shop" mentioned by Villey in his discussion of Renaissance values.[19] Santayana states flatly, in "The Absence of Religion in Shakespeare," that "There are only two or three short passages in the plays, and one sonnet, in which true religious feeling seem to break forth."[20] Santayana goes much too far here. He leaves out, for example, Portia's speech on mercy in *The Merchant of Venice*. Certainly Lear's attainment of greater humility after the storm scene indicates that his initial arrogance has been purged through suffering. This may or may not be an expression of Christian humility. In any case, it is akin to it in spirit, although it also resembles the purgation of the hero in Greek tragedy. (I shall not attempt to answer

[19] See quotation on p. 57 from Villey on the nature of Renaissance values. See also section on Christian themes in *King Leir* and *King Lear* at end of Chapter 9, below.
[20] Singer, p. 138.

the complex question as to whether or not the religious view of life and the tragic view of life are compatible.)

Quantitative measurement of the extent to which Shakespeare makes use of the Christian virtues is impossible—the classical virtues of gentility, affability, and mercy blend too easily (and very frequently in Renaissance moral treatises) with the Christian virtues of mercy and charity to make it possible to separate the two strands completely. But it can be stated that by all odds the greatest proportion of Shakespeare's virtues are classical in origin; it is only the extent of the area in which Christian and classical virtues blend together which is in question. Santayana suggests in the essay mentioned that Shakespeare had to choose between Christianity and nothing—and chose nothing. T. S. Eliot, in his invidious comparisons between Dante (a great artist backed by the great spiritual thought of St. Thomas Aquinas) and Shakespeare (a great artist backed by the inferior moral thought of Machiavelli, Montaigne, and Seneca) also implies that Shakespeare had to choose between Christianity and nihilism. Eliot even goes so far as to suggest that the Marlovian hero is preferable to Shakespeare's because Marlowe's protagonists deliberately defy Christian values and thus indicate a possible awareness of their damnation.[21] These attitudes of Santayana and Eliot almost summarize the popular critical fallacies in our century's view of the Renaissance and Shakespeare.

The concept of honor and nobility, as we have seen, stems principally from a system of values which is largely independent of the Christian ethics yet is as positive, affirmative, and social in its implications as it is individualistic. (Eliot, whose views I shall treat more fully in Chapter 8, sees only the extreme individualism of the Renaissance.) Shakespeare's morality, in other words, is derived from the philosophy of Renaissance pagan humanism. The ethics of Plato, Aristotle, and Cicero (and, to a lesser extent, the Stoics) were amalgamated into a definite

---

[21] "Shakespeare and the Stoicism of Seneca," *Selected Essays*, p. 114.

system of values—one which, however "muddled" and "derivative," was essentially a reiteration of those values which had upheld the great civilizations of Greece and Rome for a good many centuries without benefit of clergy. The virtues of the Shakespearean hero, and of his virtuous associates, are drawn predominantly from the classical ethics; the vices of the villains come almost equally from that source. With the exception of King Lear, the cardinal Christian virtue of humility is not of major importance in his shaping of the tragic hero, nor is the greatest of evils in the Christian ethics, pride, the fundamental vice which motivates his villains in the tragedies. (Aristocratic pride is, to be sure, the major tragic flaw in the character of Coriolanus.) Shakespeare is concerned, by and large, with another system of values.

We need not dwell on the so familiar "courtier, scholar, soldier" depicted by Shakespeare in his various plays as the embodiment of the Renaissance ideal of the well-rounded gentleman. But it is important to make explicit the fact that Shakespeare's hero, his man of honor, is primarily drawn along classical lines. Chapman's heroes are so explicitly classical and so obviously comparable to the heroes of antiquity that the resemblance is not missed; in the case of Shakespeare, it is missed, to a considerable extent, because it is too obvious. The virtues of valor, justice, wisdom, liberality, gratitude, modesty, courtesy, constancy, resolution, and greatness of heart are referred to so carelessly, so unsystematically, that we hardly notice that Shakespeare is dealing with the classical virtues. Only occasionally, outside of the Roman plays, is this made explicit, as in the passage cited early in this chapter where Bassanio described Antonio to Portia as a friend whose honor is so great as to be "ancient Roman." (III. ii. 292-296)

Another reason that these virtues are overlooked in Shakespeare is, of course, the dramatic medium. Spenser's indebtedness to the classical virtues is obvious; when he writes of the humanist virtue of friendship, the particular book of *The Faerie Queene* is labeled with that title. The didactic intent is as evident as when Montaigne writes an essay on friendship. But when Shakespeare wishes to embody the same virtue in appropriate dramatic form, and explain the same Renaissance concept of friendship—that a friend is a second self—he has Horatio reach for the poisoned cup with the exclamation that he is "more an antique Roman than a Dane." (V. ii. 352) Shakespeare is just as concerned with the virtue in question as is Spenser or Montaigne, but there is no tag or label to identify it. Horatio's impulsive gesture is a perfect dramatic presentation of the classical ideal of friendship—an ideal which the Renaissance derived from the entire pagan-humanist tradition.

Let us now consider the various classical virtues presented by Shakespeare.

Magnificence. Because the classical virtues are not labeled, the modern critic often considers a particular action blameworthy—which it would be by purely ascetic religious standards, although highly praiseworthy when judged by the pagan humanist. Thus, for example, Cleopatra says,

> Show me, my women, like a queen. Go fetch
> My best attires. I am again for Cydnus,
> To meet Mark Antony. (V. ii. 227-229)

This is an excellent example of the Aristotelian virtue of magnificence (the doing of things on a large scale and in a brilliant way for honor's sake). Granville-Barker, judging apparently by puritanical Christian standards, describes this action as "a flash of glorious, of transcendent vanity."[22] This would hardly have been the reaction of the Elizabethan or Jacobean audience; as Segar observes, "the magnificence of her Majesties Court is equall or exceeding the Courts of other Kings her noble predecessors."[23]

Wisdom. Lack of wisdom is a central theme of the first scene of King Lear. Lear's error of judgment, in not being able to distinguish between his faithful daughter and the hypocritical

---

[22] *Prefaces to Shakespeare,* I, 446.
[23] *The Booke of Honor and Armes,* p. 100.

flatterers, accords with Aristotle's dictum in the *Poetics* that the hero should be a man who "through no badness or villainy of his own . . . falls into . . . misfortune, but rather through some flaw in him, he being one of those who are in high station and good fortune."[24] (In general, it should be noted, Shakespearean tragedy seems to defy Aristotle's categories.) In the fourth scene of the first act, Lear already realizes how terribly he has erred. He contrasts the hideous ingratitude of Goneril with Cordelia's "small fault." In anguished remorse, he exclaims,

> O Lear, Lear, Lear!
> Beat at this gate that let thy folly in
> [strikes his head]
> And thy dear judgment out! Go, go, my people.
> (I. iv. 292-294)

Whether we are intended to feel that this folly indicates a "puerile intellect," as Wilson Knight suggests, seems dubious.[25] A few lines earlier, Lear had remarked: "by the marks of sovereignty,/ Knowledge, and reason, I should be false persuaded/ I had daughters." (I. iv. 253-255) Earlier in the same scene, when the Knight pointed out to Lear that there was a general abatement of ceremonious affection, Lear indicated that he was well aware of the state of things. When the Knight adds that Lear's fool has pined away since Cordelia has been gone, Lear's response, "No more of that; I have noted it well," (I. iv. 81) hardly suggests insensitivity or puerility of intellect. Edgar's, Gloucester's, and Othello's credulity have likewise been taken as signs of a fundamental stupidity. But for the Elizabethans to be open, free, and generous was, on the contrary, a sign of great nobility. The issue at stake is moral, not intellectual. As Sidney observes, "The only disadvantage of an honest heart is credulity."[26] The remedy against credulity was to be distrustful of others; but such suspiciousness would be mean and ignoble. Needless to say, our feelings of admiration for a particular hero

---

[24] *The Poetics* . . . , Loeb Library, Cambridge, Mass., 1953, XIII.
[25] *The Wheel of Fire*, p. 162.   [26] *Aphorisms*, I, 23.

are necessarily weakened if we think of him as stupid. (This remark particularly applies to contemporary Anglo-Saxon critics of Shakespeare who have been steeped in the French tradition in which lack of erudition, sophistication, and intellectual brilliance are often considered unforgivable sins. Even Aldous Huxley, who has foregone any rationalistic approach to the truth, attests to the premium 20th century British intellectuals place on being a sophisticated man.)

Intellectual brilliance and worldly sophistication are not the primary qualities involved in Shakespeare's notion of the good man. Moral earnestness and goodness of heart are more important attributes; for better or worse, the modern mind seems to revolt against these qualities, so sentimentally presented to us by our Victorian grandparents. Hence, we sometimes find a contemporary reviewer, in the sophisticated periodicals of our century, hardly able to cover his yawn when he writes about a Shakespearean revival. This is the temper of our time.[27] It is perhaps safe to generalize that man will never again be able to take moral ideas as seriously as the Greeks and Elizabethans did. Our prejudices, nevertheless, should not lead us to distort the work of art. Nothing in the text of *Lear* indicates that Gloucester or Edgar is to be considered stupid; a simple, plain Englishman, with no great subtlety of character, yes, but not stupid. Granville-Barker repeatedly suggests that Lear is almost in his dotage, yet he himself admits that Lear's defense against his daughters rests in "irony, the fine mind's weapon."[28] Irony is, indeed, an important mode of expression for the Shakespearean tragic hero; through it he is communicating the ambiguity, the complexity, and the subtlety of his emotional response to his predicament. Of all the Greek philosophers, Socrates appeals to us most because, as the unimaginative Cicero himself surprisingly observes, he was a mighty artist at hiding his meaning under witty ironies and droll expressions. This is precisely the

---

[27] See Joseph Wood Krutch, *The Modern Temper*, New York, 1933. (Krutch analyzes the reasons why modern writers usually fail when they attempt to write in the tragic vein.)

[28] *Prefaces to Shakespeare*, I, 287.

quality we feel in Richard the Second, in Hamlet, in Lear (and in his fool, who is a sort of reflection of himself). Othello is less capable of irony, but he is cruelest to Desdemona in the scene in which he imagines her as the madam of a brothel, where his sarcasm is just as bitter as Hamlet's against the innocent Ophelia, and where he is using the "fine mind's weapon" as the means of release of a small portion of the intense, inner pain. This resort to irony on the part of the Shakespearean hero is hardly an indication of stupidity.

Justice. Justice is the central theme of Plato's *Republic.* Critics, however, are in disagreement over what Plato meant when he tried to define the nature of the just man. Cicero is not quite so perplexing. He lumps honesty, faith, trust, liberality and gratitude together as essential components of this virtue. But his most important requirement is that no one should do any hurt to another, unless by way of reasonable and just retribution for some injury received from him. Surprising as it may seem to the modern reader or critic, justice is a matter of central concern in the concluding scenes of *Othello.* When the protagonist enters the bedroom, for example, he is obviously trying to maintain his poise and dignity, and to base his actions on what appear to him to be objective reasons. Hence, he exclaims, "It is the cause." (V. ii. 1) In similar vein, we soon discover that the sight of the sleeping Desdemona almost persuades "Justice to break her sword." (V. ii. 17) Later, when the truth of Desdemona's innocence begins to dawn on him, he continues to point to what he considers a solid ethical basis for his behavior. He exclaims:

> O, I were damn'd beneath all depth in hell
> But that I did proceed upon just ground
> To this extremity. (V. ii. 137-139)

The concept of justice is, therefore, of paramount importance throughout the entire scene. If Desdemona has slept with Cassio and ruined her husband's honor, his murder of her, at least according to the Renaissance code of honor, would be reasonable and just retribution. English law did not, of course, allow it, but, as Fynes Moryson points out, the Italians commonly took private revenge for adultery upon just grounds of jealousy.

Othello's statement at the end of the play is thus supremely comprehensible, at least in terms of Renaissance ethics. In response to the question, "What shall be said to thee?", he asserts:

> Why, anything;
> An honourable murderer, if you will;
> For naught did I in hate, but all in honour.
> (V. ii. 293-396)

The Jacobean audience would immediately relate Othello's claim that he acted honorably to his belief that he had proceeded on just grounds—and they would, at least partially, exonerate him for what must seem to our humanitarian age a hideous "crime." They would feel that, as in Lear's rejection of Cordelia, an error of judgment is at the root of Othello's dreadful deed. Othello has human failings and he becomes almost savage when he is mad with jealousy, but he is neither vicious nor wicked. This is made explicit when Lodovico states: "You shall close prisoner rest/ Till that the nature of your *fault* be known/ To the Venetian state." (V. ii. 335-337) [Italics mine.]

Bounty. Bounty and liberality are frequently referred to in the plays of Shakespeare. Cicero had defined this aspect of justice: "For generosity is of two kinds: doing a kindness and requiting one. Whether we do the kindness or not is optional; but to fail to requite one is not allowable to a good man."[29] For the Roman and Renaissance moralists, nothing was considered more contemptible than to be stingy and avaricious. Yet these same moralists insisted that one should be prudent in bestowing gifts and favors. Hence Ulysses' praise of Troilus: "For what he has he gives, what thinks he shows,/ Yet gives he not till judgment guide his bounty." (IV. v. 101-102)

The bountiful qualities of the protagonist of *Antony and*

---

[29] *De Officiis*, I. 7.

Cleopatra receive especial comment since they counterbalance, at least to some extent, the hero's many defects. When Eno-barbus deserts, Antony sends all his treasure after him. Caesar's soldier delivers it with the observation: "Antony/ Hath after thee sent all thy treasure, with/ His bounty overplus." (IV. vi. 20-22) Enobarbus considers Antony's extreme generosity "Jove-like" and so he is covered with shame and remorse when he thinks how he has deserted this "mine of bounty." (IV. vi. 32) Cleopatra, in her great eulogy which is one of the most stirring poetic passages in the play, comments once more on this particular quality:

> For his bounty,
> There was no winter in't; an autumn 'twas
> That grew the more by reaping. (V. ii. 86-88)

Gratitude. Gratitude, which is closely allied to bounty and liberality, is referred to frequently in the opening scenes of *Macbeth*. The King, for example, speaks of "the sin of [his] ingratitude" when he first meets Macbeth and promises swift reward for Macbeth's great services. (I. iv. 15) Lady Macbeth, however hypocritical she may be, goes out of her way to seem to be both a courteous hostess and a grateful subject (whereas Goneril and Regan are as rude as they are ungrateful). She tells her royal guest:

> All our service
> In every point twice done, and then done double,
> Were poor and single business to contend
> Against those honours deep and broad wherewith
> Your majesty loads our house. For those of old,
> And the late dignities heap'd up to them,
> We rest your hermits. (I. vi. 14-20)

This eloquent speech turns out to be just as insincere as Iago's famous speech on "good name in man and woman." The facts that Duncan is her guest and that she should be grateful to him do not cause her to pause an instant in her plot to gain the crown. But Macbeth's conscience is bothered deeply because these facts will make the crime that much more dastardly. He

tells his wife: "We will proceed no further in this business./
He hath honour'd me of late." (I. vii. 31-32) His wife sees
that the quickest way to override his troubled conscience is to
accuse him of lack of valor and manhood. She realizes that the
imputation of cowardice will cut as deep as his original scruple
against ingratitude.

Temperance. Hurault defines the virtue of temperance as
"the brideler of bodilie pleasures; because all passions are
moderated by that Vertue."[30] The difference between temperance and intemperance is indicated by the sharp contrast between Othello's love for Desdemona and Antony's for Cleopatra. Othello requests the Senate to permit him to take his
newly married wife with him without the least fear that his
love for Desdemona will keep his mind from the tasks of war.
He assures the Senate:

> When light-wing'd toys
> Of feather'd Cupid seel with wanton dullness
> My speculative and offic'd instruments,
> That my disports corrupt and taint my business,
> Let housewives make a skillet of my helm,
> And all indign and base adversities
> Make head against my estimation! (I. iii. 269-275)

Antony is certainly as great a general as Othello, but his intemperance is obvious from the very beginning of the play—
indeed, the story would be so familiar to the audience that this
characteristic would be taken for granted. *The French Academie,*
among other well-known Renaissance readings, cites Antony
as one of the celebrated examples of intemperance among the
men of antiquity.[31] In Shakespeare's play, Antony's great passion
for Cleopatra causes him to lose the first battle against Caesar.
The shame he feels in this disgrace finally brings him to check
his hitherto unbridled passion and to turn on the cause of his
inglorious defeat. He lashes out in anger at this Circe who has
seduced so many kings:

---

[30] *Discourses,* p. 298.
[31] La Primaudaye, p. 184.

I found you as a morsel cold upon
Dead Caesar's trencher. Nay, you were a fragment
Of Gneius Pompey's, besides what hotter hours,
Unregist'red in vulgar fame, you have
Luxuriously pick'd out: for I am sure,
Though you can guess what temperance should be,
You know not what it is. (III. xiii. 116-122)

But Antony can never gain full control over his passions. Enobarbus is serving as a testimonial character when he points out that Antony's will is lord of his reason. (According to the Renaissance view, temperance and self-control depended on the sovereignty of the reason over the will and the affections.) In a discussion of "art military," *The Courtier's Academie* points to one of the central issues of the play: "Temperance . . . is necessary to the perfection of this arte: in that he can hardly subdue his enemie, which hath not first an habite in conquering himselfe."[32]

Gentility. Cicero includes under the virtue of temperance "bashfulness, . . . modesty, government of the passions, and the observing a just order as to time and place in our words and actions." Decorum, good breeding, and gentility were, for him and for the Renaissance, important components of the gentlemanly ideal. Proteus is sent to court in *The Two Gentlemen of Verona* so that he may "hear sweet discourse, converse with noblemen,/ And be in eye of every exercise." (I. iii. 31-32) Orlando in *As You Like It* complains to his older brother, Oliver: "My father charg'd you in his will to give me good education. You have train'd me like a peasant, obscuring and hiding from me all gentlemanlike qualities. The spirit of my father grows strong in me, and I will no longer endure it." (I. i. 70-75) The importance of good breeding, etiquette, and courtesy for the Elizabethans can not be overemphasized; the popularity of translations of Italian books of courtesy and etiquette indicates the extent to which England looked to Italy

---

[32] Count Romei, p. 276.

as the model of a more civilized and gracious mode of living than the English had hitherto been accustomed to. As Guazzo observes, the very word "gentleman" should indicate two qualities: "The first is vertue, the other curtesie, the right ornament of a Gentleman: For of curtesie and gentlenes he is termed a gentleman."[33]

In the first section of *The Gouernour*, Elyot describes the various arts and exercises, such as hunting, wrestling, and dancing, in which the Renaissance gentleman should become skillful. Similarly, Troilus, who never figured in Homer's original tales, warns Cressida as she prepares to depart for the Greek camp that

> The Grecian youths are full of quality;
> They're loving, well compos'd with gifts of nature,
> And flowing o'er with arts and exercise. (IV. iv. 78-80)

Shakespeare's Trojan hero is obviously fearful that his beloved may be ensnared by the more sophisticated charms of the Greeks. Many of his compatriots must have recognized their own inadequacies (vis-à-vis Renaissance France and Renaissance Italy) when Troilus admits his own uncouthness:

> I cannot sing,
> Nor heel the high lavolt, nor sweeten talk,
> Nor play at subtile games—fair virtues all. (IV. iv. 87-89) ·

Troilus is aware of his own plainness and simplicity; he fears that Cressida will esteem the sophisticated talents of the Greeks more highly, and he is, of course, right.

Beauty and Other Outer Graces. Shakespeare lays great stress on the primary importance of such simple virtues as Troilus' honesty and faithfulness. But granted that prerequisite, he never deprecates the value of outer graces and accomplishments to accompany it. As Othello says,

> 'Tis not to make me jealous
> To say my wife is fair, feeds well, loves company,

[33] *The Civile Conversation*, II, 41.

Is free of speech, sings, plays, and dances well.
Where virtue is, these are more virtuous.

(III. iii. 183-186)

The Renaissance aristocrat rejected any and every ascetic doctrine; Puritan and Stoic alike are held in scorn. Ascham, for example, says: "I was never, either Stoick in doctrine, or Anabaptist in Religion to mislike a merie, pleasant, and playfull nature, if no outrage be committed."[34] Montaigne, too, indicates how highly selective the Renaissance indebtedness to the Stoics was. In answer to the "austere turn of mind" of the Catos, he points out that the ability to relax "doth, in my conceit, greatly honour and is best befitting a magnanimos and noble minde. Epaminondas thought it no scorne, to thrust himselfe amongst the boyes of his citie, and dance with them, yea and to sing and play, and with attention busie himselfe."[35] This is the dominant attitude in most of Shakespeare's plays. The celebration of Othello's marriage and of the triumph over the Turks—"some to dance, some to make bonfires, each man to what sport and revels his addiction leads him" (II. ii. 5-7)—is an example in the tragedies of that spirit of festivity and mirth with which so many of the comedies close. Since the soldiers are on duty, Othello requests Cassio to watch the guards: "Let's teach ourselves that honourable stop,/ Not to outsport discretion." (II. iii. 2-3) The revelries of Claudius in *Hamlet*, and the epicurean and amorous banquets of Antony and Cleopatra, are palpably in excess and arouse the disgust of others.

Beauty of body and comeliness of features were not scorned as accompaniments to the virtues, any more than gracefulness in dancing or skill in sport. Again, the Stoics are taken to task. In the words of Bryskett, "For although vertue of it selfe be lovely and to be highly esteemed, yet when she is accompanied with the beauty of the bodie, she is more amiable (whatsoever, Seneca the Stoicke, more severe then need, please to say.)"[36]

[34] *The Scholemaster*, pp. 63, 64.
[35] *Essayes*, III, 13.
[36] *A Discourse of Civill Life*, p. 38.

Shakespeare's women are particularly commended for their beauty, nor is Shakespeare blind to the fact that the male figure can also be attractive. Indeed, he seldom refers to a woman's virtues without also mentioning her qualities of sheer physical attractiveness. Often the impression is given indirectly and with rich use of hyperbole, as in Enobarbus' description of Cleopatra on her barge and in Cassio's of Desdemona's safe arrival in Cyprus. Even Othello, entering the bedchamber to murder his wife, is so taken with her beauty that he can not stab and thus disfigure her. So he exclaims,

> Yet I'll not shed her blood,
> Nor scar that whiter skin of hers than snow,
> And smooth as monumental alabaster.
>
> (V. ii. 3-5)

However praiseworthy external beauty and comeliness might be to the men of Shakespeare's age, it could never be treated on the same plane as inner nobility of mind, heart, and spirit. As Bryskett suggests: "the exterior beauty of the body prepareth the way to the knowledge of the other inward of the mind, which . . . is indeed the true man."[37] The Renaissance aristocrat hated Puritan or Stoic asceticism and enjoyed living in a magnificent style. But all outward signs of nobility were wholly secondary, at least in ethical theory, to the inner nobility of spirit which should result from the cultivation of the moral virtues. Once again there was a definite hierarchy of values, thanks to the pains the Renaissance moralists took to define their values (many of these moralists are unread today, having passed into that oblivion they so much abhorred). If a choice had to be made between the exterior beauty of the body and the inner beauty of mind and soul, it was made immediately. For the Jacobean audience, the old mad Lear, stripped almost naked, was more noble and more honorable by far than the wicked daughters sitting comfortably, warm and well attended in Gloucester's castle. Wilson Knight observes that in *Hamlet*

---

[37] *ibid.*, p. 225.

the color, brilliance, and majesty of the court of Denmark are presented as a deliberate contrast to the sincere grief of the pale-faced, mourning hero who alone wears black.[38] Hamlet, a study in ironic ambiguity, doubles the contrast by pointing out that even the garb of mourning does not represent the true man: "But I have that within which passeth show—/ These but the trappings and the suits of woe." (I. ii. 85-86)[39]

[38] *The Wheel of Fire*, p. 17.
[39] See Chapter 8 for a discussion of magnanimity, the master-virtue.

CHAPTER 7

SHAKESPEARE AND THE RENAISSANCE CONCEPT OF HONOR

(continued)

VALOR AND PATRIOTISM

T S. ELIOT takes exception to Wyndham Lewis' thesis that we possess a good deal of evidence as to what Shakespeare thought about military glory. "Do we?" Eliot replies, "Or rather, did Shakespeare think anything at all? He was occupied with turning human actions into poetry."[1] He is quite right that, as a dramatist and poet, Shakespeare could hardly have had time to construct an elaborate philosophical system of his own, and that we shall never know what Shakespeare, as a private individual, thought. But Eliot errs in stating that Shakespearean drama reflects an absence of values. The plays are actually, to no inconsiderable extent, organized artistically as a conflict between good and evil. That these notions of good and evil largely reflect the general cultural values of the Elizabethan age does not deny that, as Shakespeare turned human actions into poetry, he was constantly evaluating those actions.

It is in the chronicle histories that the hero tends to be admired, both by the other characters in the play and by the audience, primarily for his display of brute force and physical courage. (This probably explains why the modern audience finds the history plays less interesting than the comedies or tragedies. Many of us no longer consider mere military prowess a sign of greatness.) But the same heroic ideal is also apparent in *Troilus and Cressida* despite the modern note of sour cynicism resulting from the failure of both the Greek and the Trojan

[1] "Shakespeare and the Stoicism of Seneca," *Selected Essays*, p. 115.

leaders to uphold their own ideals. Shakespeare, like his fellow Englishmen, tends to be particularly critical of the Greeks; his presentation of the Trojans is, relatively speaking, much more sympathetic. The question as to whether Helen is worth keeping involves the Trojan leaders in a protracted debate. Troilus' argument in favor of doing so is in harmony with the typical Renaissance attitude apparent in Raleigh's previously mentioned description of the zealous rivalry for honor among the great nobles in the military action against Spain:

> But, worthy Hector,
> She is a theme of honour and renown,
> A spur to valiant and magnanimous deeds,
> Whose present courage may beat down our foes,
> And fame in time to come canonize us.
>
> (II. ii. 198-202)

It is for this reason that Hector insists on going forth to battle even though Cassandra prophesies his death.

Examples of this sort abound throughout Shakespeare's plays. Nothing was considered more damaging to the hero's prestige than to refuse the call to arms. Nor could one rest on laurels won in past battles. Thus Ulysses admonishes Achilles that "Perseverance, dear my lord,/ Keeps honour bright." (III. iii. 150-151) The cowardly Parolles speaks contemptuously of the man who stays at home. He tells Bertram:

> To th' wars, my boy, to the wars!
> He wears his honour in a box unseen
> That hugs his kicky-wicky here at home.
>
> (II. iii. 295-297)

In the Roman plays even the women are steeped in this spirit of fortitude. When Volumnia, for example, is asked by Virgilia how she would feel if her son were killed in action, her response is unhesitating: "Then his good report should have been my son; I therein would have found issue. Hear me profess sincerely, had I a dozen sons, each in my love alike, and none less dear than thine and my good Marcius, I had rather had eleven die nobly for their country than one voluptuously surfeit out of action." (I. iii. 22-28)

Shakespeare's soldier-hero is usually presented on a canvas of gigantic dimensions. Antony, for example, in battle fights as if a God; elsewhere he is described as "plated Mars." (I. i. 4) So, likewise, Coriolanus leads the Volscians as "their God." Indeed,

> He leads them like a thing
> Made by some other deity than Nature,
> That shapes man better; and they follow him
> Against us brats with no less confidence
> Than boys pursuing summer butterflies
> Or butchers killing flies. (IV. vi. 90-95)

Hotspur's unique combination of youthful impetuosity and soldierly greatness is admirably summed up when the King describes him as a "Mars in swathling clothes." (III. ii. 112) The glorious qualities of the great military leaders of antiquity are not only made explicit by the plots of *Julius Caesar, Troilus and Cressida*, and *Antony and Cleopatra* but are also indicated by Antony's compliment to his own men when they win a victory over Caesar. He tells them: "You have shown all Hectors." (IV. viii. 7) The strong links between the cultural values of Homeric Greece, of Rome, and of the Renaissance are casually, but significantly, reflected in this remark.

It is through dramatic action, however, that the high prestige of the great Renaissance soldier is most clearly portrayed. Brabantio's power as a Senator of the Venetian state is pointed up in the opening scenes: Iago informs Othello "That the magnifico is much belov'd,/ And hath in his effect a voice potential—/ As double as the Duke's." (I. ii. 12-14) In the next scene, the Senate is in session preparing for war against the Turk. Othello's towering prestige as the general responsible for the security of the Venetian Republic is underscored by the Duke's slighting of Brabantio as he and Othello enter the stage together:

1 SEN. Here comes Brabantio and the valiant
  Moor.
DUKE. Valiant Othello, we must straight employ
  you
  Against the general enemy Ottoman.
  [To Brabantio] I did not see you. Welcome,
  gentle signior.
  We lack'd your counsel and your help to-
  night.   (I. iii. 47-51)

Othello has an equally high opinion of his own qualities as a
military leader. He tells Iago at the beginning of the play that
he gave up his life as a bachelor soldier only as a result of the
great love he bore for Desdemona. Hitherto his arms "have
us'd/ Their dearest action in the tented field," a hint that he
perhaps still longs for the field of battle. (I. iii. 84-85) His
long speech on the glory of military life ("Farewell the plumed
troops, and the big wars") is strikingly similar to Montaigne's
lengthy eulogies of the soldier's existence. (III. iii. 349)

The hardships which the soldier in our century tends to
bear stoically or with evident exasperation were sources of
exhilaration to the Renaissance man of honor. Thus Shakespeare
contrasts the harsh exertions of battle with the soft pleasures
of amorous love—frequently his hero is more enamored of the
former. Hotspur becomes melancholic at home with his wife
and dreams of his past exploits on the field of battle. The
Chorus in the second act of *King Henry the Fifth* suggests
that this was a common attitude among English youth:

Now all the youth of England are on fire,
And silken dalliance in the wardrobe lies.
Now thrive the armourers, and honour's thought
Reigns solely in the breast of every man.
        (II. chorus, 1-4)

Othello's love of the spartan and austere existence of the soldier
leads him to observe: "The tyrant custom, most grave senators,/

Hath made the flinty and steel couch of war/ My thrice-driven bed of down." (I. iii. 230-232) We remember, too, that even the epicurean Antony's palate once had known the bark of trees. (I. iv. 63-64)

Manhood or Virility. Manhood or manliness was in the Renaissance a popular synonym for valor. The term stems from the notion that a man, by his very nature, will manifest more courage than women or boys ("virtue" and *virtu*, as well as "virility," are derived from the Latin word for man). As we learned from Aristotle: "a man would be thought a coward if he were only as brave as a brave woman."[2]

Shakespeare places particular emphasis on this synonym in *Macbeth*; obviously his intention is to contrast the physical courage of the hero with his imaginary apprehensions and moral scruples. Thus at the end of the first act, when Lady Macbeth accuses her husband of cowardice, his response is immediate and unqualified:

> Prithee peace!
> I dare do all that may become a man.
> Who dares do more is none. (I. vii. 45-47)

In the murder scene Lady Macbeth again remonstrates with her husband for his yielding to remorse and to fear of the consequences of his deed. But Macbeth hears a voice crying "Sleep no more." (II. ii. 35) He becomes more and more wrought up by these imaginary fears so his wife again tries to appeal to his manly spirit: Why, worthy Thane,

> You do unbend your noble strength to think
> So brainsickly of things. (II. ii. 44-46)

But it is in the banquet scene that the contrast becomes most striking between Macbeth's manly physical courage and the domination of his mind by the apprehensions his troubled conscience has provoked. As Macbeth recoils in horror from the ghost, his wife asks: "Are you a man?" (III. iv. 58) Soon it is

[2] *Politics* III. 2.

evident that he is "quite unmann'd in folly." (III. iv. 73)
Macbeth himself, imagining the ghost before him, exclaims,

> What man dare, I dare.
> Approach thou like the rugged Russian bear,
> The arm'd rhinoceros, or th' Hyrcan tiger;
> Take any shape but that, and my firm nerves
> Shall never tremble. Or be alive again
> And dare me to the desert with thy sword.
> If trembling I inhabit then, protest me
> The baby of a girl. Hence, horrible shadow!
> Unreal mock'ry, hence!
> [Exit Ghost.]
> Why, so! Being gone,
> I am a man again. (III. iv. 99-108)

Macbeth is not the only character in the play whose manhood is called in question. Macduff, on learning of the death of his wife and children, is so grief-stricken that Malcolm admonishes him to "dispute it like a man." (IV. iii. 219) But Macduff continues to lament his fate; again Malcolm tries to cut him short with the plea, "Let grief/ Convert to anger." (IV. iii. 228-229) Macduff finally steels himself to seek revenge, but only after confessing that "I could play the woman with mine eyes." (IV. iii. 230)

For the Elizabethan, grief which led to tears was an indication of lack of manliness. Exeter's description of the death of the Duke of York in *King Henry the Fifth* concludes, however, with the admission that he was so stirred by the courage and nobility of York, and by the pity of his death, that

> The pretty and sweet manner of it forc'd
> These waters from me which I would have stopp'd
> But I had not so much of man in me,
> And all my mother came into mine eyes
> And gave me up to tears. (IV. vi. 28-32)

In *King Lear* this notion of manly dignity finds its most subtle expression. Lear's years would make permissible the surrendering to grief and tears, whereas in Richard the Second's case, as he follows Bolingbroke in his royal triumph, it is an obvious sign of weakness. But Lear's heroic stature—in contrast to that of the deposed Richard—is revealed by his intense inner struggle to maintain dignity and patience and not to give way to womanish tears. Finally, Goneril's insulting attempt to reduce his kingly train destroys his inner control. Lear weeps, involuntarily, but with a burning sense of shame. He tells Goneril:

> Life and death! I am asham'd
> That thou hast power to shake my manhood thus;
> That these hot tears, which break from me perforce,
> Should make thee worth them. (I. iv. 318-321)

Lear proceeds to curse his daughters savagely. Again grief converts to anger. Where many modern critics consider this a sign that Lear is in his dotage, for the Jacobeans the expression of anger and the desire for revenge against injuries were highly appropriate to his predicament and far more dignified than womanly tears. This great fortitude of spirit, which either bears suffering through heroic endurance or else lashes out in anger and seeks revenge, lies behind Lear's final great speech just before his departure into the storm. Manly courage calls for patient endurance and self-control, or for the manifestation of anger and the seeking of revenge. But Lear is too old and infirm to seek revenge himself.

The only other alternative is madness. Lear is too heroic, too determined to maintain at all costs his inner dignity and integrity, however great the abuses heaped upon him, to permit either tears or a meek acceptance. Again, too many present-day critics interpret his next magnificent speech as a sign of his distraction, as something pathetic and almost ridiculous.

> You heavens, give me that patience, patience I need!
> You see me here, you gods, a poor old man,

As full of grief as age; wretched in both.
If it be you that stir these daughters' hearts
Against their father, fool me not so much
To bear it tamely; touch me with noble anger,
And let not women's weapons, water drops,
Stain my man's cheeks! No, you unnatural hags!
I will have such revenges on you both
That all the world shall—I will do such things—
What they are yet, I know not; but they shall be
The terrors of the earth! You think I'll weep.
No, I'll not weep.
I have full cause of weeping, but this heart
Shall break into a hundred thousand flaws
Or ere I'll weep. O fool, I shall go mad.

(II. iv. 274-289)

Proper appreciation of this passage depends on a close knowledge of the specific meaning of the ethical concepts involved. Patience, for example, is so general and vague a notion that a precise knowledge of the way in which it would be interpreted by the Jacobeans is required. It is scarcely to be equated with the Christian sense of meekness—Lear does not intend "to bear it tamely." Its meaning to the Jacobean audience, in this context, is that of Bryskett: "Patience is but a branch of fortitude through which men bear stoutly all injuries, whether they proceed from wicked persons, or from the inconstancies and changeablenesse of fortune; but remaineth alwayes invincible and constant against all the crosses, thwarts, and despites of fortune."[3] This passage is a close parallel to Montaigne's definition of constancy as "valor, not of armes and legs, but of minde and courage."[4] In this sense, the old, infirm Lear manifests more heroic fortitude than the youthful Hotspur could display

---

[3] *A Discourse*, p. 88. Danby finds the ideal of Christian patience the key to a proper understanding of *King Lear*. In addition, he suggests that this play demonstrates the inadequacy of pagan concepts of patience such as the one here quoted from Bryskett. See essay "King Lear and Christian Patience: a Culmination," in John Danby, *Poets on Fortune's Hill*, London, 1952.

[4] *Essayes*, I, 30.

by a thousand victories in battle. As Montaigne also observes, "the reputation and worth of a man consisteth in his heart and will: therein consists true honour."[5]

In his maturest writing, Shakespeare wastes no time with didactic explanations of ethical concepts, for he can rest assured that his audience has been soundly indoctrinated in the moral disciplines and will immediately understand the exact meaning of "patience," of "noble anger," of "women's weapons," and of "my man's cheeks." But the 20th century audience will grasp the essential meaning of the play only if it bothers to study the definitions of anger, grief, patience, and revenge in the Renaissance textbooks on moral philosophy. Our interpretation of a specific action, a particular emotion, or an individual character too often depends on our own moral bias. Behavior which seemed eminently dignified to Shakespeare and his audience may seem thoroughly undignified to us. Thus Wilson Knight speaks of Lear's desire for revenge in the above passage as "painfully incongruous" and "not far from the ridiculous."[6]

The concept of manhood is also an important theme in the final scene of *Coriolanus*. Aufidius gathers a faction of conspirators around him in preparation for the murder of the hero. He tells them that Coriolanus has betrayed them, sold out their cause. He intentionally insults the hero by suggesting that it was the mere tears of women which caused him to change his mind:

> At a few drops of women's rheum, which are
> As cheap as lies, he sold the blood and labour
> Of our great action. (V. vi. 45-47)

[5] *ibid.*

[6] *The Wheel of Fire*, p. 163. Granville-Barker's defense of Goneril and Regan—prior to their "discourtesy" when they blind Gloucester—provides an interesting parallel to Knight: "How then can we call Regan and Goneril double-dyed friends? They played the hypocrite for a kingdom; but which of us might not? Having got what they wanted and more than they expected they found good excuse for not paying the price for it. Like failings have been known in the most reputable people. Their conduct so far, it could be argued, has been eminently respectable, level-headed and worldly wise. They do seem somewhat hard-hearted, but that is all." (*Prefaces to Shakespeare*, I, 302.)

When Coriolanus appears on the stage, Aufidius formally accuses him of treachery. The charge is as much an intentional display of contempt for Coriolanus as it is an accusation of treason. Indeed, the hero is less incensed by the charge of treachery than by the imputation that he is lacking in manhood.

AUF.   But at his nurse's tears
        He whin'd and roar'd away your victory,
        That pages blush'd at him, and men of heart
        Look'd wondring each at other.
COR.   Hear'st thou, Mars?
AUF. Name not the god, thou boy of tears!
COR.   Ha!
AUF. No more.
COR. Measureless liar, thou hast made my heart
        Too great for what contains it. Boy? O slave!
                      (V. vi. 96-103)

Once again, the fact that in the Renaissance honor was the most precious of possessions makes itself apparent. This accusation of lack of manhood and valor cuts so deep that mere life becomes a matter of negligible concern. Coriolanus almost asks for his own murder in the speech which follows. (We should bear in mind Lear's " 'Tis worse than murther.") Coriolanus cries out,

Cut me to pieces, Volsces. Men and lads,
Stain all your edges on me. Boy? False hound!
If you have writ your annals true, 'tis there,
That, like an eagle in a dovecote, I
Flutter'd your Volscians in Corioles,
Alone I did it. Boy? (V. vi. 111-116)

Coriolanus suffers throughout the play from the fault of pride, hence never wins our full admiration. But the Jacobean audience would have been in entire sympathy with him in his indignant rejection of this false imputation of lack of manhood.

The Jacobeans knew their Aristotle and well knew that it

was cowardly and dishonorable for the soldier not to be more courageous than women or boys. The cardinal significance of this dictum is apparent once again in Antony's remarks to Eros when he hears that the Queen is dead:

> Since Cleopatra died
> I have liv'd in such dishonour that the gods
> Detest my baseness. I, that with my sword
> Quarter'd the world and o'er green Neptune's back
> With ships made cities, condemn myself to lack
> The courage of a woman. (IV. xiv. 55-60)

Antony is soon to discover that Cleopatra is not dead. But when she does prepare for her own suicide, she in turn displays the courage of a man. At the end of the play, she has at last mounted to a plane of tragic grandeur and can truly say of herself: "My resolution's plac'd, and I have nothing/ Of woman in me." (V. ii. 238-239) Shakespeare's greatest portrayal of feminine fickleness concludes with a death indeed befitting a princess of a line of many royal kings. (V. ii. 329-330) (Here we should compare the description of the death of Mary Queen of Scots on p. 117) Many critics can not believe that this is a sincere manifestation of heroic courage. Surely Caesar's comment is testimonial:

> Bravest at the last!
> She levell'd at our purposes, and being royal,
> Took her own way. (V. ii. 338-340)

The basis for this transformation in Cleopatra's character lies, to no inconsiderable extent, in the notion that the possession of royal blood gave a particular inclination to courage. The king was compared to the lion and eagle because he was as sovereign and as courageous as they (Richard the Lion-Hearted, for example). A similar transformation takes place in *King Richard the Second*. During the course of the play, the king evinces no qualities of strength and is incapable of resisting the astute Bolingbroke. But at the play's close, he does fight his assailants and kills two of them before he is finally struck down by Exton. So, as he dies, Exton confesses that the king is "as full of valour as of royal blood./ Both have I spill'd." (V. v. 113-114)

Similarly, too, Hamlet becomes more courageous as the play draws to a close. The man who leaps into the grave with the cry, "This is I,/ Hamlet the Dane," is an altogether different figure from the youth accusing himself of inaction and cowardice earlier in the play. (V. i. 280-281) Hamlet, grappling with Laertes, warns him to take his fingers from his throat:

> For though I am not splenitive and rash,
> Yet have I in me something dangerous,
> Which let thy wisdom fear. (V. i. 284-286)

In the next scene Hamlet tells Horatio that he feels no remorse for the deaths of Rosencrantz and Guildenstern, for

> 'Tis dangerous when the baser nature comes
> Between the pass and fell incensed points
> Of mighty opposites. (V. ii. 60-62)

The final eulogy by Fortinbras emphasizes Hamlet's potentialities for heroic leadership.

> Let four captains
> Bear Hamlet like a soldier to the stage;
> For he was likely, had he been put on,
> To have prov'd most royally; and for his passage
> The soldiers' music and the rites of war
> Speak loudly for him. (V. ii. 406-411)

Patriotism. Shakespeare does not fail to give expression to the patriotic sentiment of his age. Although the great tragedies place the hero repeatedly in the spotlight, his actions are never divorced from the social background of the play. Even if our interest focuses on the exceptional aspects of his personality, and on his relationship to a relatively small number of associates, we can never completely lose sight of the fact that he is the leader of a state. Always there are figures in the background who symbolize his relationship to a whole society (for example, the Duke of Venice, Lodovico, and Montano).

The spirit of patriotism is, as we should expect, particularly evident in the Roman tragedies. Cominius' speech to the tribunes in *Coriolanus* is a characteristic reflection of the Roman sense of patriotic obligation which Cicero emphasizes in the *Offices*. Cominius says,

> I do love
> My country's good with a respect more tender,
> More holy and profound, than mine own life,
> My dear wive's estimate, her wombs increase
> And treasure of my loins. (III. iii. 111-115)

Coriolanus expresses the same sentiment in the opening act of the play: he too holds "his country dearer than himself." (I. vi. 72) But it is Brutus, in *Julius Caesar*, who most clearly exemplifies the exalted patriotism of the Roman. He justifies his slaying of Caesar with the statement: "Not that I lov'd Caesar less, but that I lov'd Rome more." (III. ii. 22) Antony's final eulogy indicates that even his enemies could clearly recognize the high idealism of his motives.

In the chronicle histories, the spirit of patriotism manifests itself in almost every act. Gaunt's speech in *King Richard the Second* ("This precious stone set in the silver sea") which rebukes England for failing to live up to its traditional grandeur and the inherent advantages which nature has given it, is the most famous purple passage on this theme. (II. i. 46) But perhaps as significant an indication of Renaissance chauvinism is the preceding speech in which York complains how basely "our tardy apish nation" imitates the fashions of proud Italy. (II. i. 22) Henry the Fifth's speech before Harfleur inflames his soldiers with the spirit of militant nationalism: "God for Harry! England and Saint George!" (III. i. 34) In *Cymbeline*, even the great prestige of the Romans as a military might is dimmed perceptibly by the English victory. Indeed, wherever the English state is involved in war against a foreign nation in Shakespeare's plays, its ultimate triumph never seems in doubt. Civil war and internal dissension appear as the chief sources of English weakness. As the Bastard Faulconbridge says in the closing speech of *King John*:

> This England never did, nor never shall
> Lie at the proud foot of a conqueror
> But when it first did help to wound itself.
>
> Naught shall make us rue
> If England to itself do rest but true.
> (V. vii. 112-114, 117-118)

HONOR AS HONESTY, INTEGRITY

For the Elizabethans, to be honest and to be honorable were, in effect, one and the same thing. Honor was sometimes used as a synonym for honesty and integrity; conversely, the word honesty had both its present meaning and the more inclusive one of honor and moral rectitude. The importance of this ideal of complete sincerity can not be overstressed in considering the relation between Renaissance moral values and those of Shakespeare. He has been criticized for depending so frequently on borrowed plots, and for incorporating their looseness of structure into his own plays. But his close adherence to his source for plot does not mean that Shakespeare is dependent on its values. Thus, the earlier Lear play refers again and again to specific Christian doctrine, whereas Shakespeare's version presents, as its major theme, unmerited suffering and calls the very gods into question.[7] Shakespeare also remolds the tale of Cinthio, the source for *Othello*, by making its conventional Italian villain into the magnificent character of Iago, whose knavery is so well cloaked by the appearance of gentlemanly honesty and trust that not only Othello ("my friend, honest, honest Iago"), but also all Venice, assumes his integrity to be beyond question. Where values are concerned, *Othello* is being shaped not by its source, but by themes shared in common by

[7] See the discussion of *King Lear* and *King Leir* at the end of Chapter 9.

254

Cicero and the Renaissance humanist philosophers: the ideal of complete gentlemanly integrity, the preciousness of reputation, and the necessity of being able to distinguish between a true friend and a false one.

We live in an age so much more sophisticated and cynical than Shakespeare's that our Shakespearean critics can rarely be sympathetic to Othello's credulity, which they tend to consider his tragic flaw. (Bacon's scientific appraisal of human nature in the "Idols of the Theatre," the biting, acid quality of Restoration comedy, and the artificiality of Restoration heroic drama all indicate that present-day scepticism in regard to human moral potentialities is not new but was to become a dominant attitude almost as soon as Shakespeare stopped writing.) Properly to appreciate *Othello*, particularly to understand why the Renaissance audience would so readily accept Othello's unsuspecting reliance on Iago as a friend and trustworthy counsellor, depends on an awareness of the Renaissance ideal of integrity and honesty. As we have seen, it was an absolute ideal; to be a little dishonest was utterly to destroy one's credit and reputation as an honest man. Brutus once again serves as prototype for the virtue in question. His anger on learning that Cassius has been selling offices is matched only by his incredulity that anyone could act in such a way. The same spirit of unquestioned personal integrity comes out in his scorn of Cassius' desire to bind the conspirators by oath. Brutus' response indicates how important unswerving honesty was to the Romans. He asks Cassius what other oath is needed "than honesty to honesty engag'd?" (II. i. 127) He goes on to say,

> Do not stain
> The even virtue of our enterprise,
> Nor th'insuppressive mettle of our spirits,
> To think that or our cause or our performance
> Did need an oath; when every drop of blood
> That every Roman bears, and nobly bears,
> Is guilty of a several bastardy

> If he do break the smallest particle
> Of any promise that hath pass'd from him.
>
> (II. i. 132-140)

We need only compare this passage with Hurault's observations on honesty and faith to appreciate the extent to which Shakespeare is mirroring the classical values of the Renaissance. Hurault reminds his readers, with some nostalgia, of the golden age of antiquity when "there was neither ooth nor promise, but only a good and sincere will, to keep touch with such as had relied upon the trust of their faithfulnesse."[8] Brutus, as presented by Shakespeare, embodies, in dramatic form, the common Renaissance admiration for the republican virtues of ancient Rome.

That the chronicle histories are more realistic in their depiction of character than the tragedies is apparent upon a brief consideration of the difference between the unswerving honesty of Brutus, Hamlet, or Othello, and the mixture of professed idealism and actual cunning involved in Bolingbroke's self-advancement. When he returns from banishment, Richard the Second is assured that he has come back simply to recover his lost lands. Indeed, his emissary, Northumberland, tells the king that Bolingbroke swears "by the royalties of both your bloods" and "by the worth and honour of himself" to be a true and faithful subject. (III. iii. 107, 110) Northumberland also asserts,

> His coming hither hath no further scope
> Than for his lineal royalties, and to beg
> Enfranchisement immediate on his knees;
> Which on thy royal party granted once,
> His glittering arms he will commend to rust,
> His barbed steeds to stables, and his heart
> To faithful service of your Majesty.
> This swears he, as he is a prince, is just;
> And as I am a gentleman, I credit him.
>
> (III. iii. 112-120)

---

[8] p. 95.

The whole aristocratic code of the Renaissance is summed up in these last two lines. But Richard the Second realizes that this is mere hollow rhetoric and that Bolingbroke seeks his throne. In the tragedies, such falseness to the ideal of absolute honesty would thoroughly discredit Bolingbroke; in the chronicle histories, a more realistic view and the need for a patriotic interpretation of English history, permit Shakespeare to condone, at least partially, Henry the Fourth's actions here, as they are condoned to some extent, later on, when Richard the Second is murdered. It is of the utmost moral significance, however, that the new king never ceases to feel guilty about the fact that he had used dishonest means to gain his crown. On his deathbed, he tells Hal:

> By what bypaths and indirect crook'd ways
> I met this crown; and I myself know well
> How troublesome it sat upon my head.
> To thee it shall descend with better quiet,
> Better opinion, better confirmation;
> For all the soil of the achievement goes
> With me into the earth. (IV. v. 185-191)

Shakespeare's queen, too, asserted that it was never fitting to royalty to dissemble, but actually proved herself one of the most cunning monarchs in all history. Shakespeare's Bolingbroke is a historical study in the inconsistent mingling of ideal and reality, of professed sincerity and actual diplomatic cunning. He lies halfway between the idealized dramatic portrayal of a Brutus (for a modern audience unbelievably self-righteous in his behavior, hence neither sympathetic nor convincing) and the unqualified villainy of a Richard the Third.

The Ideal of Plainspeaking. Another humanist commonplace closely related to the notion of the sanctity of the pledged word stated that the nobleman "never has one thing in his mouth, and another in his heart."[9] In *Coriolanus*, both Menenius and Volumnia complain that the hero adheres too scrupulously to this maxim. Menenius protests that

[9] Bryskett, p. 63.

His nature is too noble for the world.
He would not flatter Neptune for his trident
Or Jove for's power to thunder. His heart's his mouth;
What his breast forges, that his tongue must vent.

(III. i. 255-258)

Volumnia tries to persuade her son to pretend that he does not
hold the populace in contempt. She believes that policy demands
it and so he reluctantly agrees with his "base tongue" to "give
to my noble heart/ A lie that it must bear." (III. ii. 100-101)
But soon he balks at this polluting of the truth:

I will not do't,
Lest I surcease to honour mine own truth
And by my body's action teach my mind
A most inherent baseness. (III. ii. 120-123)

Volumnia considers this scrupulous insistence on complete honesty a mere matter of pride. Once again, she tries to persuade
him to speak to the people. When he does so in the next scene,
however, he can not long endure hearing the people's accusations against him. His patrician contempt for the populace
soon breaks forth despite his efforts to check himself.

Is Volumnia right in considering her son's uncompromising
plainspokenness a manifestation of pride? As is often the case,
Shakespeare's presentation of plot and character is ambiguous
here. A similar ambiguity exists in the proper interpretation of
Cordelia's behavior in the opening scene of *King Lear.*
Cordelia, like Coriolanus, insists on an honesty which comes
close to being plain rudeness. Evaluation of the Jacobean response is difficult in this instance because ambiguity also exists
in the books on ethics and etiquette. On the one hand, plainness,
simplicity, and outspokenness are praised because, even at the
risk of rudeness, they avoid the most hated of all vices, deceit,
flattery, and hypocrisy. On the other hand, as Sidney points out,
"there is a great difference between rudeness and plainness."[10]

---

[10] *Aphorisms,* I, 106. Cf. G. B. Gello, *Circe,* trans. Henry Iden, London, 1557,
5th Dialogue. "Yet I know that it so much displeseth a noble hart, to have one
thing in the mouth, and another in the breast, that I will take courage to spéke
frelye, although I should perchaunce in some parte . . . offend the."

Shakespeare apparently wants to suggest that both King Lear and his daughter are at fault. When the King disowns Cordelia, he refers specifically to her pride "which she calls plainness." (I. i. 131) This is precisely the same charge of willful obstinacy that Volumnia places against her son. The Jacobean audience would probably recognize this as a just criticism, though viewing it, as Lear himself later does, as "a most small fault" compared to the monstrous viciousness of Goneril and Regan.

The same ambiguity exists in regard to Kent's behavior. He insists that "To plainness honour's bound/ When majesty falls to folly." (I. i. 150-151) His statement accords perfectly with the notion of the Renaissance moral philosophers that a leader should "reverence, honour, and admire those who for our good deliver their minds frankly unto us."[11] On the other hand, the audience could hardly fail to remember that their own Queen resented the slightest diminution of her authority. Lear's wrath in this scene would probably be taken as a sign of unnecessary arrogance and impetuosity akin to that of Julius Caesar. Clearly both Lear and Cordelia are somewhat at fault in this opening scene. According to the Renaissance kingly ideal, the sovereign should combine authority with gentleness and affability so that he would be both feared and loved by his subjects. The combination of kingly majesty and courtly graciousness, so lacking in the early Lear, is illustrated by the great Venetian general, Othello, who courteously asserts his power by reminding the influential Senator, Brabantio, "Good signior, you shall more command with years/ Than with your weapons." (I. ii. 60-61)

The whole humanist ethics rested on the fundamental first principle that "in vertue may be nothing fucate or counterfaite but therein is onely the image of veritie, called simplicitie."[12] The moralists put such a premium on the plain, unadorned truth that the very show of eloquence aroused a certain amount of suspicion. The cunning of Antony when he addresses the

[11] Plutarch, *Moralia*, trans. Philemon Holland, London, 1911, p. 81.
[12] Elyot, *The Gouernour*, III, 4.

Roman populace is particularly evident in his initial assertion that

> I am no orator, as Brutus is,
> But (as you know me all) a plain blunt man
> That love my friend. (III. ii. 222-224)

He then delivers a speech which is the epitome of persuasive rhetoric. Even Othello, who is anything but cunning, waxes rhetorical when he tells the Venetian Senate about his elopement with Desdemona. Twice he refers to himself as a plain, blunt soldier ("Rude am I in my speech" and "little shall I grace my cause/ In speaking for myself") (I. iii. 81, 88-89) but he carries his case not only by the obvious sincerity of his tale but equally by its moving eloquence.

The same humanist virtues are treated humorously in the comedies. Benedick, for example, complains that his love-sick friend, Claudio, "was wont to speak plain and to the purpose," like an honest man and a soldier but that now he "is . . . turn'd orthography." (II. iii. 19-21) There is also humor, grim and ironic though it be, in Richard the Third's complaint in the third scene of the first act that

> Because I cannot flatter and look fair,
> Smile in men's faces, smooth, deceive, and cog,
> Duck with French nods and apish courtesy,
> I must be held a rancorous enemy,
> Cannot a plain man live and think no harm
> But thus his simple truth must be abus'd
> With silken, sly, insinuating Jacks? (I. iii. 47-53)

Trust and Fidelity. "Fidelity" is derived from the Latin word *fides*, but Elyot assures his reader that faith, trust, loyalty, and fidelity all "shall appere to a studious reder to signifie one vertue or qualitie, all thoughe they seme to have some diversitie."[13] Both Aristotle and Cicero had stressed the possibility of a trust so complete and absolute that suspicion of lack of integrity becomes practically impossible. In the words of Cicero,

---

[13] *ibid.*, III, 6.

"confidence is reposed in men who are just and true—that is, good men—on the definite assumption that their characters admit of no suspicion of dishonesty or wrong-doing."[14] This passage is of cardinal importance when we are trying to understand the degree of intimacy and confidence which Shakespeare, in his plays, assumed could exist between men. Duncan, for example, refers to the Thane of Cawdor as "a gentleman on whom I built/ An absolute trust." (I. iv. 13-14) Prospero speaks in *The Tempest* of his trust in his brother Antonio as one "which had indeed no limit,/ A confidence sans bound." (I. ii. 96-97) Leontes' courtiers in *The Winter's Tale* manifest a like certainty as to the integrity and purity of their queen. Antonio assures his King that

> every inch of woman in the world,
> Ay, every dram of woman's flesh is false,
> If she be. (II. i. 137-139)

Clearly humanist philosophy could, at times, be utterly individualistic (permitting T. S. Eliot to speak of the vice of individualism when he writes of Shakespeare and the Renaissance), although at other times it was just as social in its emphasis, as in the discussion of man's civic and patriotic obligations (an aspect of Renaissance morality overlooked by Eliot, Werner Jaeger, and many other modern scholars). Just as Othello and Cleopatra could place so high a moral value on their loved ones that they appeared to equal the whole world in worth, so, likewise, the Shakespearean protagonist could be convinced of the trustworthiness and integrity of a single person to such an extent that to suspect that person's honesty would throw into question the integrity of the whole human race. This is particularly true for the pagan-humanist philosophers in their writings on the virtue of friendship. No Renaissance book on moral philosophy is without a discussion of this virtue and it is usually exalted to the skies. For the moralists of that age, the nature of friendship is so demanding of complete integrity

[14] *De Officiis*, II. 9.

and high idealism—a friend being a second self—that only the most rare and excellent persons will be capable of it. Indeed, friendship was sometimes placed in the hierarchy of values far ahead of all other social obligations, at times even ahead of the relation between man and wife.[15]

It is difficult in our age to conceive of the tremendous intensity and concentration of emotional affection involved in this individualistic classical ideal. Yet without a proper appreciation of it, one can not comprehend the relationship of Hamlet to Horatio or of Othello to Iago. Friendship, in the Renaissance sense, also plays its part in *The Two Gentlemen of Verona* and in *The Merchant of Venice*. Indeed, Valentine's reaction to the falseness of Proteus is a minor foreshadowing of Shakespeare's tragic characterization of Horatio, the true friend, and Iago, the false one. Valentine exclaims bitterly, "Who should be trusted when one's own right hand/ Is perjured to the bosom?" (V. iv. 67-68) Bassanio's high esteem for his friend Antonio leads to a dialogue in which comedy and tragedy are blended in equal proportions. But the value of friendship and the importance of a hierarchy of values are nonetheless evident:

> BASS. Antonio, I am married to a wife
> Which is as dear to me as life itself;
> But life itself, my wife, and all the world
> Are not with me esteem'd above thy life.
> I would lose all, ay, sacrifice them all
> Here to this devil, to deliver you.
>
> POR. Your wife would give you little thanks for that
> If she were by to hear you make the offer.
>
> GRA. I have a wife who I protest I love.
> I would she were in heaven, so she could
> Entreat some power to change this currish Jew.
>
> NER. 'Tis well you offer it behind her back.
> The wish would make else an unquiet house.

[15] See Cicero *De Amicitia*, XXI.

SHY. [aside] These be the Christian husbands! I have a
   daughter—
   Would any of the stock of Barrabas
   Had been her husband rather than a Christian!
                                        (IV. i. 282-297)

But if we are concerned with what may well be Shakespeare's
personal sentiments, rather than with the dramatic exemplifi-
cation of common Renaissance ideals, we should turn to *The
Sonnets* to see the extent to which he could exalt the virtue of
friendship and make of it a focused, intense emotion in regard
to another individual. This leads the "speaker" in *The Sonnets*
to deprecate all other worldly attachments for their relative
inconsequentiality.

   Hamlet, in the depths of despair and disgust with the world,
tells Polonius that "To be honest, as this world goes, is to be
one man pick'd out of ten thousand." (II. ii. 178-180) For
Hamlet, that one man is his friend Horatio. Throughout the
greater portion of the play, Hamlet hardly conceals his disdain
for the rest of the world—Polonius, Rosencrantz, Guildenstern,
and Osric. But at the moment of utter disillusionment, his love
and his confidence in Horatio remain unchanged and undimin-
ished. He wears Horatio, he says, "in my heart's core, ay, in my
heart of hearts." (III. ii. 77-78) Hamlet feels morally isolated
from the rest of the world. Horatio's devotion and steady reliability represent the only constant beam to brighten a world
which would otherwise be completely immersed in spiritual
darkness. In such a predicament, the honesty and virtue of a
worthy friend can do much, indeed, to relieve one from a
sense of overwhelming isolation.

   In *Othello,* the moral situation is reversed. Othello feels
himself surrounded by friends, as he is indeed; and he towers
above his associates as the heroic general on whose great soldiership all Venice depends in its fight against the Turks. In contrast to the spiritual isolation of a Hamlet, gloom-ridden in a

court full of brilliance, color and gaiety, Othello stands out as
the great central figure amidst a crowd of admirers and followers. Instead of the cynicism, suspicion, and distrust which
characterize Hamlet's every contact with his fellow men,
Othello displays the greatest confidence and love toward all
who surround him. Even toward Brabantio he is always courteous and generous, never acrimonious.

But different as Othello's world is, one marked and significant comparison to *Hamlet* exists. Iago's relation to Othello
becomes precisely that of Horatio to Hamlet. Cicero's remark,
already quoted, that one should be able to place so much trust
and confidence in truly good and just men "on the definite
assumption that their characters admit of no suspicion of dishonesty, or wrong-doing" applies equally in both cases.[16] Because the Renaissance concept of friendship placed such emphasis on the *exclusive* nature of true friendship (compare, for
example, Montaigne's remarks in regard to Etienne de la
Boétie), Othello can come to place complete confidence in a
single person. He is exceedingly friendly to Cassio; indeed he
had initially preferred him to Iago when he selected his lieutenant. But as early as the end of the first act, Othello is confid-
ing his wife into the hands of "honest Iago" whom he significantly characterizes as completely honest and trustworthy. The
storm scene ensues, then the quarrel between Roderigo and
Cassio. This leads to Othello's dismissal of Cassio and to his
placing complete reliance on Iago:

> I know, Iago,
> Thy honesty and love doth mince this matter,
> Making it light to Cassio. Cassio, I love thee;
> But never more be officer of mine. (II. iii. 246-249)

From this moment until the very last scene, Iago stands in the
special relation of trusted counselor and friend—Horatio's relationship to Hamlet which so much sustains the Prince of
Denmark during the period of his bitter disillusionment. Iago
creates Othello's plight—and then ironically appears on the

[16] *De Officiis* II. 9.

scene as the one person whom Othello can most trust and rely upon to extricate him from it. Slowly but inexorably, Shakespeare brings Othello into closer and closer intimacy with Iago. Not until the third scene of the third act does Othello speak of their relationship as that of friendship. (III. iii. 142) But by the beginning of the fifth act, the bond between the hero and the villain has been firmly cemented. When Othello hears Cassio crying for help, he believes that Iago has taken revenge and exclaims:

O brave Iago, honest and just,
That hast such noble sense of thy friend's wrong!
Thou teachest me. (V. i. 31-33)

Just as Hamlet discovered that Horatio was "e'en as just a man/ As e'er my conversation cop'd withal," (III. ii. 59-60) so Othello becomes more and more persuaded of Iago's love, wisdom of counsel, and honesty, and so comes to depend ever more strongly on him. Earlier he had at moments doubted Iago, and even threatened him with the direst consequences if his insinuations regarding Desdemona should prove false. But by the fifth act he is completely convinced of Iago's integrity. When Emilia seems sceptical that her husband could ever have told him that Desdemona and Cassio had committed adultery, Othello responds with utmost self-assurance that it was indeed, "My friend, thy husband; honest, honest, Iago." (V. ii. 154)

The difference between Horatio and Iago is the difference between the true and the false friend—a theme which no Renaissance moralist failed to discuss fully if he discussed friendship at all.[17] Since that relationship involved complete intimacy and confidence, it was of the greatest importance to be certain of the friend's trustworthiness. Out of such a banal theme, Shakespeare creates his most deceptive villain, whose superhuman art takes in not only the tragic protagonist but equally the other characters in the play. Coleridge rightly insists that in judging Othello's credulity we must place our-

---

[17] Cleland, *The Institution of a Nobleman*, p. 195.

selves in the hero's shoes, not in the position of the omniscient
spectator in the audience who is informed by Iago himself of
his villainous qualities at the outset of the play. It is equally
necessary, if we are interested in understanding the reaction
of the Jacobean audience, to bear in mind the role of the true
friend in a time of adversity.

Although family ties were sometimes subordinated to the
exalted virtue of friendship, they, too, involved the Elizabethan in a bond and moral obligation of the strongest sort.
Cicero, for example, in the *Offices*, had placed the child's obligation to the parent second only to his obligation to his country.
Hence, the same themes of intimacy, confidence, love, and
trust were of vital significance in the discussion of the obligations
of one member of a family to another. Falseness and infidelity
to one's family were viewed by the Elizabethan as among the
most abhorrent of crimes. Once again, the alarm with which
infidelity was viewed was but a measure of the boundless love,
devotion, and trust which manifested itself in the ideal family.
As Prospero tells Miranda, his retirement

> in my false brother
> Awak'd an evil nature, and my trust,
> Like a good parent, did beget of him
> A falsehood in its contrary as great
> As my trust was, which had indeed no limit,
> A confidence sans bound. (I. ii. 92-97)

In the tragedies, the discovery of falseness in a member of
one's immediate family often becomes the source of a moral
shock of such intensity that the hero is jolted by it into a state
of utmost distraction. As in the humanist definition of friendship, identification and closeness make of this other member
of the family a second self. Thus, for Othello, Desdemona is
the place

> where I have garner'd up my heart,
> Where either I must live or bear no life,
> The fountain from the which my current runs.
> (IV. ii. 57-59)

Lear departs from Goneril with the consolation, "Yet have I left a daughter." (I. iv. 276) But when he discovers Kent in the stocks, he becomes completely disillusioned as to the possibility of human goodness. Yet, as in the case of Othello when Emilia speaks of Iago's falseness, he can not at first believe or admit what is patently true. He thunders "no!" to every assertion Kent makes about Regan's responsibility for shaming her father in this ignominious fashion. (II. iv. 15-24) His stubborn insistence that Regan can not be so malicious and ungrateful bears a striking resemblance to Troilus' refusal to accept the evidence of his own eyes as to the falseness of Cressida. Troilus exclaims,

> there is a credence in my heart,
> An esperance so obstinately strong,
> That doth invert th' attest of eyes and ears,
> As if those organs were deceptious functions.
> (V. ii. 120-123)

This persistent denial on the hero's part of manifest falseness is simply a measure of the intense love, devotion, and confidence which he showers on a particular person—whether it be Cressida, Desdemona, or Regan. The identification becomes so great that the manifestation of evil in another person becomes a manifestation of evil in oneself. As Lear says when he finally recognizes Regan's true nature:

> We'll no more meet, no more see one another.
> But yet thou art my flesh, my blood, my daughter;
> Or rather a disease that's in my flesh,
> Which I must needs call mine. Thou art a boil,
> A plague sore, an embossed carbuncle
> In my corrupted blood. (II. iv. 223-228)

To discover evil and falseness in one so dearly loved, so completely trusted, at first brings incredulity, then a moral revulsion which can not be purged by an outpouring of hatred and the impulse for revenge since one's own blood is tainted

by it and the revulsion includes oneself. Lear, Hamlet, and
Othello come to feel a moral uncleanness, which involves themselves as well as all mankind, when they discover daughters,
mother, and wife to be false. This, in large part, accounts for
the abundance of sickness imagery which Caroline Spurgeon
and Wilson Knight discover in these plays. Hamlet's melancholy and longing for death, Othello's distraction and trance,
and Lear's madness spring primarily from this nausea at discovering a self-involving evil in those they had so dearly, so
whole-heartedly loved.

Loss of Faith and Consequent Misanthropy. Where trust
has been betrayed, misanthropy often results—disillusionment
in the single person, loved and trusted so completely, leads to
disillusionment with the whole human race. This is individualism with a vengeance, and from a rational point of view is
quite absurd. As Plato remarks, "misanthropy arises from trust-
ing someone implicitly without sufficient knowledge. You think
the man is perfectly true and sound and trustworthy, and afterwards you find him base and false. Then you have the same
experience with another person. By the time this has happened
to a man a good many times, especially if it happens among
those whom he might regard as his nearest and dearest friends,
he ends by being in continual quarrels and by hating everybody
and thinking there is nothing sound in anyone at all."[18] Plato
considers this misanthropy foolish since actually few men are
perfect and few are absolutely wicked, the vast majority lie
somewhere between the two extremes.

But the emotions do not follow logic. As Horace Walpole
remarked, "this world is a comedy to those who think, a tragedy
to those who feel."[19] In his tragedies Shakespeare, like Cicero
and other humanist moralists who write on friendship, tends
to focus on the isolated few, the moral elite at the top of the

[18] *Phaedo* 90.
[19] Letter from Horace Walpole to Horace Mann dated 5 March 1772, Mrs.
Paget Toynbee's edn., VIII, 153.

pyramid of society.[20] The resulting idealization is so great that the discovery of lack of integrity in a single person can throw into question the moral rightness of all humanity.

There are touches of a general disillusionment in Shakespeare's earlier plays. When Valentine discovers that his friend, Proteus, has been false, he demands: "Who should be trusted when one's own right hand/ Is perjured to the bosom?" (V. iv. 67, 68) When Juliet hears that Romeo has slain Tybalt she is most vituperative and her nurse immediately generalizes: "There's no trust,/ No faith, no honesty in men." (III. ii. 85-86) In *Measure for Measure*, the Duke answers Escalus' question as to what news is abroad in the world: "None, but that there is so great a fever on goodness that the dissolution of it must cure it. . . . There is scarce truth enough alive to make societies secure, but security enough to make fellowships accurst." (III. ii. 235-242) In the late comedies, the same tone of weary disillusionment is sometimes evident. Antonio tells Leontes that if Hermione is false, then

> We need no grave to bury honesty,
> There's not a grain of it the face to sweeten
> Of the whole dungy earth. (II. i. 155-157)

As in the sonnet, "Tir'd with all these, for restful death I cry," the general immorality of mankind leaves one single solace, the goodness of a single individual. (Sonnet 66) When this person proves false, disillusionment becomes all-pervasive.

This dichotomy between the confidence, admiration, and love felt for the individual and the disdain and distrust of the

---

[20] Cf. Cicero *De Amicitia* XXI. "Now, he alone is worthy [of friendship] whose personal merit, independent of all other considerations, renders him the just object of affection and esteem. Characters of this sort, it must be confessed, are extremely rare, as indeed every other species of excellence generally is, nothing being more uncommon than to meet with what is perfect in its kind in any subject whatsoever. But the misfortune is that the generality of the world have no conception of any other merit than what may be turned to interest. They love their friends upon the same principle, and in the same proportion, as they love their flocks and their herds."

world in general is most evident in the tragedies. Thus, in the final act of *Antony and Cleopatra* the heroine asks, "Shall I abide/ In this dull world, which in thy absence is/ No better than a sty?" (IV. xv. 60-62) Finally she exclaims:

> It were for me
> To throw my sceptre at the injurious gods,
> To tell them that this world did equal theirs
> Till they had stol'n our jewel. (IV. xv. 75-78)

Othello is just as idealistic about the woman he loves. At the end of the first act, when Brabantio warns him that his daughter may deceive her husband as she has deceived her father, Othello's boundless confidence in Desdemona evokes the brief, but impassioned, retort, "My life upon her faith." (I. iii. 295) As Iago spins his devilish web and gradually corrodes his great trust in Desdemona, Othello's love for his wife nonetheless continues to reveal itself in intermittent flashes. In the third act he exclaims as Desdemona leaves the stage,

> Excellent wretch! Perdition catch my soul
> But I do love thee! and when I love thee not,
> Chaos is come again. (III. iii. 90-92)

In the ensuing conversation between Othello and Iago, his suspicions are aroused once again. But when she reenters, the very sight of her convinces Othello that it is folly to suspect her. He cries out, "If she be false, O, then heaven mocks itself!/ I'll not believe it." (III. iii. 278-279) For Othello, everything hinges on the question of Desdemona's fidelity and honesty. Even when he is finally convinced of her infidelity by what he considers to be factual evidence, his love remains as intense as ever. Indeed, it is the very intensity of his affection for the person he has almost idolized which makes it impossible for him to endure the tortured uncertainty of the play's middle scenes in which Iago is gradually building up such a damning case against his wife. Iago, astute psychologist that he is, is aware of this aspect of Othello's nature and takes advantage of the fact that Othello must either love and trust his wife completely or else utterly deny her. For Othello, there can be no partial, qualified emotional attachment. Hence in the last scene, just before he is made to realize how grossly he has erred, he exclaims,

> Nay, had she been true,
> If heaven would make me such another world
> Of one entire and perfect chrysolite,
> I'ld not have sold her for it. (V. ii. 143-146)

It is clear from Hamlet's first soliloquy that his disdain for life and his contempt for the world closely relate to his disillusionment over Gertrude's hasty remarriage. This first soliloquy also makes explicit that it is not merely the hasty remarriage, but particularly the worthlessness of Claudius compared to Gertrude's first husband, which fills Hamlet with such disgust and loathing. The Ghost reveals that he too had had his illusions shattered when she remarried and he too stresses the blindness of the queen to the difference in moral stature between himself and his brother. He tells Hamlet that Claudius

> won to his shameful lust
> The will of my most seeming-virtuous queen.
> O Hamlet, what a falling-off was there,
> From me, whose love was of that dignity
> That it went hand in hand even with the vow
> I made to her in marriage, and to decline
> Upon a wretch whose natural gifts were poor
> To those of mine! (I. v. 45-52)

Both father and son had obviously held Gertrude in high esteem. They had expected of her the passionate attachment which Hecuba shows for Priam (the play within the play) or the constancy and fidelity which Brutus' wife, Portia, shows to her husband in both Elyot's *A Defense of Good Women* and Shakespeare's *Julius Caesar*. Her fickle behavior is the source of their bitter disillusionment—and hence of Hamlet's deliberately vulgar remarks to Ophelia. But even the Ghost can not completely forget his former love for his wife and so he admonishes Hamlet not to take revenge upon her.

From the beginning of the play, the target of Hamlet's most acid sarcasm is infidelity and lack of integrity in women. Indeed, in his first soliloquy, after commenting on Gertrude's behavior, he has reached the conclusion, "Frailty, thy name is woman." (I. ii. 146) When he meets Ophelia at the beginning of the third act, he delivers a harsh lecture to the woman he had once loved so deeply. "I have heard of your paintings too, well enough. God hath given you one face, and you make yourselves another. You jig, you amble, and you lisp; you nickname God's creatures and make your wantonness your ignorance. Go to, I'll no more on't! it hath made me mad. I say, we will have no moe marriages. Those that are married already—all but one—shall live; the rest shall keep as they are. To a nunnery, go." (III. i. 148-157)

In the closet scene, Hamlet's indignation over his mother's blindness to the obvious moral disparity between his father and his uncle reaches its height. He tells Gertrude that she has made "marriage vows/ As false as dicers' oaths." (III. iv. 44-45) As in *Othello*, this manifestation of domestic infidelity assumes such great significance that the heavens themselves seem disturbed by it.

> Heaven's face doth glow;
> Yea, this solidity and compound mass,
> With tristful visage, as against the doom,
> Is thought-sick at the act. (III. iv. 48-51)

Obviously Gertrude's impurity, not Claudius' villainy, is the source of Hamlet's sickness of heart. His disillusionment stems from an original illusion of goodness; not once in the entire play does he ever indicate that he held his uncle in high esteem. But even in the most heart-rending scenes he obviously senses remnants of virtue in his mother. When she laments, "O Hamlet, thou hast cleft my heart in twain," he replies, "O,

throw away the worser part of it,/ And live the purer with
the other half." (III. iv. 156-158) Although he reminds her
once more of her grossness, it is evident that he also trusts her
since he confides in her that he is not really mad. He bids her
not

> Let the bloat King tempt you again to bed;
> Pinch wanton on your cheek; call you his mouse;
> And let him, for a pair of reechy kisses,
> Or paddling in your neck with his damn'd fingers,
> Make you to ravel all this matter out,
> That I essentially am not in madness,
> But mad in craft. (III. iv. 182-188)

When Gertrude assures him that she will not reveal his secret,
she, in effect, enters into conspiracy with Hamlet against her
second husband. Thus, when Claudius questions her at the
beginning of the fourth act as to Hamlet's condition, she deliberately lies on her son's behalf. She informs the king that
he is "Mad as the sea and wind when both contend/ Which
is the mightier." (IV. i. 7-8)

Lear perceives the malice and ingratitude of Goneril before
the conclusion of the first act of the play. But distrustful as he
may be of the one sister, he retains the utmost confidence in
the other until Goneril joins Regan at Gloucester's castle,
bringing him at last to the realization that they are in league
against him. Until that time, despite the fact that Kent is
placed in the stocks and that Lear himself is greeted with utmost discourtesy, he entertains the illusion that Regan is a
faithful daughter. Hence he assures her:

> thou shalt never have my curse,
> Thy tender-hefted nature shall not give
> Thee o'er to harshness. Her eyes are fierce;
>   but thine
> Do comfort, and not burn. 'Tis not in thee
> To grudge my pleasures, to cut off my train,
> To bandy hasty words, to scant my sizes,

> And, in conclusion, to oppose the bolt
> Against my coming in. Thou better know'st
> The offices of nature, bond of childhood,
> Effects of courtesy, dues of gratitude.
> (II. iv. 173-182)

Once the old king realizes that both his daughters are pernicious he, like Hamlet, lets his shattered trust in those he had loved so dearly lead to a general questioning of the integrity of all humanity. The shock to Lear is so great that, for him, the whole moral order is thrown out of kilter.[21] As in the case of *Timon of Athens*, a play which becomes an unhappy caricature of misanthropic attitudes, the hurt and anguish which result from this vicious ingratitude lead to a general hatred of mankind—and a "benevolent" or "malevolent" wish to have all human society destroyed. Hence, Lear appeals to the heavens asking for universal destruction:

> And thou, all-shaking thunder,
> Strike flat the thick rotundity o' th' world,
> Crack Nature's moulds, all germains spill at once,
> That make ingrateful man. (III. ii. 6-9)

In the mock trial which ensues, both Goneril and Regan are specifically arraigned for their guilt. But all women are equally called into question, and, as in Hamlet, they are particularly indicted for their sexual appetites:

> The fitchew nor the soiled horse goes to't
> With a more riotous appetite.
> Down from the waist they are Centaurs,
> Though women all above. (IV. vi. 124-127)

Finally his moral nausea encompasses all mankind, male as well as female. When Gloucester pleads, "O let me kiss that

---

[21] Cf. P. H. Frye's concept of a tragic qualm, the "feeling of insecurity and confusion, as it were a sort of moral dizziness and nausea, due to the vivid realization, in the dramatic fable, of a suspicion which is always lurking uncomfortably near the threshold of consciousness, that the world is somehow out of plumb." Prosser Hall Frye, *Romance and Tragedy*, Boston, 1922, pp. 146-147.

hand," Lear replies tersely, "Let me wipe it first; it smells of mortality." (IV. vi. 135-136)

The misanthropy of Hamlet and Lear becomes truly all-embracing. Ignoring Plato's sane observation that the vast majority of men are neither wholly good nor wholly bad, and that one's disillusionment with a few false friends should not lead to a general condemnation of all mankind, they place a boundless confidence in their kin and loved ones. When they discover that these confidences are misplaced, the jolt results in a profound distrust of all humanity. After this shattering of all illusions about the possible goodness of the human race, Hamlet proceeds to contemplate the horrible finality of death and the gruesome process of physical rotting and of mental or even of spiritual decay which often precedes it. *King Lear*, which is sometimes considered Shakespeare's greatest tragedy, and which certainly contains his starkest and bleakest view of existence, not only dwells on this unpleasant theme but also calls into question the justice of the gods.

The Tragic Codas—Trust and Fidelity Reaffirmed. Frequently, Shakespeare's view of human existence is assumed to be Gloucester's conclusion, "As flies to wanton boys are we to the Gods/ They kill us for their sport" (IV. i. 36-37) and Edgar's, "Men must endure/ Their going hence, even as their coming hither;/ Ripeness is all." (V. ii. 9-11) These lines do relate to one of the major themes of *King Lear*, but they are counterbalanced by two themes of powerful affirmation which should receive equal stress. One of these is the character of the titanic protagonist himself, who demonstrates by his fortitude and greatness of soul the pagan-humanist conviction that, though a man may be crushed by adversity through weakness of the body or the maliciousness of fate, he can endure the most horrible of catastrophes through inner nobility of heart and mind. In the final scene, Lear still displays the same intrinsic nobility, the same moral grandeur, with which he had first confronted his daughter's maledictions.

The other positive theme, equally an affirmation of man's moral potentialities, is quite simply—though not so banally as the 20th century audience would like to think—that of fidelity: the fidelity of Cordelia, Kent, the Fool, and of Edgar. Just as Desdemona remains true to her husband even after he has smothered her, so Cordelia faithfully persists in her conviction of her father's fundamental goodness despite the cruelty with which she has been rejected by him in the opening scene. In the subplot, Edgar, too, never falters in his loyalty to his father despite the fact that Gloucester disowns him. Kent and the Fool serve the same role as does Horatio in *Hamlet*. By their fidelity to their masters they provide dramatic proof for Guazzo's maxim that though a Prince's servants "be not all of the civillest, yet they are faithfull and trustie, which is a thing more to bee set by, then civilitie, finenesse, or bravery."[22] The final scene of *King Lear*, which reveals that the king's whole-hearted love for his one faithful daughter has become almost an obsession, also leaves room for him to show how deeply he cares for Kent. Lear's concern for his faithful servants is the dramatic embodiment of Guazzo's admonition to the Prince not to "forget to reward the good Servant, and keepe him always about him as a precious thing: remembering that the servaunte is in a certaine sorte one parte of the maister, and that there is in this life nothinge more necessary than a good Servaunte: Whereupon it is written, if you have a trusty servant, let him be unto thee as thine own soule."[23]

Truth, in the sense of trueness, trust, fidelity, loyalty, and integrity, upholds Shakespeare's virtuous characters even in the midst of upheaval, as it had been the cement which bound Roman society. Without this, Hurault asks, "how could man's frailtie be upheld among so many waves and storms. . . . Among fellowes, faithfulnesse maintaineth friendship. It maketh servants to obey their maisters with all integritie."[24] This

[22] *The Civile Conversatione*, III, 53.
[23] *ibid.*, III, 54.
[24] p. 90.

is one of the codas at the conclusion of many of Shakespeare's great tragedies. If the tragic protagonist can not always share the optimism of Brutus who found no man that was not true, he can nevertheless find considerable solace in the fact that many of his followers are loyal and devoted. Thus Horatio in *Hamlet*, Desdemona and Cassio in *Othello*, Cordelia, Kent, and the Fool in *King Lear*, Eros, Iras, and Charmian in *Antony and Cleopatra* show utmost loyalty to their leader through all his tribulations. Their devotion to the protagonist is so intense and fervent that Horatio, Iras, and Charmian wish to die with their masters, and Kent indicates that he will shortly follow his. Desdemona is faithful until the very moment that she dies; she prefers to lie to Emilia, pretending that she has killed herself, rather than betray Othello.

Macbeth's tragedy in large measure results from the fact that he is so terribly isolated as the play reaches its close. Like the other heroes, he is completely sick at heart because of his tragic predicament—but in his case his isolation is much more complete since he can not look to have "honour, love, obedience, troops of friends." (V. iii. 25) Macbeth has had a troubled conscience from the very beginning of the play, but he is particularly unnerved near the close of the play because he has no Horatio, Cassio, or Kent to sustain him during the bitter moments when he comes to realize that he is the cause of his own tragedy. Hence, even the news of his wife's death leaves him relatively indifferent, and leads to perhaps the most cynical view of life and of human nature in all Shakespeare, the "to-morrow" soliloquy. But Macbeth's cynicism springs primarily from his realization that he has lost all those values which uphold the other tragic heroes in adversity—their conviction of their intrinsic nobility and their consequent self-esteem, their sense of possessing a "good name" in the human community, and their reliance on the love, devotion, and fidelity of trusted associates. Hamlet, the disillusioned idealist, has ample reason to hold an equally bleak view of existence and indeed he does so until the graveyard scene. But at the very close of the play he can nonetheless affirm the high value he places on Horatio's friendship and ask his friend to live on to see to it that Hamlet's wounded name be cleared. Macbeth is keenly aware that he has lost his right to "good report" and so life is indeed "a tale/ Told by an idiot, full of sound and fury,/ Signifying nothing." (V. v. 26-28)

CHAPTER 8

SHAKESPEARE'S AMBIVALENCE IN REGARD TO CHRISTIAN AND PAGAN-HUMANIST VALUES

THE NOTION OF GODLIKE EXCELLENCE

HE propensity of the Roman moralists to ascribe such great moral excellence to man that he might challenge comparison with the Gods led to the creation by the Renaissance pagan humanists of a race of heroes and demi-gods— of men who surpassed the ordinary bounds of possible human virtue. With his customary subtlety and ambiguity, Shakespeare makes significant use of this common Renaissance notion.

In *Cymbeline*, Iachimo, returning from Italy, has tried unsuccessfully to slander Posthumus' character. He then tells Imogen,

> He sits 'mongst men like a descended god.
> He hath a kind of honour sets him off
> More than a mortal seeming. (I. vi. 169-171)

The spectator must take care to evaluate a particular speech in its dramatic context. These lines might be taken for false flattery—since Iachimo's aim is to gain Imogen's good will— if the testimony of the two gentlemen who discuss Posthumus' character in the opening lines of the play had not indicated that his stature is, indeed, as great as this. For the first gentleman had said that Posthumus is

> a creature such
> As, to seek through the regions of the earth
> For one his like, there would be something failing
> In him that should compare. (I. i. 19-22)

This theme of godlike excellence is of cardinal importance in *Hamlet*. It is the son's intense moral admiration for his great,

279

kingly father (the first scenes indicate that the world shared his high opinion) which leads to Hamlet's bitterness and nausea about his mother's hasty remarriage. If Hamlet's only problem had been to track down the murderers of his father, and the criminal had not replaced his father in his mother's bed, he would not have become so frantic. His hysterical behavior is at least partially the result of the shock caused by his discovery of the incestuous relationship which exists between his mother and his uncle.

Hamlet's first soliloquy centers on two themes: the son's worship of his father as a man of almost godlike perfection and his bitter disillusionment about Gertrude's blindness to this fact.

> That it should come to this!
> But two months dead! Nay, not so much, not two.
> So excellent a king, that was to this
> Hyperion to a satyr. (I. ii. 137-140)

Later on in the same soliloquy he comments again on the obvious disparity in the moral worth of the two brothers. Hamlet describes Claudius as "My father's brother, but no more like my father/ Than I to Hercules." (I. ii. 152-153) The first soliloquy is interrupted by Horatio's unexpected arrival:

> HOR. My Lord, I came to see your father's funeral.
> HAM. I prithee do not mock me, fellow student.
>   I think it was to see my mother's wedding.
>
>   My father—methinks I see my father.
> HOR. O, where, my lord?
> HAM.   In my mind's eye, Horatio.
> HOR. I saw him once. He was a goodly king.
> HAM. He was a man, take him for all in all.
>   I shall not look upon his like again.
>   (I. ii. 176-178, 183-188)

In this passage, Hamlet does not compare his father to the gods, but in the play scene it becomes obvious that Hamlet did revere his father almost as if he had been a god. The jaunty tune of the song, instead of destroying the serious import of the passage, makes more sharply edged the contrasting emotions of utmost reverence for the father and contempt and loathing for the uncle.

> For thou dost know, O Damon dear,
>   This realm dismantled was
> Of Jove himself; and now reigns here
>   A very, very—pajock.
>
> (III. ii. 292-295)

That Shakespeare here has chosen the classical analogue of the Damon-Phintias friendship over the Biblical David-Jonathan one equally familiar to his contemporaries is also significant.

In the closet scene Hamlet finally points out to his mother the enormity of her offense. Again it is not the mere fact that Gertrude has married her husband's murderer, but rather her moral blindness to the relative worth of the two brothers, which cuts so deeply. So Hamlet says,

> Look here upon this picture, and on this,
> The counterfeit presentment of two brothers,
> See what a grace was seated on this brow;
> Hyperion's curls; the front of Jove himself;
> An eye like Mars, to threaten and command;
> A station like the herald Mercury
> New lighted on a heaven-kissing hill:
> A combination and a form indeed
> Where every god did seem to set his seal
> To give the world assurance of a man.
> This was your husband. (III. iv. 53-63)

Here, in this passage, Shakespeare makes most telling use of the pagan-humanist notion that man can achieve an almost godlike excellence.[1] Hamlet's extreme idealism, perhaps in-

---

[1] Cf. Guazzo, III, 36. "Next unto God, there is nothing more to bee honoured then the Father and Mother"; also Fenton, *Golden Epistles*, p. 77. "To ye old

comprehensible to the modern mind, is a direct reflection of
Renaissance pagan-humanist values; thus Hurault remarks
that among the ancients "such as were good men, have not
only beene esteemed, but also worshipped as gods, as Theseus,
Hercules, and others."[2]

Shakespeare, however, is as ambivalent as his age. When
it suits his purpose, he utilizes the Christian ethics even where
it involves him in inconsistency in the portrayal of character.
In order to make the crimes of Claudius appear more loath-
some, he has the ghost say,

> Thus was I, sleeping, by a brother's hand
> Of life, of crown, of queen, at once dispatch'd;
> Cut off even in the blossoms of my sin,
> Unhous'led, disappointed, unanel'd,
> No reck'ning made, but sent to my account
> With all my imperfections on my head.
>
> (I. v. 74-79)

In the prayer scene, Hamlet even speaks of his father's crimes.
He remarks when he discovers Claudius kneeling in prayer:

> He took my father grossly, full of bread,
> With all his crimes broad blown, as flush as May;
> And how his audit stands, who know save heaven?
>
> (III. iii. 80-82)

Shakespeare thus makes use of both Christian and pagan-humanist values, even though this involves him in contradiction. To
some extent, the question of the relative importance of each
scale of values must be left to the individual reader's judgment.
In this case, however, it may be pointed out that the central
focus of these passages which refer to the sinfulness and imperfection of the elder Hamlet is not on the fact of his sinful

---

men in ages past were borne such honorable respects, that as Gods they were
reverenced, and holden in the place and reputation of fathers."

Queen Elizabeth, while still a princess, held her father in such great respect,
that she knelt five times in succession to him before sitting down in his presence.

[2] *Politicke, Moral, and Martial Discourses*, p. 54.

condition but rather on the extent to which his uncle's crimes become more heinous because Hamlet's father was given no opportunity to repent his sins. Hamlet's acid bitterness about Gertrude's blindness to the differing moral stature of her two husbands loses much of its significance if we really view his father as a man with "crimes broad blown, as flush as May." (III. iii. 81) In isolation and interpreted literally, these lines can be cited as evidence that Shakespeare was an intensely religious person, thoroughly imbued with a sense of original sin and damnation, who believed that man's only hope for salvation rests in the grace of God. In recent years such critics as S. N. Bethell, Wilson Knight, W. C. Curry, Kenneth Myrick, John Vyvyan, and G. R. Elliott thus arrive at the conclusion that the Christian ethic provides the key to a proper interpretation of Shakespearean tragic values.[3] In "The Theme of Damnation in Shakespearean Tragedy," for example, Myrick comes to the conclusion that *Hamlet* is a thoroughly religious play. He uses in evidence beyond these passages Hamlet's fear of hell, Claudius' would-be prayer of repentance, and the spirit of contrition manifested by Gertrude and Laertes at the moment of their deaths.[4] But if instead are stressed the high regard shown by Horatio and the soldiers of the watch in the

---

[3] Myrick's Christian interpretation stands in sharp contrast to the concept of tragedy which Farnham elaborates after a careful study of medieval literature in *The Medieval Heritage of Elizabethan Tragedy*. Farnham discovers the beginnings of the Renaissance view of tragedy in Boccaccio: "The stories of Hannibal and Alcibiades are, in all the *De Casibus*, the closest to profound dramatic tragedy. Both of these men, as Boccaccio sees them, are admirably heroic and in no sense vicious; they are not even sinners in the moralist's sense of the term. They are great souls with failings to make them human, and their failings become tragic only because of the positions in which their ability has placed them." (p. 97)

I compare these two critics simply to point out how radical the differences are between those who view the Renaissance as fundamentally Christian and those who view it as fundamentally humanist. Lecky's rule of thumb is convenient here; he differentiates the Christian position from the humanist by distinguishing between the sense of sin and the sense of vice. Both are present in Shakespearean tragedy. Whether we side with Myrick or Farnham depends on the relative emphasis given to each in our judgment of the work of art as a whole.

[4] Kenneth O. Myrick, *The Theme of Damnation in Shakespearean Tragedy*, Studies in Philology, Chapel Hill, 1941, XXXVIII, 233-234.

first scene of the play, and Hamlet's intense admiration for his father, the lines attesting to the sinfulness and "radical imperfection" of the dead king cease to have any great significance, since they play false the high esteem instilled into us in reflection of Horatio's and Hamlet's attitudes.

Although *Coriolanus* is not a Christian play, considerable ambiguity exists as to the moral excellence or moral imperfectibility of the hero. Toward the end of the fourth act, Cominius reports to the terror-stricken Romans not only that Coriolanus has joined the Volscians, but also that

> He is their god. He leads them like a thing
> Made by some other deity than Nature,
> That shapes man better. (IV. vi. 90-92)

Cominius proceeds to scold Brutus for being so ungrateful to Coriolanus: "He will shake/ Your Rome about your ears." (IV. vi. 98-99) To which Menenius adds, "As Hercules/ Did shake down mellow fruit." (IV. vi. 99-100) The major stress, both in the Roman tragedies and in the chronicle histories, is not on the moral excellence of the hero but on his superhuman qualities as a soldier. (Brutus in *Julius Caesar* is, of course, a significant exception.) Thus York, in *King Richard the Second*, speaks of the Black Prince as that "young Mars of men," (II. iii. 101) and Exeter in *King Henry the Fifth* warns the French Dauphin that, unless he submits, the English king is coming "in thunder and in earthquake, like a Jove." (II. iv. 100) So, likewise, Cleopatra is told, in the battle preceding Antony's final defeat, that

> He hath fought to-day
> As if a god in hate of mankind had
> Destroyed in such a shape. (IV. viii. 24-26)

Shakespeare does not refer directly to the sort of pagan heaven described in Scipio's dream in the sixth book of the *Republic*, which deified the Roman heroes. But Belarius does deem his two adopted sons, Guiderius and Arviragus, princes

who are "worthy/ To inlay heaven with stars." (V. v. 351-352)
Horatio's moving farewell, "Now cracks a noble heart. Good
night, sweet prince,/ And flights of angels sing thee to thy
rest" is a typical Renaissance weaving of Christian and pagan-
humanist strands. (V. ii. 370-371) Antony's invocation to the
presumably dead Cleopatra suggests, on the other hand, a
thoroughly pagan heaven.

> I come, my queen.—Eros!—Stay for me.
> Where souls do couch on flowers, we'll hand in hand
> And with our sprightly port make the ghosts gaze.
> Dido and her Aeneas shall want troops,
> And all the haunt be ours. (IV. xiv. 50-54)

This passage depicts a completely romanticized heaven for the
great lovers of antiquity. The description of Cleopatra's death
demonstrates how easily Shakespeare could intertwine heroic
and purely romantic elements into the dramatic and poetic
texture of the play. At one moment her suicide is an act of
heroic grandeur:

> Yare, yare, good Iras; quick. Methinks I hear
> Antony call. I see him rouse himself
> To praise my noble act. (V. ii. 286-288)

At the next, it is purely romantic. She says of the Iras who is
dead at her feet:

> If she first meet the curled Antony,
> He'll make demand of her, and spend that kiss
> Which is my heaven to have. (V. ii. 304-306)

Shakespeare's genius reveals itself particularly in his ability
to mix the realistic and the fanciful in such a way that neither
the demands of drama for a realistic depiction of human nature
nor the demands of poetry for imaginative grandeur are denied.
Sidney, in *An Apology for Poetry*, had made much of the
poet's ability to ignore the historian's concern for reality
and thus to build a race of heroes and demigods such as never

were in nature.[5] Shakespeare's most poetically eloquent expression of man's superhuman capabilities, Cleopatra's eulogy over the dead Antony, admits to the unreality of the heroic proportions which she ascribes to Antony, and yet the audience is made to feel that her poetic conception bears relation to the hero who has just died.

> CLEO. I dreamt there was an Emperor Antony—
> O, such another sleep, that I might see
> But such another man!
> DOL.   If it might please ye—
> CLEO. His face was as the heav'ns, and therein
>   stuck
> A sun and moon, which kept their course
>   and lighted
> The little O, the earth.
> DOL.   Most sovereign creature—
> CLEO. His legs bestrid the ocean: his rear'd arm
> Crested the world. (V. ii. 76-83)

Cleopatra asks Dolabella whether it is possible that a man of such tremendous proportions could have existed. To his negative answer, she replies with the sort of daring ambiguity which permits Shakespeare to join Sidney's fictitious, idealized world of poetry with his realistic presentation of flesh and blood characters. She says,

> You lie, up to the hearing of the gods!
> But, if there be or ever were one such,
> It's past the size of dreaming. Nature wants stuff
> To vie strange forms with fancy; yet, t'imagine
> An Antony were nature's piece 'gainst fancy,
> Condemning shadows quite. (V. ii. 95-100)

Montaigne and La Primaudaye, speaking for the Christian tradition, had bitterly attacked the notion that man could attain

---

[5] In *Works*, III, 8.

a godlike excellence, for they had considered it a manifestation of his utter vanity and insolence.[6] (This view is closely akin to the *hybris* which so often leads to the downfall of the hero in Greek tragedy.) Shakespeare only once creates a character whose claims to godlike qualities really suggest arrogance, and even in that case, the characterization of Julius Caesar leaves room for considerable ambiguity. Cassius says sneeringly, in a passage similar to the one just quoted (the utter contrast of tone indicates how little the literal idea of a passage means in Shakespeare):

> Why, man, he doth bestride the narrow world
> Like a Colossus, and we petty men
> Walk under his huge legs and peep about
> To find ourselves dishonourable graves.
>
> (I. ii. 135-138)

Just prior to this, Cassius had been eager to point out to Brutus that this man, who has become a god, had formerly shown many signs of ordinary human weakness, particularly when he became tired while in swimming and depended on Cassius to bring him to shore.

There is no doubt that Shakespeare intends his audience to view Caesar's arrogance as a cause of his downfall, since Caesar becomes exceedingly boastful and obstinate when he decides to attend the Senate. His pride in making this decision is as closely related to his downfall as is Agamemnon's when he steps on the purple carpet. Yet immediately after the assassination, Shakespeare, subtly accomplishing a major shift of focus so that the ambiguity passes almost unnoticed, has Antony refer to Julius Caesar as the mighty Caesar—without in any way intimating that Caesar should not be revered for his absolute power. Indeed, Caesar's ghost becomes, in a sense, the hero of the play. So when Brutus finds Titinius slain, he exclaims,

---

[6] Montaigne, *Essayes*, II, 12. La Primaudaye, p. 15.

O Julius Caesar, thou art mighty yet!
Thy spirit walks abroad and turns our swords
In our own proper entrails. (V. iii. 94-96)

THE HEROES

Castiglione and other Renaissance moralists often spoke of a race of demi-gods and heroes, surpassing the bounds of ordinary virtue, who were above and apart from the rest of humanity. Shakespeare does not draw any distinct line between the heroes and his other characters, but does manage to suggest that there is something exceptional about his central tragic figures so that they are placed apart from those who surround them, even from such perfectly loyal and devoted followers as Horatio, Kent, or Emilia. He is not necessarily suggesting that the hero is closer to perfection than the other characters, though such a distinction is present when Desdemona and Emilia discuss the question of adultery. Emilia admits to the ordinary human temptation to be a little sinful for a great reward, whereas Desdemona shows herself completely beyond temptation. (IV. iii. 60 ff.)

Shakespeare makes his tragic heroes exceptional, however, primarily by the strength of their emotions and the intensity of their feelings. The greatness of their capacity to love and the tremendous depths to which they can be hurt separate them from the rest of the characters, good or bad. Their emotional responses are in large measure moral responses, and suggest exalted moral stature. That the tragic heroes are great of heart, both in the moral and the emotional sense (indeed, for the Shakespearean tragic hero, the two are inextricably intertwined), makes them heroic and exceptional. Castiglione had defined his race of heroes as a race with an excess of moral perfection in accordance with the Aristotelian definitions of magnanimity and greatness of heart. Shakespeare presents heroes who have major flaws (Agrippa had said of Antony, "But you gods will give us/ Some faults to make us men"); in this sense, they are not perfect. (V. i. 32-33) As a result, the philistine critic often finds it difficult to view the Cleopatra of the final act as a genuine tragic heroine—she has committed too many misdeeds earlier in the play for him to feel in her any genuine tragic grandeur.

Shakespeare, however, readily admitting faults in his tragic heroes, makes these faults seem trivial by the splendor and greatness of the character as a whole. Only infrequently employing the phrases "heroic," "magnanimous," or "great-souled," Shakespeare manages through the poetic and dramatic medium to convey precisely these qualities to the audience; indeed, it is these attributes which distinguish Hamlet, Lear, Antony, Cleopatra, and Coriolanus from the other characters in the play in question. Essex had said that "little minds tho' never so full of virtue, can be but a little virtuous," and elsewhere that it is as "vain to seek to enlarge or enflame" the ordinary person to high virtue as it is "to go about to plough the rock."[7] The quality of heroic grandeur is missing from the Antony of *Julius Caesar*, a lack which distinguishes him markedly from the Antony of *Antony and Cleopatra*. This quality causes us to identify with Cleopatra in her great sorrow over her Antony's death, to share in her contempt for the coldly calculating victorious Caesar, and to exult in the magnificence and moral grandeur of her noble suicide. Caesar has been a more "virtuous" character than she, but is almost completely devoid of the greatness of heart which arouses such strong feelings of admiration and grief in us when the hero and heroine die.

T. S. Eliot is convinced of the Stoic self-sufficiency of Shakespeare's tragic heroes, but if we examine their reactions to the deaths of their loved ones, we feel the intensity of their at-

---

[7] Devereux, ed. *Lives of the Devereux* I, 487, 325. Cf. Butcher's interpretation of Aristotle. "According to Aristotle, the characters portrayed by epic and tragic poetry have their basis in moral goodness; but the goodness is of the heroic order. It is quite distinct from plain, uninspiring virtue. It has nothing in it common or mean. Whatever be the moral imperfections in the characters, they are such as impress our imagination, and arouse the sense of grandeur: we are lifted above the reality of daily life." (A. H. Butcher, *Aristotle's Theory of Poetry*, London, 1902, p. 233. Cf. Chapter II, below, n. 24.)

tachment and devotion to be the antithesis of Stoic detach-
ment. Brutus' response to the news of Portia's death is indeed
Stoic and can only evoke feelings of cold wonder:

> Why, farewell, Portia. We must die, Messala,
> With meditating that she must die once,
> I have the patience to endure it now.
>
> (IV. iii. 190-192)

But in the tragedies of Shakespeare's maturity, the response
is anything but Stoic. The Othello of the early part of the play,
on discovering that Desdemona has come safely through the
storm, shows the most intense attachment to his loved one:

> If it were now to die,
> 'Twere now to be most happy; for I fear
> My soul hath her content so absolute
> That not another comfort like to this
> Succeeds in unknown fate. (II. i. 191-195)

This is the direct opposite of Stoic deprecation of passion and
of worldly attachments. As Howard Baker remarks in answer
to Eliot's criticism: "Needless to say, it is not stoicism; it is
active while stoicism is passive, it is the opposite of an apart-
ness from the world; and it is a firm, genuinely tragic attitude."[8]
Even after Othello has murdered Desdemona, in his "had she
been true" speech the completeness, the depth, and the whole-
heartedness of his love for her are only too apparent.

Similar greatness of heart is apparent in the devotion of the
other tragic heroes. Obvious as this may seem, it is essential
to document it; otherwise the moral greatness of the heroes of
the mature tragedies eludes definition. It is the capacity for an
ultimately steadfast, noble, and yet passionate devotion which
makes Antony and Cleopatra greater in stature than the Brutus
of *Julius Caesar* who in the cold Stoic fashion is a far nobler
man. Contrast Brutus' impassive reception of the news of

---

[8] *Induction to Tragedy*, Baton Rouge, 1939, p. 201.

Portia's death with this response of Cleopatra to Charmian's plea, "Be comforted, dear madam."

> No, I will not
> All strange and terrible events are welcome,
> But comforts we despise. Our size of sorrow,
> Proportion'd to our cause, must be as great
> As that which makes it. (IV. xv. 2-6)

So, likewise, the Hamlet of the closing scenes of the play becomes a genuinely heroic figure as the result of his capacity for passion. It is no sickly weakling who leaps into the grave, wrestles with Laertes, and, revealing for the first time the depth of the passion he had felt for Ophelia, makes us feel that Laertes' devotion is trifling in comparison.

> I lov'd Ophelia. Forty thousand brothers
> Could not (with all their quantity of love)
> Make up my sum. (V. i. 292-294)

In the case of King Lear, the hero's tragic stature depends almost entirely on his capacity for love and grief. It is no "poor, infirm, weak, and despis'd old man" (III. ii. 20) who enters in the last scene with Cordelia dead in his arms and exclaims:

> Howl, howl, howl, howl! O, you are men of stone.
> Had I your tongues and eyes, I'ld use them so
> That heaven's vault should crack. (V. iii. 257-259)

Shakespeare on one level presents a world of very human people—a world which, because of the emphasis on circumstance and detail, seems very real to us. But on another level we are involved in action exceptional in nature since we are dealing with human beings who are superhuman in the intensity of their emotions. The central values and emotional bonds which are the source of this intense feeling are few, but are of such supreme moment and such great strength that the disturbance of them is, we feel, world shaking. These values and these emotions are universal, calling forth our instant allegiance. When they are destroyed, we feel equally with the hero and other good characters that something has happened of catastrophic significance. From this point of view, the events which happen in the little tragic world come to take on the greatest general significance. Every man can share these emotions although they are presented on a heroic plane far above him.

It is at the moment of death that Shakespeare particularly points to the great-hearted quality of the hero, at the moment when the hero, the other characters, and the audience are most conscious of his intrinsic nobility. Hal's eulogy of the dead Hotspur indicates the pattern Shakespeare is to follow in portraying the deaths of his later heroes. Prince Hal says, "Fare thee well, great heart!" (V. iv. 87), and then adds:

> When that this body did contain a spirit,
> A kingdom for it was too small a bound;
> But now two paces of the vilest earth
> Is room enough. (V. iv. 89-92)

Hal's speech, or Antony's reference to Julius Caesar's death, "Then burst his mighty heart," (III. ii. 191) does not have the emotional impact of the eulogies of the great tragedies because we do not feel that the hero's character has fully revealed the moral grandeur suggested by the eulogy. But Horatio's "Now cracks a noble heart" (V. ii. 370) and Cassio's "For he was great of heart" (V. ii. 361) evoke intense feelings of mingled terror, pity, and admiration, for they sum up our own feelings about the death of a character of truly heroic proportions. This is so, too, in Octavius Caesar's reaction to the news that Antony is dead: "The breaking of so great a thing should make/ A greater crack." (V. i. 14-15) Cleopatra's response to Antony's death, like Hal's, points to the paradoxical discrepancy between the greatness of the living hero and the inconsequentiality of the corpse: "This case of that huge spirit now is cold." (IV. xv. 89) In many instances, the hero provides self-testimony to his own noble stature. The dying Antony speaks of himself as "the noblest" and "the greatest prince o' th' world," (IV. xv. 54-55) and, just before he is murdered, Coriolanus responds to Aufidius' insulting epithet, "Measureless liar, thou hast made my heart/ Too great for what contains it." (V. vi. 102-103)

In large measure it is the hero's capacity for bearing torture of mind and spirit which makes us aware of his heroic stature. In proportion as this capacity is lacking in their heroes, *Julius Caesar* and *Romeo and Juliet* suffer by contrast with the great tragedies. As Aristotle said, "even in adversity nobility shines through, when a man endures repeated and severe misfortune with patience, not owing to insensibility but from generosity and greatness of soul."[9] For this reason, death often comes as a welcome relief to the Shakespearean tragic hero. Santayana rightly singles out Macbeth's soliloquy following the murder of Duncan as fundamental to the spirit of Shakespearean tragedy. He errs, however, in suggesting that such a nihilistic speech can be considered a full accounting of the nature of that tragedy.[10] The sentiments of the Shakespearean hero are akin to those of Mary Queen of Scots who tells her weeping servants, "You ought to rejoice rather then weepe for that the end of Mary Stewards troubles is now come."[11] In a similar spirit, Macbeth says, in the soliloquy to which Santayana refers,

> Better be with the dead,
> Whom we, to gain our peace, have sent to peace,
> Than on the torture of the mind to lie
> In restless ecstasy. Duncan is in his grave;
> After life's fitful fever he sleeps well.
> Treason has done his worst. Nor steel nor poison,
> Malice domestic, foreign levy, nothing,
> Can touch him further. (III. ii. 19-26)

All the Shakespearean heroes, at the moment of death, find it not something to be feared but rather a welcome release

[9] *Nicomachean Ethics* I. 10.
[10] Singer, *Santayana*, p. 142 (cf. pp. 266-269).
[11] *Source Book of English History*, ed. Kendall, p. 173.

from the suffering and anguish they have endured. Othello tells Iago, "I'ld have thee live;/ For in my sense, 'tis happiness to die." (V. ii. 289-290) Hamlet admonishes Horatio,

> Absent thee from felicity awhile,
> And in this harsh world draw thy breath in pain,
> To tell my story. (V. ii. 358-360)

Cleopatra implores the asp at her breast, "With thy sharp teeth this knot intrinsicate/ Of life at once untie," (V. ii. 307, 308) and calms the weeping Charmian, as Mary Queen of Scots had calmed her servants,

> Peace, peace!
> Dost thou not see my baby at my breast,
> That sucks the nurse asleep. (V. ii. 311-313)

As Lear dies, Kent merely implores, "Break, heart; I prithee break!" (V. iii. 312) and rebukes Edgar for trying to revive him:

> Vex not his ghost. O, let him pass! He hates him
> That would upon the rack of this tough world
> Stretch him out longer. (V. iii. 313-315)

In the tragi-comedies, portrayal of character is not heroic—at least not in the sense in which Castiglione and Count Romei had defined that term. *Troilus and Cressida*, as much as *Julius Caesar* or *Antony and Cleopatra*, is a story of the great heroes of antiquity, but, as has been observed, the tone of the play is somewhat cynical, since the Greek and Trojan heroes frequently fail to adhere to their own ideals. The chronicle histories are too involved in the realistic presentation of the weaknesses of a Richard the Second or the politic cunning of a King Henry the Fourth for us to feel full-measured greatness of character. Even in Prince Hal's eulogy of Hotspur, criticism of his "ill-weav'd ambition" is mingled with praise of his great heart. King Henry the Fifth receives handsome tribute from the French king, but only as a warrior hero. He lacks the subtlety and depth of the Shakespearean tragic hero and therefore fails to merit our full admiration. The king warns his dauphin son that King Harry is a strong opponent, for

> He is bred out of that bloody strain
> That haunted us in our familiar paths.
> Witness our too much memorable shame
> When Cressy battle fatally was struck,
> And all our princes captiv'd, by the hand
> Of that black name, Edward, Black Prince of Wales;
> Whiles that his mountain sire—on mountain standing,
> Up in the air, crown'd with the golden sun—
> Saw his heroical seed, and smil'd to see him,
> Mangle the work of nature.
>
> > > This is a stem
> Of that victorious stock; and let us fear
> The native mightiness and fate of him.
> > > > (II. iv. 51-60, 62-64)

In the next scene King Harry even compares the heroic qualities of his soldiers to the heroes of Greece. Fluellen, in the battle which ensues, is asked whether the Duke of Exeter is safe and replies with the irrelevant tribute that "the Duke of Exeter is as magnanimous as Agamemnon" and, after finally getting around to an answer to the question, goes on to suggest that Pistol is "as valiant a man as Mark Antony!" (III. vi. 6-7, 15) The English soldiers quite self-consciously compared their military prowess to that of the heroes of Greece and Rome whom they so much admired. This feeling of rivalry, and even of superiority, is particularly evident in *Cymbeline*, where Posthumus says to the Roman Philario,

> > > Our countrymen
> Are men more order'd than when Julius Caesar
> Smil'd at their lack of skill but found their courage
> Worthy his frowning at. Their discipline
> (Now wing-led with their courages) will make known

> To their approvers they are people such
> That mend upon the world. (II. iv. 20-26)

To some extent, the lavish terms of praise in the eulogies at the close of Shakespeare's plays can be discounted, since both ordinary etiquette and theatrical practice introduce an element of conventionality for which allowances have to be made. Even with such allowances, however, the basic concept of excelling virtue still remains. When, in addition, the eulogy is supported by an abundance of praise from other characters, as in Antony's eulogy of Brutus, we can not dismiss the encomiastic speeches as mere conventional rhetoric. A given speech even takes on added meaning if it accords with our evaluation of a particular character, as is the case when Antony and Octavius Caesar praise their dead enemy, Brutus.

Perhaps an equally important means by which the admiration felt for the dead hero can be conveyed is through the rich effect of the poetry. The final eulogies in *Antony and Cleopatra* demonstrate that out of one of the most banal of humanist commonplaces, the concept of rare and excelling virtue, Shakespeare has created some of his most magnificent poetry. Cleopatra says to the dying Antony,

> Noblest of men, woo't die?
> Hast thou no care of me? Shall I abide
> In this dull world, which in thy absence is
> No better than a sty? O, see, my women,
> [Antony dies.]
> The crown o' th' earth doth melt. My lord!
> O, wither'd is the garland of the war,
> The soldier's pole is fall'n. Young boys and girls
> Are level now with men. The odds is gone,
> And there is nothing left remarkable
> Beneath the visiting moon. (IV. xv. 59-68)

When Cleopatra herself dies, one of her serving maids describes her incomparable beauty and greatness. Again the idea is simple and conventional, but Shakespeare manages to convey, nonetheless, a wealth of poetic feeling. Charmian says,

> So fare thee well,
> Now boast thee, death, in thy possession lies
> A lass unparallel'd. Downy windows, close;
> And golden Phoebus never be beheld
> Of eyes again so royal! (V. ii. 317-321)

ARE SHAKESPEARE'S HEROES EGOTISTS AND INDIVIDUALISTS?

Shakespeare's frequent tendency to focus on the hero, or on the individual who excels in virtue, leads us to conclude that individualism was an important aspect of his system of values. T. S. Eliot suggests that this individualism is a combination of the Senecan attitude of self-sufficiency and of the moral anarchism expressed by Montaigne and Machiavelli. I shall try to show that Shakespeare here is much closer to the concepts of Aristotle and Cicero, and that, even as they do, he places as much stress on the individual's awareness of social obligations as on his involvement in his own predicament.

First let us look at Eliot's position. In "Shakespeare and the Stoicism of Seneca," Eliot states: "In Elizabethan England we have conditions apparently utterly different from those of imperial Rome. But it was a period of dissolution and chaos; and in such a period any emotional attitude which seems to give a man something firm, even if it be only the attitude of 'I am myself alone,' is eagerly taken up. I hardly need—and it is beyond my present scope—to point out how readily, in a period like the Elizabethan, the Senecan attitude of Pride, the Montaigne attitude of Scepticism, and the Machiavelli attitude of Cynicism, arrived at a kind of fusion in the Elizabethan individualism."[12] Eliot relates "this individualism, this vice of Pride" to Hamlet's final speech—the hero, he observes, "dies fairly well pleased with himself." He then

---

12 "Shakespeare and the Stoicism of Seneca," *Selected Essays*, p. 112.

297

points out that Antony says, "I am Antony still," and the Duchess, "I am Duchess of Malfy still." He asks, "would either of them have said that unless Medea had said *Medea superest?*"[13] Eliot soon comes to the conclusion that the Elizabethan hero "is much more Stoical and Senecan, in this way, then the Senecan hero."[14]

In his essay on Seneca, Eliot observes, "Shakespeare and Dante were both merely poets. . . . Our estimate of the intellectual material they absorbed does not affect our estimate of their poetry, either absolutely or relatively to each other. But it must affect our vision of them and the use we make of them, the fact that Dante, for instance, had behind him an Aquinas, and Shakespeare behind him a Seneca. Perhaps it was Shakespeare's special role in history to have effected this peculiar union— perhaps it is a part of his special eminence to have expressed an inferior philosophy in the greatest poetry."[15] In this essay, Eliot commits himself definitely to the opinion that Shakespeare was influenced by Seneca, whereas in the essay on Stoicism the idea is presented tentatively, almost whimsically.

In addition to Senecan individualism, self-sufficiency, and self-pride, Eliot senses an element of anarchy in Shakespeare and his fellow Elizabethans: "Shakespeare, hardly knowing it, became the representative of the end of the sixteenth century, of a turning point in history. . . . The end of the sixteenth century is an epoch when it is particularly difficult to associate poetry with systems of thought or reasoned views of life."[16] Eliot goes on to state that he has found it "quite impossible to come to the conclusion that Donne believed anything," as elsewhere he observes "not that Montaigne had any philosophy whatever."[17]

Shakespeare is consigned to a position where, at one moment, he seems to be believing in inferior Senecan philosophy and,

[13] *ibid.,* pp. 112-113. See my discussion of "I am Antony yet" on p. 199.
[14] *ibid.,* p. 113.
[15] "Seneca in Elizabethan Translation," *Selected Essays,* p. 80.
[16] "Shakespeare and the Stoicism of Seneca," *Selected Essays,* pp. 117-118.
[17] *ibid.,* pp. 118, 109.

at the next, is anarchistic and nihilistic, believing, like Donne and Montaigne, in nothing at all. "There was a general philosophy of life," says Eliot, "if it may be called such, based on Seneca and other influences, which we find in Shakespeare as in the others. It is a philosophy which, as Santayana observed in an essay which passed almost unheeded, may be summarized in the statement that Duncan is in his grave. Even the philosophical basis, the general attitude toward life of the Elizabethans, is one of anarchism, of dissolution, of decay. It is in fact exactly parallel and indeed one and the same thing with their artistic greediness, their desire for every sort of effect together, their unwillingness to accept any limitation and abide by it."[18]

For Eliot, apparently, the only choice for the men of the Renaissance was between Christian values and the very inferior values of Seneca which easily led to no values at all.[19] If we accept this false dichotomy and Eliot's suggestion that Shakespeare's age was one of nihilism, scepticism, and a vulgarized Stoicism, we can equate Hamlet morally with Tamburlaine, and, by inference, the moral values of Shakespeare with those of Marlowe. Eliot, we remember, prefers the Marlovian hero who is at least aware of the possibility of damnation. Again and again, Eliot speaks of the Renaissance as an age of "mixed and muddled scepticism," of "anarchism," of "dissolution." Since Shakespeare belongs to this disintegrating age, Shakespeare can only represent the disintegration of all values. Eliot even suggests that Machiavelli contributes to the disintegrating philosophy of Shakespeare.[20] For Shakespeare, "the element of Seneca is the most completely absorbed and transmogrified, because it was already the most diffused throughout Shakespeare's world. The element of Machiavelli is probably the most indirect, the element of Montaigne the most immediate. . . . What influence the work of Seneca and Machiavelli and

[18] "Four Elizabethan Dramatists," *Selected Essays*, p. 98.
[19] *ibid.*, pp. 98, 119-120.
[20] "Shakespeare and the Stoicism of Seneca," *Selected Essays*, p. 119.

Montaigne seems to me to exert in common on that time, and most conspicuously through Shakespeare, is an influence toward a kind of self-dramatization of the Shakespearean hero, of whom Hamlet is only one. It seems to mark a stage, even if not a very agreeable one, in human history, or progress, or deterioration, or change."[21]

To this dark age of dissolution and chaos, Eliot holds in contrast the greatness of the whole 13th century, and, as far as philosophy is concerned, the greatness of Dante over Shakespeare. (He admits that Shakespeare is as great an artist.) "The difference between Shakespeare and Dante," Eliot writes, "is that Dante had one coherent system of thought behind him; but that was just his luck, and from the point of view of poetry is an irrelevant accident. It happened that at Dante's time thought was orderly and strong and beautiful, and that it was concentrated in one man of the greatest genius; Dante's poetry receives a boost which in a sense it does not merit, from the fact that the thought behind it is the thought of a man as great and lovely as Dante himself: St. Thomas. The thought behind Shakespeare is of men far inferior to Shakespeare himself."[22] In *Second Thoughts on Humanism*, he again compares Dante and Shakespeare and states openly what is implied here—that one must "depreciate Shakespeare for his lower view of life."[23] He hastily adds that he is not criticizing the man so much as the age. He concludes with the admission that: "I prefer the culture which produced Dante to the culture which produced Shakespeare."[24] This conclusion, which makes the Middle Ages rather than the Renaissance the golden age of European civilization, is shared by a good many recent literary critics and cultural historians.[25]

Here we see that Eliot's view of Shakespeare rests on his view of the culture which surrounded him. Our first question necessarily, then, is whether his view of that culture is sound. Do the positive values of the age truly consist of Senecan in-

[21] *ibid.*   [22] *ibid.*, p. 116.   [23] *Selected Essays*, p. 399.
[24] *ibid.*   [25] See E. M. W. Tillyard, *English Renaissance*, pp. 10-19.

dividualism and a "mixed and muddled scepticism"? If so, Eliot can rightly term them "anarchic" and "dissolute." But if we examine the treatises on moral philosophy of the age, we find that it is Aristotle and Cicero, rather than Seneca, who provide the Renaissance humanists with the cardinal definitions of their values. Elyot's *The Gouernour* quotes preponderantly from Cicero (sixty-three quotations, with Aristotle second with twenty-four); so, likewise, does Ascham's *Toxiphilus* (twenty-three quotations from Cicero, eighteen from Aristotle).[26] As Baldwin points out in *Small Latine and Lesse Greeke*, the ethical training of a prince (in this case Edward, but it would be equally true of Elizabeth) was centered on the grammar school collection of Cicero's *Offices*, *The Tuscalan Questions*, and Aristotle's *Nicomachean Ethics*.[27] For the ordinary schoolboy, training in ethics and moral philosophy, as distinguished from religious education, focused on Cicero. In the age of Shakespeare, in other words, Cicero's *Offices* was by far the most important single treatise on moral philosophy for prince and schoolboy alike.[28]

[26] Buckley, *Atheism in the English Renaissance*, p. 13.

[27] T. W. Baldwin, *William Shakspere's Small Latine and Lesse Greeke*, Urbana, Illinois, 1944, I, 246-247.

[28] Baldwin discusses the curriculum of the English grammar school (which Shakespeare probably attended) as well as the studies of the Renaissance prince who had private tutors. His conclusions leave no doubt as to the central importance of Cicero. Consider the following:

"The ethical or moral training of upper grammar school, as distinguished from the specifically religious, centered upon Cicero." (II, 581)

"Three out of the four known copies [of Cicero's *De Officiis*] have been thoroughly used throughout; the fourth copy has not been so heavily used. But as a rule seventeenth century copies show their scars only on selected passages. . . . In Shakespeare's day, however, *De Officiis* was the pinnacle of moral philosophy." (II, 589-590)

If Baldwin is accurate, it is difficult to understand that school of historical interpretation which insists that the "classical humanism of the Renaissance was fundamentally medieval and fundamentally Christian." (See Douglas Bush, *The Renaissance and English Humanism*, Toronto, 1939, p. 68.)

As C. H. Haskins has pointed out in *The Rise of the Universities* theology was the supreme subject of medieval study. The organized, systematic study of moral philosophy—except as a handmaiden to theology—was unthinkable in the medieval school curriculum. Of course, Aristotle was being studied in 1254, but he was always being reconciled with Christian dogmas.

Bush makes much of the humanistic interests of John of Salisbury. Haskins does indeed suggest that a few individuals such as John of Salisbury can maintain a

We can readily agree with Eliot that the moral values of Shakespeare's age were eclectic, derivative (in an important sense, Aquinas is the greatest derivative philosopher of all time), and even to some extent muddled. We can also readily admit that an element of Stoicism exists in most Renaissance moralists and that there are elements of scepticism in Donne and Montaigne. But this does not mean that the Englishman and the Frenchman believed in nothing. Consider, for example, the remarks of Villey on Montaigne and French humanism: "The majority of the intellectuals who worked for the revolution which we have just discussed remained Christian, at least they believed that they remained Christian; they acknowledged the dogmas of Christianity. . . . And yet, it is the way of life of the pagan philosophers which Montaigne revived as completely as one could do so. His work is the crowning achievement of French humanism."[29] Certainly there are elements of scepticism in Montaigne, just as there are elements of Christianity. But we need only consider his great love of Rome, or of the heroes of antiquity—Caesar, Brutus, Epaminondas, Alexander, and Scipio—not to mention his repeated references to all of the great classical authors and his frequent allusions to the Aristotelian virtues of liberality, magnificence, greatness of heart, and friendship (and his close relationship to Etienne de la Boétie), to sense that, however mixed and muddled Montaigne

humanistic attitude in the so-called "Dark Ages." But Haskins does not suggest that the Renaissance of the twelfth century in any way challenges the supremacy of Christian theology. His remarks do not accord with the findings of Bush in *The Renaissance and English Humanism*. For example, Haskins states that the "absence of the classical works of literature and history from this list of translations from the Greek is as significant as it is from the curriculum of the medieval universities. We are in the twelfth, not the fifteenth century, and the interest in medicine, mathematics, philosophy, and theology, reflects the practical and ecclesiastical preoccupations of the age rather than the wider interests of the humanists." (C. H. Haskins, *The Renaissance of the 12th Century*, p. 300)

Both Haskins and Huizinga criticize Burckhardt for failing to acknowledge the fact that Rome was a subject of the greatest interest for the educated man of the Middle Ages. But they hasten to add that the Romans were depicted as medieval knights and that the pagan poets were allegorized consistently so that their themes would accord with medieval Christian doctrines.

[29] Pierre Villey, *Les Sources et l'Evolution des Essais de Montaigne*, I, 32-33.

may have been, he did believe in something positive, and that many of his positive values came from his close knowledge and deep love of Greek and Roman humanism.

Eliot does not explain what he means when he speaks of a Machiavellian influence on Shakespeare's depiction of the tragic hero. But, as Mario Praz has pointed out, the Elizabethans knew as little of Machiavelli's real philosophy as the average American knows of Marx's or Lenin's. The symbol of Machiavelli loomed as ominously on the horizon of Elizabethan England as the symbol of atheistic Marxist Communism does for the man in the street today—as a foreign threat, both politically and in the realm of ideas, and as a symbol of the diabolical, not as a positive influence on the philosophy of Elizabethan England. Praz observes, "Machiavelli never supplied a pattern of heroism for the Elizabethan dramatists; such figures as Tamburlaine and Bryon were expressions of the same spirit of *Wille zur Macht* which produced the Prince, but they did not derive from it directly. Machiavelli only supplied characteristics of the political villain, who, from the very beginning was loathed at the same time as ridiculed."[30] King Richard the Third is such a villain. He is not a hero with whom the author identifies, as Tamburlaine is for Marlowe. It is difficult to perceive in what sense Machiavelli had a positive, shaping influence on the creation of the Shakespearean hero.

The essential question here is the nature of Shakespeare's individualism. Is it a manifestation of Stoic self-sufficiency? Is the hero in his hour of trial drawing into a shell and satisfying himself, like the Stoic sage, with the feeling that he alone matters? Does he argue, like Chapman's hero, Clermont, that man should Love nothing outward,

> Or not within our own powers to command
> And so being sure of everything we love,
> Who cares to lose the rest?[31]

[30] Mario Praz, *Machiavelli and the Elizabethans*, London, 1928, p. 26.
[31] George Chapman, *The Revenge of Bussy d'Ambois*, IV, v, 4-8.

To answer this question, we must examine further the nature of the hero's self-esteem, his feelings toward his intimate friends and loved ones, and his concern or lack of concern for society as a whole. Since Eliot refers particularly to the deaths of the heroes in *Hamlet, Othello*, and *Antony and Cleopatra*, I shall focus my discussion on these plays.

To begin with, we must freely admit that the tragic hero is keenly aware of his own virtuous endowments. But this quality of self-appreciation is common to all classical and Renaissance pagan-humanist philosophy. The issue which separates Stoic attitudes from those of Aristotle and Cicero is whether the virtuous individual is exclusively concerned with the sense of his intrinsic nobility, or whether he is concerned as well with the opinion of others. The dying Hamlet is anything but a self-sufficient Stoic. He snatches the cup of poison from his friend, and exclaims,

> Give me the cup. Let go! By heaven, I'll ha't,
> O good Horatio, what a wounded name
> (Things standing thus unknown) shall live behind me!
>
> (V. ii. 354-356)

The men of the Renaissance, like Hamlet, were passionately solicitous of the good opinion of the human community, their attitude the antithesis of Stoic indifference to public opinion and withdrawal into self-righteous shells.

Another accusation which Eliot makes against the dying Shakespearean hero is that he thinks only of himself when he dies. Othello, he says, in his final long speech "has ceased to think about Desdemona, and is thinking about himself."[32] If Eliot were talking of Brutus' reception of the news of his wife's death, we could agree to a Stoic influence, although even there the implications do not point to a self-pride which leaves the hero indifferent to his wife's death. Control of grief is surely not to be equated with incapacity to feel sorrow. But in *Othello*, the hero is keenly conscious of his dead wife. His greatest cry

---

[32] p. 111.

of anguish and remorse comes some time before his final long speech, when he exclaims, "O Desdemona, Desdemona! dead!/ O! O! O!" His very last speech shows that he has not forgotten her during the intervening period. He says, "I kiss'd thee ere I kill'd thee. No way but this—/ Killing myself, to die upon a kiss." (V. ii. 358, 359) Does this not indicate that Othello sees in his own suicide some sort of atonement for his murder of his wife?

Antony, whom Eliot also singles out as an example of the Senecan superman, whose death is a mere matter of postures and self-dramatization, is scarcely forgetful of the woman he loved.[33] When he hears that the Queen is dead, he says,

> I will o'ertake thee, Cleopatra, and
> Weep for my pardon.
>
>   Seal then, and all is done.
> Eros!—I come, my queen.—Eros!—Stay for me.
> Where souls do couch on flowers, we'll hand in hand
> And with our sprightly port make the ghosts gaze.
>
>   (IV. xiv. 44-45, 49-52)

Cleopatra likewise is thinking of Antony as she dies. Romantic these deaths may be; they are hardly instances of Stoic self-sufficiency. Nonetheless Eliot insists, "If you compare the deaths of several of Shakespeare's heroes—I do not say *all*, for there are very few generalizations that can be applied to the

---

[33] Eliot, in his criticism of Antony, Othello, and Hamlet, refers to the complacent and self-loving spirit in which they die. He calls this spirit "the odour of Seneca." Lecky's remarks on the idealism of the pagan Romans may be just as full of personal bias but they provide a remarkable contrast to the tendency of many modern critics to cast aspersions on idealistic systems which are not Christian. Lecky writes,

"The spirit of patriotism has this peculiar characteristic, that, while it has evoked acts of heroism which are both very numerous and very sublime, it has done so without presenting any prospect of personal immortality as a reward. Of all the forms of human heroism, it is probably the most unselfish. The Spartan and the Roman died for his country because he loved it. The martyr's ecstasy of hope had no place in his dying hour. He gave up all he had, he closed his eyes, as he believed, forever, and he asked for no reward in this world or in the next. Even the hope of posthumous fame—the most refined and supersensual of all that can be called reward—could exist only for the most conspicuous leaders." (W. E. H. Lecky, *A History of European Morals*, I, 177-178.)

whole of Shakespeare's work—but notably Othello, Coriolanus, and Antony—with the deaths of heroes of dramatists such as Marston and Chapman, consciously under Senecan influence, you will find a strong similarity—except only that Shakespeare does it both more poetically and more lifelike. But he adds: "You may say that Shakespeare is merely illustrating, consciously or unconsciously, human nature, not Seneca. But I am not so much concerned with the influence of Seneca on Shakespeare as with Shakespeare's illustration of Senecan and stoical principles."[34]

There is, of course, a Senecan or Stoic element in Shakespeare. But this Stoic influence is limited to the sympathetic presentation of suicide and to the Stoic fatalism of the "as flies to wanton boys" speech in *King Lear*. Eliot agrees with Cunliffe that *King Lear* is the most Senecan of the tragedies. But in what respects are the deaths of Gloucester and Lear examples of Stoic self-sufficiency? Each is completely involved in the fate of another—Edgar and Cordelia. As Howard Baker has observed, rather than being a manifestation of Stoic pride, "the self-conscious speeches of Shakespeare's dying heroes are statements of tragic relationships to other human beings."[35]

Finally, let us consider the attitude of the dying hero toward society as a whole. Eliot contrasts to the Stoic and Elizabethan attitude of "I am myself alone" the point of view of what he considers less self-centered philosophies of antiquity. "The Roman's training [aside from Stoicism] was that of devotion to the State, his virtues were public virtues." The Greeks were not, generally speaking, Stoics, identifying themselves with the Universe, since "men who could take part in the life of a

---

[34] "Shakespeare and the Stoicism of Seneca," *Selected Essays*, pp. 111-112.
[35] Howard Baker, *Induction to Tragedy*, p. 182. Cf. Janet Spens, *Shakespeare and Tradition*, Oxford, 1916, p. 89. "Morally Brutus is saved just by his capacity for giving and arousing love, and by his consciousness not merely of his own nobility, but of that of those about him. . . . The Senecan superman is solitary, self-sustained, incapable of appreciating others, a unit in an alien universe; to Shakespeare greatness and egotism never go together, and his heroes 'live along' every thread of human connection."

thriving Greek city-state had something better to join them-selves to."[36]

Brutus is assuredly as Stoic as any of Shakespeare's heroes. Yet throughout the play, Brutus' idealism is primarily a re-flection of his devotion to the common good, that is, a reflection of the Roman patriotic virtues, not of Stoic self-sufficiency. Antony's eulogy stresses this fact: "He, only in a general honest thought/ And common good to all, made one of them." (V. v. 71-72) Service to the state was, in the opinion of Cicero and many of his Renaissance disciples, the shortest path to the attainment of honor and one of the surest ways by which one could manifest one's own nobility. In the Elizabethan period (Eliot's age of self-centered individualism), patriotism, con-cern for the welfare of the whole of society, was considered among the noblest of sentiments. Thus Othello, in his final "egoistical" speech, justifies himself largely in terms of his long and faithful service to the Venetian state. For he says,

> Soft you! a word or two before you go.
> I have done the state some service, and they know't—
> No more of that.   Set you down this;
> And say besides that in Aleppo once,
> Where a malignant and a turban'd Turk
> Beat a Venetian and traduc'd the state,
> I took by th' throat the circumcised dog
> And smote him—thus. [He stabs himself.]
>   (V. ii. 338-340, 351-356)

This is self-justification, but hardly in Stoic terms. No more is Hamlet's dying speech,

[36] *Selected Essays*, pp. 56, 112. Cf. Lecky, *A History of European Morals*, I, 173-174, "Patriotism and military honour were indissolubly connected in the Roman mind . . . [Patriotism leads men] to subordinate their personal wishes to the interests of the society in which they live. It extends the horizon of life, teaching men to dwell among the great men of the past, to derive their moral strength from the study of heroic lives, to look forward continually, through the vistas of a distant future, to the welfare of an organisation which will continue when they have passed away. Patriotism, in the absence of any strong theological passion, had assumed a transcendent power."

> I cannot live to hear the news from England,
> But I do prophesy th'election lights
> On Fortinbras. He has my dying voice.
> So tell him, with th'occurrents, more and less,
> Which have solicited—the rest is silence. [Dies.]
>
> (V. ii. 365-369)

Shakespeare's heroes do not die in a spirit of remorse, contrition, and Christian martyrdom. This, however, does not mean that when they die they are necessarily obsessed by self-love. For the Renaissance, there were other alternatives between the extreme of sheer altruism and the opposite extreme of sheer egoism. Thus Essex observes that "martyrs for religion, heathens for glory, some for love of their country, others for affection to one special person, have encountered death without fear, and suffered it without shew of alteration. . . . For the virtues which are proper unto it are liberality or magnificence, and fortitude or magnanimity."[37] Essex's pronouncements apply equally to the magnificence of Cleopatra's death and the magnanimity of Othello's. These are classical, not Christian, virtues. But all values which are not Christian do not necessarily reduce themselves to pride—and if the Christian critic does not like *megalopsychia* (Aristotelian "pride," magnanimity, high-mindedness), he should attack it as such, and show the inferiority of the philosopher who conceived it. Indeed, Fulke Greville made just such an attack in the Renaissance:

> For where the father of Philosophie,
> Upon the common vertues, but above,
> Doth raise and build his *Magnanimity*.
>
> Let Truth examine where this vertue lives.
>
> For Mans chiefe vertue is *Humilitie*;
> True knowledge of his wants, his height of merit;
> This pride of minde, this *Magnanimity*
> His greatest vice, his first seducing spirit;

---

[37] Devereux, ed., *Lives and Letters of the Devereux*, I, 325.

Further we urge against this masters grounds,
That our first *Adam*, imag'd is to us,
In that mixt pride, that worth-exceeding bounds,
Where on Schooles build their true Magnanimous:
    Since to be like his Maker he affected,
    And being lesse still thought himselfe neglected

Which spiritual pride (no doubt) possesseth still
All fleshly hearts, where thirst of *Honour* raves.[38]

Individualism has, then, an important place in the pagan-humanist scheme of values which provided the Renaissance, including Shakespeare, with so much of its moral philosophy. But this individualism was disciplined, not anarchic. For Aristotle, for Cicero, and for the Renaissance, the individual of preeminent moral endowments was as worthy of high admiration as a hero as were the saint and martyr for the Catholic in the Middle Ages. The heroic protagonist had a definite place in the social scheme; as Theodore Spencer and E. M. W. Tillyard have pointed out, the Elizabethans had a strong sense of order, of a hierarchic and disciplined society. The age had its anarchic and disintegrative elements, but even in Shakespearean tragedy, perhaps especially there, these disruptive elements were clearly viewed as evil: Claudius, Iago, Goneril, Regan, and Edmund. And as A. C. Bradley has significantly observed, the Shakespearean type of tragedy closes not only with the downfall of the great-hearted hero but also with the overthrow of the forces of evil and disruption. Hero and villain have alike vanished at the end of the tragedy, but an ordered society does remain. In Bradley's words,

"Evil exhibits itself everywhere as something negative, barren, weakening, destructive, a principle of death. It isolates, disunites, and tends to annihilate not only its opposite but itself. . . . What remains is a family, a city, a country, ex-

---

[38] Fulke Greville, *Poems & Dramas*, ed. Geoffrey Bullough, London, 1939, I, 199-200. See Bénichou's comments on humility and aristocratic pride in introduction, p. 9.

hausted, pale and feeble, but alive through the principle of good which animates it; and within it, individuals who, if they have not the brilliance or greatness of the tragic character, still have won our respect and confidence. And the inference would seem clear. If existence in an order depends on good, and if the presence of evil is hostile to such existence, the inner being or soul of this order must be akin to good."[39]

Tillyard and Spencer have rendered a noteworthy service in placing Bradley's concept of order, which is theoretical and philosophical, on a historical basis. In both *The Elizabethan World Picture* and *Shakespeare and the Nature of Man*, evidence is presented to indicate that the notion of Elizabethan England as "a period of dissolution and chaos" is ill-grounded, and that Elizabethan individualism, both as it relates to Renaissance moral philosophy in general and to Shakespeare in particular, was an integrated part of a social philosophy which emphasized the importance and value of the individual but never at the cost of society as a whole. The Shakespearean hero would not fit very happily into the world of *The Divine Comedy* (in fact, Brutus is to be found in the lowest circle of Hell), but until further evidence is submitted, he can not be categorized as an egoistic Senecan superman, nor can one justly, except on grounds of pure personal preference, decide that Shakespeare, in a comparison with Dante, can be depreciated for "his lower view of life," or for the "inferior," or even the "rag-bag" philosophy, on which his writings are presumably based.[40]

MAGNANIMITY OR GREATNESS OF HEART

That Shakespeare's tragic hero is great of heart is indicated by the magnitude of his every emotional response. In this respect, Shakespeare's values eschew the classical virtues of moderation and temperance; in many cases the love of hero or

---

[39] *Shakespearean Tragedy*, p. 35.
[40] Eliot, "Second Thoughts on Humanism," *Selected Essays*, p. 399.

heroine is limitless. Even in the early light comedies, an extreme degree of passion is sometimes revealed. Consider the dialogue between Julia and Lucetta in the second act of *The Two Gentlemen of Verona*:

> LUC. I do not seek to quench your love's hot fire,
> But qualify the fire's extreme rage,
> Lest it should burn above the bounds of reason.
> JUL. The more thou dam'st it up, the more it burns.
>
> (II. vii. 21-24)

The same intensity of love for another individual is, of course, the major theme of *The Sonnets*; considerable ambiguity exists as to whether this wholehearted attachment is merely one of friendship. Friendship, in any case, could lead to an identification as great as that of love; indeed, for the classical moralists of pagan antiquity, romantic love was frequently considered inferior to the lasting attachment of two friends.

The love which the tragic hero feels for those close and dear to him is as steadfast as it is intense. Hamlet's devotion to his revered father, and his friendship for Horatio, are never diminished one iota by his disillusionment with mankind in general. Even though his bitterness toward women becomes so great, as a result of Gertrude's hasty remarriage, that it poisons and corrodes his love for Ophelia, in the graveyard scene he can still attest to the magnitude of that love. Othello's "brutal" murder of Desdemona leads some critics to wonder whether he truly loved her; but, as Coleridge points out, it is the very intensity of Othello's love for his wife which makes it impossible for him to accept patiently her apparent falseness.[41] The bitter disillusionment and the mounting and swelling pain which lead to the distracted states of mind of Hamlet, Othello, or Lear, all stem from a greatness of heart which had not only led to intense emotional involvement in other human beings, but also to an expectation that those to whom the hero

---

[41] S. T. Coleridge, *Lectures and Notes on Shakespeare and Other English Poets*, ed. T. Ashe, London, 1902, pp. 393-394.

was devoted would display a like high-mindedness. The pain and the mental anguish are largely the result of the shock of disillusionment when one finds viciousness or infidelity where one had expected high nobility.

The Shakespearean hero, however, is not shocked to the point of insanity when his emotions are disengaged from the antagonist who is destroying him. Brutus, for example, is unruffled by Octavius and Antony; when they finally defeat him, his self-composure is untouched, his inner integrity unshaken. But when Brutus kills his friend Caesar, Shakespeare provides touches of what is to become a major tragic theme. Caesar's "Et tu, Brute" is followed by his dying words, "Then fall Caesar!" (III. i. 71) Antony amplifies this theme of betrayal by a dear friend for the benefit of the Roman populace:

> For Brutus, as you know, was Caesar's angel.
> Judge, O you gods, how dearly Caesar lov'd him!
> This was the most unkindest cut of all;
> For when the noble Caesar saw him stab,
> Ingratitude, more strong than traitors' arms,
> Quite vanquish'd him. Then burst his mighty
>   heart. (III. ii. 186-191)

The anguish of the Shakespearean hero frequently stems from the shock of discovering that those he dearly loves are in league with his enemies. Since his identification with them has been so great that they have become almost a second self (a common humanist definition of friendship), he is led to feel that he is engaged in war against himself. Overwhelming love turns into overwhelming sickness of heart and sometimes the hero is completely torn asunder. Hamlet, for example, is emotionally disengaged from Claudius throughout the play, and hence can feel a steady hatred toward an external enemy. ("Bloody, bawdy villain! / Remorseless, treacherous, lecherous, kindless villain!") (II. ii. 607-608) But his emotional involvement in Gertrude leads to self-hatred. As Eliot has observed in his perceptive essay on *Hamlet*, Hamlet's incapacity for action stems largely from emotions which can not be dragged out into the sunlight. And as Spencer has pointed out in *Shakespeare and the Nature of Man*, since he feels that it is beyond the limits of plausibility, the hero can not conceive that the apparent falseness of Gertrude, of Desdemona, of Goneril and Regan, and of Cressida is real. His unbearable torture of mind results largely from his discovery that the person whom he had loved with such greathearted passion is unworthy of that love. The disintegration of the hero is, in other words, closely related to this inability to admit that the reality can be so hideous. Thus, as early as the fourth scene of the first act of *King Lear*, the old king asks in bewilderment:

> Doth any here know me? This is not Lear.
> Doth Lear walk thus? speak thus? Where are his
>   eyes?
> Either his notion weakens, his discernings
> Are lethargied—Ha! waking? 'Tis not so!
> Who is it that can tell me who I am?
>
> (I. iv. 246-250)

Patience. The emotional distintegration of the great-souled hero is not achieved easily or rapidly. The humanist ethics laid great stress on the virtue of patience which was usually associated with fortitude, magnanimity, and constancy; almost every Renaissance book on moral philosophy had counsels for adversity which taught men to bear it with a constant mind and princely courage. Aristotle and Cicero, as well as the Stoics, believed that nobility and greatness of soul were manifested by the endurance of misfortune—even if one could not turn to God for consolation as the devout Christian could. Thus Cicero observes in the *Offices* that "it takes a brave and resolute spirit not to be disconcerted in times of difficulty or ruffled and thrown off one's feet, as the saying is, but to keep one's presence of mind and one's self-possession."[42]

[42] I. 23.

Antonio displays this spirit of patient fortitude in the court-room scene of *The Merchant of Venice*. He tells the Duke that he is prepared to face Shylock's vengeance:

> I do oppose
> My patience to his fury, and am arm'd
> To suffer with a quietness of spirit
> The very tyranny and rage of his.
>
> (IV. i. 10-13)

Brutus' reception of the news of Portia's death is, as we have seen, a reflection of the Stoic philosophy of the Romans. He informs Messala that his former meditations on the inevitability of her death allow him to bear the news now with philosophic patience. In *The Winter's Tale*, Perdita assures Camillo that "affliction may subdue the cheek,/ But not take in the mind," (IV. iv. 587-588) as she prepares for flight with Florizel. Coriolanus, finding his mother torn between tears and anger when he is banished from Rome, admonishes her,

> Nay, mother,
> Where is your ancient courage? You were us'd
> To say extremity was the trier of spirits;
> That common chances common men could bear;
> That when the sea was calm, all boats alike
> Show'd mastership in floating.
>
> You were us'd to load me
> With precepts that would make invincible
> The heart that conn'd them. (IV. i. 2-7, 9-11)

Patience and fortitude are the pagan humanist's answer to the problem of adversity and affliction. Again Shakespeare is closer to the pagan-humanist than to the Christian solution of a crucial ethical problem. The Christian instinctively turns first to the solace and security provided by his trust in a beneficent and omniscient God. The Shakespearean hero frequently echoes the moral philosophy of the Renaissance humanists who taught men to bear stoutly all injuries and to remain "always invincible and constant against the crosses, thwarts, and despites of fortune."[48]

Such discipline upholds Antonio, Brutus, and Coriolanus in their hours of trial. But it does not prevent the heroes of the great tragedies from being torn asunder. Their response to their particular predicament is heroic and they show super-human endurance in bearing misfortune. But the burden becomes too great. They are torn by a sense of inner disintegration which finally makes it impossible for them to maintain self-composure. This is particularly evident in *Othello*. At the beginning of the play he is the very embodiment of self-assurance; nonetheless the poisons of the supersubtle villain gradually destroy his poise until finally he falls into a trance. Othello here, as at the end of the play, provides self-testimony to the reasons for his disintegration:

> Had it pleas'd heaven
> To try me with affliction, had they rain'd
> All kinds of sores and shames on my bare head,
> Steep'd me in poverty to the very lips,
> Given to captivity me and my utmost hopes,
> I should have found in some place of my soul
> A drop of patience. But, alas, to make me
> A fixed figure for the time of scorn
> To point his slow unmoving finger at!
> Yet could I bear that too; well, very well.
> But there where I have garner'd up my heart,
> Where either I must live or bear no life,
> The fountain from the which my current runs
> Or else dries up—to be discarded thence,
> Or keep it as a cistern for foul toads
> To knot and gender in—turn thy complexion there,
> Patience, thou young and rose-lipp'd cherubin!
> Ay, there look grim as hell! (IV. ii. 47-64)

[48] Bryskett, pp. 88-89.

More than any other tragedy, *King Lear* presents an inner, spiritual conflict in which the hero is fighting primarily the possibility of his own disintegration. Clearly it is the aged King's intention to maintain dignity and poise during the first two acts of the play; that is, from the moment that he has recognized the folly of his behavior in the fourth scene of the first act. Hence, he fights off the indignity of weeping in womanish fashion, and, for a long time, if with the greatest effort, madness is held off. This inner conflict dominates the first acts of the play. Modern critics tend to lose sight of the heroic fight Lear wages to maintain dignified self-control despite the mounting abuses his enemies heap upon him. Without a proper appreciation of the intensity of Lear's capacity for love (which is to become the central theme, particularly in the last scene of the play when he appears with Cordelia dead in his arms), one can not begin to appreciate the horror of the daughters' ingratitude. The mainspring of Lear's disintegration is precisely the same as Othello's or Hamlet's—these heroes are torn apart by the realization of evil in those whom they had loved so intensely, so wholeheartedly, with such a great degree of emotional identification, that the awareness of evil in the person loved destroys their own mental stability. Patience and fortitude can not prevent this disintegration.

The gradual development of Lear's madness is worthy of close scrutiny. In the discussion of manhood, reference was made to the first signs of Lear's shaken spirit. Just before he departs to visit Regan, he tells Goneril his shame that she should have the power to "shake his manhood." (I. iv. 318-321) And in the next scene he cries out: "O, let me not be mad, sweet heaven! / Keep me in temper; I would not be mad!" (I. v. 49-50) When he arrives in front of Gloucester's castle, only to find that his other, presumably worthier, daughter has stocked his messenger, the rising inner turmoil is again indicated:

O, how this mother swells up toward my heart!
Hysterica passio! Down, thou climbing sorrow!
Thy element's below! (II. iv. 56-58)

When Goneril arrives, in the same scene, Regan tells the old king to return and live with her. To which he replies, "I prithee, daughter, do not make me mad." (II. iv. 221) At the end of the scene, as Lear prepares to depart into the storm, once again the inner conflict is brought to the fore. Lear pleads for patience, fights off tears, and foresees the possibility of madness.

You heavens, give me that patience, patience I need!
You see me here, you gods, a poor old man,
As full of grief as age; wretched in both.

No, I'll not weep.   You think I'll weep.
I have full cause of weeping, but this heart
Shall break into a hundred thousand flaws
Or ere I'll weep. O fool, I shall go mad.
                    (II. iv. 274-276, 286-289)

When Lear first appears in the storm, he is in high rage and calls on Nature to destroy "ingrateful man." (III. ii. 9) Yet even at this point Lear returns at times to the ideal of patient endurance; as Kent enters, he remarks, "No, I will be the pattern of all patience; / I will say nothing." (III. ii. 37) Later in the scene he realizes that his wits are beginning to unsettle. (III. ii. 67) In the fourth scene of the third act the conflict within him still continues:

No, I will weep no more. In such a night
To shut me out! Pour on; I will endure.
In such a night as this! O Regan, Goneril!
Your old kind father, whose frank heart gave all!
O, that way madness lies; let me shun that!
No more of that. (III. iv. 17-22)

"Patience," Cornwallis writes, "keepeth the reputation un-
spotted; though outward forces be destroyed, this makes the
mind invincible."[44] Unless we keep in mind this typically
humanist counsel for adversity, we lose sight of much of Lear's
tragedy. It is the power of endurance, Perdita's affliction sub-
duing the cheek but not the mind, (*The Winter's Tale*, IV. iv.
587-588) which makes the Lear of the first three acts a tragic
figure of the greatest stature. Weak and infirm he is, but, for
the Renaissance moralists, magnanimity did not depend upon
bodily strength, but on greatness of soul, of mind, heart, and
will, which Lear manifests in abundance. After his initial arrogance in the first scene of the play, his every response is an
indication of such greatness. His anger, his desire for revenge,
and his attempt to endure affliction patiently would have met
with a completely sympathetic response from the Jacobean
audience.[45] For them, he was a figure of the greatest tragic
dignity and stature. For many a modern critic, he is instead
a pathetic figure. Granville-Barker sees Lear as "an old man
on the verge of dotage. His self-knowledge has never been
strong, and infirmity of years has made bad discrimination
worse. Further, the decay of age renders him all the more
liable to attacks of choler, and thereby to the overclouding of
reason."[46]

Contempt for Ordinary Humanity (*Not Cynicism, Contempt
for Human Values*). The Shakespearean hero despised the
trivial emotions of ordinary humanity; indeed, since he valued
only virtue, at moments he appears to be utterly misanthropic.
Thus Hamlet is nauseated by the very sight of other human
beings, not from mere cynicism, or as the result of his melancholic mood, but because they seem to lack the virtue he admires. Rosencrantz, Guildenstern, and Osric are for him the
very embodiment of the expediency and insincerity which he
feels to be typical of human nature. His loathing of man is the

---

[44] *Essayes*, p. 194. Cf. Chapter 7, above, p. 248.
[45] Segar, *The Booke of Honor and Armes*, p. 35.
[46] *Prefaces to Shakespeare*, I, 301.

natural and inevitable consequence. So, too, is his callous indifference to the fate he had engineered for the two courtiers
who accompany him to England. Hamlet's misogyny also
springs from his nauseated disgust with his mother's behavior,
which leads to distrust of Ophelia, of all womankind, and
finally to an all-embracing hatred of mankind. Yet not once
does this alter his affection and high esteem for that one man
in ten thousand who is honest—his feeling for his noble father
and his friendship for Horatio are not altered by his general
disillusionment and weariness of life. At the play's close he
is still concerned to maintain his own reputation, so he insists
that Horatio live on to restore his wounded name. Needless to
say, Hamlet's seeming misanthropy (i.e., his willingness to
admire only those who are truly virtuous—including himself!)
is not equivalent to the nihilism which George Santayana and
T. S. Eliot find in Shakespeare. There is a world of difference
between the "cynicism" of the disillusioned idealist such as
Hamlet (or, to mention one of the greatest of English writers
from another age, Jonathan Swift), and the Machiavellian
cynicism of Eliot's straw hero or the easy-going, epicurean
denial of values which Santayana ascribes to Shakespeare.[47]

Likewise in *King Lear*, the recognition that life has many
horrible aspects does not lead to a negation of all values. The

[47] Cf. Theodore Spencer, *Shakespeare and the Nature of Man*, pp. 93-109.
W. B. C. Watkins, in his comparison of Swift and Shakespeare also emphasizes
the theme of disillusioned idealism: "Swift's melancholia is the melancholia of
Hamlet, and its root is very much the same—a dichotomy of personality expressing itself in an abnormal sensitivity to the disparity between the world as
it should be and the world as one sees it. This theme is not limited in Shakespeare's plays to *Hamlet*; it recurs so frequently that, without falling into dangerous speculation about Shakespeare the man, we can certainly in all safety say
that it is a theme which interested him profoundly and over a period of years. . . .

"Disillusioned idealism is, of course, the state of mind which usually generates
the satiric spirit. Mr. Willey puts the case succinctly: 'The temper which views
all things in their theory rather than in their historical setting must also see
little, as it gazes upon human institutions, but failure and futility, and as it
contemplates human actions, little but departure from the rational norms.' This
'temper' of Mr. Willey's at times goes beyond satire and produces tragedy,
especially if the 'rational norm' is passionately idealized."
(In "Absent Thee From Felicity," *Southern Review*, v, Baton Rouge, La.,
1939, pp. 346, 348.)

importance for the Jacobeans of a disciplined hierarchy of values, which they acquired both from their Christian training and from their education in pagan-humanist moral philosophy, can not be overstated. Lear's constant appeals to the heavens for assistance prove to be of no avail. Gloucester's conclusion that the gods kill men for their sport (IV. i. 36-37) seems, at least momentarily, to be the answer the play gives to the question of the meaning of life.

Both Gloucester and Lear discover that patient endurance of *la condition humaine* is the chief answer to the problems of adversity and evil. Lear tells Gloucester:

> Thou must be patient. We came crying
>   hither;
> Thou know'st, the first time that we smell
>   the air
> We wawl and cry. I will preach to thee.
>   Mark.
> GLOU. Alack, alack the day!
> LEAR. When we are born, we cry that we are come
>   To this great stage of fools
>   (IV. vi. 182-187)

When Lear's friends lose the battle, Gloucester refuses to flee and Edgar gives him "counsel for adversity":

> GLOU.   A man may rot even here.
> EDG.   What, in ill thoughts again? Men must
>   endure
>   Their going hence, even as their coming
>   hither;
>   Ripeness is all. (V. ii. 8-11)

The malignancy and destructiveness of the powers which rule human life seem even further borne out in the final scene in which the impact of Cordelia's death leads to the final dissolution of the old King. Yet, once again, the unmistakable stress on the wanton cruelty of life does not lead to a nihilistic denial of the significance of human values. Indeed, the horror and the tragedy spring largely from the fact that Lear can still place such a high value on Cordelia despite everything that has happened. No cynical negation of human worth lies behind Lear's great cry as he enters the stage with Cordelia dead in his arms:

> Howl, howl, howl, howl! O, you are men of stone.
> Had I your tongues and eyes, I'ld use them so
> That heaven's vault should crack. (V. iii. 257-259)

Constancy, Resolution. "Constancy" was often treated by the Renaissance moralists as an aspect of magnanimity, although it was sometimes treated as a separate virtue. Since these moralists held that the moral laws were constant and immutable, they felt that nothing was more contemptible or more womanish than to be fickle and vacillating. The irresolution of the introspective, melancholy Hamlet has, of course, been a subject for critical discussion for several centuries. There will probably never be any completely satisfying explanation of the cause of Hamlet's lack of resolution. Clearly he blames himself for his own vacillation:

> Thus conscience does make cowards of us all,
> And thus the native hue of resolution
> Is sicklied o'er with the pale cast of thought.
> (III. i. 83-85)

Hamlet's remarks bear a striking resemblance to those of the Renaissance moralists. Guicciardini, for example, says, "Actions once resolved, like fixed starres, should hold one and the same station of firmnesse, they should not be subject to irregular and retrograde motions. For the vacillation and irresolution of a Prince, whose thoughts are whirled about the voluble Sphaere of several persuasions, and never fixed in one Center of resolved Constancy, turnes to his dishonour, and prejudice of the affaire in hand."[48]

[48] *Aphorismes*, p. 190.

In Hamlet's final soliloquy, the hero again criticizes himself for "some craven scruple/ Of thinking too precisely on th' event." (IV. iv. 40-41) But the concluding lines of the soliloquy are portents of an altogether different Hamlet: "O, from this time forth,/ My thoughts be bloody, or be nothing worth." (IV. iv. 65-66) During the remainder of the play, Hamlet is as resolute, determined, and active as he had been at the beginning when he warned Horatio and the soldiers of the watch that he would permit no man to prevent him from following the ghost. This is the Hamlet who grapples with Laertes in the graveyard, who tells Horatio that the conflict between Claudius and himself is one of mighty opposites, and who informs the King's messenger, "I am constant to my purposes." (V. ii. 208)

The change in Cleopatra's character is even more striking, in the final act of *Antony and Cleopatra*. I have already pointed out that inconstancy, fickleness, and mutability were considered by the Elizabethans to be typically feminine traits. Clearly Shakespeare's portrayal of Cleopatra in the early scenes of the play is intended to make her the epitome of feminine infidelity. As Antony prepares to depart for Rome, for example, she sends Charmian to him to report her evanescent moods:

> If you find him sad,
> Say I am dancing; if in mirth, report
> That I am sudden sick. (I. iii. 3-5)

But at the moment of Antony's death, fickleness and inconstancy are suddenly replaced by a steady, constant attachment to Antony and by a fixed resolve to join him in death. Thus, when the dying Antony warns her that Proculeius alone of Caesar's men is to be trusted, she retorts, "My resolution and my hands I'll trust;/ None about Caesar." (IV. xv. 49-50) At the close of the fourth act she again refers to her determination to commit suicide; she tells her women she has "no friend/ But resolution and the briefest end." (IV. xv. 90-91)

Hence, the Cleopatra of the final act is a woman of the

greatest tragic dignity. She has but two goals in mind: to avoid Caesar's triumph in Rome and to join Antony in death. Even when Caesar's guards surprise her and overwhelm her she remains constant in the course she has set for herself. She is not misled for an instant by Caesar's flattery. As he leaves, she tells her women: "He words me, girls, he words me, that I should not/ Be noble to myself!" (V. ii. 191-192) Soon the clown brings the figs. Cleopatra once again provides self-testimony to the great transformation of character which has taken place:

> What poor an instrument
> May do a noble deed! He brings me liberty.
> My resolution's plac'd, and I have nothing
> Of woman in me. Now from head to foot
> I am marble-constant. Now the fleeting moon
> No planet is of mine. (V. ii. 236-241)

However fickle Cleopatra may have been, it should be obvious that she becomes a clear illustration of the "greatness and strength of a noble and invincible spirit."[49] Many critics can not believe that such a sudden transformation of character is possible.[50] But the change in Prince Hal is just as unprepared, and, in that case, Shakespeare makes quite explicit the fact that it is possible for major transformations of character to occur. In the opening scene of *King Henry the Fifth*, the Archbishop observes:

> Never came reformation in a flood
> With such a heady currance scouring faults;
> Nor never hydra-headed wilfulness
> So soon did lose his seat, and all at once,
> As in this king. (I. i. 33-37)

Horatio, of course, is Shakespeare's supreme dramatic portrayal of the classical ideal of steadfast friendship. In the midst of Hamlet's confusion and perplexities, his melancholy and

---

[49] Cicero *De Officiis* I. 5.
[50] Granville-Barker, *Prefaces to Shakespeare*, I, 445-447. See also Chapter 11, n. 23.

cynicism, and his bitter disillusionment with mankind, the hero can still display an absolute, unwavering faith in this one constant friend.

> Since my dear soul was mistress of her choice
> And could of men distinguish, her election
> Hath seal'd thee for herself.
>
>   Give me that man
> That is not passion's slave, and I will wear him
> In my heart's core, ay, in my heart of hearts,
> As I do thee. (III. ii. 68-70, 76-79)

Antony and Cleopatra are both slaves of passion; the constancy and resolution which they display at the very end of their lives, although a sort of redemption in pagan terms, can not be compared with Horatio's steadfast reliability. Horatio, the Dane, is more of an "antique Roman" than is Shakespeare's Antony.

Majesty in Adversity. Hurault writes that the magnanimous man, in the hour of adversity, does not esteem any worldly thing in comparison with himself. For "Magnanimitie is an ornament to all vertues, because it maketh them the greater, in that the honor whereon the nobleminded man setteth his eye, surmounteth all things."[51] For the pagan-humanist philosophers of the Renaissance, in other words, the primary compensation for the great trials and sufferings to which a man was subjected by adversity was the knowledge and certainty of his own virtue. Hence, at the close of the tragedies, the hero does, as T. S. Eliot suggests, take refuge in the fact of his own nobility. The dying Hamlet, for example, requests Horatio to redeem his wounded name. Othello speaks of himself as an "honourable murderer" (V. ii. 294), and Antony tells Cleopatra to

>   please your thoughts
> In feeding them with those my former fortunes,
> Wherein I liv'd the greatest prince o' th' world,

[51] p. 287.

> The noblest; and do now not basely die.
>
> (IV. xv. 52-55)

Cleopatra, in similar vein, implores death to come and "take a queen/ Worth many babes and beggars!" (V. ii. 47-48)

These are the dying speeches to which Eliot so strongly objects. Obviously they are not speeches of contrition, remorse, humility, and repentance. It must be admitted that a wide gulf sometimes separated Christian from pagan-humanist values in the Renaissance. Indeed, it is often of crucial importance that we recognize this gulf if we are properly to interpret Elizabethan works of art. In *The French Academie*, La Primaudaye quotes a remark of Cicero's which indicates the fundamental reason for this cleavage. Cicero had said that in adversity man could have "a certain and sure hope in himself."[52] In answer to this self-assurance of the pagan humanists, La Primaudaye argues: "we knowe that this Hope is weake and uncertaine, if it be not setled and grounded upon a sure expectation of the helpe and grace of God."[53]

The Shakespearean tragic hero, in accordance with Renaissance pagan-humanist philosophy, frequently is lofty in adversity. He admits the superior might of the adverse fate which has brought him low, he may also acknowledge that death can bring high and low alike to the ground, and he sometimes confesses that he has been physically conquered by his enemies. But he can still assert a moral superiority so long as he remains true to himself—and to his conviction of innate nobility. La Primaudaye quotes Cato as saying that "I wil account my selfe invincible so long as in right justice I shal be mightier than Caesar."[54] It is in exactly the same spirit that Brutus assures his followers,

> I shall have glory by this losing day
> More than Octavius and Mark Antony
> By this vile conquest shall attain unto.
>
> (V. v. 36-38)

[52] p. 284. [53] *ibid.* [54] *ibid.*, p. 275.

Cleopatra mocks Caesar's triumph by pointing out that he, too, is but a subject of all-powerful Fortune. She exclaims,

> 'Tis paltry to be Caesar,
> Not being Fortune, he's but Fortune's knave,
> A minister of her will. (V. ii. 2-4)

In the final scene of the play it becomes particularly evident that she holds him in low regard. As he leaves after their audience together, she calls him with utmost irony, "My master and my lord!" (V. ii. 189) But as Iras dresses her in her regal garments, she envisages Antony awaiting her in heaven and she extols the high nobility of his death, since by it he has managed to outwit the omnipotent Caesar. She tells Iras that she hears Antony

> mock
> The luck of Caesar, which the gods give men
> To excuse their after wrath. (V. ii. 288-290)

As she applies the asp to her bosom, she once more calls "great Caesar ass/ Unpolicied!" (V. ii. 310-311)

These speeches are a dramatic presentation of the Renaissance concept that the honor on which the magnanimous man fixes his eye surmounts all things. Montaigne's descriptions of the deaths of the great-souled princes of Mexico emphasize exactly the same heroic quality.[55] For, as Montaigne remarks elsewhere, "He that in danger of imminent death, is no whit danted in his assurednesse; he that in yeelding up his ghost beholding his enemie with a scornefull and fierce looke, he is vanquished, not by us, but by fortune, he is slaine, but not conquered."[56] This passage from the essayist and the description of Cleopatra's death are noteworthy parallels.

[55] *Essayes*, III, 7.   [56] *ibid.*, I, 30.

CHAPTER 9

SHAKESPEARE'S AMBIVALENCE IN REGARD TO CHRISTIAN AND PAGAN-HUMANIST VALUES

(continued)

HONOR AND SELF-ESTEEM

T. S. ELIOT in "Shakespeare and the Stoicism of Seneca," and L. L. Schücking in the chapter on "direct self-explanation" in his book on *Character Problems in Shakespeare's Plays,* both discuss the self-esteem of the Shakespearean protagonist but neither enters into a serious discussion of the discrepancy between Christian and pagan-humanist attitudes on this matter. Can self-esteem be equated with egoism, as so many Shakespearean critics have recently suggested?

Shakespeare, as a representative of his age, was almost necessarily involved in ambivalence and inconsistency on this issue, as on so many others, because he was drawing eclectically and at times haphazardly from differing ethical traditions. The cardinal Christian virtue of humility is not directly referred to once in any of the five great tragedies; nor, as has already been pointed out, does the sin of pride constitute the major vice in Shakespeare's depiction of the villain (although many of his villains are extremely self-willed). It is true that Shakespeare refers frequently to Christian ethical doctrine, but the all-important question is to what extent each play as a whole is molded in terms of deeply held religious beliefs. In *All's Well that Ends Well,* Helena's remark, when the king expresses gratitude because she has offered to cure him, is an echoing of Christian commonplaces. She tells him that "most it is presumption in us when/ The help of heaven we count the act of men." (II. i. 154-155) But King Henry the Fifth's refusal to carry his helmet and sword as tokens of his triumph when entering London is of much greater significance, for this refusal is a specific rejection of classical values. The Chorus informs the audience at the beginning of the fifth act that

> He forbids it,
> Being free from vainness and self-glorious pride;
> Giving full trophy, signal and ostent
> Quite from himself to God. (V. Chorus, 19-22)

In the same speech, however, the Chorus states that the Mayor and his London councillors issue forth to greet their conquering Caesar "Like to the senators of th' antique Rome." (V. Chorus, 26) Within the short space of a few lines, in other words, Shakespeare can shift from the Christian position, which treats a triumphal procession as a manifestation of self-pride, to the typically Roman attitude which looks forward to the celebration which will take place when the victor returns triumphant to his native city. It should be pointed out, however, that in general the chronicle histories give expression to the Christian values of the Renaissance much more than do the tragedies or comedies, and that they frequently reflect the spirit of medieval chivalry. Thus, the same victorious Henry responds to the news of his victory at Agincourt with the curt statement: "Praised be God and not our strength for it." (IV. vii. 90)

Humility is not referred to even once in any of the great tragedies; yet it is in *King Lear* that Shakespeare presents, as a dominant motif, the theme of pride and the related themes of purgation and the attainment of wisdom and ultimate humility through suffering. *King Lear*, as has so frequently been observed, seems deliberately to have a pagan setting so that the benignity of the gods may be called into question. Yet, at the same time, it includes this major theme which suggests that man's pride can be purified through suffering. In this central moral issue, *King Lear* certainly presents a striking parallel to Christian doctrine (although the play has a pagan setting and Lear's purgatory is of an earthly sort) as it also resembles the spirit of some of the greatest tragedies of Aeschylus and Sophocles in which, through suffering, men become purged of their pride.

Yet the critics of our century should proceed with the utmost caution when they attribute pride to the old king and suggest that this defect is the key to an understanding of the play. Indeed, ever since T. S. Eliot wrote his essay "Shakespeare and the Stoicism of Seneca," the modern critic has been much too ready to refer to the "egotism" of Shakespeare's heroes, without sufficient awareness of the moral alternatives available to the Renaissance. When Granville-Barker, for example, speaks of Lear's "assertion of kingship as something not far from godhead," we must remember that it was indeed the Jacobean point of view that the prince "ought to be esteemed as a God among men."[1] Again and again, Hamlet attributes godlike qualities to his great king-father.

It is true that Lear acts too hastily in the opening scene of the play, and with too great certainty and arrogance, but it is extremely doubtful whether the Jacobean audience would have considered him a tyrant (in the Renaissance, an age in which many rulers possessed absolute sovereignty, tyranny referred not to the extent of one's power, but to the evil use of it). It is of much greater significance that Lear's pride, like Cordelia's outspokenness, is displayed only in the opening scene. When he next appears, in the fourth scene of the first act, his Knight informs him of the wrongs done him by his daughter. Lear replies that he had noticed them, but had attributed—nay, blamed—his "own jealous curiosity." (I. iv. 75) Such a response is hardly that of a proud man—especially in the light

---

[1] *Prefaces to Shakespeare*, I, 284. Hurault, p. 5. Cf. Chapter II, Part 1 of D. A. Traversi's *An Approach to Shakespeare*, which shows how uncritically Eliot's many disciples reiterate his opinion that the Renaissance, an age of "chaos," "anarchy," "undisciplined individualism," "theatrical gestures," "self-dramatization," etc., is not worthy of comparison with the age of Dante and Aquinas. Again and again, modern critics contrast the "unity" and "order" of the 13th century to the "anarchic individualism" of the 16th. (London, 1938.)

of the Knight's comments, so obviously of a testimonial character. Lear is not being treated with the ceremonious affection to which he is accustomed—Goneril's instructions to Oswald to be purposely negligent make this point clear enough—yet his initial reaction is to attribute this neglect to his own jealousy! During the fourth scene, insults to his royal dignity are repeatedly heaped upon him. Finally he can no longer stand Goneril's imputation that it is his servants who are unmannerly and so he calls her a liar.

That Lear is no longer the epitome of pride and self-righteousness is most clearly indicated by his next self-rebuke, which follows immediately on his insistence that his knights are well-behaved. He cries out,

> O most small fault,
> How ugly didst thou in Cordelia show!
> Which, like an engine, wrench'd my frame of nature
> From the fix'd place; drew from my heart all love
> And added to the gall. O Lear, Lear, Lear!
> Beat at this gate that let thy folly in
> [Strikes his head]
> And thy dear judgment out! Go, go, my people.
> (I. iv. 288-294)

Lear's mounting anger in the ensuing scenes would not have been associated by the Jacobean audience with his initial pride. Goneril and Regan have so flagrantly violated the canons of virtuous behavior by their deceitful flattery and subsequent callous ingratitude that, as mentioned previously, they could only have been viewed by Shakespeare's audience as monstrously vicious. The audience would have been completely in sympathy with Lear's hatred and anger.

In the very first scene, Lear's actions are criticized by the virtuous characters, Kent, France, and, implicitly, by her silence, Cordelia. During the remainder of the play, the criticism of the king as an idle old man who lacks wisdom, who is ill-tempered and choleric, comes from Goneril, Regan, Cornwall, and Oswald. Lear's early "critics" come to his defense, and show him all the deference and respect to which his position entitles him. Albany, whose role is neutral, makes explicit the fact that the testimony of the villains, which serves as the basis for many modern critics' judgment of the old king, is completely lacking in truth. He asks Goneril:

> What have you done?
> Tigers, not daughters, what have you perform'd?
> A father, and a gracious aged man,
> Whose reverence even the head-lugg'd bear would lick,
> Most barbarous, most degenerate, have you madded.
>
> (IV. ii. 39-43)

Lear's folly, his too great certainty of his own righteousness, which leads to his banishment of both Cordelia and Kent and to his rejection of Kent's counsel, constitutes an error of judgment, a flaw of character. But, like Cordelia's tardiness in speaking, it is a "most small fault" and one which he clearly confesses to have committed in his second appearance in the play. (I. iv.) Regan is surely not speaking as a choral character when she says as Lear goes out into the storm,

> O, sir, to wilful men
> The injuries that they themselves procure
> Must be their schoolmasters. Shut up your doors.
>
> (II. iv. 305-307)

Increased compassion for humanity and a genuine humility result from Lear's sufferings. Lear is schooled by adversity. Regan's philistine view, shared in large measure by so many modern critics, does not accord with Renaissance distinctions between good and evil. Lear is a good man with an initial fault of character; he suffers beyond all measure for that fault, and becomes more compassionate and more humble as a result of that experience. Goneril and Regan, on the other hand, are monstrously evil; they can not be condemned sufficiently, for it is their wickedness which has caused Lear's undeserved suffering.

Lear's growth of wisdom and compassion is thus a significant theme, but not the only major theme of the play, nor the main key to an interpretation of his character. Shakespeare's primary intention in this play is to portray the dignity, the nobility, and the greatness of soul which a weak and infirm old man can display when faced with the villainy of two daughters whom he had loved dearly and honored accordingly. Lear's admonition, "Take physic, pomp;/ Expose thyself to feel what wretches feel" in no sense contradicts this major theme. (III. iv. 33-34) In the subplot, Gloucester likewise grows spiritually as the result of facing adversity and is brought to a clearer view of himself and of mankind. Shortly after his blinding, he cries out,

> Heavens deal so still!
> Let the superfluous and lust-dieted man,
> That slaves your ordinance, that will not see
> Because he does not feel, feel your pow'r quickly;
> So distribution should undo excess,
> And each man have enough. (IV. i. 67-72)

But it is not Shakespeare's intention to suggest that Gloucester's sufferings are just and that this is the meting out of due punishment for his lust. Edgar does tell Edmund near the end of the play that

> The gods are just, and of our pleasant vices
> Make instruments to scourge us.
> The dark and vicious place where thee he got
> Cost him his eyes. (V. iii. 170-173)

This is severely Hebraic morality, however, not in accord with our sense of proportionate punishment. Gods who will punish mere lust with blindness shock our sense of justice, anthropomorphic as we mortals be. What is more important, this self-righteous judgment contradicts our sense of the total meaning of the play. The major themes of both the main plot and the subplot, the themes which are repeatedly emphasized, are the immeasurable viciousness and cruelty of which man is capable (indicated by the way in which Goneril, Regan, and Edmund treat their parents), the wanton cruelty of the heavens which seem so utterly callous to man's happiness (made overt in the measureless suffering which Lear and Gloucester endure), and the capacity of men for goodness, loyalty, and fidelity even when strict justice does not require it (indicated by the never-ceasing devotion of Kent, the Fool, Cordelia, and Edgar to their masters and fathers even when they have been rejected by them).

The theme of increased humility is also significant and should not be discounted. But Lear shows humility and remorse only to the one faithful daughter whom he has so grievously wronged. There is never the slightest suggestion that he should be humble and forgiving to his evil daughters— or, patiently turning the other cheek, accept the humiliation which they heap upon him. Quite simply, Lear's humility is the humility of a good man which he wishes to manifest to a good daughter whom he has wronged. As he had knelt shamefully, out of necessity, to Regan to beseech food from her, he now insists on kneeling to Cordelia freely and generously as a sign of his remorse. His remarks indicate that he has gained perceptibly in self-knowledge. They present a sharp contrast to the autocratic father who had banished Cordelia self-righteously at the beginning of the play. He characterizes himself as

> a very foolish fond old man,
> Fourscore and upward, not an hour more nor less;
> And, to deal plainly,
> I fear I am not in my perfect mind. (IV. vii. 60-63)

And again, "You must bear with me./ Pray you now, forget and forgive. I am old and foolish." (IV. vii. 83-84) Yet in this very scene in which Lear emerges from his madness with a markedly altered tone of deepened humility, he also, as Granville-Barker points out, has bestowed upon him once again

333

the outward signs of reverence appropriate to a Renaissance monarch. Lear enters the stage in a chair, carried by servants, and is addressed with utmost respect by Cordelia as "Your Majesty" and "Your Highness." Albany enhances Lear's sense of restored dignity in the final scene—too late, to be sure—by resigning to the old King his absolute power. Cordelia and Albany, in other words, freely give back to Lear what his own generosity and his daughter's greed had so monstrously deprived him of—his authority, his sense of respect, and his servants. Lear himself, in the last terrible scene, shows that increased humility and greatness of soul are not incompatible. As he enters, with Cordelia dead in his arms, his figure dominates the stage; his titanic emotions, which break forth in high anger at this final gross injustice, reduce the comments of all the other characters to mere whispers. Once again, he is every inch a king. At the play's close, he finally takes into his own hands the punishment of evil; despite his infirmity he kills the man who hanged his daughter. By this action we are reminded once again that Lear bears too great a soul to accept passively the degradation to which his evil daughters subject him. Self-assertion and high dignity blend with his recently discovered humility as he tells his listeners,

> I have seen the day, with my good biting falchion
> I would have made them skip. I am old now,
> And these same crosses spoil me. (V. iii. 276-278)

The play closes with Kent's remonstrance to Edgar to let Lear die and find peace in the grave. But this final underlining of the cruelty and anguish of Lear's lot does not negate the positive affirmation of utmost fidelity from those who surround the king at his death, nor the greatness of soul with which he faced adversity to the bitter end. From the beginning until the play's close, he never once merely whimpers. Shakespeare, in this weak and infirm old man, presents his most titanic and heroic protagonist.

Schücking, in his discussion of self-explanation and self-testimony in Shakespeare, comes to the conclusion that "pride, in Shakespeare's eyes, is a necessary attribute of the great."[2] These words can have but little import if we fail to make distinctions in the three different meanings the word possessed in the Renaissance: pride as the greatest of Christian sins, pride in the Aristotelian sense of *megalopsychia* (the unlimited self-esteem of the magnanimous man), and pride in the pejorative Aristotelian sense of unjustified self-esteem. Nor should we forget that for many Renaissance humanists, too great humility was considered but an inverted sense of pride and just as egoistical.[3] The Aristotelian and Ciceronian ideal condoned self-esteem where it was in strict accordance with one's worth.

Schücking discusses at some length the pride or, if we like, the self-esteem, of Lear, Brutus, and Julius Caesar. But he fails to distinguish between Lear's initial pride, on the one hand, and his sense of wounded dignity as he comes to realize that he is the butt for his daughters' repeated and deliberate insults, on the other. He also fails to separate the arrogance of the early Lear and of Julius Caesar from the self-esteem of the noble Brutus, whose pride is strictly in accord with the classical view of justified self-esteem albeit smacking of complacency and smugness to the modern reader who has lost such solid ethical moorings and resents and suspects any one who seems too certain of himself.

The fault which the Lear of the opening scene and Julius Caesar share in common is defined in Elyot's *The Gouernour*: "The prince of Oratours, Marcus Tullius, in his first boke of Offices, sayeth that in height and greatnesse of courage is moste soneste ingendred obstinacie, and inordinate desire of soveraignetie. Obstinacie is an affection immoveable, fixed to wille, abandoninge reason, whiche is ingendred of Pride, that is to saye, whan a man estemeth so moche him selfe above any other, that he reputeth his owne witte onely to be in perfection, and con-

[2] Levin Schücking, *Character Problems in Shakespeare's Plays*, London, 1922, p. 34.
[3] Cf. Della Casa, *Galateo*, p. 38.

temneth all other counsaile."[4] The suggestiveness of the ethical dicta in Cicero's *Offices* is once again evident; just as his linking of ambition with greatness of heart throws light on the character of Macbeth, so likewise his suggestion that obstinacy is the fault soonest engendered in the high-minded prince bears close relation to the character of Julius Caesar and to Lear's predicament in the opening scene. Both men are willful and pig-headed when they ignore the sane counsel of their followers (Shakespeare's audience would have been particularly critical of Caesar's usurping the powers which belong to the Roman Republic).

The pride of Achilles in *Troilus and Cressida* bears a resemblance to the Aristotelian extreme. Agamemnon bids Patroclus tell Achilles that

> we think him over-proud
> And under-honest, in self-assumption greater
> Than in the note of judgment. (II. iii. 132-134)

In Shakespeare's play, as in Homer's folk epic, the Greeks do not question Achilles' ability, but they do criticize him for sulking in his tent and hence, in effect, considering himself greater than he actually is. Coriolanus, too, deserves to be criticized for excessive self-pride. He has proved himself a great warrior, hence deserving of high esteem, but he vitiates his right to praise by insisting too strongly and insistently on the gulf which separates him from other human beings. Even his own mother, Volumnia, who is not without a sense of her son's great merit, finally rebukes him sharply.

In his criticism of Othello's final speech, T. S. Eliot states that "humility is the most difficult of all virtues to achieve; nothing dies harder than the desire to think well of oneself."[5] But Shakespeare's dying heroes, when they insist on their own great nobility, are obviously neither humble nor penitent; they should not be judged by Christian ethical criteria. It is entirely in keeping with Cicero's dictum "that Virtue loves her-

---

[4] III, xv.
[5] "Shakespeare and the Stoicism of Seneca," *Selected Essays*, p. 111.

self; for she best knows herself and realizes how lovable she is"[6] that Hamlet and Antony express a concern to be remembered by the human community and that Othello dares to assert that he is "an honourable murderer." Schücking shows greater sympathy for pagan-humanist values than Eliot, but his criticism of Brutus (for Brutus' assertion that it would be an honor to be slain by Brutus) indicates a similar unwillingness to accept those values which conditioned the shaping of the work of art. Aristotle and Cicero were uninhibited in this regard because they considered it perfectly natural and human to be aware of one's own nobility. They did not realize that, according to the dicta of a later ethics, pride would become the major sin. Indeed, as Werner Jaeger points out in the opening chapter of *Paideia*, justified self-love was one of the axioms of Greek ethical thought—for the Greeks did not equate self-love with mere love of the self. In Jaeger's words, "We must understand that the Self is not the physical self, but the ideal which inspires us, the ideal which every nobleman strives to realise in his own life. If we grasp that, we shall see that it is the highest kind of self-love which makes man reach out towards the highest areté."[7]

Awareness of his own great virtue did not mean that the

---

[6] *De Amicitia* XXVI.

[7] *Paideia*, I, 12. Jaeger's further remarks also are significant in that they indicate that Aristotle is, to a considerable extent, a spokesman for traditional Greek morality: "Both Aristotle and Homer justify their belief that high-mindedness is the finest expression of spiritual and moral personality, by basing it on areté as worthy of honour. 'For honour is the prize of areté; it is the tribute paid to men of ability.' Hence pride is an enhancement of areté. But it is also laid down that to attain true pride, true magnanimity is the most difficult of all human tasks.

"Here, then, we can grasp the vital significance of early aristocratic morality for the shaping of the Greek character. It is immediately clear that the Greek conception of man and his areté developed along an unbroken line throughout Greek history. . . .

"Under the guidance of Aristotle, we may here investigate some of its further implications. He explains that human effort after complete areté is the product of an ennobled self-love. . . . This doctrine is not a mere caprice of abstract speculation—if it were, it would be misleading to compare it with early conceptions of areté. Aristotle is defending the ideal of fully justified self-love as against the current beliefs of his own enlightened and 'altruistic' age; and in doing so he has laid bare one of the foundations of Greek ethical thought. In fact, he admires self-love, just as he prizes high-mindedness and the desire for honour, because his philosophy is deeply rooted in the old aristocratic code of morality."

Shakespearean hero was unaware that modesty was one of the basic humanist virtues. Thus Vernon informs Hotspur in *The First Part of King Henry the Fourth* that Hal had praised his gallant opponent to the skies but that, as became a prince, he had made "a blushing cital of himself." (V. ii. 62) When the Greeks and Trojans meet in *Troilus and Cressida,* Aeneas is about to enumerate the virtues of his fellow soldiers but checks himself with the admonition:

> But peace, Aeneas;
> Peace, Troyan! Lay thy finger on thy lips!
> The worthiness of praise disdains his worth
> If that the prais'd himself bring the praise forth;
> But what the repining enemy commends,
> That breath fame blows; that praise, sole pure,
> transcends. (I. iii. 239-244)

For the men of the Renaissance, praise bestowed by others can not be too lavish but self-praise is to be eschewed. Ulysses' characterization of Troilus as one "Speaking in deeds and deedless in his tongue" is but a corollary to this. (IV. v. 98) Boasting is not commendable.

In certain cases Shakespeare is faced with a nice dramatic problem, for he must convey information which will seem boastful if it comes from the lips of the character in question. Sometimes this is easily managed, as when Othello tells Iago:

> 'Tis yet to know—
> Which, when I know that boasting is an honour,
> I shall promulgate—I fetch my life and being
> From men of royal siege. (I. ii. 19-22)

In this fashion, essential information can be conveyed by the character himself without his modesty being called into question. But as the play closes, such techniques are not so easily managed and hence, to a considerable extent, we are required to accept self-testimony, which involves self-praise, as a necessary dramatic convention. Thus it is imperative, from the dra-

338

matic point of view, that both Lear and Othello recall their former days of prowess. Their vivid recollection of previous days of glory serves to remind us that our judgment of a character should not be based solely on his final predicament. Lear's bold assertion, quoted earlier, that "I have seen the day, with my good biting falchion/ I would have made them skip," (V. iii. 276-277) calls our attention to the fact that his final heroic slaying of Cordelia's murderer is the manifestation of a physical strength and courage which has not been revealed at any time during the play, but which he had obviously once possessed. Othello's recollection of his former prowess indicates how feeble and inadequate mere physical courage is when confronted with the web of circumstance in which he has become ensnared. He tells Gratiano,

> Behold, I have a weapon.
> A better never did itself sustain
> Upon a soldier's thigh. I have seen the day
> That with this little arm and this good sword
> I have made my way through more impediments
> Than twenty times your stop. But O vain boast!
> Who can control his fate? 'Tis not so now.
>
> (V. ii. 259-265)

Eliot complains that Othello's final long speech permits him to take his eyes off his own misdeeds, thus evading moral self-judgment. But the audience should not be judging Othello in terms of a single speech which happens to remind a certain modern critic of Emma Bovary. His reference to the killing of the turban'd Turk in Aleppo is a perfectly just reminder of the fact that he has "done the state some service, and they know't." (V. ii. 339) As Howard Baker says in answer to Eliot: "Certainly unusual self-awareness is an elemental condition in Elizabethan tragic heroes. But it seems to be a final, retrospective self-awareness, a drawing together of things, and an expository achievement handed down from the narrative tragedy; and it seems not to be manifestation of pride, of extravagant

339

and romantic individualism. For the self-identification is a means to the definitely ethical end of saying, 'Thus and thus I was, thus and thus I met my fall.' "[8]

THE HONORABLE DEATH

That Shakespeare, like the humanist moralists, links courage with magnanimity, the master virtue, is indicated by Volumnia's speech to Coriolanus when she urges him to go to the market place and address the people of Rome. She assures him that she does not fear his "dangerous stoutness; for I mock at death/ With as big heart as thou." (III. ii. 127-128) In similar vein, Caesar tells his wife that he will ignore the ominous portents which she has described so vividly and will proceed to the Capitol, for "Cowards die many times before their deaths;/ The valiant never taste of death but once." (II. ii. 32-33)

By an honorable and fearless facing of death men could redeem, in large measure, the misdeeds of a lifetime. Even criminals went to the scaffold with a display of iron nerves which drew the admiration of the spectators. This aspect of Elizabethan life is portrayed in *Macbeth* when Malcolm reports to the Scottish king that Cawdor has been executed:

> Nothing in his life
> Became him like the leaving of it. He died
> As one that had been studied in his death
> To throw away the dearest thing he ow'd
> As 'twere a careless trifle. (I. iv. 7-11)

But it was particularly on the field of battle that the Renaissance soldier sought to redeem his honor by dying nobly. We recall that Shakespeare's Antony, after his first defeat by Octavius Caesar, assures Enobarbus:

> To-morrow, soldier,
> By sea and land I'll fight. Or I will live,

---

[8] *Induction to Tragedy*, p. 177.

> Or bathe my dying honour in the blood
> Shall make it live again. (IV. ii. 4-7)

In *The First Part of King Henry the Sixth* the two Talbots, father and son, argue as to which is to stay and preserve the family honor, and finally, since neither will leave the field, they die together in battle. (IV. v.) Family ties were extremely close both in ancient Rome and in the Renaissance, but the parent nonetheless put the honor of his family ahead of the safety of his child. The mother of Coriolanus, as we have seen, tells Virgilia that she would rather have all her children killed in battle than have one of them ignobly shirk his duties. (I. iii. 21-28) And at the close of *Macbeth*, when Ross reports to Siward that his son has been killed in battle, Siward asks whether his wounds were on the front of his body. Assured that they were, and that his son died like a man, he abruptly dismisses further mourning. (V. viii. 39-53)

SUICIDE AS AN HONORABLE ACT

The extent to which the Renaissance ignores its own edict—to follow the pagan authors only when they do not contradict the Christian ethics—is evident in their frequent reference, without criticism, to Cato's suicide. The extent to which Shakespeare likewise is shaping his plays in terms of the pagan values, even when they conflict with Christianity, is illustrated in Cassio's choral commentary on Othello's suicide. As the hero dies, Cassio exclaims, "This did I fear, but thought he had no weapon; for he was great of heart." (V. ii. 360-361) The taking of one's own life, which Augustine, refuting the Roman values, had said can never be any sign of magnanimity or greatness of spirit, becomes, for Shakespeare and his audience, just that, even in a play whose setting is Christian Venice.[9]

This does not mean that Shakespeare completely ignores the Christian point of view. Indeed, insofar as *Hamlet* is concerned with the crucial moral issue of suicide, it becomes a study in

[9] *The City of God*, I, 22.

ethical ambivalence, for here Shakespeare can not fuse or harmonize the Christian and the pagan-humanist ethics. Hamlet, in his first soliloquy, alludes to the Christian canon against self-slaughter as the reason why he has not already taken his own life. (I. ii. 131-132) Yet when he next ponders the question, in his most famous soliloquy on that subject, he has ceased to think in Christian terms. His dilemma is that of the pagan-humanist philosophers: is greater nobility shown in enduring affliction and adversity or in bringing an end to it by suicide? (As I pointed out in Part I, Aristotle and Cicero adhered to the former view, while the Stoics sometimes took the latter.) In the grave-yard scene, Laertes takes violent exception to the Christian doctrine that suicides should be denied full burial rites, while the gravediggers present the orthodox view. All Christian sects and denominations have always prohibited the taking of one's own life. Shakespeare permits Laertes to give vent to his resentment against a priest (for not allowing Ophelia the full rites of burial), and to give supremacy to the pagan values of family loyalty and concern for proper burial rites, overriding Christian doctrine. Laertes exclaims:

> Lay her i' th' earth
> And from her fair and unpolluted flesh
> May violets spring! I tell thee, churlish priest,
> A minist'ring angel shall my sister be
> When thou liest howling. (V. i. 261-265)

For the Christians in Shakespeare's audience the "churlish priest" is, of course, expressing sound doctrine when he states that the suicide (in this case, Ophelia) does not deserve a Christian burial.

It is Horatio, Shakespeare's supreme dramatic embodiment of the classical virtue of friendship, who most clearly illustrates the extent to which Shakespearean tragedy is predominantly based on pagan-humanist values. Horatio, a sterling friend never subjected to the slightest criticism by anyone through the course of the play, is a Renaissance counterpart of Brutus.·

The pagan concept of fidelity and friendship is paramount as he prepares to follow Hamlet in death by drinking what remains of the poisoned cup, truly, as he says, more antique Roman than Dane. (V. ii. 352) Once again, suicide is being presented as a courageous act, and in a play which, as much as *Othello* and *Romeo and Juliet*, has a Christian setting.

In the discussion of magnanimity, I mentioned that the Shakespearean tragic hero feels lofty in adversity. Because his nobility is innate and can not be destroyed by the insolent blows of fickle fortune or malevolent fate, he feels superior to his particular predicament and spiritually invincible. But his greatness of mind also required that he refuse to make himself subject to anyone's will. Hence he resists capture and prefers death to captivity. Brutus, remember, assures Cassius:

> Think not, thou noble Roman,
> That ever Brutus will go bound to Rome.
> He bears too great a mind. (V. i. 110-112)

Othello is made a prisoner of the Venetian state. His suicide, following almost immediately, is partially motivated by the same sense of high nobility which impels him to refuse to submit himself to the shameful conditions of imprisonment. The spirit of self-conquest is particularly stressed when Antony and Cleopatra die. Caesar is informed that Antony has died

> Not by a public minister of justice
> Nor by a hired knife; but that self hand
> Which writ his honour in the acts it did
> Hath, with the courage which the heart did lend it,
> Splitted the heart. (V. i. 20-24)

Caesar himself provides the appropriate choral commentary on Cleopatra's defiant refusal to submit herself to his will and be taken to Rome in captivity:

> Bravest at the last!
> She levell'd at our purposes, and being royal,
> Took her own way. (V. ii. 338-340)

343

Here Shakespeare is definitely following the Stoic ethics; although Aristotle considered surrender shameful, he did not condone suicide. Shakespeare obviously is presenting the Stoic attitude typified by Seneca's remark that "to death alone it is due that life is not a punishment, that, erect beneath the frown of fortune, I can preserve my mind unshaken and master of itself."[10] Even Seneca, however, writing about Cato's suicide, shares in the general condemnation of this act. T. S. Eliot is right in suggesting that there is an element of Stoic individualism in the final scenes of Shakespeare's tragedies. But in Shakespeare's utilization of what may be a Senecan influence, his dying hero does not become, like Chapman's, a self-sufficient individual who finds himself alone in a totally hostile world. The suicide of the dying hero is a manifestation of the Renaissance maxim that it is unworthy of a highminded (i.e., magnanimous) man "to be subject to any man."[11] Sir Thomas Elyot speaks for the common humanist attitude of the Renaissance, derived from Aristotle and Cicero as well as the Stoics, when he says, "all way dethe is to be preferred before servitude."[12]

As we should predict, it is in the Roman plays that suicide is most explicitly presented as an honorable act. We should remember in this consideration that Shakespeare's Roman plays such as *Julius Caesar* are just as much influenced by the intense patriotic sentiments of the Romans as they are by Stoic fatalism or self-sufficiency. Cleopatra, for example, frequently refers to her anticipated suicide as a noble deed. Indeed, when she first announces her intention to kill herself at the end of the fourth act, she asks anachronistically:

> Then is it sin
> To rush into the secret house of death
> Ere death dare come to us? (IV. xv. 80-82)

Shortly thereafter she affirms that "it is great/ To do that thing that ends all other deeds." (V. ii. 4-5) Her motive

[10] *Consolation ad Marcia*, in *The Works . . . both Moral and Natural*, trans. Thomas Lodge, London, 1614, p. 20.
[11] Cicero *De Officiis* I. 20.
[12] *The Gouernour*, III, 9.

partially accords with the romantic convention of joining her lover in death, condoned even in the medieval romances. But as is the case with Antony, it also includes the desire to avoid the humiliation of Caesar's conquest and to manifest a final, magnificent display of the courage of which she is capable. She dies in a manner befitting a great-souled princess. The words of Montaigne describing Epaminandos are equally relevant to our final judgment of Cleopatra: "I have seene divers, by their death, either in good or evil, give reputation to all their fore-passed life. . . . Verily we should steale much from him, if he should be weighed without the honour and greatnesse of his end."[13]

It is interesting to note that Brutus, in a play which is surely a reflection of classical pagan values, expresses both the positive and negative view on this question (just as Hamlet and Glouces-ter do). At first he tells Cassius:

> I know not how,
> But I do find it cowardly and vile,
> For fear of what might fall, so to prevent
> The time of life—arming myself with patience
> To stay the providence of some high powers
> That govern us below. (V. i. 102-107)

But when Cassius suggests that he may, then, be led in triumph through the streets of Rome, he immediately changes his mind. He tells Cassius, as we saw a few pages back, that he bears too great a mind to accept shameful captivity.

AMBITION

In the discussion of ambition as a general Renaissance con-cept, it became evident that the word was not always used in the deprecatory sense sometimes associated with it today. The desire to emulate others, to outstrip them in the attainment of honors, was looked upon as highly commendable. As the King of Navarre remarks in the opening speech of *Love's Labour's Lost*, all men seek fame so that

---

[13] *Essayes*, I, 18.

> spite of cormorant devouring Time,
> Th'endeavour of this present breath may buy
> That honour which shall bate his scythe's keen edge
> And make us heirs of all eternity. (I. i. 4-7)

Competition and rivalry with others were not considered ignoble incentives to stir men to seek honor. Thus Aufidius speaks of the "ambitious strength" he employed in striving to win out in his struggles against Coriolanus. (IV. v. 117) Similarly, Ventidius speaks of "ambition,/ The soldier's virtue" in *Antony and Cleopatra* (III. i. 22-23) and Othello of "the big wars/That make ambition virtue!" (III. iii. 349-350)

Ambition for high honor was considered highly desirable so long as it did not involve the use of illegitimate means to attain one's end. Conversely, the ambitious man who used craft or force to achieve his goal was viewed with the greatest horror. No motive could more easily lead a man to villainy. Ambition, not pride, induces Claudius to poison his own brother treacherously and then to marry his widow. It causes Edmund to disown father and brother and to join Goneril and Regan in their attempt to undermine the royal dignity of their aged father. It is Brutus' fear of Caesar's ambition which leads him to join the conspirators in their plot and to slay the man he had dearly loved. It is clearly the driving force behind Shakespeare's most Machiavellian villain, King Richard the Third.

If ambition is such a reprehensible motive, how are we to explain the fact that our feelings toward Macbeth are a mingling of admiration and reprobation? The answer lies largely in his wife's accurate characterization of him:

> Thou wouldst be great;
> Art not without ambition, but without
> The illness should intend it. (I. v. 19-21)

In sharp contrast to Claudius and Edmund, Macbeth is reluctant to yield to his ambitious desires throughout the early scenes. He acts only when goaded sufficiently by his less conscience-bur-

dened wife, and when Fate, personified by the witches, assures
him that he is destined to gain the throne. Moreover, he is
obviously appalled by his deed. A part of himself is speaking
with utmost sincerity when he tells the Scottish lords, "Had I
but died an hour before this chance,/ I had liv'd a blessed time."
(II. iii. 96-97) Even though we can not admire the protagonist
fully, we can not refrain from identifying with his predicament
and sympathizing with the anguish of his tortured conscience
and the tremendous inner conflict which takes place between
the noble and vicious aspects of himself. Even as he hardens
in crime, our response is not fully condemnatory any more than
it is in the case of Raskolnikov in Dostoevsky's *Crime and Punishment*. The chain of events which leads to his final remorseless
and utterly callous murder of Macduff's wife and children is
too inexorable for us to judge his final actions solely by themselves, without consideration of the nexus of character and circumstance which has led him to become a savage butcher.

In addition, Macbeth never loses his greatness of soul which
is, at least partially, the very source of his ambition. As La
Primaudaye had pointed out in *The French Academie* (the idea
is a Renaissance commonplace which originated in Cicero's
Offices) "an excessive desire to rule and to excel others, commonly groweth with the greatnes of the hart."[14] Macbeth's
responses throughout the play are of an exalted nature; he is
never merely clever, diplomatic, or cunning like Claudius, Edmund, or Iago. They are remorseless by nature; he becomes
remorseless by necessity. Throughout the play we never cease
to admire his greatness of heart and his redoubtable courage.
Nor does Shakespeare ever allow his audience completely to
lose sight of the fact that he was originally a good man; the
pathos of his destroyed potentialities, of his realization that
mere power in itself is meaningless, comes through in the first
soliloquy in the fifth act: Seyton!—I am sick at heart,
   When I behold—Seyton, I say!—This push
   Will cheer me ever, or disseat me now.

[14] p. 255.

347

I have liv'd long enough. My way of life
Is fall'n into the sere, the yellow leaf;
And that which should accompany old age,
As honour, love, obedience, troops of friends,
I must not look to have; but, in their stead,
Curses not loud but deep, mouth-honour, breath,
Which the poor heart would fain deny, and dare not.
(V. iii. 19-28)

ANGER

It should now be apparent that on many crucial moral issues
the Renaissance ethos was surprisingly dexterous in defending
both the Christian and the pagan-humanist position even when
they were in complete opposition to each other. That Shakespeare's treatment of anger and revenge reflects this ambivalence
is particularly evident when Alcibiades defends the Athenian
soldier who has been condemned to death in the third act of
Timon of Athens. At first Alcibiades supports his friend, who
had killed a man in hot blood, by pointing out that his anger
is merely an indication of his great courage. Alcibiades tells
the Senate,

He is a man (setting his fault aside)
Of comely virtues;
Nor did he soil the fact with cowardice
(An honour in him which buys out his fault)
But with a noble fury and fair spirit,
Seeing his reputation touch'd to death,
He did oppose his foe. (III. v. 14-20)

Alcibiades' argument is in accord with Renaissance moral
philosophy. Hurault, for example, had associated the passion
of anger with the virtue of fortitude and Bryskett had defended
a man's right to be angry, especially in defense of honor and
reputation. But the Athenian senate is not convinced by Alcibiades' argument, so he then shifts to the Christian point of
view and admits that "to be in anger is impiety." (III. v. 56)

This shifting of ground does not help him to win his case but it does indicate how easily (and sometimes how anachronistically) Shakespeare, and his Renaissance audience, could switch from one system of values to the other. They were equally familiar with both.

Anger and the desire for revenge were naturally closely associated. Romeo deliberately ignores Tybalt's insults until Tybalt kills his friend Mercutio. He then seeks revenge with "fire-ey'd fury." (III. i. 129) Malcolm urges Macduff not to weep over the loss of his wife and child but rather to "Let grief/ Convert to anger"—which leads to the seeking of revenge against Macbeth. (IV. iii. 228-229) Hamlet, uncertain of the ghost's authenticity, postpones revenge, but gives vent to his anger with a string of curses—"Bloody, bawdy, villain!/ Remorseless, treacherous, lecherous, kindless villain." (II. ii. 607-608)

In an almost literal translation of Epictetus, Castiglione had argued that the affections "are assistant to virtue, as anger, that helpeth manlinesse: hatred against the wicked helpeth justice."[15] These statements relate particularly to King Lear's situation. When he disowns Cordelia in the first scene of the play, Kent tries to interpose, whereupon Lear speaks out sharply: "Peace, Kent!/ Come not between the dragon and his wrath." (I. i. 123-124) Lear is too arbitrary and too autocratic here; we sense that he is hasty both in his decision to banish Cordelia and in his display of temper against Kent. But we should not make the mistake of categorizing Lear as a testy old man and of dismissing his mounting anger against Goneril and Regan as mere spleen. As Goneril and Regan gradually carry out their malicious plot of heaping deliberate insults upon the old King in the second act, they would, let it be emphasized, completely lose the sympathy of the Jacobean audience. For them, Lear's curses would have seemed as appropriate as Hamlet's cursing of Claudius. The modern audience, with a more refined sensibility, is likely to be upset by Lear's violence

---

[15] *The Courtier*, p. 272.

—as, for example, when he calls Goneril a "degenerate bastard." (I. iv. 275) But our reaction is to be explained by the
fact that the vice of ingratitude has become relatively meaningless to us. For the Renaissance audience, no vice was worse
than that of ingratitude—particularly from a child. The violence of Lear's curses is in direct proportion to the violence of
the wrongs which have been inflicted on him. Shakespeare
uses his strongest metaphors to describe the wickedness of
Goneril and Regan—the daughters are called wolves, mon-
sters, and fiends. Lear tells Goneril as he prepares to leave her
that she personifies

> Ingratitude, thou marble-hearted fiend,
> More hideous when thou show'st thee in a child
> Than the sea-monster! (I. iv. 281-283)

It is of signal importance that the modern reader appreciate
the Elizabethan point of view on this matter. If we fail to
comprehend how grievously Lear has been wronged, and how
just and proper his anger and desire for revenge are, we reach
the conclusion that his "rage . . . shows him unfit to look after
himself."[16] But the modern tendency to censure Lear for his
behavior completely distorts the original meaning of the play.
With the conspicuous exception of the opening scene, Lear's
anger is in no sense a flaw. Lear's tragic greatness depends to
no inconsiderable extent on his capacity to feel indignation,
hatred, and anger toward his daughters so that he does not
tamely bear the injuries which are heaped upon him, as the
unheroic King Richard the Second does when he loses his
regal authority.

Aristotle's remarks on anger, quoted by many Renaissance
moralists, apply with close precision to Lear's situation: "And
they are angry with those who have been in the habit of honour-
ing and treating them with respect, if they no longer behave
so towards them; for they think that they are being treated
with contempt by them, otherwise they would treat them as

---

[16] Granville-Barker, *Prefaces to Shakespeare*, I, 301.

before. And with those who do not return their kindnesses."[17]
Lear's apostrophe to the heavens at the end of the second act
has already been referred to in the discussion of the concept
of "patience" and of "manhood." But since this is one of the
key passages in the greatest of Shakespeare's tragedies, it deserves extended critical scrutiny. When Lear cries out to the
heavens, "fool me not so much/ To bear it tamely," he clearly
is dissociating himself from the tame, meek, and weak acceptance of insult and deposition which characterizes King Richard
the Second and King Henry the Sixth. (II. iv. 278-279) This
nonacceptance becomes ever clearer in the lines which follow:

> touch me with noble anger,
> And let not women's weapons, water drops
> Stain my man's cheeks! No, you unnatural hags!
> I will have such revenges on you both
> That all the world shall—I will do such things—
> What they are yet, I know not; but they shall be
> The terrors of the earth. (II. iv. 279-285)

In order to understand this passage properly, we have only
to turn to Aristotle's definition of anger so frequently para-
phrased in Renaissance moral treatises. Aristotle defines anger
"as a longing, accompanied by pain, for a real or apparent
revenge for a real or apparent slight, affecting a man himself
or one of his friends, when such a slight is undeserved."[18] This
is a precise statement of Lear's situation and of Lear's emotional reaction to his predicament. He has been wronged grievously; his daughters have shown themselves, by Elizabethan
standards, vicious. Hence, they richly deserve the hatred and
anger he vents on them. (Even the New Testament contains
the story of Christ driving the money changers from the
temple.) That for the Renaissance aristocrat the meek acceptance of insult was a sign of great cowardice and weakness is
illustrated by the obvious contempt which the Queen feels
for her timid husband at the beginning of the fifth act of *King*

---

[17] *Rhetoric* II. 2.   [18] *ibid.*

Richard the Second. When he meekly accepts his fate and suggests that she retire to a cloister, she rebukes him sharply for his lack of manly anger.

> What, is my Richard both in shape and mind
> Transform'd and weak'ned? Hath Bolingbroke
> depos'd
> Thine intellect? Hath he been in thy heart?
> The lion dying thrusteth forth his paw
> And wounds the earth, if nothing else, with rage
> To be o'erpow'r'd; and wilt thou pupil-like
> Take thy correction, mildly kiss the rod,
> And fawn on rage with base humility,
> Which art a lion and the king of beasts.
>
> (V. i. 26-34)

Her rebuke is to no avail. In the next scene Shakespeare describes King Richard the Second as he follows Bolingbroke in the triumphal procession and suffers dust to be thrown ignominiously on his head by the populace. Meekly, with gentle tears, he accepts his plight. Shakespeare's Henry the Sixth is perhaps even more cowardly at the moment of his deposition, for he sits passively musing about his predicament while the battle rages which is to decide his future. (II. v.)

In the Renaissance, the capacity for sustained passion was admired both in the lover and in the soldier. It is his quality of sustained indignation which makes the aged Lear such a great-souled hero despite his bodily infirmities. It is the never-flagging resolution of Cleopatra, in the final act of the play, which lifts her to the heights of a great tragic heroine. We should note, however, that the Renaissance moralists, echoing the Aristotelian ideal, were just as prone to disparage a hasty temper as they were to censure somebody incapable of displaying indignation and anger when the occasion demanded it. This "golden mean" is reflected in Ulysses' characterization of Troilus as one "Not soon provok'd, nor being provok'd soon calm'd." (IV. v. 99)

Although the gentle and meek responses of King Richard the Second and King Henry the Sixth to their depositions are treated as signs of weakness, still gentleness, gentility, courtesy, and kindness, in their proper place, are considered among the most praiseworthy of the Shakespearean virtues. In the Renaissance nothing was thought to be more discourteous than an unnecessary display of force, as Duke Senior reminds Orlando when that hungry man roughly demands food from the outlaws. Othello's gentle admonition to Brabantio that his years will command more deference than his weapons also demonstrates the view that good manners are preferable to a peremptory display of ill temper. (I. ii. 60-61) Shakespeare's odd combination of opposite qualities such as gentleness and anger, each to be displayed in its proper place, is particularly evident in Belarius' characterization of Arviragus and Guiderius:

> They are as gentle
> As Zephyrs blowing before the violet,
> Not wagging his sweet head; and yet as rough
> (Their royal blood enchaf'd) as the rud'st wind
> That by the top doth take the mountain pine
> And make him stoop to th' vale.
>
> (IV. ii. 171-176)

"Anger," says Bryskett, "might accompany fortitude . . . so long as reason did temper them."[19] Coriolanus, like Lear in the first scene of the play, gives way to anger uncontrolled by reason. Brutus, the tribune, points out to Sicinius that if they can manage to infuriate Coriolanus when he appears before the populace, he will no longer be able to control his emotions and will arouse their ill will. Volumnia is aware of this weakness in her son's character and so urges him to control his ire when he appears before the people. In fact, she assures him that she has as little love for the plebeians and is just as angry toward them, but that she has "a brain that leads my use of anger/ To better vantage." (III. ii. 30-31) When Coriolanus

[19] p. 88.

is banished from Rome, however, she blazes with righteous indignation. Volumnia does not mince words any more than **Lear** does toward his daughters, than Hamlet does toward Claudius, or than Emilia in *Othello* and Paulina in *The Winter's Tale* do when they discover that their mistresses have been wronged. Volumnia heaps verbal abuses on Brutus and Sicinius, curses them to unclog her heart; in short, she answers wrong with wrong, insult with insult, as the Renaissance aristocrat did in actual life when he felt he had been insulted or injured. These emotions may be neither genteel nor Christian, but they are the stuff of which tragedy is made. When the tribunes leave the stage sulking, Menenius invites her to supper. She curtly replies,

> Anger's my meat. I sup upon myself,
> And so shall starve with feeding.—Come, let's go.
> Leave this faint puling, and lament as I do,
> In anger, Juno-like. Come, come, come.
>
> (IV. ii. 50-53)

It is in the same spirit that Paulina in *The Winter's Tale* prepares to face Leontes in order to inform him finally how grievously he has wronged his Queen. She tells Emilia,

> If I prove honey-mouth'd, let my tongue blister,
> And never to my red-look'd anger be
> The trumpet any more. (II. ii. 33-35)

REVENGE

Revenge, like suicide, is a touchstone which helps us to determine the values of a particular Renaissance writer. Hence, it reveals Shakespeare's relation to the cultural mores of his age much more clearly than anger.

When Shakespeare's protagonists seek revenge, their aim is usually in strict accord with Cicero's dictum that no one should do "harm to another, unless provoked by wrong."[20]

---

[20] Cicero *De Officiis* I. 7.

Thus, Hamlet, Laertes, and Macduff seek revenge for the death of a kinsman, Romeo for the death of a friend, Coriolanus and Alcibiades for the ingratitude shown them by their country, and Othello and Posthumus for the presumed adultery of their wives which will rob them of their honor. Even though private and illegal revenge may be involved, the question of right and wrong, in pagan-humanist terms, is still of the utmost importance. When Laertes uses the poisoned weapon, for example, he obviously feels guilty about his own duplicity. When the weapons are exchanged and he is wounded by the poisoned sword, he freely admits that he is justly killed by his own treachery.

In his *Elizabethan Revenge Tragedy*, F. T. Bowers stresses the native tradition which laid a heavy obligation on a son to avenge the death of a murdered father.[21] This sacred duty is vividly expressed when Laertes receives the news of his father's death; the Christian taboo against revenge is admitted and defied:

> Conscience and grace, to the profoundest pit!
> I dare damnation. To this point I stand,
> That both the worlds I give to negligence,
> Let come what comes; only I'll be revenged
> Most throughly for my father.
>
> (IV. v. 132-136)

When Polonius was killed, Hamlet had felt no remorse, but now once again Hamlet becomes the generous and kindly courtier. This sudden change in his attitude toward Laertes corresponds with his sudden willingness to express openly the intensity of his love for Ophelia; both events indicate the extent to which Gertrude's remarriage had soured a normally sweet disposition. When Horatio says, "Good night, sweet prince,/ And flights of angels sing thee to thy rest!" (V. ii. 370-371) his eulogy, which may seem, like some of the sonnets, slightly sentimental to modern readers, is clearly intended as an accurate appraisal of Hamlet's normal character.

[21] pp. 39-40.

In the closet scene Hamlet refers to himself as "the scourge and minister" of heaven. (III. iv. 175) His remarks, an echo of one of the Christian commonplaces on revenge, show how nimbly Shakespeare, wittingly or unwittingly, could shift from the pagan-humanist point of view to the Christian (the same ambiguity is evident in Hamlet's remarks on suicide; in his characterization of his father as a man of godlike excellence, later as a man who shares in Christian imperfection; also in his conflicting and contradictory attitudes toward the afterlife).

The same ethical ambiguity is apparent in *Romeo and Juliet.* Romeo turns the other cheek like a Christian pacifist when Tybalt first insults him, both because the Prince has forbidden private feuds and because Tybalt is a kinsman of Juliet. (III. i. 69-75) Mercutio, on the other hand, is the very embodiment of the Renaissance man of honor. He calls his friend's meek acceptance of Tybalt's slander a "calm, dishonorable, vile submission!" (III. i. 76) When Romeo discovers that his naive hope that he can prevent a duel has resulted in Mercutio's death, he, too, is transformed into the man of honor. His alteration from a peacemaker into an irate and vengeful swordsman is strong indication of the high value which the Renaissance humanists placed on friendship, reputation, and fortitude.

> This gentleman, the Prince's near ally,
> My very friend, hath got this mortal hurt
> In my behalf—my reputation stain'd
> With Tybalt's slander—Tybalt, that an hour
> Hath been my kinsman. O sweet Juliet,
> Thy beauty hath made me effeminate
> And in my temper soft'ned valour's steel!
>
> (III. i. 114-120)

Since the Renaissance aristocrat valued nothing more highly than honor, he was extremely sensitive to the slightest indication of contempt or disdain. If the modern reader is unwilling to follow Coleridge's dictum and lay aside momentarily his own values, he will misread many of the central speeches of the play which provide the key to the interpretation of both character and motivation. Thus Coriolanus' violent response to Aufidius' insulting epithet "boy" should not be considered merely a manifestation of his proud nature, but also the instinctive response of any Renaissance man of honor to the imputation that he lacks manhood. Macbeth's response is just as violent when his wife suggests that his failure to act is a sign of cowardice. (I. vii. 45-47) Antony tells Octavius that he wars against Caesar because he "Spoke scantly of me; when perforce he could not/ But pay me terms of honour." (III. iv. 6-7) Othello's passion for revenge reaches its height of savagery when, standing at one side of the stage, he watches Cassio apparently regaling Iago with the story of his easy conquest over Desdemona and marks "the fleers, the gibes, and notable scorns/ That dwell in every region of his face." (IV. i. 83-84) Lear's mounting wrath which leads ultimately to his madness stems primarily from his daughters' deliberate, coolly calculated plot to surpass each insult by a greater one; before the old King recovers from the shock of one conspicuous slight, he is confronted with another. Oswald sets off the chain of shameful indignities when he deliberately walks off the stage as Lear addresses him. When he returns, he calls the old King "my lady's father." (I. iv. 87) Goneril then suggests that Lear's kingly retinue is riotous, debauched, and epicurean. (It is noteworthy that only the villainous characters testify to Lear's senility or suggest that his retinue has misbehaved; yet many modern critics accept their accusations against Lear's own assertion that his train are men of choice and rarest parts.) (I. iv. 262-268, 284-288) The stocking of Kent is perhaps the crowning insult, as Kent himself suggests:

> I serve the King
> On whose employment I was sent to you.
> You shall do small respect, show too bold malice
> Against the grace and person of my master,
> Stocking his messenger. (II. ii. 135-139)

A few lines later he adds:

> The King must take it ill
> That he, so slightly valued in his messenger,
> Should have him thus restrain'd.
>
> (II. ii. 152-154)

To understand Lear's predicament in the first acts of the play, we should bear in mind, as the aristocratic members of Shakespeare's audience possibly would have done, Aristotle's statement that "Slighting is an actualization of opinion in regard to something which appears valueless; for things which are . . . of no importance we ignore. Now there are three kinds of slight: disdain, spitefulness, and insult. For he who disdains, slights, since men disdain those things which they consider valueless and slight what is of no account. . . . And the spiteful man appears to show disdain; for spitefulness consists in placing obstacles in the way of another's wishes."[22] Aristotle's observations, echoed and reechoed by the Renaissance moralists, throw a flood of light on Coriolanus' violent reaction to Aufidius' imputation that he is a mere boy, on the extent to which Othello's seething hatred is heightened still further when he believes that Cassio is bragging about his amorous conquests over Desdemona, and on the reasonableness for the Jacobean audience of Antony's bringing the whole world into conflict when he hears that Octavius Caesar has spoken meanly of him in his address to the people of Rome. Of course, if we judge the work of art solely in terms of modern values, the violence of the reaction to insult and ridicule is bound to seem absurd. In this respect, at least, Shakespearean tragedy would have been better understood by a Periclean audience, or by a modern Japanese audience, since, like the Elizabethans, they would consider honor a matter of cardinal importance.

Antonio de Guevara, echoing both the classical moralists and common Renaissance opinion, had said that although a man might forgive all other injuries, ingratitude could never be

[22] *Rhetoric* II. 2.

forgiven.[23] His remark, merely repeating the sayings of Cicero and Seneca, applies particularly to *King Lear* in that ingratitude, as much as deliberate insult, has caused his "heart-struck injuries." (III. i. 17) Albany, testimonial character that he is, makes it a major point that the two daughters are under heavy obligation to their father both because every child should be grateful to his parents and because Lear has been their benefactor. Lear had invoked the aid of the heavens but to no avail. Albany now predicts,

> If that the heavens do not their visible spirits
> Send quickly down to tame these vile offences,
> It will come,
> Humanity must perforce prey on itself,
> Like monsters of the deep. (IV. ii. 46-50)

Indeed, he threatens to take vengeance into his own hands, even against his own wife: Were't my fitness
> To let these hands obey my blood,
> They are apt enough to dislocate and tear
> Thy flesh and bones. Howe'er thou art a fiend,
> A woman's shape doth shield thee.
>
> (IV. ii. 63-67)

Shakespeare's gentlest characters can be savage in their hatred of evil. Hamlet never once shows the least pity for Claudius. When Emilia discovers the truth about her own husband, she expresses the hope that his pernicious soul may rot half a grain a day. At the close of the play, both Gratiano and Lodovico speak unabashedly of the torture which lies in store for him. For the Elizabethans and Jacobeans, this was the vindictive punishment which evil deserved.

Gloucester, in the third act of *King Lear*, tells of the gathering of the forces of France and predicts that the King's injuries will be revenged. But at the end of the play, France and Cordelia lose the battle and Gloucester refuses even to

---

[23] Hellowes, *Familiar Epistles*, p. 71.

consider the possibility of further flight. In a mood of utter fatalism he tells Edgar that "a man may rot even here." (V. ii. 8) In no other of Shakespeare's great tragedies do the forces of good seem so impotent; as Theodore Spencer has pointed out, good seems to have to hide from the powers of evil. Yet ultimately evil is self-destructive; Goneril poisons Regan, and soon thereafter kills herself. Edmund proves to be less Machiavellian than Iago or King Richard the Third, yet his repentance is most curious. The gods do not defend Cordelia as Albany had hoped. Vengeance on evil is much more clear-cut as the curtain falls on *Hamlet*, on *Macbeth*, and on *Othello*. In none of the other tragedies is there so grim, so stark a view of human existence, although this grimness is not to be equated with cynical nihilism. In answer to those who can perceive only the nihilistic aspects of Shakespearean tragedy, we must point out the devotion of Kent, the Fool, Albany, Edgar, and Cordelia to the aged king. Their positive affirmation of human potentialities receives marked stress in the terrible closing scene. Even in his bleakest tragedy, Shakespeare, like one of the great European writers and moralists of our own century, Albert Camus, obviously believed that "there are more things to admire in men than to despise."[24]

The Christian Denial of Revenge in Shakespeare's Plays

King Richard the Second opens with a bitter quarrel between Bolingbroke and Mowbray. Since each accuses the other of treason, the king himself finally has to act as a peacemaker. His remarks are a clear reflection of Christian teachings in regard to anger and revenge:

> Wrath-kindled gentlemen, be rul'd by me;
> Let's purge this choler without letting blood.
> This we prescribe, though no physician;
> Deep malice makes too deep incision.
> Forget, forgive. (I. i. 152-156)

[24] *The Plague*, trans. Stuart Gilbert, New York, 1948, p. 278.

Mowbray's response indicates once again how likely the Renaissance nobleman was to uphold his good name, even if it involved outright defiance of his king:

> Myself I throw, dread sovereign, at thy foot.
> My life thou shalt command, but not my shame.
> The one my duty owes; but my fair name,
> Despite of death that lives upon my grave,
> To dark dishonour's use thou shalt not have.
>
> (I. i. 165-169)

Both Mowbray and Bolingbroke feel themselves slandered and disgraced, hence flatly refuse to accept the king's intercession. In his next speech, Mowbray reiterates the Renaissance commonplace which, as we have seen, was also deeply held conviction, that honor is more important than life itself. So the king finally appoints a day for trial by combat. (It should be remembered that the play has a feudal setting.) But when that trial begins, two scenes later, he suddenly puts a stop to it and banishes both of them from England. In this play, as in *Romeo and Juliet*, the ruler supposedly has the power to prevent private feuds and has the right to banish the offenders in order to preserve the country's peace. For these particular sovereigns, the law of the land takes precedence over the code of honor, therefore private revenge is prohibited. The second scene of the first act of this same play, however, presents a conflict between the opposing views toward private revenge. The Duchess of Gloucester implores old Gaunt to avenge the death of her husband. He refuses because of the Christian interdiction:

> God's is the quarrel; for God's substitute,
> His deputy anointed in his sight,
> Hath caus'd his death; the which if wrongfully,
> Let heaven revenge; for I may never lift
> An angry arm against his minister.
>
> (I. ii. 37-41)

The Stoics shared the Christian view of revenge. It is probably their point of view being expressed, at least momentarily, in *Timon of Athens*. When Alcibiades decides to argue with the Athenian senate, one of the Senators tells him that anger is not a sign of courage, and that, indeed, "to revenge is no valour, but to bear." (III. v. 39) With the same thought, Prospero, at the beginning of the fifth act of *The Tempest*, tells Ariel to release the king and his followers:

> Though with their high wrongs I am struck to
>   th' quick,
> Yet with my nobler reason 'gainst my fury
> Do I take part. The rarer action is
> In virtue than in vengeance. (V. i. 25-28)

Prospero's remarks accord with the forgiving spirit with which so many of the comedies end. Indeed, unforeseen repentance and unpredicted mercy bring many of the comedies to a close. The tragedies, however, are made of sterner stuff. They reflect, primarily, the quick sensitivity to affront which the Renaissance had acquired from Aristotle through his numerous Renaissance disciples. Indignation, anger, and the desire for revenge are not, therefore, disparaged.

CHRISTIAN THEMES IN *KING LEAR* AND *KING LEIR*

Since we have been discussing Shakespeare's ambivalence in his use of Christian and pagan doctrines at some length, it is appropriate here to point to the striking contrast between Shakespeare's *King Lear* and the *True Chronicle Historie of King Leir and His Three Daughters*. The old play is as deeply saturated in Christian themes as Shakespeare's is lacking in precise religious doctrines. As E. E. Stoll observes, Shakespeare's "heroes and heroines alike are not supported in their hour of trial by the thought of the life beyond or even by trust in God and his righteous but unsearchable counsels." For substantiation of this statement, let us here contrast the tone of the two plays, written within about twelve years of each other.[25]

The Old Play	*Topic*	*Shakespeare's* King Lear

Religious Retirement from the World

King Leir (I. i. 24-26)	King Lear (I. i. 38-42)
The world of me, I of the world am weary,	Know we have divided In three our kingdom; and 'tis our fast intent
And I would faine resigne these earthly cares,	To shake all cares and business from our age,
And think upon the welfare of my soule.	Conferring them on younger strengths while we Unburthen'd crawl toward death.

The Sense of Intimate Communion with God

King Leir (I. iii. 6-7)	King Lear (II. iv. 228-231)
How dear my daughters are unto my soul,	But I'll not chide thee Let shame come when it will, I do not call it.
None knows, but He, that knows my thought and secret deeds.	I do not bid the Thunder-bearer shoot Nor tell tales of thee to high-judging Jove.

Turning to God in Adversity

Cordella (I. iii. 129-132)	King Lear (II. iv. 192-194)
Wither shall I go?	O heavens!
. . . . Unto Him that doth protect the just	If you do love old men, if your sweet sway
In Him will poor Cordella put her trust.	Allow obedience—if yourselves are old,
	Make it your cause! Send down, and take my part!

[25] In *Shakespeare and Other Masters*, Cambridge, Mass., 1940, p. 77. See also Tolstoy's essay on Shakespeare in which Shakespeare is vigorously denounced by the Russian novelist for his aristocratic bias and lack of Christianity. Tolstoy compares *King Lear* to the earlier version and finds the Christian doctrine of *King Leir* infinitely preferable to the moral assumptions of Shakespeare's tragedy. (Leo Tolstoy, *Collected Works*, Oxford, 1937, Vol. 21, pp. 338-364.)

Acceptance of Earthly Injustice
as the Divine Will

Cordella (II. iv. 26-28)

But why accuse I Fortune and my
    father?
No, no, it is the pleasure of my God;
And I do willingly embrace the rod.

Gloucester (IV. i. 36-37)

As flies to wanton boys are we to th'
    gods.
They kill us for their sport.

King Leir (IV. vii. 211-214)

Ah, my true friend in all extremity,
Let us submit us to the will of God:
Things past all sense, let us not seek
    to know;
It is God's will, and therefore must
    be so.

Lear (II. ii. 275-279)

You see me here, you gods, a poor
    old man,
As full of grief as age; wretched
    in both.
If it be you that stirs these daughters'
    hearts
Against their father, fool me not so
    much
To bear it tamely.

The Efficacy of Prayer

King Leir (IV. vii. 17)

For fervent prayer much ill hap
    withstands.
[Leir's would-be murderers drop their
knives miraculously at the sound of
heavenly thunder.]

Albany (V. iii. 256)

The gods defend her! . . .
    Enter Lear, with Cordelia
    [dead] in his arms.

Exaltation of Man's
Immortal Life

King Leir (III. iii. 3-4)

The nearer we do grow unto our
    graves,
The less we do delight in worldly
    joys.

Edgar (V. ii. 9-11)

            Men must endure
Their going hence, even as their
    coming hither;
Ripeness is all.

Salvation from God

Cordella (III. iv. 31-32)

I will to church and pray unto my
    Saviour,

King Lear (V. iii. 257-259)

Howl, howl, howl, howl! O you
    are men of stone

That ere I die, I may obtain his favour.

Had I your tongues and eyes,
    I'ld use them so
That heaven's vault should crack.
    She's gone forever!

King Leir (IV. vii. 226-227)

Now, Lord, receive me, for I come
    to thee
And die, I hope, in perfit charity.

King Lear (V. iii. 305-308)

And my poor fool is hang'd!
    No, no, no life!
Why should a dog, a horse, a rat,
    have life,
And thou no breath at all?
    Thou'lt come no more,
Never, never, never, never, never!

Perillus (IV. vii. 323-324)

No worldly gifts, but grace from God
    on high,
Doth nourish virtue and true charity.

The Ending—
Happy or Tragic

King of Gallia

Thanks be to God; our foes are
    overcome.
And you againe possessed of your
    right.

Kent (V. iii. 313-315)

Vex not his ghost. O, let him pass!
    He hates him
That would upon the rack of this
    tough world
Stretch him out longer.

King Leir

First to the heavens; next, thanks
    to you, my sonne.

The True Chronicle Historie of King Leir is saturated in Christian doctrine and has an all-pervasive religious atmosphere. Not only are the protagonists turning to God in their hour of trial, but also the tone and sentiment throughout the play are colored by true Christian feeling. All fundamental ethical dilemmas are resolved by reference to the Christian notions of good and evil. As Leo Tolstoy observed, this is not true of

Shakespeare's tragic world. Yet, in a representative piece of modern criticism of this play, John Danby can write that *King Lear* "is not only our profoundest tragedy; it is also our profoundest expression of an essentially Christian comment on man's world and his socicty, using the terms and benefiting by the formulations of the Christian tradition. *King Lear*, I feel, is at least as Christian as *The Divine Comedy*."[26]

[26] *Shakespeare's Doctrine of Nature*, London, 1944, p. 204.

CHAPTER 10

HONOR AS PUBLIC ESTEEM

HONOR AS RESPECT AND DUTY

C ICERO reminds his reader at the very beginning of the *Offices*, the textbook on moral philosophy which the Elizabethan schoolboy, hence very likely Shakespeare, read in grammar school, that he lies constantly under the obligation of showing reverence and respect to his superiors and that his honor depends on his performance of these duties.[1] For both Roman and Renaissance society, these "duties" were defined in accordance with the hierarchical ordering of society; thus, the king was to be shown respect and esteem because of his political superiority, the elder because of his superiority in age, and the father or husband because of his supreme position in the family group. Since the general structure of Elizabethan society was patriarchical and the family unit closely knit, Shakespeare usually considers the duty to respect, honor, and obey one's father comparable to the duty to obey one's king. When Theseus reprimands Hermia at the beginning of *A Midsummer's Night's Dream* because she refuses to follow her father's bidding and marry Demetrius, he goes even further than this:

> To you your father should be as a god;
> One that compos'd your beauties; yea, and one
> To whom you are but as a form in wax,
> By him imprinted, and within his power
> To leave the figure, or disfigure it. (I. i. 47-51)

The absolute power of the father, and the extent to which disobedience to his orders is hence treated as an unspeakable offense,

[1] I. 2.

367

is indicated by Theseus' ensuing action; he gives Hermia the choice of obeying her father's will, retiring for life to a nunnery, or being sentenced to death. The Renaissance child was expected to revere his father almost as if he were a god, as Theseus reminds Hermia, and to obey him as if he were a king. When Juliet disobeys her father, the Elizabethan audience would be sympathetic toward her only because of her marriage to Romeo. In a similar situation, Desdemona defends herself by pointing out to Brabantio the superiority of her obligations to her husband whenever there is a conflict of duties, yet she is careful to treat her father with the utmost respect. She tells him,

> My noble father,
> I do perceive here a divided duty.
> To you I am bound for life and education;
> My life and education both do learn me
> How to respect you; you are the lord of duty;
> I am hitherto your daughter. But here's my husband;
> And so much duty as my mother show'd
> To you, preferring you before her father,
> So much I challenge that I may profess
> Due to the Moor my lord. (I. iii. 180-189)

Shakespeare frequently presents a conflict between the romantic involvements of the child and the contrary wishes of the father, but he usually manages to reconcile the two before the close of the play. Posthumus is banished because of Cymbeline's displeasure that Imogen has chosen a poor gentleman for a husband. Cloten, who hopes to annul the marriage, tells the heroine when she persists in her loyalty to her husband that she sins against obedience. But by the end of the play Posthumus has proved his worth and so the king indicates that he is happy to have him as a son-in-law.

The question whether Hector shall go forth in battle against the Greeks involves him in the sharp, irreconcilable conflict which Corneille was so fond of depicting. Which is to come first: his duty to his father or his duty to uphold his honor? When

Cassandra prophesies fatal consequences if he engages in battle, Priam tells him that he must not go. Hector feels that his honor is at stake since he has pledged his word that he will fight. However, like Desdemona, he shows utmost courtesy when he refuses to obey his father. He resolves the conflict by pointing to the hierarchy of values involved; breaking faith will be a greater offense than disobedience:

> I must not break my faith.
> You know me dutiful; therefore, dear sir,
> Let me not shame respect, but give me leave
> To take that course by your consent and voice
> Which you do here forbid me, royal Priam,
> (V. iii. 71-75)

Coriolanus feels equally torn because of a conflict of duties. Even though deeply stirred when he first sees his wife, mother, and child, he is resolved to take revenge on the Romans for their ingratitude. So he admonishes himself; "But out, affection! / All bond and privilege of nature, break!" (V. iii. 24-25) When Volumnia bows to him he is visibly stirred and responds by bowing to her as a dutiful child should. Yet all her arguments are to no avail and so she finally complains,

> There's no man in the world
> More bound to's mother; yet here he lets me prate
> Like one i' th' stocks. (V. iii. 158-160)

Like all of Shakespeare's virtuous characters, Coriolanus is fully aware of his own misconduct—in this case, that his behavior is unnatural, ungrateful, and unkind. (Even Macbeth and his wife are conscious of the moral laws which they are violating, which is not true of Shakespeare's really Machiavellian figures—Iago, Goneril, Regan, and King Richard the Third.) He finally breaks under the strain and consents to spare Rome. The strength of the pull of affection which leads him to retract is made plain in his comment to Aufidius: "Sir, it is no little thing to make/ Mine eyes to sweat compassion." (V.

iii. 195-196) Aufidius admits that he too was moved, but uses this unforeseen opportunity to destroy his opponent.

The wife's duty to the husband is satirically treated in *The Taming of the Shrew* and we become aware that, as in Chaucer's description of the Wyf of Bath, universal types have existed in all ages which do not necessarily conform to the social mores of their time. In Katherine's final speech she lectures Bianca and the widow on the responsibilities which she herself has but recently learned. The Renaissance fondness for analogical reasoning is illustrated by her reference to the husband's role as that of lord, king, and governor.

> Such duty as the subject owes the prince,
> Even such a woman oweth to her husband;
> And when she is froward, peevish, sullen, sour,
> And not obedient to his honest will,
> What is she but a foul contending rebel
> And graceless traitor to her loving lord?
>
> (V. ii. 155-160)

There is considerable irony in the fact that it is Katherine who delivers this sermon, but the ideas themselves could be found in almost any Renaissance book on moral philosophy.

At the beginning of the third act of *The Two Gentlemen of Verona*, the Duke of Milan tells Valentine that his daughter has been "Proud, disobedient, stubborn, lacking duty." (III. i. 69) The Duke's accusations against Sylvia, when she refuses to comply with her father's wishes, are precisely those which Lear lodges against Cordelia. In the case of *King Lear*, the Jacobean audience would have sympathized partially with the father and partially with the daughter. Since the authority of the father was, indeed, great in that age, Lear complains with some justice of Cordelia's willfulness, which even the King of France recognizes in her but minimizes by attributing it to a mere slowness of temperament. On the other hand, Renaissance moralists, especially in England, placed a special premium on plainspoken honesty. Shakespeare's audience would thus at once have switched their sympathies to Cordelia on discovering at the end of the first scene that Goneril and Regan are deceitful flatterers.

One of the central ethical themes of *King Lear* is, quite simply, the duty—love, honor, obedience, and reverence—which the child owed to the parent. This theme, like the other major themes in the play, is reiterated frequently. Gloucester speaks, for example, of the eclipses of recent occurrence which foreshadow disunity in the social order and mentions particularly the cracking of the bond between father and child. The same theme is treated with large irony when Edmund tells Gloucester that he had lectured Edgar "with how manifold and strong a bond/ The child was bound to th' father." (II. i. 49-50) The treatment becomes even more heavily ironic when Cornwall praises Edmund for having "shown your father/ A childlike office"; Edmund brushes off the compliment with the compliant response, " 'Twas my duty, sir." (II. i. 107-108) Shakespeare's villains often pronounce piously all the proper platitudes.

Regan's hyperbolical professions of love and devotion in the opening scene are not forgotten by her old father when he discovers that her sister, Goneril, is a faithless and disloyal child. He comes to Gloucester's castle harboring the illusion that Regan at least is dutiful. He assures her,

> Thou better know'st
> The offices of nature, bond of childhood,
> Effects of courtesy, dues of gratitude.
> Thy half of th' kingdom hast thou not forgot,
> Wherein I thee endow'd. (II. iv. 180-184)

Just as Duncan's trust in Macbeth resulted from the multiple obligations of subject, kinsman, and host, so too Regan's obligations reflect a commingling of the natural bond of child to parent, the obligations of courtesy, and the debt of gratitude to a benefactor. Indeed, even if Lear had been unjust to Goneril and Regan (which was not the case), their duty would have

371

been to tolerate the vilification which he heaped upon them. In the words of Guazzo, "If the father bee churlish and curst unto [his children], let the manifold benefites received of him, countervaile that crueltye, and continue them in their duetye, by the example of the young man, who, as one cast in his teeth that his Father spake ill of him, answered, That, he would not do it, if he had not cause."[2]

There are innumerable instances in Shakespeare where a member of a particular family is reviled and even disowned when his immediate kin discover that he has been false to the honor of the family. Isabella, chaste, pure, and merciful (and hence in recent criticism often considered the prototype of Shakespeare's Christian protagonists) immediately imputes bastardy to her own brother, Claudius, when he indicates that he wishes to live even at the expense of her shame. (The term bastard is often used merely as a form of insult and should not always be considered a serious charge leveled at another person.) The tendency to disown that which was so wholeheartedly loved that it was practically a part of oneself is manifest both in Othello's treatment of Desdemona and in Leonato's treatment of the presumably false Hero in *Much Ado About Nothing*. Leonato is possibly even more savage than Othello in his revulsion; he tells the Friar that if his daughter has been false he hopes that she will not revive, and that if she does, he will tear her limb from limb with his own hands. Indeed, he wishes that he had never had a child or had adopted that of a beggar. Then he could have said, " 'No part of it is mine;/ This shame derives itself from unknown loins.' " (IV. i. 135-136) But as it is, he feels an identity with his child—through the oneness of their blood—which is so great that he must say,

> But mine, and mine I lov'd, and mine I prais'd,
> And mine that I was proud on—mine so much
> That I myself was to myself not mine,
> Valuing of her—why, she, O, she is fall'n

---

[2] *The Civile Conversation*, III, 36. Cf. Aristotle *Nicomachean Ethics* VIII. 12.

> Into a pit of ink, that the wide sea
> Hath drops too few to wash her clean again,
> And salt too little which may season give
> To her foul tainted flesh! (IV. i. 137-144)

It is this sense of close identity with one's flesh and blood which leads Lear to revile the daughters he had once loved. The modern critics who condemn Lear fail to realize that for the Elizabethan and Jacobean, shameful behavior on the part of members of one's own family was just as reprehensible as offences which one commits oneself. In the Elizabethan family children were, in an important sense, but a projection of oneself. Hence, the moral treatises were constantly warning children to "so behave themselves, [that] their father have no cause to curse them, and wish ill of them, as Oedipus did to his children, for it is a thing most certaine, that God heareth the prayers of the Father against his children."[3] As this passage indicates, it is a natural progression for Lear to pass from the cursing of his children to the apostrophizing of the heavens:

> Hear, Nature, hear! dear goddess, hear!
> Suspend thy purpose, if thou didst intend
> To make this creature fruitful. (I. iv. 297-299)

Just before he is blinded, Gloucester likewise cries out in protest: "But I shall see/ The winged vengeance overtake such children." (III. vii. 65-66) But the exhortations of both wronged fathers are bootless—in no other tragedy is the theme so clearly that of the wanton indifference of the heavens to the affairs of men. Lear and Gloucester both find that the only support and only recompense for the malignancy of their evil children and the blows of an indifferent fate lie in the devotion and loyalty of the children they had discarded. But the compensation of discovering fidelity where they had anticipated in-

---

[3] Guazzo, *The Civile Conversation*, III, 36. Guazzo also writes in this passage: "Lastly, let them stick to their parentes, in all troubles and adversitye, assuring themselves, that they which shall abandon their parentes, shall be forsaken of God, and that it is the greatest offence that may be committed."

fidelity more than atones for the anguish of trust betrayed. Both Gloucester and Lear die from heartbreak, but their hearts break from joy as much as from grief. Nothing more clearly refutes Santayana's assertion that Shakespeare's philosophy was essentially cynical and pessimistic than the alteration which takes place in Gloucester in the final scene of the play. At the end of the second scene of the fifth act, refusing to attempt further flight when he heard that Lear's forces had lost the battle, he had told Edgar, "A man may rot even here." (V. ii. 8) This is, indeed, the mood of weary cynicism and futile fatality which Santayana and Eliot would have as the essence of Shakespeare's "philosophy." But in the final scene, Edgar's report of his father's death indicates that Gloucester, like Lear, found a powerful, positive affirmation in the love and devotion of his one faithful child. Edgar's revelation to his father of his true identity provokes a response anything but cynical. The shock of reunion is too great and so

> his flaw'd heart
> (Alack, too weak the conflict to support!)
> 'Twixt two extremes of passion, joy and grief,
> Burst smilingly. (V. iii. 196-199)

In the cruelest of Shakespeare's tragedies there is compensation for the burden of existence, simple yet great—human love and fidelity.

Respect for Elders. The Elizabethan child was taught not only the Fifth Commandment, "Honor thy father and thy mother," but also that he should "imitate the youth of Rome, which had age in such reverence, that every one did honour to elder, as to his parent."[4] Once again, Goneril, Regan, and Edmund completely defy the ethical canons of their age. Goneril calls Lear "an idle old man," and Edmund is equally contemptuous of old Gloucester. (I. iii. 16) Shakespeare interweaves the two themes of respect for the parent and respect for the elder. Thus Albany arraigns Goneril, as we saw in Chapter 9, with:

---

[4] *ibid.*, II, 33.

Tigers, not daughters, what have you perform'd?
A father, and a gracious aged man,
Whose reverence even the head-lugg'd bear would lick,
Most barbarous, most degenerate, have you madded.

(IV. ii. 40-43)

The Spanish bishop, Antonio de Guevara, had remarked, in a typical passage from a representative Elizabethan textbook on moral philosophy, that "there hath bene no nation of such barbarous rudeness, nor any people so intractable, which have . . . withholden reverence from old age."[5] The failure of the eminent Shakespearean critics of our century to pay sufficient attention to the cultural values of the Renaissance in their interpretation of the Shakespearean text is particularly evident when they comment on Lear's "senility." Let us look at a few representative passages:

"Old age has weakened [Lear's] capacity for self-control, making him as soon as he is crossed the prey of an anger definitely rooted in the 'blood.' "—D. A. Traversi, *An Approach to Shakespeare*.

"We are told that Lear is uneducated; he has not grown up: the play will have the painful theme of the education of a man old and hence so set that only the most violent methods can succeed."—E. M. W. Tillyard, *The Elizabethan World Picture*.

"At the outset Lear is an old man on the verge of dotage. His self-knowledge has never been strong, and infirmity of years has made bad discrimination worse. Further, the decay of age renders him all the more liable to attacks of choler, and thereby to the overclouding of reason. . . . Old fools are babes again. In the first scene Lear's conduct was that of the neurotic—his neurosis one of old age and absolute power combined."—John Danby, *Shakespeare's Doctrine of Nature*.

"[Lear] was almost in his dotage; unbalanced certainly. His outbursts of ironic rage, the cursing of Goneril, his subsequent ravings—his whole conduct shows him unfit to look after him-

---

[5] Fenton, *The Golden Epistles*, p. 77.

self. For his own sake, then, how much better for his daughter's servants to wait on him."—Harley Granville-Barker, *Prefaces to Shakespeare*.[6]

In Shakespeare's England, wisdom and years were usually closely associated and stupidity was as frequently considered an attribute of youth as of senility. Because of our 20th century values, the modern audience tends to turn Renaissance attitudes topsy-turvy and our most eminent critics hence come to sympathize with the Shakespearean villain for his unfortunate predicament in being burdened with a silly old father. But Portia's letter of recommendation to the Venetian court in *The Merchant of Venice* surely indicates that it was Elizabethan youth whose wisdom and maturity were held suspect. For she says: "I beseech you let his lack of years be no impediment to let him lack a reverend estimation; for I never knew so young a body with so old a head." (IV. i. 161-164) Disrespect for, and maltreatment of, the aged is (or was) one of the major charges against Goneril, Regan, and Edmund, although not the most monstrous of their many crimes.[7] That the early chronicle histories reflect a similar attitude is evident from a significant passage in *The Second Part of King Henry the Sixth*. Young Clifford, arriving on the field of battle to discover the corpse of his dead father, cries out in protest and lamentation:

> Wast thou ordain'd, dear father,
> To lose thy youth in peace and to achieve
> The silver livery of advised age,
> And in thy reverence and thy chair-days thus
> To die in ruffian battle? Even at this sight
> My heart is turn'd to stone; and while 'tis mine,
> It shall be stony. York not our old men spares;
> No more will I their babes. (V. ii. 45-52)

---

[6] Traversi, p. 184; Tillyard, p. 66; John F. Danby, *Shakespeare's Doctrine of Nature*, pp. 175-176; Granville-Barker, I, 301.

[7] "Shakespeare uses the word 'unnatural' 37 times in all his plays; one fifth of these uses is in *Lear*." (Theodore Spencer, *Shakespeare and the Nature of Man*, p. 142.)

REPUTATION

As has been indicated, the sophisticated criticism of our age tends to show less sympathy for Shakespeare's heroes and less awareness of Shakespearean values than did the critics of the 18th century, who were still immersed in a vital humanist tradition and who still thought in terms of honor, greatness of soul, fortitude, resolution, and revenge.[8] As the result of our blindness today to pagan-humanist values—and, in some cases, of our bias in favor of Christian values—Granville-Barker's generally excellent criticism goes astray when he attempts to defend Goneril and Regan; Eliot's criticism of the Shakespearean dying hero, perceptive in its detailed analysis, misrepresents the true nature of the Shakespearean protagonist when it comes to larger generalizations; Santayana distorts the essential spirit of Shakespearean tragedy by turning it into a mere justification of nihilism, cynicism, or bourgeois orthodoxy; and Curry's scholarly approach becomes a source of confusion rather than elucidation since, in tracing a Thomistic framework for Macbeth he overlooks the ethical attitudes of Shakespeare's own age toward honor.

Othello, for some reason, refers more frequently to the theme of reputation than any other play by Shakespeare. When Othello, in the third act, had proclaimed a night of festivity, he warned the soldiers of the guard not to sport beyond the bounds of discretion. Disturbed in his sleep, he comes to the scene of brawl to discover the cause of the uproar and to punish the offender. When Cassio refuses to tell him what has happened, he turns to Montano:

[8] Ever since Burckhardt wrote *The Civilization of the Renaissance*, modern scholars, whether literary critics or cultural historians, have tended to be thoroughly unsympathetic to the concept of honor. Indeed, they often link the thirst for fame with Renaissance "egotism" and "individualism." The following passages are representative: Burckhardt, p. 93; T. S. Eliot, pp. 110-113; D. A. Traversi, *An Approach to Shakespeare*, p. 148; Brents Stirling, *Unity in Shakespearian Tragedy* (Chapter on "Reputation, reputation, reputation!"), New York, 1957, pp. 111-138; G. R. Elliott, *Flaming Minister*, pp. xiii, xvi, and xix; Franklin M. Dickey, *Not Wisely but Too Well*, San Marino, 1957, pp. 177-202; John F. Danby, *Shakespeare's Doctrine of Nature*, p. 41.

> Worthy Montano, you were wont be civil;
> The gravity and stillness of your youth
> The world hath noted, and your name is great
> In mouths of wisest censure. What's the matter
> That you unlace your reputation thus
> And spend your rich opinion for the name
> Of a night-brawler? Give me answer to't.
>
> (II. iii. 190-196)

This passage is a veritable gold mine of allusions to the concept of honor, although the word itself is not once mentioned. If he is unaware of Renaissance values, the modern reader is likely to pass over the speech hastily and inattentively since it lacks sharp dramatic focus. But it would not have been treated casually by the Jacobean audience since it speaks of a matter which was a central concern—indeed, almost an obsession.

Cassio's rueful lament when Othello abruptly dismisses him from his service is a striking dramatic illustration of this same cardinal theme. Iago asks,

> What, are you hurt, Lieutenant?
> CAS. Ay, past all surgery.
> IAGO. Marry, God forbid!
> CAS. Reputation, reputation, reputation! O, I have lost my reputation! I have lost the immortal part of myself, and what remains is bestial. My reputation, Iago, my reputation!
> IAGO. As I am an honest man, I thought you had receiv'd some bodily wound. There is more sense in that than in reputation. Reputation is an idle and most false imposition; oft got without merit and lost without deserving. (II. iii. 259-270)

Cassio's lament over the loss of the "immortal part of himself" does not have the slightest connection with the Christian conception of the immortal soul. (As a matter of fact, the very intensity with which the Greeks and Romans clung to the notion of immortality through posthumous reputation was a reflection of their uncertainty as to the possibility of personal survival. The men of the Renaissance usually were equally concerned with the Christian and pagan concepts of survival beyond the grave.)

Iago's cynical response to Cassio's laments, in which he lightly dismisses his lamentations about his wounded reputation, is but another indication of the extent to which Shakespeare's villains either blatantly ignore or attempt to destroy the very positive values which the virtuous characters share in their allegiance to the Renaissance ideal of honor and reputation. The nihilism Santayana attributes to Shakespeare can, with justice, be attributed to his villains, just as the self-love Eliot ascribes to the tragic heroes applies to an Iago or a Richard the Third. But if we consider the work of art as a unit, and within its own context, then the self-love, nihilism, and cynicism of the villains are clearly to be viewed as evil, and as a sinister challenge to the values which the good characters share (i.e., Lodovico, Cassio, Montano, as well as Othello and Desdemona, who are so much in the spotlight that one tends to forget how much they have in common with their virtuous associates). Bradley's remarks are pertinent here; the malevolent forces fulfill a role which is solely destructive. There is no reason to assume that Shakespeare's audience would have felt that they were deserving of any sympathy, as so many modern critics suggest, or that their comments would have been considered impartial because they would have been considered testimonial characters.

But the Shakespearean villains, who show such a shocking and callous contempt for all the moral imperatives of their society, are often as crafty as the fox and hence are capable of professions of utmost virtue. They may be devils, but they can moralize and even quote Scripture with the greatest ease. For example, the Iago who informs Cassio that a bodily wound is far worse than a wounded reputation—and thus completely reverses the Renaissance hierarchy of values according to which a physical wound should be considered as relatively inconse-

quential compared to the wounding of a man's honor—can in
the very next act tell Othello,

> Good name in man and woman, dear my lord,
> Is the immediate jewel of their souls.
> Who steals my purse steals trash; 'tis something, nothing;
> 'Twas mine, 'tis his, and has been slave to thousands;
> But he that filches from me my good name
> Robs me of that which not enriches him
> And makes me poor indeed. (III. iii. 155-161)

In the Renaissance, as in classical Greece and Rome, a man's
real value could not be enhanced by the possession of wealth
(the realities of Elizabethan social history did not thoroughly
accord with this aristocratic ideal). Reputation, on the other
hand, was a priceless commodity.

Reputation is mentioned in *King Richard the Second* almost
as frequently as in *Othello*. In the very first scene, Bolingbroke
and Mowbray wish to engage in combat in order to prove which
of them is the traitor. The King, as did Queen Elizabeth in
real life, tries to put a stop to their bitter quarrel, but Mowbray,
like a Sidney or an Essex, refuses to permit his allegiance to
his monarch to extend so far that he allows another nobleman
to sully his fair name. In defence of his refusal he tells King
Richard that "The purest treasure mortal times afford/ Is
spotless reputation." (I. i. 177-178) In the second act, in one
of the most celebrated speeches in the play, the dying John of
Gaunt suggests that the honor of the entire English nation has
become spotted:

> This land of such dear souls, this dear dear land,
> Dear for her reputation through the world,
> Is now leas'd out (I die pronouncing it)
> Like to a tenement or pelting farm.
> England, bound in with the triumphant sea,
> Whose rocky shore beats back the envious siege
> Of wat'ry Neptune, is now bound in with shame.
>
> (II. i. 57-63)

Opinion. Opinion (as a synonym for reputation and with a much more precise meaning than "public opinion" has today) is also frequently referred to in the chronicle history plays, particularly in connection with the deposition of King Richard the Second and the rise of Bolingbroke to power. (Bolingbroke, who contemplates a pilgrimage to the Holy Land, gradually effaces his sense of guilt at having achieved his end by such devious means, but he can never completely blot out the stain on his own honor.) At the beginning of *The First Part of King Henry the Fourth*, Worcester, Northumberland, and Hotspur complain that as participants in the plot against Richard they, too, have lost the good opinion of the world. When Worcester states that "we in the world's wide mouth/ Live scandaliz'd and foully spoken of," Hotspur concurs and speaks out strongly against the new king who has been so ungrateful in failing to reward them for having sacrificed their honor. (I. iii. 153-154) He exhorts his associates to take action and assures them that

> yet time serves wherein you may redeem
> Your banished honours and restore yourselves
> Into the good thoughts of the world again.
> (I. iii. 180-182)

Hotspur consistently puts honor ahead of all else. When the news reaches them that his father will not join them in their fight against the new king, Worcester fears that their success will be jeopardized by this diminution of their forces, but Hotspur welcomes the news since "It lends a lustre and more great opinion,/ A larger dare to our great enterprise." (IV. i. 77-78) And in his very dying words, he informs Prince Hal that he is more regretful about the loss of his proud titles than of life itself.

Bolingbroke, who has none of the impetuous, youthful idealism of Hotspur, is no less concerned with the opinion of the world. When he returns to England, at the beginning of the third act of *King Richard the Second*, he discovers that Bushy and Green have taken over his family lands and destroyed his coat-of-arms. He complains, just before he has them led off to execution, that they have left him no sign "Save men's opinions and my living blood,/ To show the world I am a gentleman." (III. i. 26-27) At the end of the same play, he tells Exton that the murder of King Richard the Second leaves him subject to the world's slander; his decision to make a pilgrimage to the Holy Land to atone for his crime is a typical blending of religious and secular motives since the pilgrimage will partially serve the purpose of reestablishing his reputation.

The pilgrimage never takes place. Instead, King Henry the Fourth carefully and craftily restores his lost "credit" by the strict propriety of his behavior. And so he can tell Hal, who has provoked his father's displeasure by his own wanton conduct,

> Had I so lavish of my presence been,
> So common-hackney'd in the eyes of men,
> So stale and cheap to vulgar company,
> Opinion, that did help me to the crown
> Had still kept loyal to possession
> And left me in reputeless banishment
> A fellow of no mark nor likelihood.
>
> (III. ii. 39-45)

He then gives his son a lecture on royal diplomacy, comparing at great length the manner in which Richard the Second had lost the world's esteem, by associating with the common people, with the dignified and scrupulous propriety of his own actions since he has gained the throne. He warns Hal that he, too, will lose the world's favor if he continues to associate with vulgar cronies. When Hal rescues his father from the Douglas, in the battle which takes place near the end of the play, the King remarks, "Thou hast redeem'd thy lost opinion." (V. iv. 48) But it is especially by his victory over Hotspur that Hal atones for his past misdemeanors, the victory which Hal had prophesied earlier in the play when his father had rebuked him and compared him unfavorably to the gallant Hotspur.

In the death-bed scene of *The Second Part of King Henry the*

Fourth, both father and son allude once again to their concern about public opinion. Both feel guilt-laden as a result of the moral irresponsibility of their behavior and both desire to establish a finer reputation for their family. In telling his father that his suspicions were unjustified (Henry had feared that his son had taken up the crown from the pillow because he hoped and believed his father already dead), Hal exclaims,

> If I do feign,
> O, let me in my present wildness die,
> And never live to show th' incredulous world
> The noble change that I have purposed.
> (IV. v. 152-155)

The dying father replies by predicting, in his final speech, that the prince will indeed bestow on their royal line,

> Better opinion, better confirmation;
> For all the soil of the achievement goes
> With me into the earth. (IV. v. 189-191)

Bolingbroke's diplomatic cunning, which contrasts so sharply with Hotspur's impulsive and idealistic concern for honor and fame, reveals itself once again at the very end of his life. He shrewdly suggests to his son that he busy the minds of his subjects with foreign quarrels (which Hal does in *King Henry the Fifth*) and thus erase from their memories the shameful means by which Hal's father had acquired the crown.

Hal's rejection of Falstaff at the end of the play has upset many of Shakespeare's warmest admirers, but this rejection should certainly be interpreted as an indication of the extent to which the former Prince is willing to forego all his youthful pleasures for the responsibilities of kingship—not the least of which is the maintenance of a high reputation in the world's eyes (although he thus loses the esteem of many a modern reader). Again, he makes it clear that the opinion of the world is a matter of utmost concern to him. He tells Falstaff:

Presume not that I am the thing I was;
For God doth know (so shall the world perceive)
That I have turn'd away my former self;
So will I those that kept me company.

(V. v. 60-63)

The new King is heeding the advice given him by his father in
The First Part of King Henry the Fourth; he will not, like
Richard the Second, be "a companion to the common streets."
(III. ii. 68) Much as this rejection may lower Hal in our
opinion, it was necessary in order to prepare the Elizabethan
audience for the royal greatness of King Henry the Fifth, who,
in the next play in this historical sequence, is to appear as
Shakespeare's most complete dramatic embodiment of the
Renaissance kingly ideal.

Hector's challenge to the Greeks in *Troilus and Cressida*
provokes one of the many interminable intellectual discussions
among the Greek chieftains. Nestor proposes that Achilles be
matched with Hector since

Who may you else oppose,
That can from Hector bring those honours off,
If not Achilles? Though't be a sportful combat,
Yet in the trial much opinion dwells;
For here the Troyans taste our dear'st repute
With their fin'st palate. (I. iii. 333-338)

Ulysses, however, objects to Nestor's scheme. With the diplomatic cunning for which he has always been famous—a cunning
far surpassing that of Bolingbroke—he suggests that the Greeks
will be much safer if they pit Ajax against Hector since then,
if he is defeated, they can say that Hector has not defeated their
best man. Once again, it is obviously a major concern of Shakespeare's leaders to establish a high opinion for themselves in the
eyes of the world. Ulysses argues,

If the dull brainless Ajax come safe off,
We'll dress him up in voices; if he fail,

> Yet go we under our opinion still
> That we have better men. (I. iii. 381-384)

The attitude of Shakespeare's heroes and of his Elizabethan audience is, in other words, strikingly similar to that of Greek and Roman society; hence, it is not necessary here to raise the question whether Shakespeare is guilty of anachronisms or aware of historical differences between his own and earlier societies. Cicero's opinion that there is "nothing more desirable than the opinion of good men, nothing sweeter than genuine glory" is in complete agreement with the thirst for honor and jealous concern for reputation manifested by so many of Shakespeare's characters.[9]

These attitudes are of the greatest importance to a proper interpretation of Macbeth's character. As the result of his great bravery when he conquers the rebel thanes, he is held in the highest esteem by his king and fellow countrymen at the beginning of the play. The Sergeant who describes Macbeth's actions refers to him as "brave Macbeth (well he deserves that name)," (I. ii. 16) and the King himself calls him a "peerless kinsman." (I. iv. 58) Because so many honors have been showered upon him, Macbeth balks at the murder of Duncan. He tells his wife:

> We will proceed no further in this business.
> He hath honour'd me of late, and I have bought
> Golden opinions from all sorts of people,
> Which would be worn now in their newest gloss,
> Not cast aside so soon. (I. vii. 31-35)

Macbeth has often been accused of love of adulation, but the question must be asked whether his love of adulation is any greater than that of his age as a whole? For his pleasure in acquiring new honors, as long as he does so by legitimate means, accords strictly with Du Vair's definition of honor (the clearest and most complete of all the Renaissance definitions of the

---

[9] *Philippics* v. 18.

concept) which I referred to in the introduction to this book: "True honour is the glittering and beaming brightnes of a good and vertuous action, which rebounds from our consciences unto the sight of them with whom wee live, and so by a reflexion in our selves, brings us a testimonie from others of the good opinion which they have of us, which makes us enjoy great comfort of minde."[10] Shakespeare's audience, so familiar with this view, would scarcely have accused Macbeth of love of adulation and lack of humility—unless they judged him by strictly Christian standards.

Curry uses these standards in his interpretation of the play in *Shakespeare's Philosophical Patterns*, which tries to discover a moral framework for the play in the ethics of St. Thomas Aquinas. Judging by medieval Christian criteria, Curry accuses Macbeth of the desire of "flattering his inordinate love of self."[11] Curry goes on to say that "Macbeth is actuated in his conduct mainly by an inordinate desire for worldly honors."[12] These judgments, based on a Christianized Aristotelian ethics, simply do not accord with the cultural values of Shakespeare or his age. In his plays, honor is never a "mutable good," an "evanescent satisfaction," as Curry would have it.[13] On the contrary, it is one of man's primary goals in life to acquire ever greater honor, since by means of it the Renaissance "man of honor" can leave behind him a name which will possibly be as immortal as Scipio's or Cato's.

Good Report. "Good report" is frequently referred to in *Cymbeline*. Since the hero is in Italy when the play begins, Shakespeare makes use of the services of two gentlemen so that the audience may be made aware of his preeminent virtue. After the first gentleman has lauded his rare qualities, the second replies, "I honour him/ Even out of your report." (I. i. 54-55) Later on in the first act, when Iachimo tries to slander Posthumus' character, Imogen curtly rejects his testimony. She tells him, "Thou wrong'st a gentleman who is as far/ From thy report as thou from honour." (I. vi. 145-146)

[10] pp. 74-75.   [11] p. 113.   [12] *ibid.*   [13] *ibid.*, p. 131.

In the third act Belarius informs his two adopted sons that he did not always live in a forest but that he was once a great soldier whose honorable deeds were unjustly rewarded with slander. He concludes,

> O boys, this story
> The world may read in me. My body's mark'd
> With Roman swords, and my report was once
> First with the best of note. Cymbeline lov'd me;
> And when a soldier was the theme, my name
> Was not far off. (III. iii. 55-60)

In adversity, in other words, the Shakespearean hero takes solace not only in his innate nobility but also in the fact that he had once been held in high esteem by the world. These compensations for "the slings and arrows of outrageous fortune" are particularly evident at the close of *Othello* and *Hamlet*. Othello reminds his listeners of the great services which he has done his country (for which he is just as entitled to "good report" as Belarius):

> Soft you! a word or two before you go.
> I have done the state some service, and they know't—
> No more of that. I pray you, in your letters,
> When you shall these unlucky deeds relate,
> Speak of me as I am. Nothing extenuate,
> Nor set down aught in malice. Then must you speak
> Of one that lov'd not wisely, but too well;
> Of one not easily jealous, but, being wrought,
> Perplex'd in the extreme. (V. ii. 338-346)

Hamlet also insists on his right to a good report. At the moment of his death, it is his major concern to see to it that the Danish nation does not misjudge his actions:

> Horatio, I am dead;
> Thou liv'st; report me and my cause aright,
> To the unsatisfied. (V. ii. 349-351)

Hamlet can insist that Horatio live on to restore his

wounded name and to tell the world his story because neither in his intentions nor in his actions has he been essentially vicious. (Did Hamlet have uncanny foreknowledge of what certain eminent modern critics would say to wound his name?)[14] Even if he is completely misjudging his own character, his concern about public opinion is surely the antithesis of Stoic self-sufficiency. Cicero, not Seneca, provides us with the key to an understanding of the dying speeches of the Shakespearean protagonist. Cicero praises those "states in which the best men seek praise and glory, and avoid disgrace and dishonour. Nor indeed are they deterred from crime so much by the fear of the penalties ordained by law as by the sense of shame which Nature has given to man in the form of a certain fear of justified censure."[15]

POSTHUMOUS REPUTATION

When Scipio died, Cicero insisted that death had not deprived him of his highly esteemed countryman since "For me, indeed, though he was suddenly snatched away, Scipio still lives and will always live; for it was his virtue that caused my love and that is not dead."[16] Hamlet is similarly transfixed by his vivid memory of his great father and finds it just as impossible to forget his presence. (I. ii. 184-188) Claudius and Gertrude suggest that Hamlet's prolonged grief is unnatural, but Hamlet can understand neither how the Danish court can be so festive nor how Gertrude can change husbands with such great ease. It is Gertrude's fickleness and quick forgetfulness of her first husband (it should not be forgotten that Hamlet's intense admiration for his father was the perfectly normal attitude of many a Renaissance child toward his own father) which are the main source of Hamlet's sour disillusionment and acrid sarcasm:

---

[14] See T. S. Eliot, "Shakespeare and the Stoicism of Seneca," *Selected Essays*, pp. 110-113.
[15] *De Re Publica* v. 4.
[16] *De Amicitia* XXVII.

OPH. You are merry, my lord.

HAM. Who, I?

OPH. Ay, my lord.

HAM. O God, your only jig-maker! What should a man do but be merry? For look you how cheerfully my mother looks, and my father died within's two hours.

OPH. Nay, 'tis twice two months, my lord.

HAM. So long? Nay then, let the devil wear black, for I'll have a suit of sables. O heavens! die two months ago, and not forgotten yet? Then there's hope a great man's memory may outlive his life half a year. (III. ii. 129-141)

All of Hamlet's bitterness—his sarcasm and irony toward his fellow courtiers, his nausea over his mother's remarriage, his contempt for Ophelia's father, and, finally, his general misanthropy and distrust of the world and consequent longing for death—springs from one central source, his tremendous admiration for the heroic qualities of his great king-father.

For the Elizabethans, the bonds which linked father and son were of enormous intensity and were similar to the links which bound king and subject. The Elizabethan audience would therefore have grasped immediately that Hamlet's grief over the death of his father was as limitless as his admiration for him. If Hamlet's grief seems excessive to a modern audience, we need only consider the Elizabethan response to Sir Philip Sidney's death:

"Boundless the flood of tears poured out since that time; constant the mourning of the nobility; continuous the grief of the knightly order; nor was the self-possession of University men so firm but that once and again they filled all eyes and ears with mournful dirge and lamentation. Even to the present time the cities mourn, towns weep, settlements are saddened, the Muses falter, letters lie prone; and our Queen, common mother of all, at the most casual mention of Sidney gives way to sorrow and lament. Nor has Nature, the artificer of things, engendered Scots so arid or Frenchmen so stony but that long and greatly they bewept the death of Sidney, and even to this day have attended his virtue with most thankful memory. Do you deem it proper, I ask, in the presence of such a bereavement, to be sparing of the eyes, to staunch tears, to seek for consolements, and (what exceeds every measure of inhumanity) to strive after a reputation of calmness in the midst of public grief? Verily, God forfend that this which has nearly destroyed the eyes of the public and wrung tears from foreigners, this which the stronger sex of men and the hardened hearts of soldiers have lamented aloud, I should pass over with dry eyes—that I should fall asleep in the midst of such a shipwreck of the commonwealth."[17]

If we bear in mind the importance both the Romans and the Elizabethans attached to posthumous reputation as a means by which heroic leaders can achieve immortality, we need not search through Elizabethan books on the psychology of the melancholy man for clinical parallels to modern case histories in order to ascertain the cause of Hamlet's grief and distraction. At the beginning of the play, Hamlet finds that he alone is cherishing the memory of the great dead king and mourning his death appropriately. (I. ii. 176-188) The rest of the court seems to have forgotten him almost as if he had never lived. That his mother has failed to join with him in his mournings is surely the root cause of his disillusionment. His misanthropy is an inevitable result.

Both in classical antiquity and in the Renaissance, posthumous fame depended on remembrance by contemporaries and by posterity. Hamlet finds that the whole court has forgotten this common Renaissance ideal. To understand Hamlet's disillusionment, we need only consider the passages in *The Sonnets* where Shakespeare assures his friend that he shall "outlive a gilded tomb," that his praise "shall still find room/ Even in the eyes of all posterity," and that he "still shall live . . ./

[17] Thomas Moffet, *Nobilis*, p. 69.

390

Where breath most breathes, even in the mouths of men."
(Sonnets 101, 55, 81) Immortality through posthumous memory obviously depends on the willingness of men of future ages
to honor the outstanding virtues of the eminent men of past
times. Denmark fails to do so and hence Denmark becomes,
for Hamlet, a prison. His father is treated, most injustly, as
Delio predicts the villains in *The Duchess of Malfi* will be
treated after their deaths. Delio says,

> These wretched eminent things
> Leave no more fame behind 'em, than should one
> Fall in a frost, and leave his print in snow—
> As soone as the sun shines, it ever melts,
> Both forme and matter.[18]

For everyone except Hamlet, the sun is shining once again in
Denmark. Is it any wonder that he becomes a misanthrope?

Hamlet is particularly bitter about his mother's behavior.
This bitterness spreads out and finally encompasses all women.
Here, too, the key to an understanding of Hamlet's emotion
lies in an appreciation of the esteem in which he held his father,
and the consequent intensity of the shock when he discovers
that his own mother is among the first to forget her dead
husband and hastily remarry. This is the subject of Hamlet's
first soliloquy:

> Frailty, thy name is woman!—
> A little month, or ere those shoes were old
> With which she followed my poor father's body
> Like Niobe, all tears—why she, even she
> (O God! a beast that wants discourse of reason
> Would have mourn'd longer) married with my uncle.

> (I. ii. 146-151)

As a result of Gertrude's fickleness, Hamlet becomes a mis-
ogynist who finally comes to distrust even the innocent Ophelia,
advising her to get to a nunnery so that she will not be a
breeder of sinners. Gertrude's failure to fulfill her obligations

---

[18] *The Tragedy of the Dutchesse of Malfy*, v, v, 138-142, in John Webster,
The Complete Works, ed. F. L. Lucas, London, 1927.

to her dead husband (that is, to mourn properly and to honor his memory) provoke emotions in Hamlet which can find no satisfactory outlet. He can not hate her, as he does Claudius, without also hating himself. It is in this sense, not in the Freudian sense of an Oedipal attachment, that he finds himself entangled by his close relationship to his own mother. Sigmund Freud, J. M. Robertson, T. S. Eliot, Ernest Jones, and Sir Laurence Olivier fail to perceive that it is Hamlet's great admiration for, if we like, a "father figure" and the inadequacy of Claudius as a "father substitute" which provide the key to an understanding of the personality of this most famous of disillusioned idealists. It is Claudius who is in a sense Hamlet's "rival" for Gertrude's love; nowhere in the play is there the slightest suggestion that Hamlet feels, either on the conscious or unconscious level, even the slightest bit of envy or hatred toward the dead king. Seldom in world literature has a son admired a father with such overwhelming intensity. Never once in the play is it suggested that his feelings are ambivalent—hence, the Freudian "party line" is as ridiculous as a Marxian interpretation of the play would be.

In a way, the situation in *Hamlet* is the exact reverse of that in *Antony and Cleopatra*. In the former play, a queen whose constancy her son had taken for granted proves fickle and unfaithful; in the latter, a queen who has been the epitome of feminine fickleness proves herself, following her lover's death, to be suddenly capable of utmost fidelity. It is Cleopatra herself who, in some of Shakespeare's most moving lines of poetry, eulogizes the dead lover and who suggests that the memory of such a great man can outlast his death. As Antony dies, she exclaims,

> Noblest of men, woo't die?
> Hast thou no care of me? Shall I abide
> In this dull world, which in thy absence is
> No better than a sty? O, see, my women,
>   [Antony dies]
> The crown o' th' earth doth melt.

(IV. xv. 59-63)

In the final act, in her conversation with Dolabella, she refers once again, in a purple passage too famous to need extended quoting, to the tremendous proportions of the dead hero whose "face was as the heav'ns" which lighted "the little O, the earth." (V. ii. 79, 81) For Hamlet, as for Cleopatra, the world is indeed a sty—and an unweeded garden besides—but it is Gertrude's blindness to the remarkable qualities of the dead king hero, not the mere fact of his father's death, which is the source of his sickness of heart. Neither of these plays can be properly understood without keeping in mind the Elizabethan ideal of unaltered admiration and profound grief at the moment of the death of a heroic leader. The Elizabethans believed that such attachments should last beyond the grave; as we have already observed, frequently in Shakespeare's plays the feeling of fidelity is so great that the followers wish to follow their master in death, as Cleopatra and then her maidservants do. Indeed, even Antony's great adversary, Octavius Caesar, (who had said when the news was brought to him of Antony's death that "The breaking of so great a thing should make/ A greater crack") (V. i. 14, 15) is so moved by Cleopatra's noble suicide that he gives instructions to

Take up her bed,
And bear her women from the monument.
She shall be buried by her Antony.
No grave upon the earth shall clip in it
A pair so famous. (V. ii. 359-363)

Unlike the fickle Gertrude and the wicked Claudius whose court is festive while the dead Hamlet's memory should still be "green," (II. i. 2) Octavius gives instructions, at the very close of the play, that his "army shall/ In solemn show attend this funeral." (V. ii. 366-367)

In the other plays, the theme of posthumous reputation is often alluded to but never has the central significance it holds in these two plays. Julius Caesar, cited by Montaigne and Etienne Dolet as evidence that it is possible to achieve immortality through honored remembrance in later times, is also

393

singled out by the Prince of Wales in *King Richard the Third* as a man who has outlived death.[19]

> That Julius Caesar was a famous man.
> With what his valour did enrich his wit,
> His wit set down to make his valour live.
> Death makes no conquest of this conqueror,
> For now he lives in fame, though not in life.
>
> (III. i. 84-88)

Aufidius, in like manner, decides that Coriolanus deserves a "noble memory" despite the fact that he has been a bitter enemy of the Volscians. (V. vi. 154) This attitude at the close of the tragedies becomes indeed a dramatic convention. Even *Timon of Athens* closes with the assurance that more will be said in honor of Timon's memory after the curtain falls. Statements of this sort at the close of the tragedies are partially mere convention, but 20th century critics have made perhaps no greater mistake than to assume that for Shakespeare and his audience the conventional was not important, or that the feelings expressed were necessarily artificial and insincere because they were conventional.

There are even suggestions of a pagan heaven, a sort of ethereal hall of fame, for the great heroes, which bears a resemblance to Cicero's description of Scipio's dream. During the battle of Agincourt, for example, King Henry the Fifth tells the French herald that

> A many of our bodies shall no doubt
> Find native graves; upon the which, I trust,
> Shall witness live in brass of this day's work;
> And those that leave their valiant bones in France
> Dying like men, though buried in your dunghills,
> They shall be fam'd; for there the sun shall greet
>   them

---

[19] Cf. *Cymbeline*, III, i. 2-4. "Julius Caesar (whose remembrance yet/ Lives in men's eyes and will to ears and tongues/ Be theme and hearing ever)."

And draw their honours reeking up to heaven
Leaving their earthly parts to choke your clime.

(IV. iii. 95-112[20])

Arviragus and Guiderius are referred to as princes "worthy/ To inlay heaven with stars." (V. v. 351-352) Antony, as he dies, looks forward to meeting Cleopatra again in a heaven apparently reserved for the great lovers of antiquity. He asserts that "Dido and her Aeneas shall want troops,/ And all the haunt be ours." (IV. xiv. 53-54)

Burial Rites. For the Elizabethans, remembrance of the dead also called for more tangible signs that they were being held in honor: funeral rites, a tomb, and an appropriate epitaph. The privilege of a high and solemn funeral was not every man's; here, as in almost every other aspect of Renaissance life, one's rank in the aristocratic hierarchy determined exactly how elaborate the funeral was to be. Belarius, for example, decides that Cloten should be buried like a prince. At the end of *King Richard the Third*, the victorious Richmond orders the bodies of the slain soldiers to be interred as becomes their birth.

The right to a high and stately funeral burial also depended, however, on the nobility of one's character. Thus, at the end of *Titus Andronicus*, Lucius decides,

As for that ravenous tiger, Tamora,
No funeral rite, nor man in mourning weeds,
No mournful bell shall ring her burial;
But throw her forth to beasts and birds of prey.

(V. iii. 195-198)

This is frequently the fate meted out to Shakespeare's villains. When someone has displayed a mixture of good and evil qualities, the response is sometimes accordingly divided, as in Hal's

---

[20] Cf. *The First Part of King Henry the Sixth*, IV. iii. 47-52. "Thus, while the vulture of sedition/ Feeds in the bosom of such great commanders,/ Sleeping neglection doth betray to loss/ The conquest of our scarce-cold conqueror,/ That ever living man of memory,/ Henry the Fifth." (I. i. 52-56)

Cf. *ibid.*, I. i. 52-56. "Henry the Fifth, thy ghost I invocate:/ Prosper this realm, keep it from civil broils!/ Contrast with adverse planets in the heavens!/ A far more glorious star thy soul will make/ Than Julius Caesar or Bright—"

395

final words in regard to Hotspur: "Thy ignominy sleep with thee in the grave/ But not rememb'red in thy epitaph!" (V. iv. 100-101) But if the hero has been truly noble, even the enemy shows utmost respect. Thus *Julius Caesar* closes with Octavius' command:

> According to his virtue let us use him,
> With all respect and rites of burial.
> Within my tent his bones to-night shall lie,
> Most like a soldier, ordered honourably.
>
> (V. v. 76-79)

Christian and pagan-humanist elements are blended after Joan of Arc's victory in *The First Part of King Henry the Sixth*. The Dauphin assures her that after her death not only will she be honored as France's greatest saint but that also he will erect a pyramid to her more stately "than Rhodope's of Memphis ever was." (I. vi. 22)

Nothing was more abhorrent to the Elizabethans than the fate of Tamora—death without funeral rites and without a grave. (Again, the similarity is striking between the cultural values of Greece and Rome and those of the Renaissance. *Antigone* portrays a like concern for funeral rites and for an honorable grave. Indeed, its plot raises the same essential questions as that of *Hamlet*, of one's duty to the recognized leaders of the state as against one's obligations to one's family. It should be added that Shakespeare never makes it as difficult as Sophocles does in *Antigone* to resolve a conflict of loyalties.)

Although the Elizabethans had an almost obsessive concern for posthumous reputation, funeral rites, and a proper burial, Shakespeare's protagonists can, on occasion, display a heroic indifference to them. Thus, King Henry the Fifth asserts as he prepares to invade France that he will either conquer that country

> Or lay these bones in an unworthy urn,
> Tombless, with no remembrance over them.
> Either our history shall have full mouth

Speak freely of our acts, or else our grave,
Like Turkish mute, shall have a tongueless mouth,
Not worshipp'd with a waxen epitaph.
                            (I. ii. 228-233)

Similarly, Cleopatra, who rises to the height of a true tragic
heroine in the final act, prefers the horrible fate of lying grave-
less on the open plains of Egypt to the indignity of being led
in Caesar's triumphal procession in Rome. She states, with a
hyperbole which does not belie her sincerity, that in preference
to such indignity   Rather a ditch in Egypt
    Be gentle grave unto me! Rather on Nilus' mud
    Lay me stark-nak'd and let the waterflies
    Blow me into abhorring! (V. ii. 57-60)

In *The Winter's Tale*, the shepherd reveals that he fears
that Florizel has betrayed him, since Camillo threatens him
with death. He anticipates a shameful execution where "Some
hangman must put on my shroud and lay me/ Where no
priest shovels-in dust," (IV. iv. 468-469) whereas he had
hoped to die in his father's bed and to lie by his honest bones.
In this brief speech the importance of the family idea to the
Elizabethans is once again indicated; the desire for closeness
and intimacy with the family group lasts beyond death. As Cicero
had said in the *Offices* (a major Renaissance textbook in moral
philosophy): "The bonds of common blood hold men fast
through good-will and affection; for it means much to share in
common the same family traditions, the same forms of domestic
worship, and the same ancestral tombs."[21]

The strength of the feeling of family solidarity is particularly
apparent in *Hamlet*. Laertes deliberately defies all Christian
canons in his determination to avenge his father and his sister.
He tells Claudius, on his return to Denmark, that he will risk
damnation in order to fulfill his filial obligation to revenge his
father's death. He reacts with particular vehemence to the news
of Polonius' death because of his

---

[21] I. 17.

obscure funeral—
No trophy, sword, nor hatchment o'er his bones,
No noble rite nor formal ostentation.

(IV. v. 213-215)

His rage reaches new heights when he discovers that Ophelia, too, is being subjected to shameful burial because of her suicide. The priest, in accordance with common Christian doctrine, defends his refusal to permit full burial rites.

PRIEST   No more be done.
  We should profane the service of the dead
  To sing a requiem and such rest to her
  As to peace-parted souls.
LAERTES   Lay her i' th' earth;
  And from her fair and unpolluted flesh
  May violets spring! I tell thee, churlish
      priest,
  A minist'ring angel shall my sister be
  When thou liest howling. (V. i. 258-264)

This is a clear defiance of Christian values; loyalty to one's family is placed ahead of obedience to the laws of God. (Christianity has always been aware of this possible conflict of loyalties and has always insisted that the love for human creatures must never be greater than the love of God.) Here again, the ethical ambivalence of the Renaissance is revealed, for here is presented a dramatic clash between Christian values and the family obligations to honor the dead, even if they died by their own hands, and to avenge their deaths. As F. T. Bowers has pointed out, even Renaissance law was inconsistent on this matter. The Church and the law of the land were presumably in complete accord in their absolute condemnation of private revenge, but both in France and England a law also existed which in effect supported the private revenge of the death of one's father. An anonymous author (perhaps the Earl of Northhampton), writing against dueling, acknowledges the fact that

398

the civil law denies the father's inheritance to that son which will not revenge the death of his father. The ethical inconsistencies in Shakespeare's dramas are, in other words, but a reflection of the profound inconsistencies in the age itself.

Oblivion. Just as the lack of a grave and an appropriate epitaph deprived the Elizabethan of the feeling that he had continued physical contact with his family, so, too, the idea of "oblivion" (forgetfulness) filled him with horror, since he might thus be deprived of the posthumous remembrance he so much craved. Shakespeare refers frequently to the image of "blind oblivion" and he usually associates it with the ideas of time and death. The hold these themes had on the Elizabethan imagination is apparent to the sensitive reader of the drama of that age, since not only Shakespeare but also Webster, Tourneur, and many other poets frequently produce some of their finest poetry when dealing with them.

Since Shakespeare may be expressing his more intimate feelings in *The Sonnets* (no one will ever be able to prove this), it is particularly interesting to observe the view of life which he expresses when he uses this lyric form. In both *The Sonnets* and the tragedies, the short span of human life seems to be surrounded by an enveloping gloom (time, death, oblivion, and chaos) which heightens and intensifies man's need for love, fidelity, and nobility. If we can view Shakespeare's works with sufficient perspective, it may seem perhaps that he is saying that man should do everything possible to maintain a sort of purity (not Puritanism) and high idealism in his relations with his fellow men, since human loyalty, human fellowship, and the faith one can have in other human beings alone provide man with any security or give any meaning to his existence. Even after death, man strives by every possible means to be remembered by posterity—by tombs, epitaphs, biographies, and chronicles (autobiographies were less popular than in our day but the Renaissance painters, unlike their medieval brethren, were not averse to "hiding" themselves somewhere in their own pictures). For the same reason, childlessness was viewed with dismay, since it was sometimes suggested that only through off-spring could men perpetuate themselves. This is one of the major themes of *The Sonnets*.

Oblivion, physical decay, mutability, and chaos are all so terribly feared in Shakespeare's plays that even the comedies have their lightness and brightness perceptibly dimmed by them. For example, at the opening of *Love's Labour's Lost*, the King of Navarre tells his comrades:

> Let fame, that all hunt after in their lives,
> Live regist'red upon our brazen tombs
> And then grace us, in the disgrace of death,
> When, spite of cormorant devouring Time,
> Th' endeavour of this present breath may buy
> That honour which shall bate his scythe's keen edge
> And make us heirs of all eternity. (I. i. 1-7)

In *King Richard the Third*, Buckingham informs Richard of the immorality of the late King Edward. The dishonorable behavior of the king and of his family has caused them to be "almost should'red in the swallowing gulf/ Of dark forgetful-ness and deep oblivion." (III. vii. 127-128) This punishment of evil was, for the Elizabethans, just as important as the physical torture which awaited Iago. In only a few passages does Shake-speare vividly suggest the terrors of hell-fire; and when Claudio, Hamlet, and the dead Ghost allude to "the Inferno" they rarely connect it directly with the rewarding of the good and the punishing of those who are evil.[22] On the other hand, there

---

[22] It is primarily because of the absence of any strong theological passion that one comes to feel that Shakespeare was not an *ardent* Christian and had relegated religion to Villey's "back shop." The chief Christian goal is to achieve union with God, as it is in the concluding passages of *The Divine Comedy*. Is not this passionate concern to identify oneself with the Divine Being almost totally miss-ing from the Shakespearean text? The prayer of Claudius does not involve deep-seated repentance since his character remains totally unchanged. "Flights of angels" sing Hamlet to his rest; but there is no detailed doctrinal affirmation, in this passage or elsewhere, of the supreme importance of immortal bliss. "Absent thee from felicity" may seem to refer to heavenly bliss—but is Shakespeare con-cerned with theological concepts or is this the equivalent of Othello's remarks to Iago, "I'd have thee live / For in my sense 'tis happiness to die"? (v. ii. 289-290)

are numerous references to forgetfulness; evil is punished by being swallowed up in "oblivion," just as virtue is rewarded by posthumous reputation. A good king and great man is forgotten as rapidly as if he had been an utterly wicked monarch— adequate cause for neurosis in any Elizabethan son. Such oblivion is handled in a slightly different way in *Troilus and Cressida*. There Achilles' punishment for his pride is to be treated as if he had been forgotten by the other Greeks. Macbeth's penultimate soliloquy also refers, if obliquely, to his loss of any right to affection and esteem. The opening scene of *Measure for Measure* treats the same theme ironically. The Duke, feigning gratitude, informs Angelo:

> O, your desert speaks loud, and I should wrong it
> To lock it in the wards of covert bosom
> When it deserves, with characters of brass
> A forted residence 'gainst the tooth of time
> And razure of oblivion. (V. i. 9-13)

It has been suggested that Shakespeare is as nihilistic as the Russian writers of the late 19th century and that he emphasizes unduly those aspects of life which point to the overwhelmingly destructive force of death, mental and spiritual decay (and the ultimate rotting of the human body), time, and oblivion. He does, without doubt, show his keen awareness of these disintegrating forces. But this awareness does not lead to cynicism or to that flippancy in regard to all human values so characteristic of Restoration comedy and of modern satirical fiction (Aldous Huxley's early novels, for example).

In Shakespeare's tragedies the negative forces are always present; they represent a vast void of darkness, chaos, and cold on the circumference of human life, but their existence makes it more, rather than less, important to affirm the validity of human love and of man's moral potentialities. (The closest

---

Shakespeare's values are not placed in another world; he does not condemn this world in order to exalt the next. Sonnet 146 and Lorenzo's speech in *The Merchant of Venice* (v. i. 58-65) are almost unique in their exaltation of heaven and consequent deprecation of man's mortal existence.

parallel in modern literature is perhaps in the concluding pages of Camus' *The Plague*.) This surrounding void does create the conditions for a profound cynicism when the protagonist discovers that, in his special predicament, human values, human love and affection have no meaning. This is the reason for Hamlet's misanthropy and almost complete cynicism. This explains why Macbeth, when he has lost his claim to "honour, love, obedience, troops of friends" (V. iii. 25) comes to the conclusion that life is a "brief candle . . . signifying nothing." (V. v. 23, 28)

For reasons which will probably never be known to anyone except the poet himself, Shakespeare, in *Troilus and Cressida*, is as concerned as he had been in *The Sonnets* to suggest that time and oblivion are the nihilistic forces most to be feared (in *Hamlet* and *King Lear* he focuses on death and the processes of gruesome decay). Thus, when the Greeks and Trojans meet in the fourth act of the play, Agamemnon declares,

> What's past and what's to come is strew'd with husks
> And formless ruin of oblivion;
> But in this extant moment, faith and troth,
> Strain'd purely from all hollow bias-drawing,
> Bids thee with most divine integrity
> From heart of very heart, great Hector, welcome.
>
> (IV. v. 166-171)

Later in the same scene, Hector, too, refers to the omnipotence of time. He tells Ulysses,   The end crowns all,

> And that old common arbitrator, Time,
> Will one day end it. (IV. v. 224-225)

But Ulysses is not the man to be given this advice, for it was he who had warned Achilles that the deeds of the great Greek warrior are forgotten since "Time hath, my lord, a wallet at his back,/ Wherein he puts alms for oblivion." (III. iii. 145-146) Ulysses now points out that time and oblivion are ultimately supreme over all human values:

> Let not virtue seek
> Remuneration for the thing it was!
> For beauty, wit,
> High birth, vigour of bone, desert in service,
> Love, friendship, charity, are subjects all
> To envious and calumniating Time.
>
> (III. iii. 169-175)

In this passage Ulysses expresses the essence of Shakespeare's "naturalism." From this limited point of view (because it is only a part of Shakespeare's *Weltanschauung*), those who possess high virtue and royal blood are no better off than the poorest rogues and scoundrels. This is Hamlet's conclusion in the graveyard scene when he traces the dust of the noble Alexander and assumes it may ultimately be found stopping a bunghole; it is Edgar's conclusion when he decides that "ripeness is all"; (V. ii. 11) and it leads Cleopatra to observe " 'Tis paltry to be Caesar," (V. ii. 2) since he, too, is a puny subject of omnipotent Fortune. Whether Shakespeare places his emphasis on time and oblivion, as he does in Macbeth's soliloquy on "tomorow, and tomorrow, and tomorrow" and in the passages just quoted from *Troilus and Cressida*, or on other destructive factors such as death and the fickleness of fate and fortune, the theme is really one and the same: the extinction of all human values as the result of the superior power of nature which can finally grind all human values into the dust.

These sinister, nihilistic forces, however, so frequently mentioned in discussions of Shakespeare's philosophy of life, do not lead Shakespeare's characters to become pure cynics. On the contrary, the significance of human ideals becomes more intense, as in Othello's terrifying lines of prophetic irony,

> Perdition catch my soul but I do love thee,
> And when I love thee not
> Chaos is come again. (II. iii. 90-92)

In Shakespearean tragedy, everything depends on holding true to the highest nobility, to the highest love and fidelity. This is the "meaning" of *King Lear* and *Hamlet*—even though the heroes go through a period of bitter cynicism. On the brink of death, Hamlet can still count on the friendship of Horatio; indeed, he only stops Horatio from the ultimate proof of his friendship, joining him in death, because of his concern that his reputation be upheld after his death.

It is in *The Sonnets*, however, that the conflict between man's love of man—represented in its purest form in the Renaissance by the humanistic ideal of friendship—and the corrosive power of time and oblivion are most graphically portrayed. The opening lines of the fifteenth sonnet, for example, point up this theme of mutability and decay: ("When I consider everything that grows/ Holds in perfection but a little moment.") (Sonnet 15) But although he recognizes the disintegrating forces in life which make growth but the beginning of decay, the "speaker" in *The Sonnets* can still defiantly assert the worth of his love:

> Then the conceit of this inconstant stay
> Sets you most rich in youth before my sight,
> Where wasteful Time debateth with Decay
> To change your day of youth to sullied night
> And, all in war with Time for love of you,
> As he takes from you, I ingraft you new.
>
> (Sonnet 15)

In this sonnet Shakespeare suggests that he must war against Time for his friend's love; in what is perhaps his most famous sonnet he is sure that he can claim victory:

> Love's not Time's fool, though rosy lips and cheeks
> Within his bending sickle's compass come.
> Love alters not with his brief hours and weeks,
> But bears it out even to the edge of doom.
>
> (Sonnet 116)

A devotion which does not alter when it finds alteration is Shakespeare's theme both here and in his greatest tragedies.

Hamlet remains true to his father although others forget him. Desdemona and Cassio are faithful to Othello despite the fact that he turns against them. Cordelia and Kent are willing to risk the old king's further displeasure by remaining loyal in spite of his rejection of them. The fickle Cleopatra finally rises to tragic heights by manifesting her constancy.

The poet elaborates on the same theme in Sonnet 123 when he declares, "No, Time, thou shalt not boast that I do change!" in the opening lines, and reiterates the theme in the concluding couplet: "This I do vow, and this shall ever be—/ I will be true, despite thy scythe and thee." But he can not always sustain this mood in which the triumphant power of love is affirmed. In Sonnet 64, for example, the poet is forced to admit that time and chaos are superior forces and so he surrenders to his fears:

> Ruin hath taught me thus to ruminate,
> That Time will come and take my love away.
>> This thought is as a death, which cannot choose
>> But weep to have that which it fears to lose.

The next sonnet is written in the same mood but also suggests that a way may perhaps be found to evade the horrible fact that time will cause the most enduring of earthly things to decay. The poet resorts to a literary convention common to humanist expression in Renaissance Italy, France, and England; he suggests that his friend may achieve immortality through the posthumous reputation which the poet's verse will bring him:

> Where, alack,
> Shall Time's best jewel from Time's chest lie hid?
> Or what strong hand can hold his swift foot back?
> Or who his spoil of beauty can forbid?
>> O, none! unless this miracle have might,
>> That in black ink my love may still shine bright.
>>> (Sonnet 65)

In this way Shakespeare suggests that human values can triumph over the gruesome fact that each living being is ultimately subject to complete disintegration. Sonnet 81 presents this idea most fully; the poet vehemently insists that the "name" of his friend shall have immortal life despite the destructive power of time and death. He tells his friend, "You still shall live (such virtue hath my pen)/ Where breath most breathes, even in the mouths of men."

Shakespeare's boast of the power of his pen has proved no exaggeration. The nobility of Hamlet, the greatness of soul of King Lear, the magnanimity of Othello, and the curious mingling of good and evil in Macbeth have survived through the sustaining power of Shakespeare's art, which continues to fascinate and persuade in our own 20th century—an age in which so many men have yielded to the temptation to seek refuge in a thoroughly inhumane aestheticism, or political dogmatism, or religious asceticism, or intellectual withdrawal from human values. Forgetfulness and oblivion, "the most abhorred thing of Nature," as Cornwallis described them, have not conquered Shakespeare's tragic values even though they have swallowed up the aristocratic values of the society which gave them birth.[23]

Ill Fame. If the Elizabethans felt that a reputation for high virtue could outlast physical decay, they were no less convinced that it was possible for ill fame to endure beyond the grave. Because of dramatic exigencies, most of Shakespeare's villains are forgotten at the end of the play—once the audience has been assured that they will be duly punished. Albany, for example, replies when informed of Edmund's death, "That's but a trifle here." (V. iii. 295) But in *Troilus and Cressida*, the heroine has a Cassandra-like foreknowledge of her own ultimate fate at the moment when she is most ready to assert her own constancy:

> If I be false, or swerve a hair from truth,
> When time is old, and hath forgot itself,
> When water drops have worn the stones of Troy,
> And blind oblivion swallow'd cities up,

[23] *Essayes,* p. 93.

> And mighty states characterless are grated
> To dusty nothing—yet let memory,
> From false to false, among false maids in love,
> Upbraid my falsehood! (III. ii. 191-198)

In the final act, the poor young idealist who fancies "With so eternal and so fix'd a soul" (like the "speaker" in *The Sonnets*) finds that his beloved has proved to be fickle. (V. ii. 165-166) So he exclaims,

> O Cressid! O false Cressid! false, false, false!
> Let all untruths stand by thy stained name
> And they'll seem glorious. (V. ii. 178-180)

In the very last scene, he turns on Pandarus, the man who has been the cause of his ill fortune, and wishes him an equally shameful reputation. When Pandarus starts to speak, he curtly dismisses him: "Hence, broker, lackey! Ignominy and shame/ Pursue they life and live aye with thy name." (V. x. 33-34) Thus ends the play which is among Shakespeare's most bitter and disillusioned. Hamlet and Lear are subjected to much greater suffering, and their disillusionment goes much deeper, but until the very end they are sustained by the fidelity of others. But, as *Troilus and Cressida* comes to its close, the hero seems to be alone in a despicable world. The great Achilles has shamefully disgraced the corpse of Hector, Cressida has proved false, and hence the audience can not but feel that Thersites' cynical view of mankind is a sort of choral commentary. In all the gloom there is nothing noble, nothing positive to be affirmed, since both the Greek and the Trojan heroes have failed to adhere to their own ideals. It is not therefore surprising that the play ends with disjointed abruptness and without any eulogy.

Honor and the Family. In *Hasting's Encyclopedia* J. B. Carter observes that it was "the family idea, so fundamental in the social structure of Rome [which] triumphed over the grave," and that it was this idea that "possessed an immortality which the individual failed to attain."[24] Once again, the Renaissance follows in the footsteps of the Romans, although the Elizabethans were equally concerned with the Christian concept of immortality. Most Elizabethan writers give expression to both the Roman and the Christian view, although some Christians denied the pagan-humanist position and a few ardent humanists, such as Etienne Dolet, were sceptical as to the possibility of Christian immortality.

In Shakespeare, allusion is frequently made to man's eternal soul, but there is no real suggestion that the afterlife will afford permanence to man's values and that man can thereby find compensation for his insecurity while here on earth (any more than there is any genuine poetic expression of the central Christian concern for union with God). Shakespeare's unwillingness to associate the permanent principle with the notion of Deity stands in sharp contrast to Spenser's resolution of the problem of worldly mutability in the concluding stanzas of *The Faerie Queene*. For if Shakespeare tends to consider "oblivion" as man's final destiny, Spenser, on the other hand, as a true Christian humanist, rests convinced that man will find his ultimate security in his union with God.

> For, all that moveth, doth in Change delight;
> But thence-forth all shall rest eternally
> With him that is the God of Sabbaoth hight;
> O that great Sabbaoth God, graunt me that Sabbaoths
>   sight.[25]

Shakespeare, like the Romans, refers frequently to the notion that a significant sort of immortality can be achieved through the continuity of the family line. Thus Sonnet 12 concludes with his admonition to his friend: "And nothing 'gainst Time's scythe can make defence/ Save breed, to brave him when he takes thee hence." The very next sonnet expands the same

---

[24] Jesse Benedict Carter, "Ancestor Worship and the Cult of the Dead," in James Hastings, *Encyclopaedia of Religion and Ethics*, Edinburgh, 1923, I, 462.
[25] VII, xiii, 6-9.

theme; Shakespeare warns the young man of his coming end
and exhorts him to have a son:

> Then you were
> Yourself again after yourself's decease
> When your sweet issue your sweet form should bear.
> Who lets so fair a house fall to decay,
> Which husbandry in honour might uphold
> Against the stormy gusts of winter's day
> And barren rage of death's eternal cold?
> O, none but unthrifts! Dear my love, you know
> You had a father—let your son say so.
>
> (Sonnet 13)

Viola in *Twelfth Night* obviously has the same idea in mind
when she counsels Olivia,

> Lady, you are the cruell'st she alive
> If you will lead these graces to the grave,
> And leave the world no copy. (I. v. 259-261)

The passages in which the mother and wife assure Coriolanus
that they will commit suicide if he marches on Rome bear a
close resemblance to Shakespeare's source, Plutarch. Volumnia
says that she will not endure the shame of having Coriolanus
tread on his "mother's womb/ That brought thee to this world."
(V. iii. 124-125) Virgilia adds,

> Ay, and on mine,
> That brought you forth this boy to keep your name
> Living to time. (V. iii. 125-127)

The Elizabethan son felt that, if he inherited his father's
virtues and honorable name, he could perpetuate his noble
character and thus make his father immortal.[26] The strength
of this filial tie is obvious in *Hamlet*, but the anguish which
results from the tearing asunder of family bonds is an even

---

[26] Cf. Montaigne, *Essayes*, III, 9. "I am not tied with that strong bond, which
some say, bindes men to future times, by the children bearing their names."

more central theme in *King Lear*. King Lear is driven mad by his daughters precisely because of his very closeness to them. This becomes particularly evident when he turns from Goneril to Regan only to find that she, too, is unfaithful. He attempts to free himself from his entanglement by rejecting her, as she has rejected him, but finds that it is impossible for him to do so:

> I prithee, daughter, do not make me mad.
> I will not trouble thee, my child; farewell.
> We'll no more meet, no more see one another.
> But yet thou art my flesh, my blood, my daughter;
> Or rather a disease that's in my flesh,
> Which I must needs call mine. (II. iv. 221-226)

When his sanity is restored, he finds it impossible for him to see Cordelia because of the strength of his feeling for his own flesh and blood. He had rejected her; now he can not bear the thought that he deserves to be accepted by her. And so Kent informs the gentleman that the old king "by no means/ Will yield to see his daughter." (IV. iii. 42-43) The audience soon discovers that this refusal results from the fact that the wrongs he has done his daughter

>   sting
> His mind so venomously that burning shame
> Detains him from Cordelia. (IV. iii. 47-49)

Paradoxically enough, it was because of the strength of the family idea that the disowning of a member of one's own family occurred so frequently in Elizabethan times. Usually this was done by the imputation of bastardry. Thus in the third act of *Measure for Measure*, Isabella at one moment praises her brother and at the next, finding him, in her opinion, cowardly, disowns him. When he offers to die in her behalf, she exclaims, "There spake my brother! There my father's grave/ Did utter forth a voice!" (III. i. 86-87) But when he loses courage, and pleads for life even at the cost of her honor, she cries out,

> Heaven shield my mother play'd my father fair!
> For such a warped slip of wilderness
> Ne'er issu'd from his blood. (III. i. 141-143)

Once again, it is evident that for the Elizabethans honor was the most precious of earthly possessions. Despite (or perhaps, rather, because of) the strength and intensity of family feeling, a member of one's house who has stained the family honor can be rejected and disowned without a moment's hesitation. Leonato in *Much Ado About Nothing* is just as quick as Isabella to disown a member of his family who may have stained the family's honor. In the fourth act, when she is charged with adultery, he hopes that she will not recover from her fainting spell and promises to tear her with his own hands if she does revive. (IV. i. 116-144) But in the next act he discovers that she is innocent and in revenge for this slur challenges Claudio to a duel:

> I say thou hast belied mine innocent child;
> Thy slander hath gone through and through her heart,
> And she lies buried with her ancestors—
> O, in a tomb where never scandal slept,
> Save this of hers, fram'd by thy villainy!
>
> (V. i. 67-71)

It is the honor of the family name which is at stake, both when Leonato threatens his child and when he defends her. Leontes in *The Winter's Tale* shows a like sensitivity to the honor of his line when he suspects Hermione of adultery. Before the suspicion had entered his mind that his wife might be an adulteress, he had thought his son's features identical with his image of himself as a child:

> Looking on the lines
> Of my boy's face, methoughts I did recoil
> Twenty-three years, and saw myself unbreech'd,
> In my green velvet coat. (I. ii. 153-156)

But, again, the child he had loved so dearly and had even viewed as a copy of himself becomes the object of repugnance once the father suspects him of being a bastard. So he tells the child curtly:

> Go play, boy, play. Thy mother plays, and I
> Play too; but so disgrac'd a part whose issue
> Will hiss me to my grave. Contempt and clamour
> Will be my knell! (I. ii. 187-190)

In the ensuing action, Camillo hears from Polixenes of the king's depression. Here again Shakespeare stresses the closeness of family ties. The king's sad countenance, Polixenes says, looks "As he had lost some province, and a region/ Lov'd as he loves himself." (I. ii. 369-370) The suspicion of the mother's infidelity does not, however, completely destroy Leontes' love of his child. When he hears that his son is sick, he attributes his illness to a deep sense of shame:

> To see his nobleness!
> Conceiving the dishonour of his mother,
> He straight declin'd, droop'd, took it deeply,
> Fasten'd and fix'd the shame on't in himself,
> Threw off his spirit, his appetite, his sleep,
> And downright languish'd. (II. iii. 12-17)

Oddly enough, this passage could easily be inserted into *Hamlet*; it is a perfect description of the nature and cause of the Prince of Denmark's melancholic state.

Soon Leontes is planning to take revenge on Hermione. When Paulina brings the child to him again, in the vain hope of assuaging his kingly wrath, he no longer recognizes it as his own. He bids Paulina burn it, and when she hesitates, he threatens, with a ferocity equal to Leonato's in *Much Ado About Nothing*, to dash out the child's brains with his own hands. (II. iii. 139-141) When Hermione appears before the court of justice in the third act, it is clear that she is equally concerned to maintain the honor of the family. She tells the court she is willing to lose her own life, but she insists that her honor must be upheld since " 'Tis a derivative from me to mine."

(III. ii. 45) Certain of her own innocence, she tells the court with firm assurance that if any can prove that she has done one thing beyond the bounds of honor she stands ready to have her nearest of kin cry "fie upon my grave." (III. ii. 55)

This reference is but another indication of the extent to which the Elizabethans attached importance to the devotion which surviving members of one's family would supposedly show following one's death. Devotion to their fathers cause Hamlet and Laertes to give way to immeasurable grief. This grief becomes doubly intense when they discover that others have failed to share their sorrow and have not displayed proper respect for the deceased. The same intense family love provokes those terrible lines ("Howl, howl, howl, howl!") in the closing scene of *King Lear*. The same love leads Leontes, when he thinks that he has been the cause of the death of his innocent wife and child, to seek to atone for the wrongs he has done them:

> Prithee bring me
> To the dead bodies of my queen and son.
> One grave shall be for both. Upon them shall
> The causes of their death appear, unto
> Our shame perpetual. Once a day I'll visit
> The chapel where they lie, and tears shed there
> Shall be my recreation. (III. ii. 235-241)

Shakespeare's fullest presentation of family honor and family loyalty occurs in the fourth act of *The First Part of King Henry the Sixth* (which may or may not be a part written by Shakespeare). Talbot and his son are surrounded on the field of battle by the French forces. The old Talbot urges his son to flee since young Talbot is the only heir who can perpetuate the family line. Talbot tells the youth that he had brought him up "That Talbot's name might be in thee reviv'd." (IV. v. 3) (He also wants his son to survive so that he will be able to avenge his father's death.) But the son refuses his father's request. He uses exactly the same arguments which motivated the characters in the plays which have just been discussed.

> And shall I fly? O, if you love my mother,
> Dishonour not her honourable name
> To make a bastard and a slave of me!
> The world will say he is not Talbot's blood
> That basely fled when noble Talbot stood.
>
> (IV. v. 13-17)

It takes a whole scene of stichomythia for the son finally to convince his father that he will not desert him. Two scenes later they die together in battle; the continuity of the family line is destroyed, but the last of the Talbots gain immortality through posthumous fame. As the father dies, he says,

> Thou antic Death, which laugh'st us here to scorn,
> Anon, from thy insulting tyranny,
> Coupled in bonds of perpetuity,
> Two Talbots, winged through the lither sky,
> In thy despite shall scape mortality.
>
> (IV. vii. 18-22)

CHAPTER 11

HONOR AS PUBLIC ESTEEM (continued)

HONOR AS REWARD

MONG the numerous paradoxes of the Renaissance humanist ethics, one of the most striking is the contradictory exhortations: to the subject, to be virtuous regardless of whether or not his honorable service is rewarded; to the king, to be ever vigilant in bestowing honorable reward whenever it is justly merited. Shakespeare makes dramatic use of this paradox in the opening lines of *Macbeth*. When Duncan first meets his victorious general the king rebukes himself for the "sin of his ingratitude" in not having already rewarded Macbeth and hastens to add that reward will soon be forthcoming. Duncan feels heavy obligation to this great warrior:

> Would thou hadst less deserv'd,
> That the proportion both of thanks and payment
> Might have been mine. Only I have left to say,
> More is thy due than more than all can pay.
>
> (I. iv. 18-21)

Macbeth, in the becoming manner of a gentleman, responds to this gesture of royal courtesy with the humble protest that his services to his country require no payment. He assures Duncan that "The service and the loyalty I owe,/ In doing it pays itself" and that it is His "Highness part . . . to receive our duties." (I. iv. 22-24)

As Count Romei points out in *The Courtier's Academie*, one should accept honors which are offered as a reward for service rendered in a spirit of modest reticence. But, as he immediately adds, such reticence should not lead one to decline honorable titles of dignity when they are offered. For the pagan-humanist moralists of Shakespeare's age, a genuine contempt for honors was not a sign of modesty but, on the contrary, an inverted sense of pride, since it indicated that one felt disdain for one's fellow men. These observations are particularly germane to an understanding of one of Shakespeare's late tragedies, *Coriolanus*. Coriolanus displays the same commendable modesty as Macbeth in at first refusing reward for his services. His refusal to accept part of the spoils of battle should also be considered praiseworthy since, as Montaigne observes, to mingle wealth with the prize of honor lessens and degrades it. (This exaltation of honor and deprecation of riches, so characteristic of the Romans, is frequently referred to by the Renaissance moral philosophers.) It is perfectly proper, then, that Coriolanus "look'd upon things precious as they were/ The common muck of the world." (II. ii. 129-130)

But when Cominius requests the aristocratic hero to listen to his praises—"In sign of what you are, not to reward/ What you have done" (I. ix. 26-27)—Coriolanus exceeds the limits of modesty and clearly reveals his flaw of pride by refusing graciously to accept the acclaim of the populace. Hence, he is partially responsible for his banishment from Rome by the citizens of the city. This does not, however, make their actions one bit less unjust, since their punishment is shamefully ungrateful treatment of the man who has served his country so nobly. Gratitude to a benefactor is just as central a moral issue as in *Macbeth* or *King Lear*. As Menenius observes when he hears that Coriolanus has been sentenced to death:

> Now the good gods forbid
> That our renowned Rome, whose gratitude
> Towards her deserved children is enroll'd
> In Jove's own book, like an unnatural dam
> Should now eat up her own. (III. i. 290-294)

For the Renaissance moralists, as for Cicero, who provided the authoritative definition of so many of their values, no act was more monstrous than the failure to be grateful to a benefactor.

416

Many critics have taken Lear to task for the imprudent act of giving up his kingdom. But it is a convention common to many Elizabethan plays for an old king to retire and bestow his kingdom on his children. Lear's action is imprudent only in that he acted rashly and failed to see which of his daughters was faithful and deserving of such a great benefit. It can not be pointed out too frequently that he rebukes himself for this error in judgment. The act itself is viewed throughout the play as a manifestation of royal bountifulness. (Liberality was one of the major humanistic virtues and particularly appropriate to a monarch.) Thus Lear speaks of himself as an "old, kind father, whose frank heart gave all!" (III. iv. 20) Kent refers to him as the "old, kind king." (III. i. 28) And Albany, scolding Goneril for her wanton cruelty, asks indignantly, "Could my good brother suffer you to do it? / A man, a prince, by him so benefited!" (IV. ii. 44-45) The Renaissance injunction that a king should be liberal in the bestowing of reward was unequivocal, but so, too, was the injunction that "dutie bindeth all persons to esteeme as a great benefite, all favour, how little soever it bee."[1] On this issue, the Renaissance is as one; Bryskett's judgment reflects the only attitude possible for the Jacobeans toward the behavior of the two daughters: "For the ungratefull man is of the nature of the wolfe, of whom it is written, that being suckled when it was yong by an Ewe; when it grew great, in recompense of his nourishment he devoured her."[2] The attitude toward ingratitude is consistent throughout Shakespeare's plays. Consider Amiens' song in *As You Like It*:

> Blow, blow, thou winter wind,
> Thou art not so unkind
>   As man's ingratitude.
>   (II. vii. 174-176)

[1] La Primaudaye, p. 402.
[2] Bryskett, p. 237.

> Freeze, freeze, thou bitter sky,
> That dost not bite so nigh
> As benefits forgot.
> (II. vii. 184-186)

The conferring of reward for services performed involved not only the classical virtue of liberality but also that of justice. The Renaissance definition of "distributive justice," referred to so frequently by the moralists, came from the *Nicomachean Ethics*; in the words of Hurault, "it consisteth chiefly in distributing honour and promotion unto [the king's subjects] according to every man's desert."[3] The honor referred to sometimes merely involved the bestowal of public thanks, but more frequently it took the form of the conferring of dignity and title by action of the king. Sometimes it involved both. In the last act of *Measure for Measure*, for example, the Duke returns to Vienna and professes to be deeply grateful to Angelo and Escalus.

> Many and hearty thankings to you both!
> We have made enquiry of you, and we hear
> Such goodness of your justice that our soul
> Cannot but yield you forth to public thanks,
> Forerunning more requital. (V. i. 4-8)

Rewards of honor are usually gained as the result of military service. Coriolanus and Macbeth both earn their titles as a result of their great valor in battle. Report of their heroic achievements is followed by public thanks and bestowal of title. Thus, in the second act of *Coriolanus*, Menenius tells the patricians and tribunes that they have gathered

> to report
> A little of that worthy work perform'd
> By Caius Marcius Coriolanus, whom
> We met here both to thank, and to remember
> With honours like himself. (II. ii. 48-52)

[3] In Hurault, p. 179.

Once again it is apparent that the Renaissance, in stressing the importance of the public confirmation of one's nobility, is merely echoing the moral attitudes of classical antiquity. In *Shakespeare's Philosophical Patterns*, Curry criticizes Macbeth for manifesting what is merely a common Renaissance trait. Macbeth, according to Curry, "is actuated in his conduct mainly by an inordinate desire for worldly honors; his delight lies primarily in buying golden opinions from all sorts of people. . . . His nature violently demands rewards: he fights valiantly in order that he may be reported in such terms as 'valour's minion' and 'Bellona's bridegroom'; he values success because it brings spectacular fame and new titles and royal favour heaped upon him in public."[4] Curry is judging Macbeth in terms of the Christianized Aristotelianism of St. Thomas Aquinas who did indeed consider honor a "temporal" and a "mutable" good. But, as I suggested in the first chapter of this book, Renaissance pagan-humanist attitudes toward honor are usually favorable, rarely deprecatory, and go directly or indirectly back to Aristotle's original formulations: "Those on the other hand who covet being honoured by good men, and by persons who know them, do so from a desire to confirm their own opinion of themselves; so these like honour because they are assured of their worth by their confidence in the judgement of those who assert it."[5]

Curry's condemnation of Macbeth for seeking honor, as long as he is seeking it by legitimate means, is a censure which would leave few of Shakespeare's heroes untouched. In *Macbeth*, when Duncan announces his intention of naming Malcolm the Prince of Cumberland, he also promises glittering titles to those of his followers who deserve them.[6] He asserts that "signs of nobleness, like stars, shall shine/ On all deservers." (I. iv. 41-

---

[4] pp. 113-114.

[5] *Nicomachean Ethics* VIII. 8.

[6] Cf. Queen Elizabeth's promise to reward Essex: "Deem, therefore, Cousin mine, that the search of your honour, with the danger of your breath, hath not been bestowed on so ungrateful a Prince that will not consider the one and reward the other. (*The Letters of Queen Elizabeth*, ed. G. B. Harrison, p. 125.)

42) The Renaissance was not opposed to magnificent spectacles or to spectacular success. Every Renaissance court placed the greatest stress on pomp and ceremony. In his plays Shakespeare, as a man of his age, frequently describes honor with adjectives which have color and life; consider, for example, Hotspur's desire to "pluck bright honour from the pale-faced moon." (I. iii. 202) There are sufficient grounds for a lengthy and severe criticism of Macbeth's character without accusing him of possessing an insatiable thirst for honor when such a thirst was typical of all the great Elizabethan aristocrats and of most of Shakespeare's great soldier-heroes. Even Sir John Falstaff tells Hal facetiously after the battle of Shrewsbury: "If your father will do me any honour, so; if not, let him kill the next Percy himself. I look to be either earl or duke, I can assure you." (V. iv. 143-146)

MAGNIFICENCE — ACCOUTREMENTS OF HONOR

The concept of honor has been divided into many seemingly separate and distinct parts in this book so that each part can be seen as a separate entity. But it is now time to point out that the pagan-humanist morality of the Renaissance was as unified and integrated as the Thomistic ethics of the 13th century— and that this unity was largely derived from the fact that the *Nicomachean Ethics* was as responsible for Renaissance moral formulations as it was, in a Christianized form, for the ethics of St. Thomas Aquinas. As T. S. Eliot has observed, Aristotle has been the "moral pilot" of Europe, although the Renaissance interpretation, based on the direct study of his *Ethics*, was very different from Thomism. With certain conspicuous exceptions such as Sir Francis Bacon, Shakespeare's Elizabethan contemporaries were not aware, as John Donne was in the 17th century, that "the new philosophy (i.e., science) would call *all* in doubt"—classical humanism just as much as medieval scholasticism, and even the new theologies of a Luther and a Calvin— and that the Puritan middle classes, exploiting the techniques of modern science, would ultimately overthrow the whole social structure of the Renaissance nation-state, with its rigid notions of class distinction, just as completely as the Renaissance monarchs and the Italian mercantile states had overthrown medieval feudal patterns. Shakespeare stands on the threshold of modern times, but those interpretations which suggest that Hamlet is a torn and divided soul because of his awareness of new currents of thought are reading modern ideas into the play which simply are not there.

The present chapter deals with honor in its public sense. In order to see that the separate aspects of this topic actually form a single whole, it may be helpful to look at a passage from Elyot's *The Gouernour*: "Lette it be also considered that we be men and nat aungels, wherfore we knowe nothinge but by outwarde significations. Honour, wherto reverence pertaineth, is . . . the reward of vertue, which honour is but the estimation of people, which estimation is nat every where perceived, but by some exterior signe, and that is either by laudable reporte, or excellencie in vesture, or other thing semblable."[7] Honor, in its public sense, in other words, had many facets to it; the importance these external signs of honor possessed for the Elizabethan can not be exaggerated.

Apparel. In the first part of the book it was pointed out that the attitude of the Renaissance aristocracy contrasted sharply with that of the Puritan middle class. For the Elizabethan nobility, rich and costly dress was highly prized as an outward sign of one's honorable dignity so long as that magnificence was not excessive. For the Puritan, on the other hand, simplicity and extreme modesty were usually upheld as an ideal. Luxurious dress was more likely to be considered a sign of inordinate pride than of honorable dignity. These Puritan standards have been so pervasive in the last three hundred years that in the Shakespearean criticism of our time vanity is frequently ascribed to the person who dresses magnificently. Thus, as has already

[7] III, 2.

been mentioned, Granville-Barker considers Cleopatra's speech to her maidservants ("Show me, my women, like a queen") (V. ii. 227) a "flash of gorgeous, of transcendent vanity."[8] This criticism, like Curry's on Macbeth, makes the desire for the public display of honor a manifestation of mere vanity and self-love.

The Renaissance moralist, however, frequently echoed Aristotle and warned against excessive sumptuousness. Polonius, in his advice to Laertes, is representative of Renaissance taste, as defined in the Sumptuary Laws and the Homilies against Gorgeous Apparel, when he tells his son to avoid extremes:

> Costly thy habit as thy purse can buy,
> But not express'd in fancy; rich, not gaudy;
> For the apparel oft proclaims the man,
> And they in France of the best rank and station
> Are most select and generous, chief in that.
>
> (I. iii. 70-74)

Of course, on state occasions the nobility were expected to attire themselves in a magnificent and glittering fashion which can only seem excessive to our modern, democratic, middle class taste. For the aristocrat felt that what would be considered excessive display if worn for everyday occasions was perfectly appropriate when only rarely worn. This notion is reflected in Henry the Fourth's comments to his son:

> Thus did I keep my person fresh and new,
> My presence, like a robe pontifical,
> Ne'er seen but wond'red at; and so my state,
> Seldom but sumptous, show'd like a feast
> And won by rareness such solemnity.
>
> (III. ii. 55-59)

It should also be remembered that if magnificence of dress was not in itself reprehensible, the Renaissance humanists never tired of pointing out that true nobility is an inner quality of

---

[8] I, 446. Cf. Aristotle's discussion of magnificence in *Nicomachean Ethics* iy. 2.

heart and mind. Shakespeare almost literally strips Lear naked in order to emphasize this fact. The nadir of Lear's physical degradation is reached when Lear observes, "Is man no more than this? Consider him well. Thou ow'st the worm no silk, the beast no hide, the sheep no wool, the cat no perfume. Ha! Here's three on's are sophisticated! Thou art the thing itself; unaccommodated man is no more but such a poor, bare, forked animal as thou art. Off, off, you lendings! Come, unbutton here. [*Tears at his clothes.*]" (III. iv. 107-114) Undoubtedly this is the ultimate limit of adversity in Shakespearean tragedy. But it is in just such circumstances that the pagan-humanist philosophers had taught that friendship, fidelity, and nobility could best show their true worth. In this case, the pagan-humanist ethics is very close to the moral teachings of Jesus and from this point of view, *King Lear* can rightly be considered a work which emphasizes such cardinal Christian values as compassion, pity, humility, and charity.

The supremacy of inner moral values in *King Lear* does not, however, diminish the extent to which the Jacobean audience would have also insisted on the importance of outward accoutrements of honor. As Lear himself says at the end of the second act when Regan asks why he should need any train at all,

> O, reason not the need! Our basest beggars
> Are in the poorest thing superfluous.
> Allow not nature more than nature needs,
> Man's life is cheap as beast's.
>
> (II. iv. 267-270)

It is a shocking and degrading caricature of the whole aristocratic concept of honor for King Lear to have been brought to such a mean and pitiful physical condition. Hence, in a Jacobean stage presentation, the effect would have been morally appropriate, as well as dramatically striking, when Lear appears in the fourth act carried in a chair by attendants and once more garbed as befitted a king. The restitution of the physical manfestations of Lear's royalty, of which he had been stripped as the result of his daughters' meanness, would have been as important as the fact that Cordelia employs (unlike her sisters) respectful and honorable titles when she addresses him. That he is finally given public recognition of his royal position would only underline more heavily the barbarity of the affronts and indignities to which he had been subjected earlier in the play.

Retinue. The retinue of the Renaissance monarch served equally with his magnificent palaces, the royal ceremony of court, and the sumptuousness of apparel to indicate to the world the dignity of his position. Indeed, as *The Diall of Princes* observes, even the young courtier, newly come to court, will not be esteemed either as virtuous or nobly born "if hee be not also sumptuously apparelled and well accompanied."[9] In this regard, the only difference between the courtier and the monarch would have been in the amount spent on dress and the size of the retinue (the courtier himself was likely to become one of the gentlemen of the king's retinue if he was sufficiently in the king's favor to be entitled to such a high honor).

The modern critic, let it be repeated, must be aware of the ethics and social customs of Shakespeare's age if he is to give the proper interpretation of his characters. Granville-Barker writes of King Lear: "Not that Shakespeare bates us one jot of the old man's stiff-necked perversities. He no more asks our sympathy on easy terms for him than will Lear yield an inch to Goneril's reasonable requests. A hundred useless knights about the home—even though, from their master's point of view, they were men of choice and rarest parts—must have been a burden."[10] Again, it is the Puritan assumptions of the last three hundred years which are turning topsy-turvy our critical interpretations of fundamental ethical issues in Shakespeare's plays. The hundred knights about the house are of course useless and a needless expense if we choose to think in strictly utilitarian terms. But for the aristocratic culture of

---

[9] Guevara, p. 626. See table, Chapter 4, p. 153.   [10] I, 286.

the Renaissance, as for Aristotle, this utilitarian concern was base, mean, ignoble. For Greek, Roman, and Renaissance societies, the only values which really counted were intangible, and hence not monetary. In theory, at least, it was honor alone which possessed any real value. Lear's one hundred knights would have been considered but a meagre retinue for a king (the typical English nobleman had a retinue of eighty gentlemen and five hundred yeomen). Goneril's request—far from being "reasonable" as Granville-Barker states—is one of the most malicious aspects of her deliberately contrived plot to destroy Lear's kingly dignity. Nor should it be forgotten that in the first scene he had given away his kingdom with the specific reservation of "the name, and all th' additions to a king." (I. i. 138) This modern justification of the reasonableness of Lear's two daughters, which necessarily implies that Lear himself is senile and unreasonable, turns Lear into a pathetic figure and makes his "noble anger" in the first two acts mere childish irascibility. ("Noble" and all its synonyms have practically disappeared from our everyday vocabulary but that should not cause us to lose sight of the fact that, for the Elizabethans and Jacobeans, "honor" and "nobility" were practically synonymous with their concept of the good man.) Indeed, the interpretation of Wilson Knight, Granville-Barker, and Danby carries this confusing of black and white to just such an extreme; Goneril and Regan are defended for their treatment of Lear in the early scenes and Lear's indignation is hence considered ridiculous.

The issue as to whether Lear's knights are "disorder'd and debosh'd" is almost as important as that of whether he needs any retinue at all. Lear calls them "men of choice and rarest parts," but many recent critics prefer to accept Goneril's charge that they are disorderly at its face value. (I. iv. 277-288) There are a good many reasons to question whether Goneril's view would have been the view of the Jacobean audience, for it was Goneril herself who told Oswald to be deliberately insolent to the old King. Even if one assumes her charges to be fair, she would have little reason for indignation. Lear's knight —the one member of his retinue to appear on the stage—informs his master with utmost respect of the failure of Goneril's servants to show "ceremonious affection." (I. iv. 63) The knight is certainly a testimonial character; Shakespeare provides no equivalent figure to support Goneril's charge. If we wish to accept her statement, we do so on the basis of her testimony and that of her steward, Oswald. But we should not forget that she has already proved herself a liar in the very first scene of the play when she told her father how dearly she loved him— only to plot with her sister, as soon as he leaves the stage, to deprive him of the little authority he has kept for himself. Shakespeare's contemporaries were not inclined to accept the testimony of a proved liar—one lie destroyed a man's credit completely. For these reasons, it seems most likely that the audience would have been completely in agreement with Lear's indignant reply to her charges:

> Detested kite, thou liest!
> My train are men of choice and rarest parts,
> That all particulars of duty know
> And in the most exact regard support
> The worships of their name. (I. iv. 284-288)

If the audience is at this point unpersuaded as to whether it is Goneril or Lear who is telling the truth, her remarks to Oswald at the end of the scene (IV. i.) give further proof. She tells Oswald to compose a letter to Regan in which she reveals her low opinion of her old father and casually suggests that he invent additional reasons of his own to discredit Lear further. Goneril, this is to say, is capable of limitless falsehood.

When Lear is confronted by the two sisters at the end of the second act, they take turns at further insulting him, especially by whittling down his train. Finally, it occurs to Regan that amity (as though she had ever thought in those terms!) can better be preserved if there are no longer two separate commands. Goneril immediately approves of her suggestion, and hence asks Lear: "Why might not you, my lord, receive attendance/ From those that she calls servants, or from mine?" (II. iv. 246-247) There is considerable irony in a comparison of this suggestion with an apt historical parallel—Queen Elizabeth's treatment of Mary Queen of Scots while she was her prisoner. The issue is the same, although Lear, mere literary figure that he is, certainly has far more right to courteous treatment. When asked whether Mary has been honorably used "according as a Queen of her Quality," Elizabeth replied that Mary, even in imprisonment, has been continually served by her own servants—"honourably attended upon with persons of nobility, and such as were of the ancient families of our Realm."[11] The extent of this final affront to Lear's dignity (the suggestion that Lear accept the services of his daughter's servants and be deprived of his last remaining authority) can best be measured by the fact that Shakespeare's own queen allowed her rival and enemy, even in prison, to command her own retinue of noble ladies.

By this suggestion of removing his retinue, Goneril and Regan are destroying their father's last vestige of self-respect; rather than being reasonable they are committing the most shameful of acts. Lear's cry of outrage, " 'Tis worse than murther/ To do upon respect such violent outrage," applies to this final insult just as much as it did to their other affronts. (II. iv. 24-25) The destruction of the last vestiges of honor would have been considered by the Jacobean audience—at the first performance of the play a court audience—as the most hideous of all possible crimes against Lear. Yet Wilson Knight, in a representative piece of modern criticism of *King Lear*, can write:

"This old man, recently a king, and, if his speeches are fair samples, more than a little of a tyrant, now goes from daughter to daughter, furious because Goneril dares criticize

[11] *The Letters of Queen Elizabeth*, p. 71.

427

his pet knights, kneeling down before Regan, performing, as she says, 'unsightly tricks' (II. iv. 159)—the situation is excruciatingly painful, and its painfulness is exactly of that quality which embarrasses in some forms of comedy. In the theatre, one is terrified lest some one laugh: yet, if Lear could laugh—if the Lears of the world could laugh at themselves—there would be no such tragedy. In the early scenes old age and dignity suffer, and seem to deserve, the punishments of childhood: 'Now, by my life,/ Old fools are babes again.' " (I. iii. 18-19)[12]

In Shakespeare's other plays the size or quality of one's retinue is an issue of only minor importance. In the fifth act of *The Winter's Tale* the meagreness of Florizel's retinue is commented on in a dialogue between Leontes and a servant. Leontes observes,

> He comes not
> Like to his father's greatness. His approach,
> So out of circumstance and sudden, tells us
> 'Tis not a visitation fram'd, but forc'd
> By need and accident. What train?
> SERV.   But few,
> And those but mean. (V. i. 88-93)

In similar fashion, Octavius Caesar reproaches Octavia when she comes unannounced "like a market-maid to Rome." The Renaissance love of pomp and ceremony is reflected in Caesar's rebuke:

> Why have you stol'n upon us thus? You come not
> Like Caesar's sister. The wife of Antony
> Should have an army for an usher, and
> The neighs of horse to tell of her approach
> Long ere she did appear. (III. vi. 42-46)

---

[12] *The Wheel of Fire*, p. 164.

DISHONOR AND SHAME

Antony and Cleopatra is almost a study in shame. From the very beginning of the play, Antony's former reputation as a great Roman general, as austere and disciplined as any of the great military leaders of Spartan Greece, is contrasted with his present decline into an epicurean, pleasure-loving wastrel who can not break away from Cleopatra's bewitching snares. Antony, like Hamlet, is aware of the discrepancy between his ideal of himself and the irresolution and vaccillation of his present behavior. At times he defies this ideal as, for example, when he embraces the Egyptian queen with the exclamation, "The nobleness of life/ Is to do thus." (I. i. 36-37) But when the messenger brings the news of Fulvia's death and of Pompey's successes, he responds to his latent sense of honor and departs for Rome. As Caesar had hoped: "his shames quickly/ Drive him to Rome." (I. iv. 72-73) (Rowe's description of the irregular greatness of mind of Antony is thoroughly appropriate; by fits and starts he returns to his former heights, but never with the constant firmness and self-assurance he once had.)

Caesar's eulogy, early in the play, of the Spartan and austere qualities which Antony had once displayed prepares us for the alteration which takes place in Antony when he first meets Caesar in Rome. When Octavius accuses him of breaking his oath, Antony responds like a Roman: "The honour is sacred which he talks on now,/ Supposing that I lack'd it." (II. ii. 85-86) He asks pardon for his faults, but only so far as it befits his honor to stoop in such a case. In the third act, he is still the man of honor who will not brook offense. He complains to Octavia that her brother has addressed the people of Rome and "Spoke scantly of me; when perforce he could not/ But pay me terms of honour." (III. iv. 6-7) He responds by preparing to war against Caesar and thus to stain his rival's honor in revenge for this insult. For it is his view, as we have seen, that if he loses his honor, he loses himself. Octavia returns from Greece to Rome and Antony to Egypt. Caesar tells his sister that she has been abused and insulted by Antony's treatment of her; he uses this insult to his family's honor as a pretext in order to prepare for war.

In the third act, in the naval engagement, Antony allows his attachment to Cleopatra to cause him to follow her in flight. His followers are sickened by this disgraceful behavior. As Scarus tells Enobarbus,

> I never saw an action of such shame.
> Experience, manhood, honour, ne'er before
> Did violate so itself. (III. x. 22-24)

But Antony is fully aware of the disgrace which he has brought on himself. He tells his attendants, "the land bids me tread no more upon't! / It is asham'd to bear me!" (III. xi. 1-2) When Cleopatra enters, Iras informs her that "He is unqualitied with very shame." (III. xi. 44) When she approaches to comfort him, he (like Cassio in *Othello*) bemoans the fact that he has "offended reputation—/ A most unnoble swerving." (III. xi. 49-50)

Despite his shortcomings, Antony is constantly concerned to uphold his honor, and when he fails to live up to his own ideal of what he should be a sense of shame immediately seizes him. Finally Enobarbus, realizing that Antony is doomed to ultimate defeat, deserts him. When Antony sends his treasure after him, Enobarbus is so affected by his disgraceful desertion of his bountiful lord that he dies of the shame of it. (IV. ix. 1-23) The aristocratic sense of shame is also apparent when Antony receives the news of Cleopatra's "death." Antony tells Eros,

> Since Cleopatra died
> I have liv'd in such dishonour that the gods
> Detest my baseness. I, that with my sword
> Quarter'd the world and o'er green Neptune's back
> With ships made cities, condemn myself to lack
> The courage of a woman. (IV. xiv. 55-60)

Antony asks Eros to slay him: "for with a wound I must be cur'd." (IV. xiv. 78) Just as Cassio says he is hurt past surgery when he loses his reputation in the drinking scene, so Antony infers that by a bodily wound (i.e., suicide) he can regain his dying honor. Loss of life is considered trivial if by such a sacrifice honor can be restored.

Antony's shortcomings are apparent from the very moment the play begins. But, like every Renaissance aristocrat, he is constantly bothered when his behavior is shameful. This is not the case with Shakespeare's really Machiavellian villains. Both Lear and Cordelia harbor the naïve illusion that Goneril and Regan will be ashamed of their unspeakable cruelty. Thus Lear tells Regan, "But I'll not chide thee./ Let shame come when it will." (II. iv. 228-229) And Cordelia, when she hears what has happened to her father, cries out, "Shame of ladies." (IV. iii. 29) But it is not an attribute of Shakespeare's villains to feel shame for their wrong-doing; they are completely cynical. Goneril calls Albany a moral fool, just as Lady Macbeth chides her husband for his milky gentleness. Iago's disparagement of reputation, when Cassio bewails his loss of it, is perhaps the most striking indication of the extent to which the villains, generally speaking, are insensitive to loss of honor. They confirm the sayings of La Primaudaye in *The French Academie* that:

> A wicked man (saith Euripides) hath no shame in him.

> I looke for small goodnes of a yoong man (saith Seneca) except of such a one as blusheth after he hath offended.[13]

Renaissance moral philosophy taught that nothing was terrible to a noble mind but dishonour. The shock and indignation of Shakespeare's audience at seeing how coolly indifferent to dishonor Iago, Goneril, and Regan were would have reached tremendous proportions. Shakespeare could count on his audience to react violently against such cynicism; a modern audience,

[13] p. 243.

unaware of Renaissance values, can miss most of the evidence—
as for example, Iago's contemptuous remarks about the value of
reputation—which so thoroughly damns the villains. Missing
the evidence can lead us to view the villains as fairly reasonable
and decent fellows, as too many modern critics have done.[14]

Scorn. Scorn suggests much more than shame that one is
being held in contempt by others (rather than by oneself). It
is sensitivity to public shame which leads Antony to war against
Caesar when he discovers that Caesar has spoken scantly of
him. In *King Henry the Fifth,* the Dauphin's mocking gift of
tennis balls so enrages the British monarch that he informs the
French messenger

> many a thousand widows
> Shall this his mock mock out of their dear husbands,
> Mock mothers from their sons, mock castles down;
> And some are yet ungotten and unborn
> That shall have cause to curse the Dauphin's scorn.
>
> (I. ii. 284-288)

Aristotle had defined anger as "a longing, accompanied by
pain, for a real or apparent revenge for a real or apparent
slight."[15] Whether or not he had read Aristotle, Shakespeare
had an acute eye and hence frequently portrays the sensitivity
of the Renaissance aristocracy to the slighest sign of contempt,
an integral part of the code of honor of their age. That a gift
of precious treasure which royalty was accustomed to give to
royalty should be replaced by a gift of tennis balls simply
would not do. So at the end of the second act, Exeter appears
before the Dauphin, the donor of this "magnificent" gift, and
informs him of the English monarch's message:

> Scorn and defiance, slight regard, contempt,
> And anything that may not misbecome
> The mighty sender, doth he prize you at.
> Thus says my king. (II. iv. 117-120)

[14] See Danby, *Shakespeare's Doctrine of Nature*, pp. 42-43.
[15] *Rhetoric* II. 2.

In this play, the French Dauphin is to discover that, as the Italian Guazzo had warned, "It is not good to mocke any man in any maner of wise. For if he bee our better, or equall, he will by no meanes abide that we shoulde abjectly esteeme of him."[16]

The wily Ulysses counts on the same sensitivity to loss of esteem to stir the sleeping Achilles. He tells his fellow Greeks that they must deliberately ignore their great hero-leader:

> Pass strangely by him,
> As if he were forgot; and princes all,
> Lay negligent and loose regard upon him.
>   (III. iii. 39-41)

Achilles may not be quick-witted, but he is as quick as any Renaissance aristocrat to observe this intentional slighting; he realizes that he has lost reputation among his fellow Greeks. But even Ulysses' brilliant speech ("Perseverance, dear my lord, keeps honour bright") can not shake him from his great lethargy. (III. iii. 15ff.)

Even the bourgeois characters in Shakespeare's comedies often manifest a jealous concern for honor and reputation. In *The Comedy of Errors*, the goldsmith Angelo asks Antipholus of Ephesus for the money owed him for the chain which he believes he had given this twin. When Antipholus truthfully denies that he has received it, Angelo, feeling his reputation touched, bids the officer arrest him with the comment, "I would not spare my brother in this case/ If he should scorn me so apparently." (IV. i. 77-78) Shylock's famous speech in defense of his persecuted race reveals a like sensitivity to contempt. He tells Salerio that Antonio "hath disgrac'd me, and hind'red me half a million; laugh'd at my losses, mock'd at my gains, scorned my nation, thwarted my bargains, cooled my friends, heated mine enemies—and what's his reason? I am a Jew." (III. i. 56-62) Shylock is convinced that a Christian would seek

---

[16] II, 29.

revenge of a Jew if he had been wronged in this way. He sees no reason why he should not exact a like revenge.

Public Disgrace. If scorn and contempt were intolerable for the Renaissance aristocrat, they were still somewhat more bearable than an open, public disgrace in which the whole world, from king to beggar, would be able to look down on one. The letters of Queen Elizabeth, of Essex, and of Raleigh, provide abundant evidence of the dismay the aristocrats felt about possible scandal in their careers when they feared that they might be made a wonder and a spectacle to the world at large. The scorn and contempt of one's fellow aristocrats was cause for sufficient shame; to have one's inferiors also in a position to mock and condemn was, as Essex put it, a fate worse than death.[17]

This fear of the rabble's contempt is evident in Shakespeare's earliest plays. When Talbot is ransomed in *The First Part of King Henry the Sixth*, he informs Salisbury of the shameful treatment he had received from the French:

> With scoffs and scorns and contumelious taunts
> In open market place produc'd they me
> To be a public spectacle to all. (I. iv. 39-41)

He also reports to Salisbury that the French, as a sign of their contempt, were willing to ransom and exchange him for a prisoner of far lower rank. Talbot would not permit his great worth to be cheapened in this manner; therefore he disdainfully refused to accept this opportunity for liberty, "and craved death/ Rather than I would be so vile esteem'd." (I. iv. 32-33)

In *The Second Part of King Henry the Sixth*, the wife of Duke Humphrey Gloucester is sentenced to banishment. The Duke asks leave to retire from court since he fears that the dishonor to his name will cause him to die of grief. But in the next scene he is forced to stand watching his wife being led in public disgrace through the streets. He dresses himself in mourning clothes,

---

[17] G. B. Harrison, *Essex*, p. 261.

feeling this dishonor worse than his wife's death would have been. When she arrives in the procession, he has to endure the added ignominy of listening to her rebuke that he should have allowed his forlorn duchess to be made "a wonder and a pointing stock/ To every idle rascal follower." (II. iv. 46-47)

The aristocrat's dread of public disgrace is equally apparent in *Antony and Cleopatra*. Antony, for example, asks Eros to kill him and describes the public disgrace of both master and servant which will otherwise occur:

> Eros,
> Wouldst thou be window'd in great Rome and see
> Thy master thus with pleach'd arms, bending down
> His corrigible neck, his face subdu'd
> To penetrative shame, whilst the wheel'd seat
> Of fortunate Caesar, drawn before him, branded
> His baseness that ensu'd? (IV. xiv. 71-77)

It is Caesar's guard, Proculeius, who prevents Cleopatra from stabbing herself; he informs her that Caesar wishes that "the world see/ His nobleness well acted." (V. ii. 44-45) Cleopatra pretends to acquiesce and when Caesar holds audience with her calls him her lord and master. But as soon as she is with her servants again she shows that she, like Antony, is determined to avoid the breath of the stinking rabble of Rome. Essex, in disgrace with his Queen, had complained that "the prating tavern haunters speak of me what they list; they print me and make me speak to the world, and shortly they will play me upon the stage."[17] Cleopatra anticipates a like fate:

> Saucy lictors
> Will catch at us like strumpets, and scald rhymers
> Ballad us out o' tune. The quick comedians
> Extemporally will stage us and present
> Our Alexandrian revels. Antony
> Shall be brought drunken forth, and I shall see
> Some squeaking Cleopatra boy my greatness
> I' th' posture of a whore. (V. ii. 214-221)

Rather than face such public humiliation, she makes preparations for a magnificent suicide fitting to a great Queen. Caesar arrives on the scene at the end of the play only to admit that he has been outsmarted; Cleopatra, by the glory of her death, has robbed him of the glory he had anticipated in having her participate in his great triumphal procession in Rome.

The death of Macbeth, who seems to have given up all concern about human values in his final soliloquy, shows that, however vicious he may have become in his descent into ever greater crime and however much life may have lost all meaning with his loss of self-esteem, he still at the very end possesses the greatness of courage that was his at the beginning of the play. Like Brutus, he bears too great a mind to submit to the indignities of capture. When he softens momentarily, refuses to be "a Roman fool," and tells Macduff that he will not fight with him, Macduff taunts him:

> Then yield thee, coward,
> And live to be the show and gaze o' th' time!
>   (V. viii. 23-24)

> MACB.   I will not yield
> To kiss the ground before young Malcolm's feet
> And to be baited with the rabble's curse.
>   (V. viii. 27-29)

Whately's commentary on this passage gives further evidence that the critics of the 18th century, still involved in a genuine humanist tradition, had a closer awareness of Shakespearean motivation than many modern critics, since the concept of honor still had meaning in their age. Whately observes that Macbeth is still possessed of a strong sense of honor, that he shuns the thought of disgrace, and hence dies as becomes a soldier.[18]

It is, of course, Macbeth's tragedy that the enormity of his deed leaves no room for any sort of redemption. As soon as he has committed the crime, he realizes that his bloodstained

---

[18] Whately, *Remarks on Some of the Characters of Shakespeare*, p. 83.

hands can never be cleansed of their guilt. His wife, in sharp contrast, believes that "A little water clears us of this deed." But in her final appearance, she too reveals that the sense of remorse had been deeply fixed in her, even if almost buried. As she walks in her sleep, she exclaims: "Here's the smell of the blood still. All the perfumes of Arabia will not sweeten this little hand. Oh, oh, oh." In this scene there is no doubt that Shakespeare is portraying the Christian sense of sinful guilt rather than the pagan sense of shame. But except in the case of Lady Macbeth, Shakespeare's tragic heroes and heroines, when they die, are preoccupied rather with humanist concerns —honor, fidelity, and friendship. Although Macbeth admits that he has sold his soul to the common enemy of man, and although Othello speaks of himself as damned beneath all depths of Hell, Shakespeare's protagonists, when they die, do not have Christian doctrines paramount in their minds. Both Othello and Hamlet anticipate the peaceful tranquility of death; they view it as a restful oblivion, as the classic writers had, and their final concern at the moment of their death is about the reputation they will leave behind them with the human community. Even Macbeth, who knows that he has lost any claim to honor, refuses at the very end to endure any further disgrace. After he rejects the idea of suicide ("Why should I play the Roman fool and die/ On mine own sword?") (V. viii. 1-2) he refuses to live on to be "the show and gaze of th' time!" and dies fighting. At the very end he proves himself once again to be a brave soldier and a "man."

CHASTITY AND WOMAN'S HONOR

"Honour feminine is preserved by not failing onely in one of their proper particular vertues, which is honestie."[19] This definition, from the *Courtier's Academie*, is representative of the definition of chastity in all of the moral treatises of the Renaissance. As in so many other instances, Shakespeare makes use of this moral commonplace in his drama almost without

[19] Count Romei, p. 126.

alteration. In *All's Well that Ends Well*, one of the minor characters, Mariana, tells the widow and her daughter, Diana, that "the honour of a maid is her name, and no legacy is so rich as honesty." (III. v. 12-14) Diana herself tells Bertram that

> My chastity's the jewel of our house,
> Bequeathed down from many ancestors,
> Which were the greatest obloquy i' th' world
> In me to lose. (IV. ii. 46-49)

Many of the themes which have been discussed in connection with the concept of honor were paralleled in the observations on chastity. All the synonyms for honor—good name, reputation, honesty, opinion, and integrity—are commonly used in the specific sense of chastity when they are used to describe the virtue of a woman. Thus, in this same play, Diana is referred to as a "young gentlewoman . . . of a most chaste renown." (IV. iii. 17-19)

The loss of a woman's honor equally affected that of her husband since the world would "judge him ignorant, of small worth, and worthy of that contempt his wife and the adulterer procure him."[20] The jealousy of a suspicious husband in Elizabethan plays is often considered by the "hard-boiled" members of a modern audience, living in the day of Kinsey Reports, exaggerated and hence amusing. But, again our misinterpretation of Shakespeare's intended meaning results from our failure to realize the extent to which honor was cherished in the Renaissance as the most precious thing that man possessed, therefore cause for extremely violent reactions when its loss was threatened. As Ford says in *The Merry Wives of Windsor*, when he suspects that he has been betrayed by Falstaff: "See the hell of having a false woman! My bed shall be abus'd, my coffers ransack'd, my reputation gnawn at. . . . But cuckold! wittol! Cuckold! The devil himself hath not such a name. . . . God be praised for my jealousy! . . . Fie, fie, fie! Cuckold, cuckold, cuckold, cuckold!" (II. ii. 305-329)

[20] *ibid.*, p. 127.

The Elizabethans were haunted by this fear of deception and of cuckoldry. When we fail to sympathize with the suspiciousness of Othello, of Leontes, of Posthumus, or of Leonato, we must bear in mind that the theme of feminine infidelity was one of the most popular and yet most serious themes of Shakespeare's age. Donne's general scepticism is not representative of the men of his time, but his scepticism of woman's virtue is fairly representative of much male opinion in Elizabethan and Jacobean times (whether women shared in this opinion is a question we shall not attempt to answer). This suspicious attitude toward the opposite sex was one of the main subjects of Elizabethan and Jacobean plays, both comedies and tragedies, and the dramatists wrote some of their finest and most convincing poetry when dealing with this theme. Webster's Flamineo decides, for example, that women can never be trusted; his observations extend beyond his particular predicament to a generalized statement of what was so commonly felt:

> O men
> That lie upon your death-beds, and are haunted
> With howling wives, neere trust them, they'll re-marry
> Ere the worme peirce your winding sheete: ere the Spider
> Make a thinne curtaine for your Epitaphes.[21]

Elyot succinctly summarizes this typical Renaissance attitude when he observes that "we note in children inconstance, and likewise in women; the one for slendernesse of witte, the other as a natural sicknesse."[22] His *Defence of Good Women*, of course, is written to counteract the ridiculous extremes to which this view was sometimes taken. He points out that women can be true and faithful, and singles out for special mention the Roman women who committed suicide in order to join their husbands in death. Shakespeare is as ambivalent as the writers of his age on this issue. Hotspur refuses to con-

---

[21] *The White Divel*, v, vi, 155-159. These lines prove to be an excellent summary of the main theme of Shakespeare's *Hamlet*.

[22] Elyot, *The Gouernour*, III, 19.

fide his secrets to his wife; he tells her "constant you are,/ But yet a woman." (II. iii. 111-112) Brutus yields on the other hand to Portia's persuasions when she reminds him of the voluntary wound she gave herself to prove her constancy. This reminder forces him to admit that she is an honorable wife and so he confides in her. Desdemona carries fidelity to a truly tragic extreme when, in order to protect her husband, she tells Emilia that she has killed herself.

Nevertheless, Shakespeare's men often reveal a predisposition to distrust their women, because they tend to consider them naturally inconstant and fickle. The very last sonnet which "the speaker" addresses to his mistress suggests that Shakespeare may be writing from bitter personal experience:

> For I have sworn deep oaths of thy deep kindness,
> Oaths of thy love, thy truth, thy constancy;
> And to enlighten thee, gave eyes to blindness,
> Or made them swear against the thing they see;
> For I have sworn thee fair—more perjur'd I,
> To swear against the truth so foul a lie.
>
> (Sonnet 152)

As was so often the case in the Renaissance, Shakespeare suggests in *The Sonnets* that male friendship should be exalted because one can count on greater constancy and fidelity in the ideal relationship which could exist between men:

> A woman's face, with Nature's own hand painted,
> Hast thou, the master mistress of my passion;
> A woman's gentle heart, but not acquainted
> With shifting change, as is false women's fashion.
>
> (Sonnet 20)

Shakespeare's creation of character is often determined by this typically Renaissance view of woman's frailty. When the men prove false, almost invariably their infidelity results from some deep-seated vice—usually that of ambition, as in the case of Iago, of Claudius, and of Macbeth. But women's falseness

440

does not require some strong impelling motive; mere weakness and temperamental frailty can lead them almost blindly to betray their men. Not moral viciousness, but lack of awareness of the existence of moral values, lead Gertrude and Cressida to falseness. They are not strong enough to resist the temptation of the moment; hence the bitter grief and revulsion filling the hearts of Hamlet and Troilus can not be purged by hatred, for Gertrude and Cressida are too weak to justify such strong emotions of anger and hatred (Eliot's essay on *Hamlet* is rich with suggestive insights on this matter). Moral nausea engulfs both Hamlet and Troilus, leaving them bitterly disillusioned.

These generalizations do not apply to such virtuous characters as Ophelia, Desdemona, and Hermione, or to such thoroughly vicious ones as Goneril and Regan. Nevertheless, weakness and fickleness are viewed as typically feminine; hence, when the women are exceptionally virtuous they are apt to point it out, as Hermione does in asserting that she is not subject to the womanish tears characteristic of her sex. (II. i. 107-112) In like manner, Cleopatra openly admits her weakness to Caesar; she tells him that she has "been laden with like frailties which before/ Have often sham'd our sex." (V. ii. 123-124) In the final scene, when she finally renounces her feminine traits, there is a corresponding self-awareness:

> My resolution's plac'd, and I have nothing
> Of woman in me. Now from head to foot
> I am marble-constant. Now the fleeting moon
> No planet is of mine. (V. ii. 238-241)

When Posthumus finally becomes convinced of Imogen's infidelity, in *Cymbeline*, his generalizations on the nature of women indicate his particular bias which seems to be justified by his predicament, but they are also the reflection of a common Renaissance notion. He complains that

> . . . even to vice
> They are not constant, but are changing still

441

> One vice but of a minute old for one
> Not half so old as that. I'll write against them,
> Detest them, curse them. (II. v. 29-33)

Hamlet's famous line, "Frailty, thy name is woman" is a similar blanket condemnation of the whole sex. (I. ii. 146) He is ironically cruel and suspiciously aloof from Ophelia because of the convincing proof that Gertrude's marriage seems to provide that women are indeed not to be trusted. We need not look for specific indications of Ophelia's disloyalty to Hamlet; the generalized feeling that no woman can be trusted simply engulfs her, an innocent victim. Rosalind's humorous and whimsical account in *As You Like It*, in which she tells Orlando how she cured a former wooer, presents the basic Renaissance view of woman's nature and at least partially accounts for the misogyny of Hamlet, Posthumus, and of King Lear, whose misogyny is particularly evident in the "Let copulation thrive" speech in the storm scene. "At which time would I, being but a moonish youth, grieve, be effeminate, changeable, longing, and liking, proud, fantastical, apish, shallow, inconstant, full of tears, full of smiles; for every passion something and for no passion truly anything, as boys and women are for the most part cattle of this colour; would now like him, now loathe him; then entertain him, then spit at him; that I drave my suitor from his mad humour of love to a living humour of madness, which was, to forswear the full stream of the world and to live in a nook merely monastic." (III. ii. 429-442) Cleopatra, as portrayed in the early part of *Antony and Cleopatra*, is the epitome of feminine fickleness. Her artful deceptiveness, particularly her talent for shamming death on the whim of the moment, forces us to admire her for being so fascinatingly inconstant ("Age cannot wither her/ Nor custom stale her infinite variety"). Her final constancy shows, however, that the Renaissance believed woman could rise to the heights of tragic heroism and in effect belie her own nature—

as the eye-witness accounts of the death of Mary Queen of Scots unquestionably prove.[23]

If women were held suspect because of a natural tendency to fickleness, it is no wonder that their husbands were apt to spend sleepless nights. Othello, Posthumus, Leontes, and Leonato are all at some point suspicious and jealous, even though their women are innocent. Since the audience is omniscient, it is likely to find fault with these exceedingly distrustful men. But it is necessary to remember, as Coleridge pointed out long ago in regard to Othello's jealousy, that Othello kills Desdemona "in a conviction forced upon him by the almost superhuman art of Iago, such a conviction as any man would and must have entertained who had believed Iago's honesty as Othello did. We, the audience, know that Iago is a villain from the beginning; but in considering the essence of the Shakespearean Othello, we must perseveringly place ourselves in his situation, and under his circumstances."[24] If we are to relate Coleridge's perceptive remarks to the reactions of Shakespeare's original audiences, it is only necessary to point to the Elizabethan belief that woman is, by nature, an inferior creature, whose primary duty is to obey the superior in her family, whether it be her father or her husband; for "woman have not mortall vertues in that perfections as hath a man."[25]

The modern audience is apt likewise to condemn Shakespeare's jealous and distrustful men for the ferocity with

[23] See Brents Stirling, *Unity in Shakespearian Tragedy*, pp. 157-192. Stirling criticizes both hero and heroine for their imperfections and reaches the conclusion that *Antony and Cleopatra* is a "satirical tragedy." Stirling fails to perceive that Shakespeare can endow his protagonists with tragic grandeur and nonetheless give them "some faults to make them men." Shakespeare's heroes are remarkable and exceptional beings; they are not, except perhaps in the case of Brutus, consistent models of moral perfection. Corneille's heroes frequently are beyond criticism; as a result they seem to lack the qualities of warmth and humanity of the Shakespearean protagonist. Bénichou's discussion of aristocratic grandeur in *Morales du Grand Siècle* is an effective answer to the carping criticism of Shakespeare's heroes which denies them tragic stature because of the obvious defects in their characters. See note, p. 289.

[24] Samuel Taylor Coleridge, *Lectures and Notes on Shakespeare and Other English Poets*, p. 393.

[25] Count Romei, *The Courtier's Academie*, p. 235.

which they turn on their wives. Posthumus exclaims, "O, that I had her here, to tear her limbmeal!" (II. iv. 147) Othello tells Iago that he will chop Desdemona into messes. Leontes wishes to dash out the brains of his child once he has come to suspect that his wife is an adulteress. Leonato asserts that he will tear his daughter to pieces with his own hands if he finds that she has been false. Judged by the humanitarian criteria of the 20th century (which must, unfortunately, account for concentration camps which make the cruelty of the Elizabethans seem mild indeed), these irate husbands are not only subject to censure for their inability to control their passions, but equally for the savage cruelty they display toward those they had but recently loved. But the Renaissance, while it emphasized the Christian virtues of mercy and forgiveness and the classical virtues of gentility and kindliness, made no pretensions of being consistently humanitarian. Nor was the gentle Shakespeare particularly kindly in his final treatment of those characters whom he intended to be the very embodiment of evil, any more than was the Christian Dante, whose final circle of Hell may seem to a modern reader the essence of barbaric sadism.

The Elizabethan audience would not have reacted against the cruel savagery of these vengeful husbands. Not that sadism was admired for its own sake; Othello, for example, does not actually chop Desdemona into pieces but instead tries to be merciful when he decides that he must slay her. In judging Othello, we must remember that Moryson is giving expression to common Renaissance opinion when he writes, with a surprising degree of awareness of differing social customs, that the Venetians "impatient to bring their honor under publique trialls dispatch the punishment of all Jelousyes by private revenge, killing not only the men so provoking them, but their wieves, sisters or daughters dishonouring themselves in those kindes."[26] In other Elizabethan and Jacobean plays, the re-

[26] Fynes Moryson, *Shakespeare's Europe*, p. 164.

action when one discovers that one's wife has been unfaithful is just as violent. In *The Fatal Dowry*, for example, the hero discovers his wife in the very act of adultery and brings her before her own father who admits that she deserves to die. The vengeance the husbands takes on an erring wife is the same sacrifice he would demand of himself if he had to choose between life and honor. This is especially evident in *Measure for Measure*. Isabella seems a very unsympathetic sister when she asks Claudio to give up his own life to preserve her chastity. But she had made it clear to Angelo, when he first made his shameful proposition to save Claudio's life at the expense of her honor, that her demands on Claudio are no greater than those she would have made on herself.

> Were I under the terms of death,
> Th' impression of keen whips I'ld wear as rubies,
> And strip myself to death as to a bed
> That longings have been sick for, ere I'ld yield
> My body up to shame. (II. iv. 100-104)

Husband and wife, father and child, brother and sister owed a common allegiance to the honor of the family name. Because the sense of family loyalty was so great, one identified oneself completely with the other members of one's family. Hence, the pollution of one member seemed to involve the others in a like corruption. Thus, in *The Comedy of Errors*, Adriana pleads with Antipholus of Syracuse, whom she mistakes for her husband, not to be licentious since otherwise

> I am possess'd with an adulterate blot,
> My blood is mingled with the crime of lust;
> For, if we two be one, and thou play false,
> I do digest the poison of thy flesh,
> Being strumpeted by thy contagion.
> (II. ii. 142-146)

In Othello's case, he loves his wife so dearly that he is even willing to endure the dishonor she has brought upon him.

Much as he laments the fact that she has made him "A fixed finger for the time of scorn/ To point his slow unmoving finger at," he nonetheless assures Iago that he can bear even that indignity. (IV. ii. 54-55) What he can not abide is the corruption of that which he had loved so whole-heartedly:

> But there where I have garner'd up my heart,
> Where either I must live or bear no life,
> The fountain from the which my current runs
> Or else dries up—to be discarded thence,
> Or keep it as a cistern for foul toads
> To knot and gender in. (IV. ii. 57-62)

As Caroline Spurgeon and Wilson Knight have pointed out, Shakespeare frequently associates lust and uncleanness. They provide one of his most recurrent images in both *Hamlet* and *Troilus and Cressida*. In *The Rape of Lucrece*, the blood of the heroine is, in similar fashion, referred to as corrupted, tainted, and even putrefied, although the innocent Lucrece insists that her mind is still pure and immaculate. Her name stained and her blood tainted, she takes her own life rather than continue to live in dishonor.

The killing of an adulterer in Renaissance England was considered an act of manslaughter which would almost certainly be pardoned. The leniency of the law in this regard results from the fact that the husband's honor and reputation are destroyed. Hence, when Othello asks Iago to slay Cassio, his fault would have been considered primarily that of an error in judgment. Shakespeare's audience would not have considered Othello's actions, any more than his emotional reactions, beyond comprehension, for if Desdemona had actually commited adultery with Cassio, they could hardly have condemned him for his fierce hatred of the adulterer and for his desire to kill both his wife and her lover. Again let it be said that in order fully to enjoy a Shakespearean play—not to mention to be historically accurate—the modern audience must free itself of its humanitarian bias, even if we wish to pat ourselves on the back for having freed ourselves from the superstitious prejudices of the benighted Elizabethan era. If we do not follow Coleridge in his "willing suspension of disbelief," we are apt, like many modern critics, to lose all sympathy with Shakespeare's heroes and his plays, and in the loss become absurd.

HIS book has attempted to place Shakespeare's dramatic treatment of the concept of honor in its proper cultural context—the pagan-humanist values of the aristocracy of his age. To define Shakespeare's relation to the Renaissance ethos is not an easy task, nor can one ever arrive at anything like complete certainty as to the validity of his conclusions.

This study has shown that certain moral assumptions were shared by Shakespeare and his audience, and that many leading themes of particular plays, such as the ingratitude of Goneril and Regan to their royal benefactor and aged father, are clarified considerably by appropriate reference to the precepts and axioms of Renaissance moral philosophy.

It may seem that I have unduly stressed the significance of Aristotle and Cicero throughout, since there is little reason to believe that Shakespeare was directly influenced by Aristotle and no evidence to indicate a specific debt to Cicero. But it is enough to know that the English monarchs from Edward to Elizabeth made use of the *Nicomachean Ethics* as one of their principal moral works; that the numerous Italian dialogues on honor and the duel were directly indebted to Aristotle's definitions of honor, reputation, disgrace, injury, and contempt; and that Cicero's *Offices* was the grammar school textbook on moral philosophy, for us to assign these two pagan philosophers a place of central significance. Even if Shakespeare's eyes were simply on the flesh-and-blood aristocrat, he could not have missed endless opportunities to witness the actual carrying out of various cardinal aspects of the pagan-humanist ethics derived from these two philosophers. The dueling scenes involving Romeo, Tybalt, and Mercutio, and the duel between Hamlet and Laertes, are unmistakable reflections of the Renaissance code of honor and the duel, a code based on Aristotle. So, likewise, when Lear suffers insult and abuse from the steward Oswald, we should recollect that *King Lear* was first performed before the King at Whitehall and that the insult and contempt shown on the stage for a royal personage could only have been interpreted by the court audience in the light of its pagan-humanist definitions of the meaning of honor, insolence, injury, and revenge.

Finally, a word should be said about my hypothesis that Shakespeare reflects the Christian values of his age to a lesser degree than pagan-humanist morality. Unmindful of Stoll's wise admonition that "interpretation, mainly a study in emphasis, is, if worthy of the name, in faithful response to the emphasis of the poet,"[1] we can easily go astray by stressing disproportionately either the absence or presence of Christian values. Then the critic of the critic could properly say, as Stoll does of Tieck and Brooke and Nicoll, "that there has been criticism instead of interpretation and that the primary moral and emotional impression has been missed or ignored."[2] In support of my own position on this matter I would refer again to Pierre Villey's excellent description of the Renaissance state of mind:

The idea of the Eternal is too weighty and the word of God is too powerful for those who are Christian in the full sense of the word not to extend their jurisdiction over most of life's actions or forbid positive reason (that is, reason based on facts) to encroach further on their province.

But if the enticing game of giving free rein to reason in its unshackled form happens to catch men's attention and they turn their attention toward the realities of present human existence as toward a new pole, who does not see that moral philosophy, feeling hemmed in, will gnaw at the net, will extend the boundaries of the territory which has been conceded to it, will perhaps capture man's entire soul? In some cases, then, it will relegate religious faith to a back shop, where it will die out. In other cases religion, alive but completely enervated, will still be a part of life but actively participate in it only feebly and from a distance.[3]

---

[1] E. E. Stoll, *Shakespeare and Other Masters*, 1940, p. 239.   [2] *ibid.*
[3] *Les Sources et l'Evolution des Essais de Montaigne*, I, 12-13.

APPENDIX

Pierre Villey, *Les Sources et l'Evolution des Essais de Montaigne*, I, 12-13. Translation appears in Chapter 1, pp. 56, 57.

"Une trêve est signée. Ces écrits enregistrent un droit pour la philosophie morale à conduire la vie, mais en lui imposant leurs conditions. A côté et au-dessous de la morale révélée, un art de vivre peut se développer selon sa méthode propre. La révélation dira les fins de l'homme et étendra sur sa vie entière le réseau compliqué de leurs conséquences; la raison devra se contenir dans les interstices laissés libres. Adaptant les maximes des philosophes et en imaginant des nouvelles à leur imitation, elle indiquera des moyens pour exécuter ces principes sacrés, et fera la loi dans la portion d'activité que la religion abandonne comme neutre. Alors, que va-t-il se passer? Sans doute chez les véritables chrétiens, chez tous ceux, dont toutes les fibres sont imprégnées de l'obsédante préoccupation de l'au-delà, du sentiment de la présence de Dieu et de la foi en Christ, la zone neutre restera petite et la raison se limitera scrupuleusement à cette besogne subalterne. Si elle fait évoluer la morale en dépit de l'immobilité des textes, ce sera à son insu, sans toucher au principe d'autorité, ce sera en modifiant le sens des Ecritures. La pensée de l'éternité est trop lourde et le verbe de Dieu trop puissant chez celui qui est chrétien au sens plein du mot pour ne pas étendre leur juridiction sur la plupart des actes de la vie, et pour laisser la raison positive empiéter sur leurs attributions. Mais si le jeu séduisant de cette raison positive vient à captiver l'attention, à la tourner toute vers les réalités présentes comme vers un pôle nouveau, qui ne voit que la philosophie morale à l'étroit rongera les mailles, étendra la lande concédée, accaparera peut-être la conscience entière et reléguera la foi religieuse dans une arrière-boutique où elle s'éteindra parfois, ou parfois encore vivante mais énervée, elle assistera aux actes de la vie sans y participer que faiblement et de loin en loin. Alors les rôles seront intervertis, le pivot de la morale aura changé. Entre ces deux limites extrêmes, une infinité de positions intermédiaires se présente aux penseurs; sur cette échelle chacun se placera plus ou moins loin suivant son tempérament intellectuel, selon que sa raison positive aura plus ou moins de force à organiser la vie, et selon que l'autorité et les pensées métaphysiques auront plus ou moins perdu de leur prise sur la conscience.

"Entre 1550 et 1600 tout le monde se jette sur la philosophie ancienne. On en trouve partout; c'est une ivresse générale."

BIBLIOGRAPHY

CLASSICAL PHILOSOPHY AND CIVILIZATION

Aristotle. *The Art of Rhetoric*, trans. John Henry Freese, Loeb Library, Cambridge, Mass., 1957.

————. *Nicomachean Ethics*, trans. H. Rackham, Loeb Library, Cambridge, Mass., 1956.

————. *The Poetics*. "Longinus": *On the Sublime*. Demetrius: *On Style*, trans. W. Hamilton Fyfe and W. Rhys Roberts, Loeb Library, Cambridge, Mass., 1953.

————. *Politics*, trans. H. Rackham, Loeb Library, Cambridge, Mass., 1944.

Aurelius, Marcus. *Meditations*, trans. George Long, in *Great Books of the Western World*, ed. Robert Maynard Hutchins, Vol. 12, Chicago, 1952.

Cicero. *De Finibus Bonorum et Malorum*, trans. H. Rackham, Loeb Library, New York, 1921.

————. *De Officiis*, trans. Walter Miller, Loeb Library, Cambridge, Mass., 1956.

————. *De Re Publica, De Legibus*, trans. Clinton Walker Keyes, Loeb Library, Cambridge, Mass., 1951.

————. *De Senectute, De Amicitia, De Divinatione*, trans. William A. Falconer, Loeb Library, Cambridge, Mass., 1953.

————. *The Philippics*, trans. Walter C. A. Ker, Loeb Library, Cambridge, Mass., 1957.

Epictetus. *The Discourses*, trans. George Long, in *Great Books of the Western World*, ed. Robert Maynard Hutchins, Vol. 12, Chicago, 1952.

Jaeger, Werner. *Paideia*, New York, 1945, 3 vols.

Plato. *Euthyphro, Apology, Crito, Phaedo, Phaedrus*, trans. Harold North Fowler, Loeb Library, Cambridge, Mass., 1953.

————. *Lysis, Symposium, Gorgias*, trans. W. R. M. Lamb, Loeb Library, Cambridge, Mass., 1953.

————. *The Republic*, trans. Paul Shorey, Loeb Library, Cambridge, 1943.

Plutarch. *Moralia*, trans. Philemon Holland, Everyman's Library, London, 1911.

Seneca, Lucius Annaeus. *Ad Lucilium Epistulae Morales*, trans. Richard M. Gummere, Loeb Library, Cambridge, Mass., 1943, 3 vols.

Seneca, Lucius Annaeus. *Consolation ad Marcia*, in *The Workes of L. A. Seneca both Morall and Naturall*, trans. T. Lodge, London, 1614.

MEDIEVAL PHILOSOPHY AND CIVILIZATION

Aquinas, St. Thomas. *The Summa Contra Gentiles*, trans. the English Dominican Fathers from the Latest Leonine Edition, London, 1928, 4 vols.
———. *The Summa Theologica*, trans. the Fathers of the English Dominican Province, London, 1935, 22 vols.
Augustine, St. *The City of God*, trans. Marcus Dods, in *Great Books of the Western World*, ed. Robert Maynard Hutchins, Vol. 18, Chicago, 1952.

Boethius. *The Consolation of Philosophy*, trans. H. F. Stewart, New York, 1926.

Dante Alighieri. *The Divine Comedy*, trans. Alan Howell and Philip Wicksteed, London, 1936, 3 vols.
Davis, H. W. C. (ed.). *Medieval England*, Oxford, 1929.

Francis, of Assisi, St. *The Little Flowers of St. Francis of Assisi*, trans. T. W. Arnold, London, 1904.

Gilson, Etienne. *The Spirit of Medieval Philosophy*, trans. A. H. C. Downes, London, 1950.

Haskins, Charles Homer. *The Renaissance of the Twelfth Century*, Cambridge, Mass., 1927.
———. *The Rise of Universities*, New York, 1923.
Hearnshaw, F. J. C. (ed.). *The Social and Political Ideas of Some Great Medieval Thinkers*, New York, 1923.
Huizinga, Johan. *The Waning of the Middle Ages*, London, 1937.

[John of Salisbury.] *The Statesman's Book of John of Salisbury*, ed. and trans. John Dickinson, New York, 1927.
[Joinville, Jean, Sire de.] *Chronicle of the Crusades of St. Lewis*, in Villehardouin and De Joinville, *Memoirs of the Crusades*, trans. Sir Frank Marzials, Everyman's Library, London, 1955.
Jones, George. *Honor in German Literature*, Chapel Hill, N.C., 1959.

a Kempis, Thomas. *The Imitation of Christ*, trans. William Benham, in *The Harvard Classics*, ed. Charles W. Eliot, Vol. 7, New York, 1937.

Langlois, Charles Victor. *La Vie au Moyen Age d'après quelques Moralistes du Temps*, Paris, 1908.

Painter, Sidney. *French Chivalry*, Baltimore, 1940.
————. *William Marshal*, Baltimore, 1933.
Petrarch, Francis. *Petrarch's Secret; or the Soul's Conflict with Passion: Three Dialogues between Himself and S. Augustine*, trans. William H. Draper, London, 1911.

Rashdall, Hastings. *The Universities of Europe in the Middle Ages*, Oxford, 1895, 2 vols.
Read, Herbert. *The Sense of Glory*, Cambridge, England, 1929.

Taylor, Henry Osborne. *The Classical Heritage of the Middle Ages*, New York, 1901.

WORKS BY RENAISSANCE AUTHORS

Agrippa, Henry Cornelius von Nottesheim. *Of the Vanitie and Uncertaintie of Artes and Sciences*, trans. Ja[mes] San[ford], London, 1569.
Ascham, Roger. *The Scholemaster*, ed. Edward Arber, reprinted from the 1st ed. of 1570, London, 1923.
Ashley, Robert. *Of Honour*, ed. Virgil Heltzel, reprinted from the Sloane ms. 2131 (fols. 16-20), San Marino, 1947.

[Bacon, Francis.] *The Essays or Counsels, Civil and Moral, of Francis Bacon*, ed. Samuel Harvey Reynolds, Oxford, 1890.
Bryskett, Lodowick. *A Discourse of Civill Life: containing the ethike part of morall philosophie. Fit for the instructing of a gentleman in the course of a vertuous life*, London, 1606.

Castiglione, Baldassare. *The Book of the Courtier*, trans. Thomas Hoby, ed. Ernest Rhys, Everyman's Library, London, 1928.
[Chapman, George.] *The Plays and Poems of George Chapman*, ed. Thomas Marc Parrott, New York, 1910.
Cleland, James. *The Institution of a Nobleman*, Facsimile Reproduction of the 1607 ed., New York, 1948.
Cornwallis, William. *Essayes*, ed. D. C. Allen, Baltimore, 1946.

Dekker, Thomas, *The Wonderfull Yeare*, ed. G. B. Harrison, London, 1924.
Della Casa, Giovanni. *Galateo: of Manners and Behaviour in Familiar Conversation*, trans. Robert Peterson, London, 1576.

[Devereux, Robert.] *The Life and Death of Robert Devereux Earl of Essex*, ed. G. B. Harrison, New York, 1937.

Devereux, Walter B. *Lives and Letters of the Devereux, Earls of Essex, in the Reigns of Elizabeth, James I, and Charles I, 1540-1646*, London, 1853, 2 vols.

[Drayton, Michael.] *The Works of Michael Drayton*, Vol. 1, London, 1753.

Du Vair, Guillaume. *The Moral Philosophie of the Stoicks*, trans. T[homas] J[ames], London, 1598.

[Elizabeth I]. *The Letters of Queen Elizabeth*, ed. G. B. Harrison, London, 1935

Elyot, Thomas. *The Defense of Good Women*, Oxford, 1940.
———. *The Boke Named the Gouernour*, ed. Ernest Rhys, Everyman's Library, London, 1937.

Fenton, G[eoffrey]. *Golden Epistles. Containing varietie of discourse, both morall, philosophicall, and divine: gathered, as well out of the remainder of Guevarae's workes, as other authors Latine, French and Italian*, London, 1575.

Gascoigne, George. *The Complete Works*, ed. John W. Cunliffe, Vol. 2, Cambridge, England, 1910.

[Gello, J. B.] *Circes of J. B. Gello, Florentine. Translated out of Italion*, into Englishe by H[enry] Iden, London, 1557.

[Greville, Fulke.] *Poems and Dramas of Fulke Greville, First Lord Brooke*, with introduction and notes by Geoffrey Bullough, Edinburgh, 1939, 2 vols.

Guazzo, M. S. *The Civile Conversation*, trans. George Pettie, London, 1581.

[Guevara, Anthony of.] *The Familiar Epistles of Sir Anthony of Guevara*, trans. Edward Hellowes, London, 1574.

de Guevara, Antonio. *The Diall of Princes*, trans. Thomas North, 3rd ed. (1st ed. 1557), London, 1619.

Guicciardini, Francesco. *Aphorismes Civill and Militairie amplified with authorities, and exemplified with historie*, trans. Robert Dallington, London, 1613.

Hurault, Jacques. *Politicke, Moral, and Martial Discourses*, trans. Arthur Golding, London, 1595.

[James I]. *The Political Works of James I*, ed. Charles Howard McIlwain, reprinted from the 1616 ed., Cambridge, Mass., 1918.

Jonson, Ben. *Works*, ed. C. H. Herford and Percy and Evelyn Simpson, Vol. 8, Oxford, 1943.

Kendall, Elizabeth (ed.). *Source Book of English History*, New York, 1900.

[King Leir.] *The True Chronicle Historie of King Leir and His Three Daughters, Gonorill, Regan, and Cordella . . .* , London, Printed by Simon Stafford for Iohn Wright, 1605.

Lipsius, Justus. *Two Bookes of Constancie*, trans. John Stradling, London, 1595.

de Maisse, Sieur André Hurault. *Journal*, ed. G. B. Harrison and R. A. Jones, London, 1931.

Markham, Francis. *The Booke of Honour or Five Decads of Epistles of Honour*, London, 1625.

Markham, Gervase. *Honour in his Perfection*, London, 1624.

Medwall, Henry. *Fulgens and Lucres*, New York, 1920.

Moffet, Thomas. Nobilis, *A View of the Life and Death of a Sidney and* Lessus Lugubris, ed. and trans. Virgil Heltzel and Hoyt Hudson, San Marino, Calif., 1940.

[Montaigne, Michael.] *The Essayes of Michael Lord of Montaigne*, trans. John Florio, Everyman's Library, London, 1910, 3 vols.

Moryson, Fynes. *Shakespeare's Europe: Unpublished Chapters of Fynes Moryson's Itinerary*, ed. Charles Hughes, London, 1903.

Mulcaster, Richard. *Positions: wherein those primitive circumstances be examined, which are necessarie for children, either for skill in their bookes, or health in their bodies*, London, 1581.

Naunton, Robert. *Fragmenta Regalia*, ed. Edward Arber, reprinted from the 3rd posthumous ed. of 1653, London, 1870.

de la Primaudaye, Pierre. *The French Academie*, trans. T. B[owes], 4th ed. (1st ed. 1586), London, 1602-05.

Rabelais, François. *Gargantua and Pantagruel*, trans. Sir Thomas Urquhart and Peter Motteux, in *Great Books of the Western World*, ed. Robert Maynard Hutchins, Vol. 24, Chicago, 1952.

Ralegh, Sir Walter. *Works . . . To which is prefix'd a new account of his life*, by Tho[mas] Birch, London, 1751, 2 vols.

Raleigh, Sir Walter. *Selections*, ed. G. E. Hadow, Oxford, 1926.

Romei, Count Annibale. *The Courtier's Academie: Comprehending seven severall dayes discourses . . . written in Italian . . . and translated into English by J[ohn] K[epers]*, London, 1598.

R[obson], S[imon], Gent. *The Court of Civill Courtesie*, London, 1591.

Segar, Sir William. *Honor, Military and Civill, contained in foure Bookes. viz. 1. Justice, and Jurisdiction Military. 2. Knighthood in generall, and particular. 3. Combats for life, and Triumph. 4. Precedencie of great Estates, and others.* London, 1602.

———. *The Booke of Honor and Armes*, London, 1590.

Selden, John. *Table Talk, ed. Frederick Pollack*, London, 1927.

Shakespeare, William. *The Complete Works*, ed. George Lyman Kittredge, Boston, 1936.

Sidney, Sir Philip. *Aphorisms*, London, 1807, 2 vols.

———. *Collected Works*, ed. Albert Feuillerat, Cambridge, England, 1923, 3 vols.

Spenser, Edmund. *The Poetical Works*, ed. J. C. Smith and E. de Sélincourt, London, 1937.

Stubbes, Philip. *The Anatomie of Abuses*, London, 1595.

Webster, John. *The Complete Works*, ed. F. L. Lucas, London, 1927, 4 vols.

Whetstone, George. *The Honourable Reputation of a Souldier*, London, 1585.

———. *A Mirror of Treue Honnour and Christian Nobilitie*, London, 1585.

WORKS ON RENAISSANCE LITERATURE
AND CIVILIZATION

Baker, Herschel. *The Dignity of Man*, Cambridge, Mass., 1947.

Baker, Howard. *Induction to Tragedy*, Baton Rouge, La., 1939.

Baldwin, T. W. *William Shakspere's Small Latine and Lesse Greeke*, Urbana, Ill., 1944, 2 vols.

Barnet, Sylvan. "Some Limitations of a Christian Approach to Shakespeare," *The Journal of English Literary History*, Vol. 22, Baltimore, 1955.

Bénichou, Paul. *Morales du Grand Siècle*, Paris, 1948.

Black, J. B. *The Reign of Elizabeth*, Oxford, 1936.

Bowers, Fredson T. *Elizabethan Revenge Tragedy, 1587-1642*, Princeton, 1940.

Bradley, A. C. *Shakespearean Tragedy*, London, 1932.

Bryson, Frederick. *The Point of Honor in Sixteenth Century Italy: An Aspect of the Life of the Gentleman*, Chicago, 1935.

———. *The Sixteenth Century Italian Duel*, Chicago, 1938.

Buckley, George. *Atheism in the English Renaissance*, Chicago, 1932.

Burckhardt, Jacob. *The Civilization of the Renaissance in Italy*, Oxford, 1945.

Bush, Douglas. *The Renaissance and English Humanism*, Toronto, 1939.

Busson, Henri. *Les Sources et le Développement du Rationalisme dans la Littérature Francaise de la Renaissance*, Paris, 1922.

The New Cambridge Modern History, ed. Sidney Potter, Cambridge, England, 1957.

Campbell, Lily B. "Theories of Revenge in Renaissance England," *Modern Philology*, Vol. 28, Chicago, 1931.

Camden, Carroll. *The Elizabethan Woman*, London, 1952.

Coleridge, Samuel Taylor. *Lectures and Notes on Shakespeare and Other English Poets*, ed. T. Ashe, London, 1902.

Craig, Hardin. *The Enchanted Glass*, New York, 1936.

Curry, Walter Clyde. *Shakespeare's Philosophical Patterns*, Baton Rouge, La., 1937.

Danby, John. *Poets on Fortune's Hill*, London, 1952.

———. *Shakespeare's Doctrine of Nature*, London, 1944.

Dickey, Franklin M. *Not Wisely But Too Well*, San Marino, Calif., 1957.

Eisinger, Fritz. *Das Problem des Selbstmordes in der Literatur der Englischen Renaissance*, Überlingen/Bodensee, 1925.

Eliot, T. S. *Selected Essays*, New York, 1932.

Elliott, G. R. *Flaming Minister*, Durham, N.C., 1953.

Farnham, Willard. *The Medieval Heritage of Elizabethan Tragedy*, Berkeley, Calif., 1936.

Febvre, Lucien. *Le Problème de l'Incroyance au XVIe Siècle: la Religion de Rabelais*, Paris, 1947.

Ferguson, Wallace K. "Italian Humanism: Hans Baron's Contribution," *The Journal of the History of Ideas*, Vol. 19, New York, 1958.

———. *The Renaissance in Historical Thought*, Boston, Mass., 1948.

Granville-Barker, Harley. *Prefaces to Shakespeare*, Princeton, 1946-47, 2 vols.

———, and Harrison, G. B. (eds.). *A Companion to Shakespeare Studies*, New York, 1937.

Heilman, Robert B. *Magic in the Web*, Lexington, Ky., 1956.

Holzknecht, Karl. *The Backgrounds of Shakespeare's Plays*, New York, 1950.

Kelso, Ruth. *The Doctrine of the Elizabethan Gentleman in the Sixteenth Century*, Urbana, Ill., 1929.

Knight, G. Wilson. *The Imperial Theme*, 3rd ed., London, 1951.

———. *The Wheel of Fire*, 4th ed., London, 1949.

Leech, Clifford. *Shakespeare's Tragedies and Other Studies in 17th Century Drama*, London, 1950.

Lewis, C. S. *English Literature in the Sixteeenth Century*, Oxford, 1954.

Myrick, Kenneth. "The Theme of Damnation in Shakespearean Tragedy," *Studies in Philology*, Vol. 38, Chapel Hill, N.C., 1941.

Nicoll, Allardyce, et al. (eds.). *Shakespeare Survey*, Cambridge, England, 1948-60, 13 vols.

Praz, Mario. *Machiavelli and the Elizabethans*. The Annual Italian Lecture of the British Academy, London, 1928.

[Santayana, George.] *Essays in Literary Criticism of George Santayana*, ed. Irving Singer, New York, 1956.

Schücking, Levin. *Character Problems in Shakespeare's Plays*, London, 1922.

Sewell, Arthur. *Character and Society in Shakespeare*, Oxford, 1951.

Smith, D. Nichol. *Shakespeare Criticism*, Oxford, 1939.

Spencer, Theodore. *Shakespeare and the Nature of Man*, 2nd ed., New York, 1959.

Spens, Janet. "Chapman's Ethical Thought," *Essays and Studies*, Vol. 11, Oxford, 1925.

————. *Shakespeare and Tradition*, Oxford, 1916.

Stauffer, Donald A. *Shakespeare's World of Images: The Development of His Moral Ideas*, New York, 1949.

Stirling, Brents. *Unity in Shakespearian Tragedy*, New York, 1957.

Stoll, Elmer Edgar. *Shakespeare and Other Masters*, Cambridge, Mass., 1940.

Tillyard, E. M. W. *The Elizabethan World Picture*, New York, 1944.

————. *The English Renaissance: Fact or Fiction?*, London, 1952.

Tolstoy, Leo. *Collected Works*, Vol. 21, Oxford, 1937.

Traversi, D. A. *An Approach to Shakespeare*, London, 1938.

Villey, Pierre. *Les Sources et l'Evolution des Essais de Montaigne*, Paris, 1908, 2 vols.

Vyvyan, John. *The Shakespearean Ethic*, London, 1959.

Watkins, W. B. C. "Absent Thee from Felicity," *The Southern Review*, Vol. 5, Baton Rouge, La., 1939.

Whately, Thomas. *Some Remarks on the Characters of Shakespeare*, ed. Joseph Whately, London, 1785.

MISCELLANEOUS

Bloch-Michel, Jean. "The Obstinate Confidence of a Pessimistic Man," *The Reporter*, Vol. 17, November 28, 1957.

Butcher, A. H. *Aristotle's Theory of Poetry*, London, 1902.

Camus, Albert. *The Plague*, trans. Stuart Gilbert, New York, 1948.

Carter, Jesse Benedict. "Ancestor Worship and the Cult of the Dead," in *Encyclopaedia of Religion and Ethics*, ed. James Hastings, Edinburgh, 1923.

Fuller, B. A. G. *A History of Philosophy*, New York, 1955.

Frye, Prosser Hall. *Romance and Tragedy*, Boston, 1922.

Krutch, Joseph Wood. *The Modern Temper*, New York, 1933.

Lecky, William E. H. *A History of European Morals*, 3rd ed., London, 1877, 2 vols.

Legouis, Emile and Cazamian, Louis. *A History of English Literature*, New York, 1939.

Linton, Ralph. *A Study of Man*, New York, 1936.

Richards, I. A. *Principles of Literary Criticism*, London, 1925.

Shaw, George Bernard. "On Getting Married," in *The Works of Bernard Shaw*, Vol. 12, London, 1931.

de Staël-Holstein, Mme. La Baronne. *Réflexions sur le Suicide Suivies de la Défense de la Reine, et des Lettres sur J. J. Rousseau*, Paris, 1814.

Walpole, Horace. *The Letters*, ed. Mrs. Paget Toynbee, Vol. 8, Oxford, 1904.

INDEX

THIS INDEX attempts to cover the more important ideas discussed in this book. It also lists the more important writers, moralists, and critics referred to in the text. It is a selective index and does not attempt to include all the references to a topic. It should be noted that: 1) references to Shakespeare's characters are listed under the play in question; 2) almost all the references to passages in Part 2 (following p. 164) are to discussions of the Shakespearean text; 3) italic numbers indicate major discussions of a given topic which are covered by a heading or subheading in the Table of Contents.